IVOR CUTLER

Popular Music History
Series Editor: Alyn Shipton, Royal Academy of Music, London

This series publishes books that extend the field of popular music studies, examine the lives and careers of key musicians, interrogate histories of genres, focus on previously neglected forms, or engage in the formative history of popular music styles.

Published

Ivor Cutler

A Life Outside the Sitting Room

Bruce Lindsay

eⓔuınox

SHEFFIELD UK   BRISTOL CT

Published by Equinox Publishing Ltd.

UK: Office 415, The Workstation, 15 Paternoster Row, Sheffield, South Yorkshire S1 2BX

USA: ISD, 70 Enterprise Drive, Bristol, CT 06010

www.equinoxpub.com

First published 2023

ISBN-13 978 1 80050 294 9 (hardback)
         978 1 80050 295 6 (ePDF)

British Library Cataloguing-in-Publication Data

A catalogue record for this book is available from the British Library.

Library of Congress Cataloging-in-Publication Data
Names: Lindsay, Bruce (Music journalist) author.
Title: Ivor Cutler : a life outside the sitting room / Bruce Lindsay.
Description: Bristol, CT : Equinox Publishing Ltd, 2023. | Series: Popular music history | Includes bibliographical references and index. | Summary: "Ivor Cutler: A Life Outside the Sitting Room is the first biography of one of post-war Britain's most recognisable authors, poets and performers"—Provided by publisher.
Identifiers: LCCN 2022026197 (print) | LCCN 2022026198 (ebook) | ISBN 9781800502949 (hardback) | ISBN 9781800502956 (pdf)
Subjects: LCSH: Cutler, Ivor. | Singers—Great Britain—Biography. | Poets, Scottish—20th century—Biography.
Classification: LCC ML420.C93 L55 2023 (print) | LCC ML420.C93 (ebook) | DDC 782.42164092--dc23/eng/20220830
LC record available at https://lccn.loc.gov/2022026197
LC ebook record available at https://lccn.loc.gov/2022026198

Typeset by JS Typesetting Ltd, Porthcawl, Mid Glamorgan

Contents

Acknowledgements

Much of the information in this book comes from communications with individuals, by phone, Zoom, email and even face-to-face, between October 2020 and February 2022. I am deeply indebted to the following, who took time to speak or write to me about Ivor Cutler: James Allsopp; Lucy Armitage; Briony Bax; Glen Baxter; Alfie Benge; Steve Beresford; Alfio Bernabei; David Bramwell; Matt Brennan; Fiona Brodie; Sandra Brownjohn; John Burnside; Tracyanne Campbell; Neil Cargill; Joe Coles; Etienne Conod; Beverley Crew; Chris Cutler; Dan Cutler; Elicia Daly; Morag Deyes; Alan Dix; Graham Duff; Dylan Edwards; Sue Edwards; Charley Eiseman; Olwen Ellis; John-Paul Flintoff; Lee Freeman; Fred Frith; Dan Geesin; Frances Geesin; Fraser Geesin; Ron Geesin; Dave Green; Sandy Grierson; Ted Harrison; John Hegley; Linda Hirst; Gavin Hogg; Zoe Hood; Chris Huhne; Ella Huhne; Fabian Ironside; Hamish Ironside; David Jones; Ivor Kallin; Andy Kershaw; Phyllis King; John Knutas; Kate Lithgow; Mark Lynch; Gill Lyons; Raymond MacDonald; Ronald Macrae; Beth Marcuson; Roger McGough; Alastair McKay; Joyce McMillan; Adrian Mealing; Alex Mermikides; Milton Mermikides; Ewan Morrison; Anna Morshead; Brian Morton; Craig Murray-Orr; Ciara Nolan; Alison O'Kill (now Harbert); Louise Oliver; Rebecca Orr-Deas; Ashley Page; Piers Plowright; Emma Pollock; Jonathon Porritt; Zoë Readhead; Caroline Richmond; Alasdair Roberts; Xavier Russell; Lemn Sissay; Arthur Smith; Christine Stark; Charlotte Steel; Duglas T. Stewart; Ann Sylph; Trevor Tomkins; David Toop; Tony Ward; Jon Webster; David Wheeler; Kate Williams; Jo Willingham; Robert Wyatt.

My thanks also go to the following, for advice, assistance with contacts and general help and support: Rob Adams; Harri Clay and Anne Gerrish (*TimeOut*); Jeremy Cutler; Hannah Fletcher (YM&U Group); Simon Freeman; Brian Gaudet; David Ginsberg (WICN); Maisie Glazebrook (*Private Eye*);

Sara Jane Hall; Lara Harrison (Superstar PAs); Amanda Fitzalan Howard; Emma Milnes (Zoological Society of London); Louise North, archivist, BBC Written Archive; the staff of the British Library; the staff of the British Film Institute library; Sadie Williams (Ralph Steadman Art Collection Ltd.)

Thanks, also, to Alyn Shipton, Val Hall and the team at Equinox Publishing.

And, of course, my love and thanks to Julie, Sam and Alex, who have tolerated my love of Ivor and his work even though they don't share it.

BBC copyright content reproduced by courtesy of the British Broadcasting Corporation. All rights reserved.

Lyrics to "Little Red Robin Hood Hit the Road" by Robert Wyatt. Copyright and reproduced with the kind permission of Robert Wyatt.

"Uneventful Day" by Phyllis King. Taken from King, P. A. (1978) *Dust*, Morden Tower Publications. Reproduced by kind permission of Phyllis King.

Lyrics to "Yellow Fly," by Ivor Cutler. Reproduced by kind permission of the Estate of Ivor Cutler.

According to Mark Hussey, "Any biographer is a Frankenstein, assembling his creature from whatever parts are available ..."[1] This particular creature is assembled from many available parts, but there are, no doubt, other parts out there that might still be awaiting assembly. Hopefully, a future biographer can make use of this material to expand on the Ivor Cutler story.

1 An Introduction

"May I interview you, Ivor?"

"Mr Cutler to you! Only my intimate friends get to call me Ivor. When strangers call me Ivor it's like getting a French kiss from a public relations consultant."[1]

I have never knowingly been French kissed by a public relations consultant but the look which Ivor Cutler gives to his potential television interviewer – also, by the wonders of technology, Ivor Cutler – suggests that the experience would not be pleasant. But calling him "Mr Cutler" seems too formal. So I have reached a decision: when I write about his life as a schoolteacher he's Mr Cutler, for the rest of the time, he's Ivor. I hope he would approve, and I hope public relations consultants will understand.

What sort of a man was Ivor?

According to those who knew him, Ivor was sympathetic, mischievous, a bundle of contradictions, generous with praise, genuine, really beautiful, contrary, a bit of a rascal, intimidating, encouraging, supportive, deeply insecure, off the wall, a delight, magical, very normal, really special, manipulative, very entertaining, childlike, a creature of habit, an endlessly abundant barrel of jokes and wisdom, embarrassing, a Marmite humorist, a walking Dada.[2] Journalists and writers held varying opinions: according to Bernard Levin he was "admirably lugubrious"; to an anonymous journalist he was "Several chips short of a haggis supper"; Nigel Williamson declared "it is unlikely that we will see his like again."[3]

In his own words, he was a humorist, an unwitting hypocrite, extremely sensitive, intuitive, a great tease, screwed up, a pragmatist, very much an optimist, a bit of a preacher, pathetic, not an intellectual, a child, very romantic, controversial, lugubrious, a loner, a useful member of the human race. As for his talent, praised by many fans and admirers, he summed it up by saying: "If I am a genius, I'm a genius in a very small way indeed."

What about his work? In a career that lasted from the late 1950s to the 2000s, Ivor wrote poetry, children's stories, songs, plays, and tales about family life in an exaggeratedly Scottish Scotland. He performed on radio and television, played live concerts at venues large and small, and recorded a dozen or so albums, accompanying his songs on a selection of creaky harmoniums. He appeared on mainstream media, including the opening night of BBC Two, but he was also a darling of the 1960s counterculture. Paul McCartney, John Lennon and Bertrand Russell were fans, as were John Peel and Andy Kershaw, who regularly booked him for sessions on their radio shows. He enjoyed appearing in the Beatles' *Magical Mystery Tour*, but his working relationship with George Martin was strained. He grew to hate hotels and touring, but he loved flora and fauna, and often wrote poetry in London Zoo. When he died, aged 83, in 2006, the Scottish Parliament celebrated his life and work.

Ivor's fans – including most of the people who contributed to this biography – speak fondly, even passionately, about their favourite songs, stories or poems and label him "genius" or "national treasure." His detractors, of which there are quite a few, speak just as fervently but without the fondness: for them, his work sparks nothing more than a puzzled expression, or perhaps a tirade of abuse.

To me, Ivor left such an extensive body of work that it's hard to imagine how someone could fail to find something to enjoy, but then I'm biased. My love of the works of Ivor Cutler goes back for more than fifty years. Usually, the first time I became aware of a now favourite performer or band – Captain Beefheart, Fairport Convention or Charlie Parker, for example – is lost in the mists of time. With Ivor, I can pinpoint my first time to within an hour or so: 30 January 1971, at around 11.00 p.m. Leaving Lanchester Polytechnic's main hall in Coventry, where I'd just seen Centipede perform as part of the Lanchester Arts Festival, I picked up a festival programme, flicked through it as I was driven home, and read a short, silly, poem about shoes. Someone called Ivor Cutler wrote it, apparently. He was performing on the following evening, but there was no way I would be able to get back to Coventry so I missed my chance to see him on stage. Still, "Shoes" made me laugh out loud. A few months later I heard him on the radio, and the voice, once heard, has never been forgotten.

Ivor's tales often have an autobiographical foundation, but he found ordinary autobiography "fairly boring."[4] He may have said the same thing about ordinary biography. If you agree with him, I suggest that you stop reading now and listen to *Velvet Donkey* instead. If not, please continue …

2 Return to Y'Hup

Scotland, 2019. Musicians from across the country record some songs, poems and recitations for a new album. The musicians include saxophonist Raymond MacDonald, drummer Matt Brennan (aka Citizen Bravo), Tracyanne Campbell (of Camera Obscura), Emma Pollock (formerly of the Delgados), guitarist and violinist Malcolm Benzie (from bands including eagleowl and Withered Hand), and a couple of guests from south of the border, Robert Wyatt and Phyllis April King. The pieces include a song sung by a mythical bird, a suggestion to people in business about the best way to look after their joints, a stern query about damaged legwear, and a languid, gentle, song about sandwiches, rolls, and cups of tea. Every one of these tales, spoken or sung, was written by one man – the Glasgow-born Ivor Cutler.

January 2020, still in Scotland. Glasgow's Celtic Connections festival devotes an evening to a concert of those songs, poems and recitations, known collectively by the album's title, *Return to Y'Hup – the World of Ivor Cutler*.[1] Critics respond warmly to the event, praising it as a "singular show" and referring to the twenty-strong ensemble as "a murderer's row of indie and folk talent ..."[2] The album and concert title make sense to those familiar with Ivor's early work, but the rest of the world – most of the world – might be asking: "Just where or what was Y'Hup? And why would anyone want to go back to it?"

Ivor's work offered some answers, at least regarding the where and what. According to the sleeve notes of his first record, 1959's *Ivor Cutler of Y'Hup*, Y'Hup was 700–800 miles off the western coast of South America, "a richly wooded island with a flora and fauna which indicate a migration from Australasia thousands of years ago." So far, so idyllic, but Y'Hup had its drawbacks. Beware of the yam, for example, a small animal, possibly descended from the kangaroo, which moved around with a backing motion and no

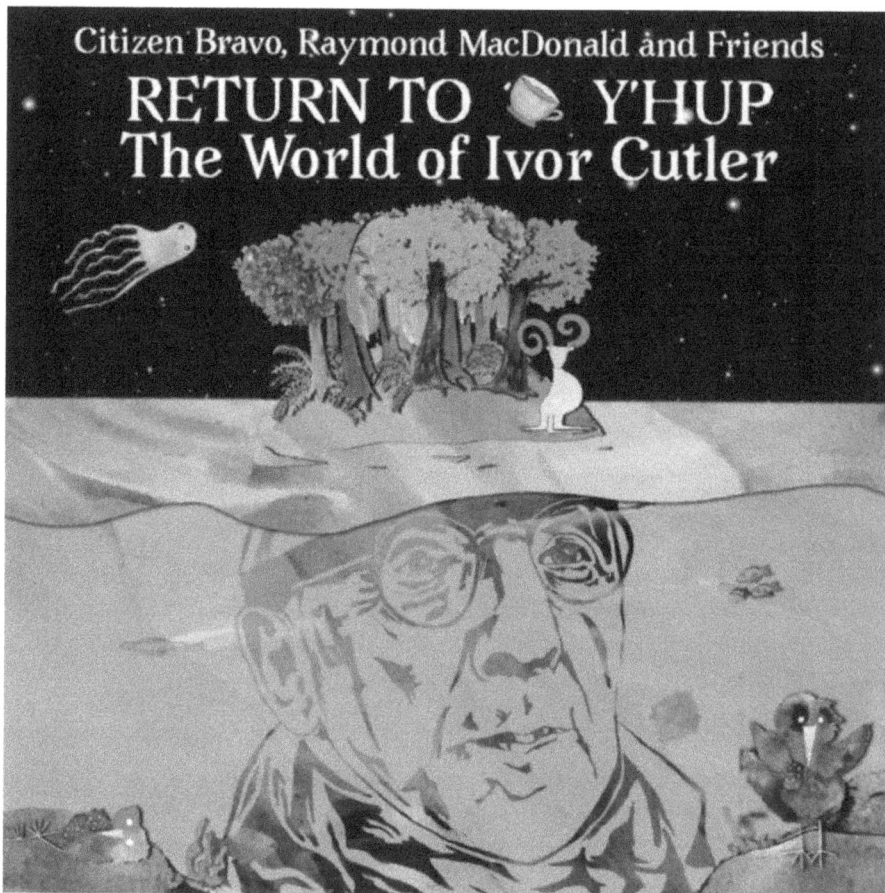

Return to Y'Hup. (Courtesy of Chemikal Underground Records and Matt Brennan. Cover designed by Anna Miles and Bertrand Mougel.)

longer had any forelegs. The weather was far from perfect: almost every day, at around 11.00 a.m., the island experienced a heavy shower of green rain, a mixture of water and plankton. Such a daily drenching was unlikely to encourage tourism, but it was vital to Y'Hup's ecological well-being, for this rain was full of Vitamin P, making it so valuable to the inhabitants that they were each allowed just a single soup bowl of the precious fluid per day. If green rain and fearsome animals failed to deter the intrepid traveller, there was one further obstacle to overcome if you wished to visit Y'Hup. Afraid of upsetting the island's natural balance, Ivor refused to divulge its latitude or longitude, rendering it practically invisible in those far-off days bereft of GPS. The island was, presumably, small, but it offered one of its inhabitants the chance to hold the title of Oblique Musical Philosopher when, every twenty-three years, a competition was held to establish who was the most oblique of all the island's musical philosophers (how many there were in total is a beguiling and un-answered question). The notes claimed that Ivor was the holder of the title, giving him the honour of being referred to as Ivor Cutler of Y'Hup, O.M.P.[3]

The main barrier to visiting Y'Hup had nothing to do with an absence of accurate coordinates. This island rich in flora and fauna was a figment of a fertile imagination, a creation whose continued existence depended not on the vagaries of nature, or the impact of climate change, but on its creator's artistic direction. Ivor first brought Y'Hup to public attention at the end of the 1950s. By the end of the 1960s, as his career took off and expanded into new artistic pathways, Ivor left Y'Hup behind, but he carried on obliquely philosophising for the rest of his life.

Sixty years after Y'Hup's first appearance, Matt Brennan and Malcolm Benzie visited *Rip it Up: The Story of Scottish Pop*, advertised as "the first major exhibition dedicated to Scottish pop music."[4] The exhibition, which took place from June to November 2018 at the National Museum of Scotland in Edinburgh, was named after one of Scottish pop's finest songs, "Rip it Up" by Orange Juice. It included 300 objects related to the country's pop music scene and clothes featured strongly: Annie Lennox's tartan trouser suit, Billy Mackenzie's beret, Alex Harvey's striped jumper, one of Clare Grogan's dresses, and more. Ivor Cutler, one of Scotland's most sartorially, musically, lyrically and vocally distinctive performers, was notable by his absence. Such an absence should not come as a surprise, for Ivor moved to England in the early 1950s and his showbiz career – if that's the right term – didn't begin until he was living and working in London. Nonetheless, Benzie and Brennan were disappointed: after all, so much of Ivor's work is drawn from his Scottish childhood. His absence from the exhibition proved to be the catalyst for the creation of *Return to Y'Hup*.

Return to Y'Hup: The World of Ivor Cutler, credited to Citizen Bravo, Raymond MacDonald and Friends, features material from *Ivor Cutler of Y'Hup*, the EP released in 1959, plus a selection from Ivor's first album, 1961's *Who Tore Your Trousers?*, and a few pieces from his later records. The songs on *Ivor Cutler of Y'Hup* offer a wealth of knowledge on many subjects, but reveal little about Y'Hup. "Here's a Health to Simon" tells us about Ivor's eldest son; "Size 9½" is a song about feet; "Pickle Your Knees" offers advice on achieving the sweetest possible knees (the pickling solution should be cheese-based), but only the final song offers insight into Ivor's fantasy island. "The Boo-Boo Bird," he explains in his introduction to the track, takes us to "the most fabulous island in the world," an island with many glories, the greatest of which is, perhaps, the Boo-Boo Bird itself. The song is sung tremulously by a member of the titular species and tells of its appearance – it has no head, tail, wings, legs or body and so is invisible, only its plaintive cry of "boo-boo" reveals its presence as it flies across the island, a welcome bird, a bird which presages good things and yet is cursed with one of the saddest calls of any winged creature. After six songs characterised by cheery, if sometimes confusing, humour and jaunty melodies, "The Boo-Boo Bird" is something of a shock, but an early reminder that among all of the silliness and absurdity in Ivor's musical world there is plenty of melancholy.

Ivor's mysterious island took shape in the 1950s. In April of 1959, the *Daily Mirror* announced that "Ivor Cutler O.M.P" had recorded his first disc.[5] By the end of the year, the BBC was referring to Ivor by his "official" title of "Ivor Cutler of Y'Hup, O.M.P." The *Daily Mirror* gave nothing away about Y'Hup's creation, but a combination of the Goons and the environment of 1950s London may have something to do with it. Ivor moved to London in 1952, when the city was still covered in bomb sites and war-damaged buildings and when the end of rationing was two years in the future. Smog was commonplace. The Great Smog of December 1952 combined fog and smoke in a lethal combination: the resulting noxious fug hung over the city for five days and is estimated to have caused up to twelve thousand deaths.[6] Ivor had spent two years living and working in rural Suffolk and the move to smog-bound London must have felt something like a return to the industrial Glasgow of his early years. On radio, *The Goon Show* was one of the few shafts of innovation and freshness in the entertainment world, a series of ridiculous and unfeasible tales first broadcast on the BBC Home Service in 1951. Its mix of strange plots, outlandish sound effects and bizarre characters soon became popular with a young generation seeking something new in comedy. Prince Charles became a fan, and so did Ivor. The invention of Y'Hup, with its exotic location and even more exotic flora and fauna, offered an escape to an altogether more desirable environment than the one offered by the smog-bound city, while Cutler's take on the island and its inhabitants was as surreal and odd as the world of the Goons. Y'Hup existed for barely a decade, but it formed a strong foundation for its creator's career.

3 Early Life

Ivor Cutler was born on 15 January 1923, in the Govan area of Glasgow, the descendant of the Kushners and the Goldbergs, Jewish families who arrived in Scotland from mainland Europe at the turn of the twentieth century. His paternal grandparents, Moris Kushner from Belarus and Shipre Dushditz from Poland, married in Łódź on 14 March 1894.[1] Their first child, Jacob, was born two years later, and within a year or two they joined thousands of Jewish families fleeing westward in the hope of a better life. Some headed to the USA, others moved to England, while a smaller number arrived in Scotland. The Kushners took young Jacob to Glasgow, home to a thriving Jewish community.[2] Many Jewish migrants fled the Russian Empire to escape pogroms and antisemitism, others emigrated to escape legal restrictions, others left to escape poverty and hardship, many probably left for a combination of these reasons.[3] It's not clear why the Kushners left their homeland, although Ivor did tell one interviewer that the family was "running away from pogroms,"[4] but once they set foot in the west of Scotland, they stayed.

There were stories about the Jewish immigrants: that they arrived in Scotland by sailing up the Clyde; that family names were changed by immigration officials who couldn't, or wouldn't, spell or pronounce the original names; that the migrants were heading for the USA but disembarked in Scotland by accident or were tricked into doing so by unscrupulous fraudsters. Ivor himself said that his grandparents (he didn't specify which ones) had been tricked into landing in Scotland.[5] The Clyde was certainly a major shipping route, but vessels from eastern Europe and the Baltic states docked on the east coast of Scotland, at Leith, not the west. The migrants booked passage under their original surnames and carried papers with those names, so officials could easily reproduce them in writing even if pronunciation might be difficult. "Kushner" is, of course, not hard to pronounce, but by the time

Moris and Shipre's second son, Joseph, was born in 1900, they had become the Cutlers.[6]

Unlike the Kushners, the Goldberg family never changed its surname. In Glasgow, Fishel Goldberg from the Russian Empire and Tilla Wolfson from Germany married in 1893.[7] Their first child, Paulina, was born two years later; she would become known as Polly and would grow up to become Ivor's mother.[8] Tilla, also known as Tilly, gave birth to a total of fifteen children. Eva, the youngest, was born in November 1915, twenty years after Polly, and as Auntie Eva she would become a crucial figure in Ivor's early life.[9]

The Cutlers and the Goldbergs settled into Scottish life with varying degrees of success. Moris Cutler worked at a variety of jobs and the family was rarely, if ever, free of financial worries. Fishel Goldberg was a master tailor, and by his early thirties he was employing others, enabling the Goldberg family to achieve a higher standard of living than the Cutlers. However, both families eventually moved to the Gorbals.[10]

As Glasgow's Jewish community grew in size it began to divide along class and income lines. The most prosperous middle-class families lived in the West End, the working class tended towards the Gorbals and the surrounding streets. Even in the Gorbals there was a division between the poorer workers, employed tailors and peddlers like Moris, and the better-off self-employed tailors and small business owners such as Fishel.[11] Home to a mix of Scots, Irish and overseas migrants, the Gorbals became notorious as one of Britain's worst slum areas. Writing in 1948, the left-wing journalist, folk singer and song collector A. L. Lloyd described it for readers of the *Picture Post*:

> North of the Gorbals are the black, rat-ridden banks of the Clyde. South is the railway jungle that spreads out from the big goods and mineral depot on Pollokshaws Road. The western end of the ward has the handsome classical terraces of Abbotsford Place and Warwick Street. The eastern end is bounded by the lowering mid-Victorian tenements of Lawmoor Street. Within these bounds live some 40,000 shockingly housed people.[12]

Ralph Glasser, the son of Jewish immigrants, grew up in the Gorbals during the 1920s. He remembered some elements of the area fondly, such as the Workers' Circle, a social and political club for Jewish immigrants where socialist and anarchist literature was always available, but malnutrition was rife and the joint deformities and bow legs that signalled rickets were an everyday sight. There was a "bustling district" of workshops, factories, pawnshops, pubs and small shops, but the streets "were slippery with refuse and often with drunken vomit." The Glassers' tenement was in decay, rats and mice were everywhere, plumbing was feeble. Six to eight flats shared two lavatories: "Going to the lavatory we had to remember to carry a supply of newspaper, not only for use as toilet paper but also to clean the soles of our boots of excrement and urine …"[13]

By 1919 the Cutlers were living at 68 Abbotsford Place, a short walk to the south of the Goldbergs' home at 66 South Portland Street. This area was, at the time, considered to be the centre of the Gorbals' Jewish community, socially and culturally, if not geographically.[14] The Cutlers shared their building with a mixed group of tenants, of various occupations or none, and with surnames suggesting Jewish or Scottish backgrounds: Bininkonsky, Bloch, Seihn, Ash, Haddon and Green. Despite Glasser and Lloyd's descriptions of the Gorbals, Moris and Shipre must have felt settled in Abbotsford Place: they stayed there until their deaths.[15]

On 25 February 1919, Jacob Cutler, now calling himself Jack Moris Cutler and employed, like his father, as a draper and jeweller, married Polly Goldberg in the South Portland Street synagogue.[16] They soon moved to 3 Ralston Drive in Govan. The area may have been a little grander than the Gorbals, but accommodation was still at a premium and the young couple began their life together in a house divided into eight properties, each one occupied by a skilled worker or a professional. Most of the tenants' surnames – Lindsay, Fraser, MacDonald, Crawford – are established Scottish ones.[17]

Jack and Polly's first child, Bernard, was born in December 1919. Jack signed the birth registration with a strong, crisp and clear signature, perhaps a sign of the young man's confidence in his family's future and his ability to rise in the world. Bernard's sister, Rita Minnie, was born two years later and then, on 15 January 1923, Isadore Cutler took his first breaths at 3 Ralston Drive: he soon became known as Ivor. Later in life, he would sometimes claim that his first screams coincided with the roar from thousands of football fans as Rangers scored a goal at the nearby Ibrox Stadium. A pleasant story, but Ivor was born at 8.40 a.m. and Rangers never played that early in the morning.[18]

Ivor never lived in the Gorbals, but he visited, perhaps several times a week when he was a young child, to see his grandparents. In the 1980s he recalled that as a child he was close to his grandfather. He didn't clarify which one, but Moris is the most likely: when asked hypothetically "You're entitled to one phone call … Who do you dial?" he replied "My father's father …"[19] In his loosely autobiographical collection of stories, *Glasgow Dreamer*, Ivor writes about staying with his Cutler grandparents for a period of recuperation when, age three, he caught an unnamed disease, considering the stay to be "a great treat." He acknowledged that his father's parents were very poor, but he still preferred their home to the slightly more upmarket Goldberg household.[20] He had intimate personal experience of the Gorbals' limited hygiene facilities. In "Gorbals 1930" he talks of Granny Goldberg giving a cooking apple to a delivery boy with snot oozing from his nose, and of Uncle Joe's lavatory, shared with seven other families, its toilet bowl full of strips of old newspaper and "strangers' diarrhoea." No one can accuse Ivor of over-romanticising life in the Gorbals, even if he did have fond memories of the place.[21]

Ivor's family moved slowly but surely up the economic and social scales. By 1925 Jack was renting an office at 72–73 Great Clyde Street. Three years later, after the birth of Ivor's youngest brother, Joseph, a notice in the *Scotsman* of 25 January 1928 listed Jack as a wholesale jeweller. Ivor told Martin Pople, a friend and an agent at Serious, the music production and development organisation, that aged nine he moved to somewhere a little nicer and became "petit bourgeois."[22] The move brought him problems: asked years later to describe his childhood in five words, he responded: "Dealing with arbitrary petit-bourgeois nonsense."[23] The idea of becoming petit bourgeois might have worried Ivor, but it was another indication that the family was on the up. As his distant cousin, Ivor Kallin, put it "A lot of the Jewish community became quite bourgeois and moved out to Whitecraigs, Giffnock, Newtonmearns, more suburban." Even before the move to Glasgow's petit bourgeois heartland, Ivor remembered, his family did not struggle financially in the way that many Glasgow families of the time had to, including his paternal grandparents. "No," he said, "I remember liking austerity, though. As a boy my two grannies used to make the same kind of cake, one making it with milk and one with water. I always preferred the one with water."[24]

"Somewhere a little nicer" for the Cutlers was a flat at 952 Pollokshaws Road, a long, wide, road that led almost symbolically from the western boundary of the Gorbals to the more desirable suburbs. The flat was opposite Queen's Park. If Ivor's memory is accurate, then the family arrived at Pollokshaws Road between 1930 and 1933. In 1935, Ivor's youngest sister, Beth, was born. Beth remembers the Pollokshaws Road apartment, her first home, as a beautiful flat where her family lived until 1943. After that, the Cutlers took another step up the property ladder when they moved to a house at 29 Redburn Avenue, nine miles or so southwest of the Gorbals, off the main Ayr Road on the border between Giffnock and Whitecraigs. Ivor's cousin Lee Freeman remembers it as "quite impressive."[25]

Jack's success brought benefits for the family beyond their quite impressive new house, including holidays and a motor car. Ivor fondly remembered holidaying in Largs, on the Firth of Clyde just thirty or so miles from Glasgow. "It is quiet and civilised and it is the sort of place where there is somewhere you can go when it rains," he said, also remembering holidays further afield, to the Isle of Man or Scarborough, resorts better suited to his family's rising social status.[26] One holiday to Scarborough, in the summer of 1938, came to a sudden conclusion before Jack and his children had crossed the English border. Polly was already at the seaside resort, looking for somewhere for the family to stay, as Jack drove his Ford Eight south with the Cutler children on board. A few miles past Jedburgh the family reached Mossburnford. Everything was going well until another car appeared, heading towards them on the wrong side of the road. Jack swerved, but it was too late. The cars collided.

Jack's practical but humble Ford Eight was wrecked. The second car, a far more upmarket 3½-litre Alvis, was relatively unscathed, its occupants unhurt. Every one of the Cutlers sustained injuries, elder brother Bernard coming off worst with a broken nose and Jack suffering a facial cut and bruising to his right side. The driver of the Alvis was charged with driving without due care and attention and the case came to Jedburgh Sheriff Court the following November. The *Jedburgh Gazette* reported on the case in detail, under the attention-grabbing headline of "Driver's Front Wheel Skid: Can it Be Corrected?"[27]

The case hinged on the issue of whether the Alvis driver could have corrected the skid which caused the crash. If he could have done so, then he faced a guilty verdict, if not, then he would go free. Three people were in the Alvis: John March Booth of Twickenham, London; his wife (referred to only as "Mrs Booth"); and their chauffeur, Reginald Williams. Surprisingly, Williams wasn't driving: Mr Booth was at the wheel. Jack Cutler gave brief evidence about his view of the accident and his futile attempt to avoid the oncoming vehicle, but the *Gazette* spent most of its report on the evidence given by Booth, Williams, Police Constable Collin and the defence's expert witness, automotive engineer Charles Wickes. The engineer's turn in the witness box produced a fleeting moment of hilarity, at least as the reporter saw it. Under questioning, Wickes opined that "inexpert" drivers and engineers could sometimes make mistakes "just as inexpert fishermen sometimes make mistakes about the size of their fish!" Once the laughter had subsided, Sheriff Baillie added "And the experts sometimes make mistakes too!" Laughter again filled the court. The verdict was never in doubt: Mr Booth, a member of the Veteran Motorists Association – "composed of motorists who drove carefully" – could not have corrected the skid and was therefore not driving without due care. Not guilty.

Beth was only three and a half when she was involved in the crash, but still recalled the incident eighty years later. Although the *Jedburgh Gazette* named Bernard as one of the injured passengers, Beth did not recall Bernard being in the car, believing that he was probably trying to earn money to help him with his medical studies. However, she did remember that Rita was in the front passenger seat while she sat in the back between Ivor and Joseph. She received a cut below her ear. Her father's reaction to the crash was understandable: even though the family escaped serious injury, the car was crucial to his livelihood. "I do remember my father being pretty mad about it," Beth recalls, "The car was not a toy. It was a large part of my father's living. And I don't think that my father otherwise ever said anything bad about anyone."

Although the incident was frightening and potentially tragic, it was not one of the childhood events that Ivor, who was fifteen at the time, recalled in interviews. There are other ways of remembering, though: a car crash forms the central event of "Phonic Poem," which emerged over thirty years later.

Ivor summed up his childhood and adolescence in a few words:

> ... every step in my development had somebody sneering or saying "No! That's stupid!" I think I was seen as a soft bloke who was an easy touch for going down the shops ... and of lesser value than my brothers. [My parents] thought I was daft. That what I was doing was just rubbish.[28]

It's a bleak view of fifteen or sixteen years of life, and it's supported by many other statements he made in later life, but it tells only part of the story. There were happy times, too, and the occasional recognition of his talents or his potential. But one of his earliest memories is of attempted fratricide.

Little Ivor enjoyed his years as the baby of the Cutler family, the focus of attention for the proud parents. A family photo, used as the cover image for his *Privilege* album, shows Jack, Polly, Bernard, Rita and Ivor seated at a tea table filled with food and drink. Jack smiles straight at the camera; big brother Bernard does the same, but his wide-eyed stare makes him look a little nervous; Rita looks at the camera too, but seems eager to turn away and grab a slice of the cake that's enticingly close. Ivor sits in shorts at the front of the group, his body at right angles to the camera but his head turned towards it: he's holding a biscuit and fixes the photographer's gaze confidently. Polly is the only one who ignores the camera: instead, she looks intently at her toddler son, a wide smile on her face. He has all her attention. There's a quotation just above the photo: "It is the baby's privilege to be the centre of the universe – until the next one comes along."[29] The phrase, according to Ivor's son Jeremy in the notes to the re-issued album, "expresses a profound issue for Ivor" who said that he never came to terms with the arrival of his younger brother and sister who, he believed, had displaced him in their parents' affections.[30] It's possible that when this photograph was taken "the next one" was already on his way.

Joseph Nathan Cutler was born in 1926, when Ivor was three years old. Young Ivor was not happy about it, even if he later credited Joe's arrival with helping his creativity: "Without that I would not have been as screwed up as I am and therefore not as creative."[31] A creative career was still some time away, and Ivor had more immediate concerns about his new sibling: deciding to remove this threat to his status, Ivor attempted to kill him. The story is repeated many times, with a consistency that isn't always apparent in many of Ivor's other oft-repeated tales. Towards the end of his life, he tied the tale to a more general feeling about his mother's lack of love for him:

> Ever since I was born, more or less, I've always seen myself as a lesser being ... It's all based on my mother's relationship with myself and her not really loving me, which is why I nearly killed my kid brother ... He was lying in a basket, couldn't do anything,

and I went over to where the fire was and I took out the poker. Auntie Eva happened to come into the kitchen at the same time. "Ivor! Put that down!" So I put it down. I wasn't going to fight over it.[32]

Eva was still a child herself. No more than eleven or twelve years old when she foiled Ivor's plans, she had already been babysitting the Cutler children for half of her life.[33]

Joseph "became the one Mammy really loved," Ivor said towards the end of his life. Ivor's long-term partner, Phyllis King, felt that he never got over this early trauma: "He was the sun, and then his brother was born and he became the sun, took the sun away from him. Ivor felt quite deserted, betrayed in a way."[34] In later years, Ivor turned events such as these into positive factors in his development, telling the audience at his final live performance, "If any of you have been brought up in an absolutely horrible way ... you're the lucky ones. You need that little bit of the awfulness to give you the kind of quality that you and the audiences might find to their taste ..."[35]

The "awfulness" continued into Ivor's primary school years. Ivor's first school was in Ibrox, the area that was also home to Rangers, the chosen football team for Protestant Glaswegians. It was a secular primary school, a mix of children from different social and cultural backgrounds: Irish, Scots, eastern European Jewish migrants. Ivor recalled being challenged to a fight

The Goldberg Family, c.1924: (Back row) Cassie, Willie, Celia, Sam, Flora, Israel, Sophia. (Front row) Polly, Tilla, Eva, Fishel. (Courtesy of Lee Freeman, photographer unknown.)

by the school bully, who knocked him down as the rest of the pupils stood and watched: "I was a gentle kinda bloke and I wasn't in the least interested in fighting with him, and I just turned my back on him and walked home. I think it left them bewildered because they hadn't realised that people would behave like that."[36]

Ivor and his fellow Jewish children were outnumbered by those from the Catholic and Protestant communities. The Protestant "Billies" and the Catholic "Dans" feuded among themselves, but both showed a hatred for the Jewish children of the neighbourhood. In the Gorbals, Ralph Glasser first became aware of their existence when a gang of boys shouted a challenge to Ralph and his friend: "'Wha' are yese – Billy or a Dan? Billy or a Dan!' Fists up, they were going to beat us to a pulp if we gave the wrong answer."[37] The challenge could sometimes be extended: "are you a Billy or a Dan or an old tin can?" The old tin can was a Jew, who could be kicked down the street by either of the other two groups.[38]

Young Ivor may not have been interested in fighting, but he was interested in music, even if this wasn't appreciated by his parents. One of his experiments with instruments involved the family piano, an experiment which was also an early attempt at composition: "I started composing when I was about seven or eight when I took the poker and stuck it in the piano keys to see if they would wrench out. It wasn't approved of and I had to give it up."[39] In 1974 he said that he came from a "musical family where there was a lot of singing taking place" but three years later he presented a slightly different picture: "We were no musicians. I tried to learn the piano but my mother stopped me – I was three – because I had the poker between two notes and I was trying to lever them."[40]

The family, in keeping with Jewish tradition, sang at home whether or not they were musically talented: "We were Orthodox Jews and so there'd be a bit of singing on Friday nights, Passover in particular. That's the first [music] I can really remember, anyway," he told his friend Brian Morton.[41] When he told the story ten years later he sounded more cynical: "Every Friday night all us Jews in the family sat round the table and my mother made the big meal and we sang all the correct songs to sing."[42] According to Beth, young Ivor "sang beautifully … Years later I had the same music teacher – and although I loved music I was never in tune. And this woman … used to tell me how good he was." The story goes that he won a prize aged six for his rendition of "My Love is Like a Red, Red Rose." He attended synagogue until his mid-teens, where he "soaked in the Jewish melodies."[43] He told Phyllis King that when he, Rita and one of his brothers walked home they would sing three-part harmonies as they went along. Phyllis feels that this made them all seem very musical.

When Ivor was thirteen he went to a piano teacher, told him he wanted to play Bach and took a few lessons: "Not many, though. Good thing, actually, because the more you're thinking of other people's work, the less you are able to find your own voice."[44] Ivor carried on and made his first serious attempt at composition when he was fifteen. In one version of the story, Ivor spoke of this first attempt as a song called "Funeral Bells," because "death has always been part of my life."[45] His mother was unimpressed: "I sat at the piano and sang it … and I turned to her and said 'Well, Mammy, what did you think?' And she gave me a funny kind of smile, sort of stiff, and she said 'Yes, it's very nice' but then she broke and said 'Ivor, couldn't you write something nice?'"[46] In another version, Ivor claimed that his first composition was a short instrumental which he called "my first Piano Concerto," just three lines long "because I didn't know what a concerto was."[47]

For his secondary education Ivor went to Shawlands Academy, a school that twenty-five years later provided teaching to Ian McGeachy, another Scottish artist who moved south to find fame, changing his name to John Martyn in the process.[48] Miss Irving, the music teacher, encouraged Ivor's musical ambition. Ivor remembered her as Marie S. Irving, and gave her credit for playing the first piece of music that really inspired him, Dvořák's ninth symphony, the New World Symphony. She played it to the class and, as Ivor remembered, "it knocked me out … I thought, 'I'm going to be a composer and I'm going to play simple melodies, as simple as you can get' and, of course, you're fifteen and you don't know any better. But to my astonishment it has come to pass."[49]

Miss Irving was the only teacher of whom Ivor spoke fondly. He played one of his early compositions to her, receiving a far more positive response than his mother's had been. Once again, there are two versions of the tale. He told Brian Morton that the composition was "Funeral Bells" and that Miss Irving "was knocked out, probably the first time in her whole career anyone had composed anything, and she went and got Miss Harper, the art teacher, down. She listened politely and went 'Wow!'." In an alternate version of the tale, it was the Piano Concerto that Ivor first played for Miss Irving: "I took it to school and showed it to the music teacher and she was knocked out. It was a load of rubbish. Then I did a serious one called 'Funeral Bells' because being a humorist I'm a naturally lugubrious kind of bloke, and suicide always has a big attraction to guys like me."[50]

Miss Irving introduced Ivor to opera, although the introduction was not as successful as she probably wished, thanks to Ivor's choice of production. "She said 'Which one do you want?' and I said *Siegfried*! And she said 'Oh, it's heavy'. You know, when you're young you're stupid, and I said 'The heavier the better'. I thought heavy was good, you know, profound. I was bored out my mind. It really put me off opera …" Later, he visited the Mitchell Library, reading the scores to a variety of songs including Russian and Spanish folk songs, "hoping for cool things like flattened sevenths." He also began learning acoustic guitar.[51]

With the notable exception of Miss Irving's encouragement, Ivor's childhood outside the home was not happy: none of his fellow pupils, the other neighbourhood children nor his teachers were well disposed to him. As a result, he felt that his local community didn't respect him: "I had a mixed upbringing," Ivor recalled, "I remember sad [memories], the sad ones come flooding in. The happy ones were, I suppose, the everyday things like mince and potatoes and pineapple chunks for my dinner ..."[52] Ivor mentioned these happy foodstuffs in his work: a dinner of mince balls, potatoes and pineapple chunks in episode 12 of *Glasgow Dreamer*, or the meal of mince and pineapple chunks that's enlivened by sauces pulled from the middens on a track from *A Flat Man* titled "Ep. 1. Doing the Bathroom."

Occasionally, happy events were more than the everyday, but even then, as Ivor tells, they rarely avoided a modicum of sadness. For his fourth or fifth birthday his parents gave him a scooter. He took it out at 6.00 a.m. next morning, riding along proudly in the quiet street, but it was inadequately lubricated, possibly because it was second-hand, and made what he described as "a Hell of a racket." Polly shouted at him out of the tenement window and ordered him upstairs: he never did it again. The racket was part of the fun, for Ivor had the love of loud noise that's common to young children, a love that the grown-up Ivor didn't hold, his ears no longer able to tolerate such sounds.[53]

Music was not Ivor's only interest, he had an aptitude for maths, particularly trigonometry.[54] At Shawlands he took lessons in Greek and he later claimed that his written letter d's, with their similarity to the lower-case Greek letter delta, were the result of this early exposure to the language.[55] At the age of twelve the "madness with words" started in earnest when he invented a new language and showed it to his Hebrew teacher, who was unimpressed with his pupil's effort. Ivor, in his turn, was unimpressed with the teacher: "He was a failure & an unhappy man."[56]

Mathematical ability, musical talent and an interest in linguistics failed to ensure a happy school life. Even if Jewish children looked no different from their fellow pupils, they were easily identifiable from their adherence to their religious practices and the cry of "Jewboy" would often follow them home.[57] Ivor Kallin went to school in Glasgow thirty years later: "I never went to an assembly at school, the Jewish kids went to another classroom ... We'd have Jewish holidays on top of the other holidays, which probably caused a bit of resentment as well." The teachers could not be relied upon to deal with bullying or name-calling, for as Ivor remembered they could be just as bullying, insulting and anti-Semitic as his fellow pupils. When journalist Damien Love asked Ivor "What is the worst thing you've ever put your name to?" he replied "Age 12, I, a practising Jew at the time, was forced by my racist teacher to sign a Church of Scotland card saying I'd never smoke nor drink."[58] One teacher made young Ivor stand in front of his class and sing the Jewish national anthem, "Hatikvah": "and he said: 'Come on out and sing "Call Out the Lifeboats"'. That was the nearest he could get to 'Kol od balevav' which was the beginning of the song." He also recalled regular corporal punishment, claiming that he was strapped two hundred times in a three-year period at Shawlands Academy: assuming a typical school year of forty weeks, Ivor was being beaten almost twice a week. The punishment was ostensibly for bad writing although Ivor later believed that there was also an underlying element of racism.[59] Ivor's handwriting may well have been perceived as "bad" by the purveyors of Scottish education simply because he was left-handed.[60]

If school and the local community were unwelcoming, the family could perhaps be relied upon to offer love and safety, but this was not always Ivor's experience. An aspirational Jewish family hoped for its children to rise above their parents' station in life and for many of these families the aspiration for their sons was a professional career, in particular a career in medicine.[61] It was not easy to achieve. Academic ability on the part of the boy, and financial resources on the part of the family, were the minimum requirements for the successful completion of medical education. Bernard and Joseph would be the sons to achieve the status of doctor. Bernard first left home at the age of thirteen, destined not for medical school but for a career as a rabbi. Four years later, remembers his sister Beth, he decided "it would be better to cure people's bodies than their souls and so returned to Glasgow and studied medicine." A few years later, Joseph followed him to Glasgow University medical school. Bernard and Joseph were seen as the cleverest members of the family – Beth recalls that Joseph was the brightest "and he let us all know about it" – but Ivor was seen as strange. "What I heard from general family chit-chat growing up was that Ivor was 'different', they didn't take him seriously," says Lee Freeman.

Ivor doesn't appear to have harboured any strong ambition to be a doctor. However, Freeman thinks he regretted that he hadn't gone to university. She was told that Jack and Polly couldn't afford to send him, which is plausible as he and Bernard would have overlapped at university, whereas Joseph didn't begin medical school until Bernard passed his final examinations in January 1945.[62] However, Ivor gave a more dramatic explanation for not following a medical career, claiming that when the war started he wanted to go into medicine until his father explained the brutality of the training: "He said if you're going to become a doctor, you've got to get hold of a frog and smash its head against a wall, like the Nazis did with babies, and then dip it into a bath of acid …"[63]

Before the outbreak of war, Ivor lost his religious faith. Aged fifteen, he heard a speaker from the Rationalist Society, went home, lay in bed "and said nasty to God and God didn't kill me."[64] Soon after, Ivor said, "[I] asked the minister of this progressive Jewish thing 'Do you know if there's a God?' He said no. Probably he'd had a rotten night or something. And that was it, really."[65] That may have been it as far as a belief in God was concerned, but his cultural background remained with him: he told the *Jewish Chronicle*, "Religion is not relevant to my life, but I was born a Jew and there is no way you can hide under the carpet, not that I want to."[66]

Then he attempted to end his life, using a packet of aspirin Bernard had brought home from medical school:

> It was a packet of six. I looked at it and it said "Maximum dose: two." So, one night I took the whole six, and then I wrote a good-bye letter ... This was the mid-1930s, when Hitler was doing his thing. And not only that, the torture of being a teenager. I woke up all refreshed the following morning and I said to my brother: "You know these aspirin? I took them all and I tried to kill myself." He told my mum and dad. God, they were deeply embarrassed.[67]

The all-refreshed Ivor soon had other decisions to make.

4 A Life in the Clouds

"I was called the Dreamer when I was a boy," Ivor recalled.[1] Dreamers are all very well, but when life requires a more practical approach they're not the most popular of people. The teenage Ivor, the lover of art and music, was rapidly approaching a time when decisions about career, family, independence, were going to be expected. If medicine wasn't on the cards, because of economic constraints, his father's fanciful description of anatomy lessons, or a lack of motivation on Ivor's part, then what would he do for a living? Final decisions were yet to be made when more pressing matters intervened.

By 1939, with the Cutlers established in their Pollokshaws Road flat, national and local plans were being developed to deal with civilian emergencies in the event of war. Major cities were seen as key targets for German bombers and evacuation plans were put in place to minimise civilian casualties. In Scotland, population centres with more than fourteen thousand people per square mile, especially those with key industries like shipbuilding or engineering, were identified as "sending areas," the biggest by far being Glasgow. Rural parts of the country, with population densities of less than one hundred people per square mile, were to become "receiving areas," ready and able to accept evacuees from sending areas. When war was declared the evacuation plan was immediately put into operation: by the end of September around 175,000 people had been evacuated from the sending areas, including over sixty thousand unaccompanied children.[2]

The younger Cutlers moved to the safer environments of country towns and villages. Ivor and Joseph went to Annan, on the north shore of the Solway Firth just eight miles from England, and Rita and Beth travelled to Carluke, just 24 miles southeast of Glasgow city centre, in Lanarkshire's Clyde Valley.[3] The evacuations were short-lived, the last few months of 1939 became known as the phoney war and there was little experience of enemy action in Scotland.

Many evacuees returned home, Ivor and his siblings among them. Beth remembers that they were back in Glasgow by January 1940 and life gradually returned to some sort of normality, although Beth started school earlier than she had expected, beginning classes that month when she was not yet five.

Ivor finished school in June 1940.[4] His father may have tried to get him to follow in his footsteps as an agent, but if so, his attempts failed. Instead, Ivor became an apprentice engineer at the Rolls-Royce factory in Hillington.[5] To those who only know Ivor from his work as a writer and performer, such an apprenticeship seems incongruous, but this was a teenager who was good at maths, especially trigonometry, so engineering would have looked like a sensible choice. Fifty years later he said that he "loved the aesthetics" of the work, but felt that he didn't fit in.[6] Drawing on memories of his time at the factory, he gave some insight into the turbulence of his teenage years to a couple of young interviewers: "Came home to me what being your age means. Saying fuck, shit and cunt just as I did, age 17, working at Rolls-Royce on aero-engines, sensitive as hell, a number one pain in the arse at home, suicidal, rejecting religion, going dancing to find girls. Thanks for bringing it back."[7]

The Rolls-Royce factory was vital to the British war effort, producing Merlin engines for Spitfires, and engineers involved in this work were in a "reserved occupation," membership of which absolved individuals from military service. However, as war progressed younger men in these occupations were encouraged to volunteer for the forces and from early in 1941 all men in reserved occupations, of whatever age, were able to apply for service with the Royal Air Force. Advertisements ran in national newspapers to tempt them to do so even if, in practice, many employers were reluctant to see their skilled employees joining up: "I was a motor fitter. But I wasn't satisfied – No sir! Thinks I, I'm fighting fit and only twenty-seven. I could be giving it back to Jerry, up there!" ran one advertisement which emphasised that "Even if reserved you can fly with the RAF."[8]

As refugees arrived in Glasgow, news of the Nazi treatment of Jews travelled through the Scottish community. Beth believes that this affected her brother, who she describes as a sensitive seventeen-year-old. In March 1941 the Luftwaffe bombed Glasgow and Clydeside for four nights, destroying or damaging thousands of properties, including many houses and tenement buildings. The Gorbals area was hit and the Goldbergs were just one of many families whose homes were attacked: Jack and Polly gave Tilly and Eva a temporary home until they were able to return.[9] Phyllis King believes Ivor's decision to volunteer was "partly because people were saying things about Jews never taking part. He was going to do his bit." Many people believed Jews were shirking their responsibilities in the war effort, a belief given credence by the fact that many Jewish men and women who served were not recorded as Jewish in official records, fearing what might happen if they were captured by German forces.[10] Ivor himself referred to a newspaper headline: "I saw in the Daily Record, a banner headline: 'Abraham Levi, Conscientious Objector', and I knew what that was about.'[11] In the middle of 1941 he travelled to Edinburgh and volunteered for service with the Royal Air Force Volunteer Reserve, registering as Isadore Cutler. Soon after, #1562357 Cutler, I. started his training programme.[12]

By the end of 1940 the need for air crew meant that recruitment widened beyond the educated middle- and upper-class men who formed the core of the pre-war service. Young men from a wider range of backgrounds could now be accepted for air crew training and even basic schooling was sufficient for entry to flying courses as long as applicants were fit and showed "an aptitude for learning."[13] Ivor had more than a basic education, showed an aptitude for mathematics and was, one assumes, physically fit: he was selected for navigator training. For many young men, pilots were the most glamorous of RAF personnel and the most aspirational role for a young volunteer would be flying Hurricanes or Spitfires. If Ivor attempted to be selected for pilot training he was unsuccessful. In later years he claimed that it had never been his aim: "I never wanted to be a pilot because I was a cocky seventeen-year-old and thought it would be like driving a bus."[14]

The first step in Ivor's preparation for a front-line role was probably attendance at an Air Crew Reception Centre, where medical and dental inspections took place along with administration. Number 1 Air Crew Reception Centre was based at Lord's Cricket Ground in London – a memorial plaque can be seen on the wall of the members' pavilion. The centre's atmosphere was relaxed, with the only real daily exercise gained by walking to Regent's Park for meals at London Zoo's restaurant.[15] Phyllis King believes that Ivor must have done some basic training in London, "because when we used to pass a big block of flats near Regent's Park he'd remember staying there." The next step was the beginning of flying training, requiring a move to an Initial Training Wing. Here, the new recruits concentrated on physical fitness, signalling, drill and aircraft recognition, before moving on to the next stage in the process, in Ivor's case to specialist navigation training. In October 1940 this training moved from Britain to Port Albert in Canada: the need for operational bases in the UK and the potential disruption to training caused by German raids meant that training bases outside the UK were vital.[16] Ivor set off for Canada, making his one and only visit to North America.

Ivor enjoyed his time in Canada, even if he was less enamoured of the actual task of navigating. He told Phyllis King "how wonderful it was when he got there, with all the food that was available. And having a weekend off, when they'd gone to Toronto. He said it was very old-fashioned. Then of course he loved the flying and being up in the sky and plotting the route." Ciara Nolan, who knew him in the 1990s, remembers Ivor telling stories about "how nice it was sitting in this glass bubble and looking at the clouds," and Christine Stark recalls him saying that he liked looking at the clouds rather than doing the navigating. Even the noise of the aircraft in flight gave him enormous pleasure.[17] The BBC television documentary, *Ivor Cutler: Looking for Truth with a Pin*, showed a number of photographs from Ivor's RAF days. In one, he's wearing his RAF cap with a white flash indicating that he's air crew; another shows him shovelling snow; in another he's one of twenty-five RAF men in front of a twin-engine plane, the teenaged Ivor looking almost stereotypically like an RAF flyer with his thick, dark, hair Brylcreemed down and swept back, a neatly clipped moustache on his upper lip – but his tie is slightly askew, not as straight as those of his comrades.

These stories and photos make life as an RAF navigator trainee seem almost idyllic – hours spent in Canadian skies, the pilot doing the hard work while the navigator could simply stare at the sky – but even training in the safety of Canada was fraught with dangers. Aircraft malfunction, pilot error, stormy weather or mid-air collisions were everyday risks as were the environmental stressors within the aircraft, such as noise, vibration, glare and cramp: if high-altitude training was undertaken these risks were compounded by the dangers of hypothermia or anoxia. Aircrew could die in training and many did: in 1943, as training intensified, 850 Allied aircrew died in 298 bomber accidents in the USA.[18]

However much Ivor enjoyed his training, the RAF was, ultimately, unimpressed by Ivor. He failed to qualify as a navigator and returned to Scotland. The story of how, or why, or even when, he failed the course is one of the most-repeated stories of Ivor's pre-fame life and his own telling of the tale changed over time. In one version, he said that he was just one flight away from qualification when two examiners decided that his route plotting was too erratic: "That was my war experience and I was deeply embarrassed at the time … But with hindsight I think the Almighty must have had it in mind for me to do something more important than getting shot to pieces." In another version he claimed that he "liked looking at cloud formations too much so I went off course all the time, so eventually they said I was dangerous and grounded me."[19] Phyllis King said that he was "too much of a dreamer," while John Knutas summarised the examiners' opinion as "too dreamy and unfocussed." Many people speak of this as if the idea of a "dreamy" navigator was rather hilarious, but front-line aircrew would have viewed the prospect of flying with a dreamy and unfocussed navigator with trepidation. Ivor did not see his dismissal as a laughing matter and was hurt by his failure: Knutas said that Ivor "told me that he'd both felt and been called a coward during the process of that rejection, which had troubled him a great deal ever since."

Later on, Ivor's friend and manager David Jones recalls, "He would say, according to which day of the week it was, that he'd been in Bomber Command or Coastal Command." As he didn't complete his specialist training and so was not sent to an operational unit, it's more likely that he was never assigned to a Command at all. It's notable, too, that while many people who served in the armed forces made friends for life and joined in reunions and remembrance services every year, Ivor seems to have done neither of these things. There is no mention of RAF friends or reunions in any of Ivor's interviews or letters I have seen and no one I spoke with told me of any. Dan Cutler knows of his father's RAF days, but is uncertain about what exactly went on: "There's a series of things that I kind of remember being said, but a discussion of, or any real understanding of what he'd actually done and where and when, I don't know. There is this sense that things were never quite clear."

Other, positive, experiences from his RAF days stayed with Ivor for many years, helping to shape his love of art and music. Early in his training, at RAF Cranwell, Ivor first heard Schubert's String Quartet Number 14 in D Minor, "Death and the Maiden," performed in somewhat incongruous circumstances by the Griller Quartet. Wearing badly cut RAF suits and looking rather pathetic and awkward, the quartet sat down and started to play, "and of course it was sheer magic. And I thought 'Hey, there's a war on and these guys are playing this utterly beautiful music with these terrible suits on' and it was just terribly sad ..."[20] Off duty time gave Ivor a chance to learn more about another musical genre he grew to love – jazz. On the bases, leisure time was spent in the Navy, Army and Air Force Institutes canteen (the NAAFI). According to Ivor, each canteen held a piano which anyone could play and he watched the skilled piano players avidly, learning a few chords, and developing his own ability.[21]

Looking beyond the clouds, Ivor saw something else that affected him deeply and that he recalled with obvious pleasure on a radio show over forty years later: "When I studied air navigation I met and fell in love with the Orion constellation and when the lonely feelings stir I've only to look out the window."[22] He wrote to John Knutas, asking him if the Orion constellation was visible in Helsinki, telling him how he could see it in the autumn sky over London in the early hours and referring to Orion as "a comforting sight."[23]

With navigator training behind him, Ivor returned to Glasgow. He took on work at the Winsor Engineering Company, at 11–39 Cogan Street in Pollokshaws, and stayed there until the end of the war. It was uninspiring work, but it did give him one source of pleasure: "I very much enjoyed the factory noises in the same way as I enjoy thunder and lightning. Whenever I see lightning I immediately start counting to see how many miles away it is and when it gets very close it's very exciting."[24] The company advertised itself as "heating, ventilation and general engineers, sheet-metal and plate workers, acetylene and electric welders."[25] Ivor became the storeman and first-aider, useful work in a factory engaged in engineering, but not the wartime work Ivor had envisaged when he volunteered. Neither was it the sort of job that would keep him engaged until he reached pensionable age. Beth, now a primary school pupil, enjoyed Ivor's presence at the family's new home in Redburn Avenue, remembering him as a sympathetic big brother who would talk with her, answer questions and explain things: "Ivor always was very nice to me ... And he was prepared to spend time explaining things like socialism and the health service." He was keen to continue with music, too, and soon after the end of the war he bought a baby grand piano for the family home. Whether or not other family members made use of the instrument is unclear, but according to his sister, Ivor would spend many hours sitting at the piano and improvising. Music, however, did not keep him gainfully employed and Winsor Engineering did not engage his creativity. He needed to find other employment. He found teaching.

In the late 1940s, Ivor attended Jordanhill Training College for Teachers in Glasgow.[26] Around that time he also went to classes at Glasgow School of Art, where, he told Phyllis King, he learned to draw. An early experiment had met with failure, he told Dan Geesin, the son of his friend and fellow musician Ron Geesin, when at Ibrox school he drew a bus driving over hills, "a 'bendy bus' that followed the contours." He was very pleased with the way the bus followed the bumps in the road, but his teacher told him that he couldn't do that because "buses are not bendy!" "So after that," he told Dan, "I just did what I wanted." A more successful attempt appears in Ivor's *Times* obituary, but this tale places Ivor at Jordanhill training college, where he drew jagged mountains before adding a larger-than-life bus that followed their contours, giving him the sensation of being in charge of the painting.[27]

Phyllis, a teacher herself, was unsure why he decided to teach "but there seems to be a lot of the teacher in him."[28] The immediate post-war years offered plenty of opportunity for would-be teachers. The 1945 Education Act raised the school leaving age from twelve to fifteen, so steps were actively taken to recruit new staff and men and women recently demobilised from the armed forces were encouraged to apply. Jordanhill Training College, already one of the largest teacher-training institutions in Britain, expanded rapidly after 1945 and by the 1960s it claimed to be one of the largest teachers' colleges in the Commonwealth, with over three thousand students.[29] Ivor trained as a secondary school teacher, as men were not admitted to the primary education course until 1967. However, all students ended their training with a period of infant teaching, giving an insight into classroom activities with younger children. Jordanhill opened in 1921 but traced its history back by almost a century to the pioneering work of the Scottish teacher and educationalist David Stow.[30] Stow aimed for learning to be enjoyable, making physical activity key to his approach, with "marching and singing, clapping hands and exercises" enabling children to let off steam so they became more obedient and more attentive. He did not award prizes, concerned that they fostered jealousy and bad feelings, and he condemned the use of corporal punishment.[31] One hundred years later, Ivor would show himself to be sympathetic to much of Stow's approach.

Two crucial events took place in 1948, when Ivor was at Jordanhill. His grandfather Moris died on 7 September at the Victoria Infirmary; his cause of death was listed as coronary thrombosis and his name recorded as "Morris Cutler (formerly Kushner)."[32] And on an unspecified date, Ivor had sex for the first time: "I never had intercourse until I was twenty-five, people gasp at that nowadays," he revealed in a radio interview.[33]

If Jordanhill's lineage still drove its 1940s curriculum, even to a small extent, then Ivor must have felt positively about taking up his place in the education of the new generation of Scots. The reality of work in the Scottish education system was very different. After qualifying, Ivor set to work in South School, Paisley: class sizes were very large – Ivor told Gavin Hogg that his first class was of fifty-two ten-year-olds – discipline was expected to be strict, and pupils who stepped out of line even slightly were punished physically.

Robert McMillan – the father of Joyce McMillan, the theatre critic of the *Scotsman* – trained at Jordanhill and taught at South School. McMillan, his best friend George Kerr and Ivor bonded together at the school: all ex-forces, critical of the establishment, and new to the profession. Joyce McMillan remembers that her father "absolutely loved Ivor" and thought that he was "incredibly droll in the staff room, keeping his fellow teachers amused at break times." A photograph from the time shows Mr Cutler and an older teacher sitting at the centre of forty boys and girls, all around ten years of age. Most of the children are smiling and the older man, straight-backed and dark-suited, seems to be doing his best to look cheery, but Ivor is less convincing. He's wearing a tweed jacket and flannels but no tie, his legs are crossed and a half-smile plays on his face. He's sporting a beard but much of the Brylcreemed hair seen in his RAF photos has gone: male-pattern baldness is in full flight. A second photo, possibly taken a little earlier, shows him standing to the left of a group of ten boys and girls (it may be cropped from a larger image). This time, he's wearing a tie and a smarter jacket. His baldness doesn't look quite so advanced, there's no beard, but he is sporting a moustache. He stares straight at the camera, no attempt at a smile. In neither picture does he look like a man who's still in his twenties.[34]

Corporal punishment was a daily occurrence at South School and Mr Cutler was expected to deliver it when necessary. He rebelled, at least at first, but eventually he was forced to give in: "I didn't use the strap and I was getting a nervous breakdown because they thought I was a softie."[35] The weapon of choice for Scottish teachers who were intent on inflicting physical punishment was the tawse, a two-foot-long leather strap split lengthways to create two or three leather tongues and used to administer a painful slap to an errant pupil's hand, legs or buttocks. It's a measure of the place of corporal punishment in the Scottish education system that each teacher bought their own tawse and that a Scottish company took pride in making the "best" ones. The Lochgelly Tawse, heavier, narrower and firmer than its rivals, was famous across the country and John J. Dick Leather Goods had a seventy percent share of the tawse market.[36] Mr Cutler ordered a Lochgelly Tawse of his own, but when it arrived he thought that it was too thick and heavy and offered to exchange it for a thinner one: one teacher, "a real sadist," made the exchange. Mr Cutler hung the thin tawse on the wall and, unsurprisingly, his pupils decided to test him out. Feeling that he had no alternative, "I hit them."[37]

There's little, if any, evidence that Ivor enjoyed his time in Paisley. Only one of his anecdotes is positive, but even this story has a cautionary aspect to it. In charge of a drawing class, he told the pupils to draw an animal. In an echo of Ivor's own "bendy bus" picture, one boy drew an ass with fourteen legs rather than the regulation four, because he thought it looked better that way: "I wanted to lift him out of his cage and put my arms around him but my intellect told me not to which was lucky, because I would probably have been sent to prison."[38] After barely two years of teaching in Paisley the combination of large class sizes, rigid teaching strategies, strict discipline and the use of the tawse became too much for Mr Cutler. He secured a new teaching position and, when he left, he cut the tawse into pieces, giving one piece to each child "so they could think, 'Thus are the mighty fallen."[39]

Ivor left Paisley, Glasgow and Scotland behind. Years later, he explained that he left Scotland not because of his disillusionment with the Scottish education system, but because "everyone thought I was a nutter."[40] Whatever the reason, he was heading south of the border to spend the next two years living and working near Leiston in Suffolk, where he experienced a radically different approach to education.

5 Back to School

Ivor's new post was at Summerhill, the school established by Scottish writer and educationalist A. S. Neill with the aim of freeing children from adult authority:

> I see that all outside compulsion is wrong, that inner compulsion is the only value. And if Mary or David wants to laze about, lazing about is the one thing necessary for their personalities at the moment. Every moment of a healthy child's life is a working moment. A child has no time to sit down and laze. Lazing is abnormal, it is a recovery, and therefore it is necessary when it exists.[1]

Neill's philosophy was far outside mainstream educational ideas and the British press found itself both shocked and fascinated by the idea of a "school with no rules" which didn't force pupils to attend lessons and reportedly let them run around without clothes.[2] How would it suit a young teacher from Scotland who had only recently owned his own tawse?

Ivor – it seems unlikely that Summerhill pupils would have called him Mr Cutler – spent around two years teaching at the school. Zoë Readhead (Neill's daughter and the current head of Summerhill) remembers Ivor visiting her father, but was very young at the time and has no detailed memories of him. Photographs of Ivor at Summerhill show a rather more raffish figure than the one pictured at school in Paisley, but he's still far from the distinctively dressed man he would become. The hair is longer at the sides, the beard and moustache are bushier and merge into one, his shirt is open-necked and casual, but on visual appearances alone he doesn't cut a very memorable figure.[3]

Phyllis King felt that Summerhill was in tune with how Ivor thought teaching should be. Ivor spoke of being deeply affected by Neill's ideas: "I couldn't believe that there could be anything like – I think I said about it, like Fairyland." As Readhead explained, the Fairyland allowed "alternative people … to express themselves and be part of the school," the environment enabling Ivor "to explore his silliness … and realise that the children really grasped it and loved it." Teachers lived on site, took part in meetings and joined the community, but staff accommodation was simple, possibly just a hut or out-building, far more basic than the Cutlers' house, but not too far removed from wartime RAF sleeping quarters.[4] Even though Leiston may be isolated from Britain's major metropolitan centres, there was plenty to occupy the music-loving teacher in his free time. Summerhill is just a short and relatively flat cycle ride from the coastal town of Aldeburgh, home to Benjamin Britten and the annual music festival which he helped to establish in 1948. If Ivor wanted to explore English traditional music then another short cycle ride would take him to the Eel's Foot pub in Eastbridge, home of regular music and song sessions.[5]

Neill's attitude to his own parents suggests that he would have some sympathy with Ivor's childhood experiences: "It is the mother who makes the Scots home an uneasy place," wrote Neill, "in which one has to think three times before one speaks … My father did not care for me as a boy. Often he was cruel to me, and I acquired a definite fear of him."[6] Ivor spoke with great fondness about Neill, telling Andy Kershaw that he was a saint. Interviewed for Neill's biography, *Neill of Summerhill*, Ivor said "When you were with him you knew that you were allowed to be yourself, that you were approved of. His being around was enough. I loved him."[7] In 1994 he spoke of how Neill would "just let you be, warts 'n' all" and described him as "the only man that was utterly saintly."[8] A liberal and forward-looking educational environment, with a much-admired head teacher, should have offered Ivor a suitable place for a long and happy career, but two years later he was on the move again.

It's unclear why Ivor left Summerhill after so short a time: no records from the early 1950s survive so any official explanation has long since disappeared.[9] John Knutas believes that there was some sort of schism, while Ivor's own explanation was brief: "I had the time of my life but my headmaster thought I was no good … I got bored after two years because there were no women there. I like women."[10] Ivor did try one new teaching strategy at Summerhill, an attempt at reverse psychology in which he rewarded bad behaviour by giving the pupil twopence (around 1p). The experiment failed, simply costing Ivor money.[11]

Ivor moved further south, to the capital and to a fresh start: "That was the beginning of my life, going down to London," he said in a television interview, although in another interview he dated the beginning of his life to a different event that took place over a decade later. The beginning or not, London became Ivor's home for the rest of his life.[12]

Ivor taught for the Inner London Education Authority (ILEA) for almost thirty years, working at a range of schools across the city and enlightening his young charges about poetry, drama and music. His thoughts on education and his approaches to teaching were not always welcomed by the senior staff – he claims to have walked out of two schools because of disagreements with the head teachers.[13] However, he seems to have found a welcome at two schools in particular: Paddington Green and Fox Primary. Ivor's teaching methods in ILEA schools owed more to A. S. Neill and his own worldview than they did to the methods preferred in Paisley. He was happy to explain his methods, whether he was speaking to the tabloids, the broadsheets or the hippest of music journalists. When Michael Watts wanted to interview him for *Melody Maker*, Ivor suggested that he visit Paddington Green Primary and observe him in action: "An hour like that, he said, and I wouldn't need to speak to him on an interview basis." The observation never happened, so Ivor and Watts met and Ivor explained one of his strategies: "in one piece of drama I demonstrated the reaction of a young child to the birth of another ... How the child hated it because it had taken its place in the mother's affections. And, see, they breathed a sigh of relief when they realised that what they thought was not unnatural." If Ivor explained where this idea may have originated, Watts didn't tell his readers. As for Ivor's desired outcome of this immersive drama: "if they go on to love the baby, wow!"[14] Another strategy was "children's revenge," when he invited pupils to call him whatever they liked: "At one time, when I asked what DC stood for in music theory, a girl stood up and said 'Dirty Cutler'. I was in a bad mood, but that really cleared the air."[15]

Almost twenty-five years after Watts's interview, and fourteen years after his retirement from teaching, Ivor still offered the same explanation for his approach to the teaching of drama and movement:

> I used it therapeutically. Because all the normal childhood traumas like sibling hatred ... and lavatories and bad smells and mother/child things and death and so on ... I was able to imbue these situations with laughter ... and it was okay to enjoy terrible smells, for instance, and they stopped feeling guilty. That was the theory.[16]

If that was the theory, what was the practice? Ivor worked part-time, as he told a journalist for *Cream*, or split his working week between two schools, two days at Fox and three at Paddington Green, for example, as Phyllis King remembers.[17] Mr Cutler's classes were greeted with joy by most of the pupils, most of the time, but he had his critics. Ivor's son Dan, who went to Fox, knew of "aggrieved parents who felt that their children weren't being taught properly, who were fended off by the then head teacher, who I think was a great supporter."[18] The head's support was important to someone with radical ideas about education: Miss Dearden, the head of Fox in the 1970s, was "pretty open-minded" according to Charlotte Steel, a pupil there in 1972–1973, and this may help to explain Ivor's long-term relationship with that school. Miss Dearden retired at the end of the 1970s, just a year or two before Ivor left teaching.[19]

Other parents were much happier with Mr Cutler's educational strategies. Poet and performer Roger McGough, a teacher himself before finding fame as a member of the Liverpool Poets and the Scaffold, moved to Notting Hill Gate and sent his children to Fox. When he found out that Ivor taught there he thought "Oh, that's good. The kids will be well looked after." When Kate Williams, the daughter of guitarist John Williams, went to Fox her parents already knew of Ivor's reputation as a performer: "they'd always ask 'Did you have a good lesson with Ivor?' They met him at parents' evenings too ... My parents maybe weren't as conventional as most ..." Film director Ken Russell also knew Ivor and told his son Xavier, one of Mr Cutler's pupils from 1968 to 1971, "Oh, keep an eye on him. He's very artistic, I like what he says. It might not always make sense ..." It's worth noting that all of these parents have careers in the arts: perhaps it was the parents in more conventional occupations that baulked at Mr Cutler's unusual approach.

Dan did not enjoy his father's classes. Teachers' children have always felt awkward when taught by a parent and Dan found the situation "created a certain amount of aggro for me, with the other kids. Not only was I in a class where my dad was the teacher, but he was teaching such weird stuff." When Dan was interviewed in 2020, he expanded on this point:

> He was my dad and he was weird and I was kind of proud of him, but when the whole class is in their serried ranks and he's sitting at the piano and everybody in turn has to run up, face the whole class and say "I'm beautiful" and then run back – he could be embarrassing.[20]

The rest of the former pupils I spoke with were unanimous in their love of Mr Cutler and his teaching, describing his classes as feeling "a bit naughty"; calling him "a very generous teacher, quite anarchic and off the wall. I don't think we realised at the time how lucky we were to have someone like that"; or referring to him more simply as "wonderful" or "magical."[21] Some of their classmates, like some parents, felt differently. Jonathon Porritt, a friend of Ivor's and an ex-teacher, was someone who would have loved to have had Ivor as a teacher, "but," Porritt recalls, "he often implied that many didn't!" One pupil, the son of *Times* critic David Wade, responded to Mr Cutler's unorthodox style by refusing to go to school. Wade discovered that the cause of his son's reluctance to attend lay in the odd things he was asked to do in Mr Cutler's drama classes. The boy's parents insisted he carry on going to classes, and eventually he became "reconciled to and even enthusiastic for the Cutler method."[22] This is a rare and extreme response, but does demonstrate the impact Mr Cutler could have on the unwary child.

At Fox, Mr Cutler's classes took place away from the main school, in a building variously described as a studio or outbuilding and called the George Hall.[23] John-Paul Flintoff, taught by Mr Cutler between 1977 and 1979, doesn't remember ever going into class and finding him unprepared: he would always be "sitting at the piano and looking quite severe" as the pupils entered the hall. Outside lesson times, Mr Cutler kept himself to himself, staying in the building during breaks rather than visiting the staff room. As was the fashion at the time when lessons involved lots of physical activity, Mr Cutler's classes might involve the pupils stripping down to vest and pants before the lesson began: photos of the classes show barely dressed boys and girls seated around Mr Cutler at the piano, or standing by a window as he explained some aspect of the day's lesson. Once ready, Mr Cutler would play piano and the children would do what Rebecca Orr-Deas calls "silly dances." Dancing had a practical purpose, she recalls, "because it was so cold. I don't think George Hall was heated."

Former Fox pupils remember various lessons and games. One game involved groups of children "killing" each other. In the early 1970s the game was called "Cowboys, Indians and Red Cross," with children in the first two groups running around the classroom killing each other, before the Red Cross group moved from pupil to pupil making them come back to life.[24] When Alex Mermikides attended Fox in the late 1970s the game had developed. Mr Cutler divided the class into two rows, the first child pretended to shoot the next child, who died dramatically, then the next child had to cry out "Oh no, you've killed my wife" [or child or husband] and shoot the first child. When Alex and Ivor met later he told her this was not a game, but "drama therapy." In another game, Mermikides recalls, one child would be a "smelly tramp" on a bench and the second child played a "posh person" drawn irresistibly to the smell of the tramp.

Poetry and music were common threads across the years. These lessons were not about the great composers or the classical poets, they were much more fun. In poetry sessions, "he'd just sort of encourage us to write down the first thing that would come into our heads ... then he'd recite [the poems] with that fantastic style of delivery ... imagine if you were the least academic kid in the class, it was like a leveller. Everyone's poem would sound amazing."[25] Milton Mermikides, Alex's younger brother, enjoyed writing poetry "where you were the centre of the poem, so you would write about yourself." This was poetry as a means of self-discovery and self-expression. Music and poetry could combine with singing, either Mr Cutler's own songs or popular songs by the Beatles and others with his new lyrics: "Fried Liver," based on "Moon River," was a favourite.[26] There was Free Music, in which he shared percussion instruments, or any other instruments to hand, among the pupils.[27] Music lessons might involve the piano, the harmonium – Mr Cutler's own – or assorted percussion instruments. Mr Cutler was an inventive musician: "he played piano for us and put newspaper between the hammers and the strings

... the idea that you could modify the medium of the music just blew an impressionable seven-year-old's mind ... He played ragtime and when he put the newspaper in the piano [it] sounded like an old record: I thought that was incredible."[28] Percussion lessons often focused on what Mr Cutler called "African drumming," including what Rebecca Orr-Deas recalls as "a syncopated rhythm that's always stayed with me: two against three."

Mr Cutler showed his pupils kindness and support. Xavier Russell recalls that if a pupil looked depressed or sad he would ask them why they were looking like that and would make something up to cheer them up: "His eye would always wander over everyone." During lunchbreaks, any pupil could pop in for a chat or a private lesson. Kate Williams and her friends would call in for ad hoc piano lessons: "we went in one day and he played us a 12-bar blues, although I didn't know that's what it was at the time. You'd just copy the chords he was playing, so there'd be three of us at the piano with him and we'd just play along." Williams was from a musical family, but these lessons helped in her musical development: she has gone on to become an award-winning jazz musician and composer.

When Ella Huhne recalls Mr Cutler's kindness and support she's not speaking as an ex-pupil, but as the daughter of Ivor's friend, the actor Ann Murray.[29] During the 1960s Ella and her brother Chris saw Ivor frequently when he visited the family home. Ella doesn't know how Ivor and her mother met, but recalls being told that they acted together on a test production for BBC colour television which involved Ivor and two or three women in a bed, with her mother as one of the women. Chris remembers Ivor as "a person and a presence" around the family home, but Ivor's presence failed to develop young Chris's musical talents: he was on his way "towards final recognition of my lack of musicality" and eventually settled for careers in business and politics. Ivor left a greater impression on Ella. Murray and her husband, Peter Paul-Huhne, often held parties: with a father in business and a mother who acted, Ella describes the mix of guests as "quite extraordinary." At one party, Ivor played the family's piano. "He said to me 'Why don't you sing along.' I must have been pretty small and I said 'I can't sing'. He said 'Everybody can sing!' I remember that so well, it was so lovely, the way he said it ... There was something about him that was very accessible to a child, because he worked with his imagination all the time."

Jo Willingham knew Ivor when she was a teenager, having moved to London in the mid-1970s and become a friend of Phyllis King's daughter Anna. She visited Anna and her mother at their flat, where she would often meet Ivor, and recalls that while he could be intimidating, he could also be kind. She stayed in touch with him for some years, firstly through Anna, then through her own sister, Sandra Brownjohn. When she successfully applied for a job after graduating, Ivor wrote her a reference. Above all, she recalls, "It was the best feeling if you could make him laugh," but this wasn't easy. To do so, "You had to be on your game."

At Fox Primary, mysterious strangers would sometimes appear in George Hall. Orr-Deas recalls days when "trendy, 'hippy', women in long dresses would come into class and watch. I don't remember them being introduced to us." Williams remembers that "Sometimes he'd have young, student-age, men with him. They'd come and sit in on the classes and he'd always refer to them as his 'sons'. We knew they weren't, they couldn't all be because there were different ones each time." Whether these were official observations, by teaching or social work students for example, is unclear: Dan Cutler is adamant that he never observed one of his father's classes. Given that Ivor was happy to invite a *Melody Maker* journalist to his classroom, it's possible that some, if not all, of these observers visited at his invitation alone. Caroline Richmond was one person who observed a class at Ivor's personal invitation, even though she had no interest in teaching. "He suggested it," she told me, "I wouldn't have dared to ask. He enjoyed encouraging [the children] to be a bit naughty." Richmond watched Mr Cutler playing a boogie-woogie version of "God Save the Queen" and encouraging the children to sing along: "Then he stopped the piano ... and asked, glaring with feigned disapproval, "Who sang 'God Shave the Queen'?" No one owned up, of course, because no one had. He ticked them off and restarted. Whereupon, of course, they all sang it."[30] Mr Cutler's sartorial style was also becoming more and more distinctive. Hats now featured regularly, perhaps a deerstalker, or a little skull cap full of badges and little bees on wires, and odd socks were commonplace.[31] Alex Mermikides thought, with reference to a popular children's television series of the time, that her teacher "dressed like a Womble." He cycled to school, arriving on his bicycle "with all his bits and bobs, ringing his bell," with his portable harmonium strapped to the bike.[32]

This oddly dressed, bicycling, liberal-minded arts teacher seems like an obvious target for pupil tricks and misbehaviours, but his former pupils remember that Mr Cutler's classes rarely lapsed into ill-discipline and, if they did, he was skilled in quashing any attempted rule-breaking. There was corporal punishment at Fox. Kate Williams recalls pupils getting hit with a ruler, or a hymn book, but not by Mr Cutler: "I don't remember Ivor ever laying a finger on anyone. I just don't think he would have done that." Mr Cutler could "convey disapproval with no words. Just stopping and looking at you in a certain way – that was quite an effective deterrent," according to Alex Mermikides. Charlotte Steel remembers another strategy:

> If people were naughty he got really cross. A few boys didn't like the classes so they'd be a bit naughty and he'd say "Right. Question Time." We'd all have to sit back in the semi-circle and he'd ask questions about the universe or something. We'd all get really pissed off if there was too much Question Time.

John-Paul Flintoff also recalls a version of Question Time, when Mr Cutler would order pupils into three rows according to height, tallest at the right of the back row, shortest at the left of the front row, and they would then sit cross-legged on the floor before the questions began.

Former pupils recall only two occasions when Mr Cutler lost his temper. In one game, in which he called out different characters to mime, one child performed a goose step and he "went livid ... absolutely livid." In another class a boy started talking about the Holocaust: Ivor quickly ordered him to stop.[33] Lessons usually ended with the theme song from the BBC TV series *Andy Pandy* on piano: if there was too much bad behaviour he would sometimes draw the class to a close by playing that tune a little earlier than usual.[34]

Ivor left teaching in 1980, feeling that he'd "psychologically outgrown" the need to teach. He told Ena Kendall he had enjoyed his time as a teacher and could count ex-pupils as his friends, but never wanted to see another child: "I suffer from empathy, I don't have the means of shutting off and then everybody's vibes just walk in and destroy me."[35] He also felt that his approach was becoming untenable in the changing climate of education, leaving before he would have been sacked for not conforming to expected practice.[36]

Ivor retained a great deal of respect for the teaching profession. A *New Musical Express* article from 1988 asked "What would you do if you ruled the world?" He responded with ten key points, one being "Teaching would be the top profession, with teachers worthy of the name, and the cream in the nursery and infants, using AS Neill's principles."[37] Ivor amused his friend Jonathon Porritt by his continued argument that the younger the age group you were teaching, the more you would be paid: "So professors teaching postgraduates would get a great deal less than teachers in Primary Schools!" Respect for the profession isn't the same as respect for its practitioners, however. Twenty years after Ivor's own career ended, he recalled that many teachers, heads and inspectors were "a pathetic lot."[38]

Teaching gave Ivor a regular salary, but his need to be creative remained unfulfilled. Soon after he arrived in London, he started attending art classes once again, this time at evening sessions in the Camberwell School of Art, whose post-war students included jazz trumpeter Humphrey Lyttelton.[39] He went with a friend, Ron Lawrence, who he met when they were teaching at adjacent schools. The class was run by Neville Smith, who favoured a mathematical approach to drawing, emphasising the marking of dots on the paper to represent specific points on the model's body, which could then be joined together accurately to create the image. William Coldstream developed this style, colloquially referred to as "dot and carry," and it was taken up enthusiastically by his followers, including some of the staff at Camberwell. The artist Victor Pasmore remembered sitting for Coldstream in the 1930s, when he arrived with "a plumb-line and ruler ... he started with the eye then measured the distance to the next eye. He measured up every detail."[40]

At the first lesson, according to Lawrence, Ivor "just sat there looking at the model ... he said he didn't know where to start." Smith suggested that he pick a point at the top of the sternum, then find the tip of the shoulder and mark another point, and so on. At the next session, Lawrence recalled, Ivor arrived with a geometry set, "protractor, set square, rulers, you name it, and there he was measuring the angles so he could get it dead accurate, put his dot, put his dot. 'I can draw!' And that's how he learned to draw."[41] It's an amusing story, and there's no reason to doubt that these events happened, but Phyllis King is sure that Ivor learnt to draw at the Glasgow School of Art and anyone familiar with his drawings might wonder when his geometry set disappeared. Ivor may have been playing tricks on Neville Smith and his point-to-point method, his cry of "I can draw!" not a declaration of a "Eureka!" moment, but a sarcastic comment on Smith's approach.

Another of Lawrence's anecdotes illustrates Ivor's potentially damaging approach to art criticism when they visited the Tate Gallery and viewed one of Francis Bacon's works. Ivor, Lawrence said with some understatement, was not a fan of Bacon and decided drastic action was required to fully express his lack of admiration: "'Ron,' he said, 'I'm gonna take out my penis and I'm gonna pee all over it.' I persuaded him not to." Ivor may have been willing to inflict urinary damage on paintings he disliked, but he could be effusive in his praise of artists he admired, although his admiration wasn't constant. He admired Giorgio Morandi so much that he wrote a poem, "To Giorgio Morandi," in tribute, but at a 1984 performance he told the audience that Morandi was "at the top of my First Eleven until two or three years ago when I psychologically outgrew him." Four years later, Ivor had apparently revised his opinion and in a *New Musical Express* article he placed Morandi in a list of favourite artists that included Joan Miró, Paul Klee, Barbara Hepworth, Henry Moore and Ivor's friend Craig Murray-Orr, as well as cartoonists Glen Larson, Bernard Kliban, Michael Leunig and Martin Honeysett.[42] Miró suffered a similar fate to Morandi a few years later. After Gavin Hogg sent him an exhibition catalogue, Ivor told him that while he'd outgrown Miró, he'd enjoyed the later drawings in the catalogue, so Hogg's thoughtfulness had not been wasted.[43]

Francis Bacon owed Ron Lawrence a debt of gratitude for preventing Ivor's urinary protest. Lawrence also played a key role in another of Ivor's major life events when, in the early 1950s, the pair went on a double – possibly blind – date. Virginia Pearson, a decade younger than Ivor, was one of the women on that date.[44] Virginia was described to me as "a lovely person," "elegant … beautiful and kind."[45] She was born in Preston, Lancashire, in 1933, the daughter of George, a factory manager, and Beryl and, as her son Dan recalls, "came down to London to look for something in life." Ivor and Virginia's first date developed into a relationship, and they married on 4 September 1954. Ivor was living in Marmora Road, in southeast London; Virginia was in Warwick Way, a short walk from the Houses of Parliament. The wedding took place in Westminster Register Office and, in contrast to his RAF recruitment record, the marriage certificate recorded the groom's name as Ivor, not Isadore. Ivor's occupation was given as "School Teacher," but no occupation was listed for Virginia. Beth was the only member of Ivor's family to attend. She was late, she recalls, and didn't know any of the other four guests, who she remembers as being two couples: "They might as well have been people from off the street ..." The party went for lunch after the ceremony, but Beth remembers little of the celebration and nothing more of her fellow guests. The two witnesses named on the marriage certificate are Ann White and Dymphna Porter, possibly fellow teachers, possibly friends of the bride or groom.[46]

In *Looking for Truth with a Pin*, Ivor's friend Jon Webster, who first met him many years after the marriage, said that because Virginia was a gentile the marriage "did not go down well with his Jewish parents." However, speaking with me in 2021, Webster did not remember this and said that Ivor never talked about his marriage with him. Ivor had long since given up on his Jewish faith, so this difference in religious background is unlikely to have troubled him. It's unclear how upset Jack and Polly were: Beth remembered that the rest of the family met with Ivor from time to time, which suggests that any upset was resolved or possibly never actually happened.

Soon after the marriage, Ivor and Virginia moved to Dunstans Road in East Dulwich, their home on 29 March 1955 when Jeremy Simon Cutler was born in Dulwich Hospital.[47] Their next home was a flat at 27 Nassington Road, which was, according to Dan Cutler, "in the top floor of what is now a very sought-after house on the edge of Hampstead Heath, but then was somewhere my father could afford." The family was living at the Nassington Road flat when, in February 1957, Dan was born at Queen Mary's Maternity Home in Hampstead.[48] A photograph from the children's early years shows Ivor, the proud father, pushing Dan in his pram and keeping a protective hand on Jeremy's back. Other photos show one of the boys wearing a kilt: an unlikely form of apparel for a toddler from the centre of London.[49] As Dan recalled on *Looking for Truth with a Pin*, Ivor was keen to pursue this style of dress for some time, to his son's dismay: "None but he would think it would be a great idea to send your kid on their very first day to their first school, in central London, wearing a fucking kilt." Speaking in 2021, he said that "It wasn't a routine thing but it's very difficult to recall." Did it actually happen? "We all believe so, but that's not always the same thing." "I still can't recall the specific memory," he added shortly afterwards.

Jeremy also remembered how his father's actions didn't always meet his son's expectations. As a young child, Jeremy wanted to go fishing: a simple and common enough wish for a small boy, but his father, who he said "didn't really want to engage with the tangible," took an unorthodox approach. Jeremy recalled how Ivor's approach to fishing involved tying a fork to a length of string and dangling it over a puddle. The result, said Jeremy, "was a kind of public humiliation, because I knew we weren't going to catch a fish." Ivor's imaginative approach was more successful when it came to telling bedtime stories, Jeremy remembered, when Ivor and his sons would "make it up as we went along. Me and my brother would be the drivers of the Royal Scot train to Scotland."[50]

By the later 1950s, Ivor was formulating a plan to leave teaching and become a full-time painter. Ivor knew what he wanted to do, but wasn't sure how he could do it. As the father of young children he needed to maintain an income and painting was, at least at first, unlikely to match his salary from the Inner London Education Authority, so a radical change of direction was needed: "'How do I make money?' so I thought 'Oh, I'll write songs and then people will sing them and I'll get royalties.'"[51] How hard could it be?

Very hard, as it turned out. Ivor wrote some songs and set about bringing them to the attention of Britain's music industry, notably the music publishers in the Denmark Street area of Soho known as Tin Pan Alley. By his own estimate, Ivor spent two years on this fruitless search for a songwriting career.[52] Then he arrived at the offices of Box & Cox.

6 A Life of Whimsical Fantasies

H. Elton Box and Desmond Cox were showbiz entrepreneurs, and writers of songs including "The Wheel of the Wagon is Broken," recorded by the Paul Whiteman Orchestra, and "I've Got a Lovely Bunch of Coconuts."[1] By the 1950s they were operating as Box & Cox, music publishers, based at 7 Denmark Street in the heart of Tin Pan Alley.[2] According to hit songwriter Bill Martin, Box and Cox were often willing to listen to new compositions, however odd they might be:

> You would be invited to play them your song, and then afterwards, one of them would say, "What do you think, Mr Box?" and the reply would be "I'm not sure Mr Cox." They then asked if you had a song like "A Lovely Bunch of Coconuts." They would do things for a laugh, and give you money.[3]

If any of Tin Pan Alley's music publishers were likely to appreciate the songs of Ivor Cutler, it was Box & Cox.

Box invited Ivor to play a song. In Ivor's words, Box had "never seen anything so funny in his life." Ivor sat at the piano with his back to Box and Cox and, having been told to sing whatever he wanted, performed "some songs about a guy with a hole in his head, or something …" Eventually, he turned round on hearing a strange noise, to find that Box was lying on the floor: "his face was purple. They said 'He wants to laugh but he daren't in case you get offended' … I said 'I meant to be funny, you can laugh.'" The audition was a success and Ivor signed with Box & Cox. He was still aiming to write songs for others to perform, but although Box offered the songs to different artists – Ivor claimed that Peter Sellers and Spike Milligan were among them – none took up the offer.[4] Ivor finally said "seven words that changed my life … 'Perhaps I ought to sing them myself.'"[5]

Around this time he made his first attempt at live performance, at a venue called the Blue Angel. It was, the story goes, an "unmitigated failure."[6] The reasons for such a disappointing debut are now lost, while the venue itself is open to debate, with most sources simply referring to it as being in London, while some give its location as Islington. There was a Blue Angel pub in Islington, on the City Road, but in the 1950s it was called the Blue Coat Boy.[7] A Mayfair club called the Blue Angel, on Berkeley Street, did exist in the 1950s and was popular with "debutantes and Guards officers."[8] This Blue Angel is the likeliest venue for Ivor's onstage debut: a year or two later David Frost performed there, with an act full of Peter Cook jokes, suggesting that it was willing to play host to the rising stars of satire.[9] Even this venue doesn't seem suited to Ivor's early musical experiments and rejection at the beginning of his intended new career probably put him off live performance.

As live performance was not yet his forte, in August 1957 Ivor wrote to the BBC offering his services as a radio star. Having heard and enjoyed a Third Programme show featuring songs by the American satirist Tom Lehrer, he felt that a programme of his own songs would prove popular with Third Programme audiences: as he put it, they would be "diverted exceeding" by such a show. He had a dozen songs ready for performance, which he described as musically sound with lyrics influenced by The Goons, Flanders and Swann, Paul Klee and Franz Kafka, and he added that he could accompany himself on harmonium, guitar or piano. Two weeks later, the BBC firmly but politely refused Ivor's kind offer.[10]

The BBC's indifference left Box with two problems to overcome: selling Ivor as a songwriter and selling Ivor as a performer. It was time to call on his friends in the media. Ned Sherrin, a BBC producer who described Box as a "Cockney–Runyonesque–Charing Cross character," was one such friend and one evening, at Box's invitation, he went to Box & Cox's "seedy premises at the end of Denmark Street" with the journalist and scriptwriter Caryl Brahms. It's clear from Sherrin's memory of the meeting that this was far from the glittering world of showbiz:

> The office appeared to be empty apart from Ivor, a fey, gnomish figure idly tinkling on a harmonium. Further into the room I spotted Boxy behind the door, peeing into the sink. Seeing Caryl he buttoned up sharpish. He explained that he had thought of me because no one else in Denmark Street could make head nor tail of a talent so original, so "way out". Caryl and I found the repertoire of surreal, Edward Lear-like, offbeat, blackish, folksy songs intriguing.[11]

Sherrin remembered that at the end of the performance, Brahms said "Oh, it's folk surrealism, isn't it?" Ivor "said something like 'I've been rumbled.'"[12]

Brahms's invention of "folk surrealism" was the earliest known occasion when Ivor's work was given a label: there would be many more.

Sherrin had a space available at short notice on *Tonight* and booked Ivor for five nights on the show, a live TV magazine programme broadcast each weekday evening after the six o'clock news and presented by Cliff Michelmore.[13] Advertising its first edition, the *Radio Times* announced that the show would feature "interviews with people in the news; views from people who never get into the news; sporting comment; reviews of the day's papers; musicians and music ..." The first week's guest list was typical of the programme's eclectic approach: singer Cy Grant, well known for performing topical calypso songs, who would become a regular performer on the show's daily music spot; satirist, doctor and *Beyond the Fringe* performer Jonathan Miller; archaeologist Sir Mortimer Wheeler; Lady Baden-Powell; and the journalist and editor Sydney Jacobson.[14] When Ivor made his debut, in March 1958, the *Radio Times* didn't forewarn viewers about his time on the show, an indication that Sherrin was filling a space at short notice.

Exactly what kind of a sensation Ivor's TV debut caused is uncertain, but there are at least three stories about the event. Sherrin's own memory suggests a low-key, five-day debut that failed to stir the nation's viewers to any sort of action: as he put it, "although he was not the overnight sensation we had hoped it did give his career an early push."[15] Ivor told a slightly different story in a 1993 radio interview: "Ned wanted me to do a week on the programme but after one night he was told 'This man is ahead of his time, forget the rest of the week.'"[16] Yet another version of the tale emerged the following year:

> Ned [Sherrin] was on a thing called *Tonight* on the telly. He put me on, he said "I'll have you on for a week". And we did the first night. And there was a three-verse song. On the middle verse, the engineer switched the sound off by mistake. So they had to give me a second night. The guy in charge said: "This guy's ahead of his time, we can't ... enough is enough."[17]

A letter sent by H. Elton Box a few months after the broadcast, in the hope of getting another TV appearance for his client, mentions that Ivor appeared on just two nights: on the first occasion the sound broke down and on the second Ivor "was on only for about 30 seconds." Further evidence comes from Ivor's BBC contract for the programme, which records that he performed only on Monday 24 and Tuesday 25 March, singing and playing the harmonium.[18]

One show, two shows or five, an accidental power failure or an engineer's error, there's little remaining evidence of Ivor's time on *Tonight*, but while he didn't set the world on fire, his TV debut wasn't a complete disaster. Box sent a letter of thanks to Donald Baverstock, the show's producer, with no mention of any mishaps or problems.[19] Barely six weeks later, Sherrin began producing a fortnightly variety show starring Henry Hall and his band and featuring an array of guest artists. The show debuted on 12 May as *The Henry Hall Show* and Sherrin booked Ivor to appear later in the series. Clearly, Sherrin's experience on *Tonight* hadn't put him off working with Ivor, but a few weeks later Sherrin wrote to tell him that "*The Henry Hall Guest Show*," as he called it, was to undergo a radical change in format and so Ivor's appearance was cancelled. The previous day, Ivor had written to Sherrin telling him of a new song, "The Dance," which he may have been planning to sing on the show, signing the letter "Yours cordially, Lemon Squash."[20] Sherrin produced the first five episodes of the programme but when it re-appeared after a four-week gap, now called *The Henry Hall Guest Night*, John Steel was the producer.

Frustrated by this setback to his artist's career, Box wrote to Sherrin asking if he could find another show for Ivor, pleading "For heaven's sake fit him in somewhere as he is driving us screwy, the same as his songs are. God bless you mate."[21] Box's plea failed to have the desired effect. Sherrin's attempts to introduce new ideas into the variety show format of Henry Hall's series were dismal failures, the audience deserted the BBC for ITV in droves and Sherrin was given the less arduous task of overseeing a popular quiz show, *Ask Me Another*.[22] Ivor's own letters also failed, perhaps because he insisted on mixing up his real-life activities and his mythical island life. He wrote to Kenneth Corden, telling him that he was now back from a trip to Y'Hup with a supply of new material. Deliberately or accidentally, Corden misread "Y'Hup" as "Europe" and decided that a programme about Ivor's trip to the continent was insufficiently interesting to feature on *Tonight*.[23]

Ivor and Box's persistence did pay off in a small way: Corden agreed to arrange a special audition for Ivor to assess his suitability for television. Ivor was given three days' notice of the audition and arrived at the appointed time to find a panel of senior BBC staff ready to watch and listen: Corden, Eric Maschwitz (the head of TV light entertainment) and producer Dennis Main Wilson. Ivor persisted in the legend that he was a resident of Y'Hup, used hats and small props, dressed "in tramp get-up," played piano, and sang "There's a Turtle in my Soup, Waiter" and "Rolling Tins and Rolling Pins." None of it entertained the judges, who concluded that Ivor failed to capture the imagination, lacked professionalism and was eccentric. Later that day Barbara Scott informed Ivor that there was no prospect of a TV engagement.[24] Ivor's television career was now on hold, but the Fontana record label had taken an interest in the "eccentric" performer.

On 9 April 1959, *Daily Mirror* pop music columnist Patrick Doncaster revealed news of two exciting "new faces of 1959." In a music world that was embracing rock 'n' roll – the top 20 for that week included records by Little Richard and Buddy Holly – Doncaster's first new face was bang on trend. This was seventeen-year-old Dickie Pride, a teenager who, Doncaster exclusively revealed, "trembles while he sings." The second new face was twice Pride's age and was pictured sporting a coconut matting hat and playing a bamboo flute.

He was an ex-RAF man who wore "baggy, trampish, costume," wrote songs with titles like "Gravity Begins at Home" and had already recorded songs that combined "crazy titles with goony lines," for release by Fontana.[25]

Ivor Cutler of Y'Hup was a vinyl EP (extended play) disc, a seven-inch record which played at forty-five r.p.m. but featured more tracks than the usual one-per-side to be found on a single. Ivor's debut featured seven tracks, with a running time of almost fifteen minutes. As was usual with EPs, it came in a sturdy cardboard sleeve rather than a flimsy paper one, which enabled the use of a cover design and sleeve notes. On the front cover, against an orange background, is a photo of the artist: he's sporting a bucket hat and what looks like a woollen blouson jacket, which covers a dark, striped shirt and a paisley-pattern tie. There's a hint of a beard under his chin. He's just slapped the right side of his face and his hand stays in place, covering his right eye: it's the sort of annoyed smack you might give yourself if you arrive home from the shops and realise you forgot the toilet rolls. The lettering above the photo reads "Ivor Cutler of Y'Hup" and underneath it is the phrase "Oblique Musical Philosopher."

A brief pen portrait on the back cover says that Ivor is "36, married, 2 children ... He has written 38 songs that might be described as a combination of Franz Kafka and the Goons." It also noted that Ivor was a painter, had appeared on television, and lived in London "when he is not visiting Y'Hup." Ivor introduces each track with a few words of explanation. His style, serious and rather paternal, is reminiscent of Oliver Postgate's narration of the children's television series *The Saga of Noggin the Nog*. In his introduction to "Gravity Begins at Home" Ivor stresses his belief in the importance of home and family and at the end of the song he acknowledges that "my wife" is responsible for two lines of the song, a rare, possibly unique, acknowledgement of Virginia's artistic influence. A question arises: if Ivor has written thirty-eight songs, why did Fontana decide to release only seven of them? Perhaps the financial risk involved in recording and releasing a full album was prohibitive; perhaps Ivor, or Box & Cox, were unwilling to allow most of his repertoire to be released at once. *Ivor Cutler of Y'Hup* failed to crack the top 20. It was Ivor's only Fontana release.

Although Ivor's debut record failed to set the world on fire, the BBC soon offered him a new opportunity. *Monday Night at Home* first appeared on the Home Service radio station in May 1959, aiming "to bring together for your entertainment interesting people with interesting things to say, and special features of drama and comedy."[26] On 19 October one of those interesting people, or perhaps one of the special comedy features, was "Ivor Cutler from Y'Hup": he pre-recorded three "humorous stories" for the show on 14 September. Ivor was in good comedy company, as Peter Ustinov and Joyce Grenfell were also on the bill.[27] It was the first of over seventy performances Ivor gave on the show, which was usually repeated on Saturday nights as *Home on Saturday*.

By November, the *Radio Times* was crediting Ivor as "Ivor Cutler of Y'Hup, O.M.P." He usually performed one or two songs or stories each week and some of them have become fan favourites: in his third show, Ivor performed "Egg Meat" and on 23 November he debuted the much-loved "Gruts for Tea," which was also broadcast on the show's Christmas edition a few weeks later. In early 1960, the *Radio Times* stopped listing specific pieces, crediting Ivor instead with "Songs of an O.M.P." perhaps because his decisions about what to perform on each show arrived too late for inclusion in the magazine. The listings reverted to their original format after a few months, detailing Ivor's performances of further favourites such as "Dirty Dinner" and "Shapely Balloon."

"The fact that he was on the radio was quite special," recalled Jeremy Cutler, who also remembered how the family would gather round the radio to listen to Ivor's performances.[28] Ivor claimed that these early radio appearances resulted in letters from people who were "stuck way out on a moor somewhere saying that I was their only contact with reality."[29] They also brought one of his earliest reviews. The show was "an enjoyable hour of assorted entertainment," wrote the radio critic of *The Times*, who singled out some of the regular contributors for praise and explained that "Mr Ivor Cutler, whose fantasies tend to the whimsical ... is quietly earnest, and one would never laugh aloud if he were with one."[30] At least, I think it's praise.

Ivor stands out as one of *Monday Night at Home*'s most innovative and radical performers: he later claimed that before his appearances on the show "My bids for attention made me an absolute pain in the neck to all," and that these appearances made him "an object of controversy."[31] His contributions made an impact: "A secretary at the BBC said I'd hit on a goldmine ... they made a lot of people very angry."[32] The goldmine wasn't a total success, however. Ivor recalled that "Because of all the people who hated what I did, they only had me three times out of four."[33] While he certainly didn't appear every week, neither did anyone else and surely if he engendered such hatred the BBC would have come up with a more effective solution than simply giving him a week off every month.

Other performers from the radical wing of British comedy appeared on the show, including the group that Patrick Doncaster and the Fontana marketing department had already identified as an influence on Ivor – the Goons. Doncaster's reference to Ivor's "goony lines" is possibly the earliest example of a link being made between Ivor and the Goons in the national press, but there were soon plenty of others, including Ivor's own references to the influence of the famed radio show and especially its main writer, Spike Milligan. For anyone in 1950s Britain who was searching for something that compared to Ivor's songs and stories, the Goons were an obvious choice, not that there were many alternatives. The four Goons – Spike Milligan, Peter Sellers, Harry Secombe and, at the beginning, Michael Bentine – brought a new brand of surreal and anarchic wit to Britain's living rooms through *The Goon Show*, which ran on the Home Service from 1951 to 1960.[34] Fans had their favourites among the actors and the characters, but Milligan was at the heart of *The Goon Show*, writing the majority of its episodes throughout the decade.

There are parallels in the lives of Milligan and Cutler. Milligan was an only child until he was seven and a half, his mental health issues affected him for much of his adult life, and when his brother Desmond was born, wrote one of his biographers, "Spike ceased to be exclusively on the receiving end of his parents' attention. You can interpret the rest of his life as a protracted and often florid attempt to get that attention back again." Milligan, unconcerned with being mistaken for a bus driver, attempted to become a fighter pilot, but failed because of poor eyesight and returned to the Royal Artillery. In an army variety show his costume was "a top hat worn over a shoulder-length wig, a black suit and a stand-up collar [that] made him look like a nineteenth-century undertaker with vampire tendencies."[35] It was a look that Ivor favoured in his early performance career: he acknowledged that he "used the Goons as a launching pad. I owe an enormous debt to Spike Milligan."[36] Milligan might well recognise himself in Ivor's description of his favourite comedy influences: "The humorists that I respect are all really very unhappy men, perhaps desperate men, who will laugh rather than sit down and feel sorry for themselves."[37]

The Marx Brothers, descended from Jewish parents who migrated from France and Germany to New York, are another possible inspiration.[38] Their on-screen energy is quite different from Ivor's stage persona, but their wordplay, absurd logic and surreal jokes can be seen as precursors of his style and their greatest movies – *Duck Soup*, *Horse Feathers*, *A Night at the Opera* – appeared in the mid-1930s, when Ivor and his friends may have seen them in Glasgow's cinemas. Ivor didn't acknowledge this influence in interviews, perhaps because they didn't fit the criteria of desperate, unhappy men, but he did declare his love of absurdity, "the making naked of oneself, acting a fool where you could bring scorn and opprobrium on yourself, taking risks in this way."[39]

Franz Kafka is a much better fit with the "desperate and unhappy" image. Born to Jewish parents in Prague in 1883, he had physical and mental health problems for much of his life – he "exuded" depression according to his friend and biographer Max Brod.[40] He doesn't have much of a reputation for silliness or daft jokes, but he was crucial to Ivor's development as a humorist. Ivor's discovery of Kafka's *The Castle* was a key event in his life: he told John Knutas that the book was his "greatest influence." He first read the book when he was thirty-four and credited it with changing his humour from amateur to professional.[41] Part of its appeal stemmed from Cutler's empathy with the lead character: "The Castle was the one I loved because it was me he was writing about. The empathy was there – I was empathising with him, but really I was thinking about myself."[42]

Established on *Monday Night at Home* and with his first recording on general release, Ivor's career began to take off. By the autumn of 1960 he was sufficiently well known to be asked to perform on a variety show in aid of the Questors Theatre's New Theatre Fund in Ealing, playing harmonium and singing "his own peculiar and particular songs."[43] It was good publicity for the up-and-coming artist, but other developments offered financial benefits as well, good news for a man who was happy to tell the press that he was "in this for the money."[44] As Ivor's showbiz career got under way, he was still teaching for the ILEA and, with Virginia, bringing up two young sons. By June of 1961 the family had moved from Nassington Road to 17B Lansdowne Crescent, in Notting Hill.[45] A couple of months later, writing for the *Kensington Post*, "A.P.S." asked Ivor "what his wife thought about having a husband who had this off-beat creative talent. 'She's fed up with it all', was the answer, 'but she's getting used to it.'"[46]

There was a lot to get used to over the next few years. Ivor's recording career was soon reinvigorated, though not by Fontana. A&R man Hugh Mendel heard Ivor on *Monday Night at Home* and signed him to Decca.[47] The resulting records, his debut album *Who Tore Your Trousers?* and his second EP, *Get Away from the Wall*, appeared in 1961, and "Disker," the pop music correspondent of the *Liverpool Echo*, looked forward to the September release of both records: "This promises to be the most hilarious pair of comedy discs made by a British artiste this year." If readers wanted a flavour of what to expect, "Disker" noted that Ivor had already performed some of the tracks on *Monday Night at Home*.[48] Across both records, at least seven songs and stories had appeared on the radio show, including perennial fan favourites "Gruts for Tea" – which Glen Baxter describes as his "gateway drug" into Ivor's works – and "Egg Meat."

Jack Bentley, show business columnist for the *Sunday Pictorial*, awarded the coveted Album of the Week title to *Who Tore Your Trousers?* jointly with *The Romantic Music of Tchaikowsky* by the Andre Kostelanetz Orchestra. Bentley claimed Ivor was "the farthest out humorist I have heard," and gave him the highest accolade available to showbiz journalists of the time: "Makes Spike Milligan seem positively ungoonish."[49] In Coventry, record reviewer Arthur Reeves passed harsher judgement on *Get Away from the Wall*, so appalled by this humourless disc that he failed to mention it by name, referring to it only by serial number (Decca DFE6677). The rest of his record review column suggests that Reeves was a middle-of-the-road fan, as he reserved his enthusiasm for the Vintage Jazz Music Society and Polkorama, apparently the world's biggest polka band. He listened "without a glimmer of a smile" to Ivor's "super-goonery" and "silky Scottish voice," wondering "if there was anything wrong with me … my wife assured me that there was nothing more wrong than usual."[50]

Ivor returned to live performance, taking to the stage of the Players' Theatre Club as part of a nightly revue called *Late Joys*, alongside Bill Owen who went on to lasting fame as Compo in the BBC TV comedy *Last of the Summer Wine*. There was to be no repeat of the Blue Angel failure. "R.B.M."

reviewed the show for *The Stage*, and was obviously impressed by the new-comer, "who sings weird songs weirdly while playing a weird-sounding musical instrument, his face a blend of surprise, resignation, boredom and latent enthusiasm – a picture, indeed, of droll comedy, very much to the liking of the audience."[51]

Ivor also managed to earn some money from his talent as a visual artist, selling cartoons to *Private Eye* and *The Observer*.[52] During 1962 he regularly contributed cartoons to *Private Eye* under the pseudonym "Knifesmith," which the magazine published as a series called "Knifesmith's Korner."[53] At the end of 1966, *International Times*, the recently established newspaper of the counter-culture, included a cartoon by an artist identified simply as "Cutler." There's no proof that it was one of Ivor's, but the style seems to fit. The drawing is of a father and son, the boy armed with a tennis racquet. A fly hovers above them and the boy asks "Dad, can I kill that fly?" Father replies, "If it gives you pleasure, son."[54]

Private Eye was barely a year old when Knifesmith joined its roster in 1962. In May 1962 the comedian and satirist Peter Cook, another fan of the Goons, bought the fortnightly magazine from its founders. The twenty-four-year-old Cook was already a star, part of the *Beyond the Fringe* team with Alan Bennett,

A Cartoon by "Cutler," *International Times*, 28 November 1966. (Courtesy of the International Times Archive at internationaltimes.it.)

Dudley Moore and Jonathan Miller. He also co-owned a nightclub in Soho, called the Establishment.[55] The Establishment seated around 120 patrons across two rooms and offered nightly cabaret and live music – the Dudley Moore Trio was resident there for much of the club's three-year existence, with Moore also acting as the club's musical director.[56] In early 1962 Ivor took up a Monday night residency. Peter Hepple, a critic for *The Stage*, was very happy with this "lugubrious Scotsman of middle-age" (Ivor was thirty-nine) and gave his readers the first detailed description of Ivor's on-stage image, describing his appearance as:

> something like Spike Milligan, except that he affects a fringe of beard that girdles his face like a guardsman's chinstrap, his vocal equipment is more like that of Alastair Sim. His playing attire is a long, green-striped robe which gives him a kind of Old Testament appearance and for each of his numbers he wears a different hat.[57]

Hepple also reported on new residents for the club's "late late show," a group of "musical assassins" called the Alberts.

A quartet of actors (John Bird, Eleanor Bron, John Fortune and Jeremy Geidt) formed the Establishment's regular troupe of players.[58] The quartet took a break in April and May of 1962 and Cook and his business partner, Nicholas Luard, booked Lenny Bruce to appear at the club during that time. This was something of a coup for the venue, and something of a risk. *The Stage* broke the news of Bruce's appearance in a story which revealed that Ivor and the Alberts were about to begin their residencies, giving the impression that Bruce was a relatively benign performer, referring to him as an "American comedian" and "foreign satirist," and noting that "Lennie [*sic*] Bruce has not previously appeared in this country, although his long-playing records have sold heavily here."[59]

Back home in the USA, Bruce was considered a sick, obscene comic and a danger to society. *Time* magazine called him "the sickest of them all."[60] In March 1962 he was in a California court, on trial for obscenity after being arrested in San Francisco for saying "cocksuckers" on stage: he devoted twenty-four pages of his autobiography to the arrest and trial.[61] Further trials for obscenity and drugs offenses would follow – he claimed to have been arrested nineteen times by 1965 – but this time he was found not guilty and so he was able to make the journey to London to take up his residency. As Cook no doubt expected, Bruce's act attracted criticism, heckling, walkouts and, on one evening, a major altercation between Cook and actor Siobhan McKenna, who was offended by Bruce's language.[62] Kenneth Tynan, who had seen Bruce in New York and was at the Establishment for his opening night, described his residency as "a few explosive weeks ... there was little room for doubt that he was the most original, free-speaking, wild-thinking gymnast of language our inhibited island had ever hired to beguile its citizens." This was not satire tucked away in the pages of a print magazine, or hidden behind funny costumes, this was satire straight from, in Tynan's words, "the nerve-fraying, jazz-digging, pain-hating, sex-loving, lie-shunning, bomb-loathing life he represents."[63] Cook was eager to book Bruce for a return engagement at the Establishment, but the other establishment had different ideas. Attempts by Cook, and even one by the Earl of Harewood who was running a conference on drama at the Edinburgh Festival, to bring Bruce back to Britain failed to impress the Home Office, which refused to allow him to enter the country.[64]

Ivor Cutler and Lenny Bruce had much in common. Bruce was just two years younger than Ivor, and both were Jewish (Lenny Bruce is the stage name of Leonard Alfred Schneider), grew up listening to relatives and neighbours speaking Yiddish, volunteered for active service (Bruce joined the US Navy and served at Anzio) and loved jazz.[65] Their stage personas were far apart, but each of them subverted the expected showbiz norms of the day. Ivor saw much to admire when he watched Bruce perform and envisaged his appointment to a government position. It's unlikely many parents of Mr Cutler's young charges would have approved, because Ivor thought that Bruce would make a great Minister of Education: "I wrote a letter to him, saying how great I thought he was, and the following night he read it to the audience. And when Lenny Bruce was banned, I asked the audience ... to write to their MPs, and they were all laughing, like bloody fools." Ivor believed that Bruce "really loved people," but he never had that feeling confirmed: "I went to speak to him one night and tell him how good he was and he just shut the door in my face. He couldn't stand that sort of thing."[66] Despite Bruce's lack of hospitality, Ivor continued to hold him in high esteem, telling Duglas T. Stewart thirty years later, "Oh, I loved that man. I loved him dearly."

In September, Ivor travelled to Scotland to appear in an Edinburgh Fringe Festival mime and music show called *Get Up and Gruts*. Part of the title may have been taken from one of Ivor's stories, but this was not a solo show as Ivor shared the bill with a group of mime artists who performed a dozen sketches and left the critic from *The Stage* underwhelmed. Thankfully, Ivor saved the day with "a superb dead-pan performance of home-made songs to what looks suspiciously like a home-made harmonium." He was a terrific theatre performer, but "G.S." thought that a wider audience was waiting: "Mr Cutler should be firmly placed in front of a television camera as soon as possible."[67] G.S. should have stayed in more often, for by the time of his Fringe performance Ivor had been in front of the cameras on half a dozen occasions after his *Tonight* debut.

Ivor first appeared on 1960s TV in an afternoon series called *Let's Imagine*, which discussed a different topic each week with an ever-changing panel of guests. Ivor appeared in a short sketch on *Let's Imagine: A Judgement on Our Time*, a discussion about the 1960s, and joined presenter Kenneth Horne on *Let's Imagine: A World of One's Own*, billed as Ivor Cutler in Y'Hup.[68] A few months later, Ivor joined *The Acker Bilk Band Show*, a tea-time BBC programme starring clarinettist and singer Acker and his Paramount Jazz Band. Bilk, from Somerset, was a popular performer famed for wearing a striped waistcoat and bowler hat, and for playing an easy listening and upbeat style of trad jazz. He'd already had half a dozen hits when, in late 1961, he reached number two in the charts with "Stranger on the Shore," an instrumental ballad from the BBC drama series of the same name.[69] Ivor appeared in all six of Bilk's shows, billed once again as Ivor Cutler of Y'Hup, O.M.P. He seems an odd choice of regular companion for Bilk's cheery but mainstream brand of entertainment, but there's a clue to the mystery in a *Melody Maker* interview, when Ivor said that Acker's brother, David Bilk, used to be his agent.[70] Casual viewers might have thought they'd spotted another family connection on the show, as A. J. Cutler also appeared each week. No relation, however. He went on to greater fame as Adge Cutler, leader of the Wurzels, whose hits include "I Am a Cider Drinker" and "Combine Harvester." Admittedly, the titles could belong to Ivor Cutler poems, but there the similarity ends.

Despite Ivor's relative inexperience, someone at the BBC was impressed enough to invite him to the corporation's sound feature and drama producers' conference. The 1962 event was the first edition of this annual get-together to offer an invitation to writers, an invitation extended not only to Ivor but to at least two dozen others, among them Caryl Churchill, Dominic Behan, John Mortimer and Stephen Potter.[71]

At the beginning of 1963 *The Tatler*, a long-established magazine aimed at readers with an interest in high society, high fashion, hunting and the royal family, interviewed Ivor. It's an unlikely publication to feature Ivor and it's an odd article. There's the usual reference to Ivor's position of Oblique Musical Philosopher, a brief mention of "his wife and two children in Notting Hill" and a description of him as a "writer and raconteur." Nothing unusual in that, but the accompanying photograph suggested there's more to this man. Ivor sits in a no smoking carriage on the London Underground, dressed conservatively but holding a block of wood and, possibly, a knife. Opposite is another passenger: she's holding on tight to her handbag and looks perturbed (or possibly asleep). She had nothing to fear, for as the article explains, whittling wood on the Underground was one of Ivor's favourite spare-time occupations. He was also, *The Tatler* exclusively revealed, a "free dancer."[72]

Ivor gained his first radio series in January 1964, a five-episode Home Service show called *The I.C. Snow*, broadcast from Monday to Friday at 10.30 p.m. The *Radio Times* described it as a show in which Ivor would present "the kind of thoughts, music, and stories that have made him so bitterly misunderstood for years."[73] It seems that the show managed to successfully continue this atmosphere of bitter misunderstanding: Ivor didn't host his own radio show again for many years.

Another aspect of Ivor's relationship with the BBC may have made producers think twice about giving him a show of his own. From the earliest days of his broadcasting career, Ivor complained about his fees: that they had not been paid, that they were paid late, that the payment was sent to his agent rather than directly to him, or, most often, that the fee offered was far too low.[74] Much of this correspondence is amusing, in particular Ivor's exchange of letters with Patrick Newman, the light entertainment booking manager, even though Newman was initially unimpressed by Ivor as an artist, finding him to be condescending, his humour often puerile and better suited to a Chelsea party than to BBC broadcasts.[75] During 1961 the pair engaged in spirited correspondence regarding fees for appearing on *Monday Night at Home*. Ivor ended one of his letters by quoting the Athenian statesman Alcibiades in the original Greek. Newman, unskilled in Greek, found a colleague who was able to translate the phrase ("An artist has to live, the same as everybody else") and continued the debate about the fees.[76]

Ivor wrote to a Miss Alexander in 1965, complaining that the seven-guinea fee offered for an appearance should be raised to twelve guineas and noting, in support of his claim but without further evidence, that some of his stories were earning him "several hundreds" of pounds. Ivor and the BBC finally agreed on nine guineas.[77] Eighteen months later he complained about the fee offered for writing a series of scripts, referring to himself as a producer of "highly concentrated gems" who was upset by the way BBC fees were based on the length of a contribution rather than its quality.[78]

There was no need to worry if the BBC fees were too low, or disappeared, for there were plenty more fish in the entertainment sea. Live performance, for example, for which Ivor was acquiring a taste. After Ivor and the Alberts had become Establishment Club regulars, they combined their powers in a new theatrical revue, *An Evening of British Rubbish*, at the Comedy Theatre. They were joined by Joyce Grant and Bruce Lacey, and as far as the theatre critic of *The Times* was concerned, *An Evening of British Rubbish* was an accurate title. It was, the critic wrote, no more than an attempt to copy a far more successful American show, *Hellzapoppin'*, and it fell far short of its aim. There were highlights, however, with Grant and Lacey drawing positive comments, but the critic praised Ivor's performance above all others. Ivor's contributions seemed to exist in isolation from the rest of the cast and were a "shining exception" to the disorganised chaos of much of the show, his comedy was "weird, wholly personal, and often of a somewhat sinister cast … and delivered with cool authority and the flawless timing the rest of the cast signally lack." Ivor's confidence and on-stage authority were on the rise. His sartorial style as he sat at his harmonium brought to mind a legend of British horror film: "His physical presence [was] suggestive of Peter Cushing disguised as Burke and/or Hare."[79]

J. C. Trewin, writing for the *Birmingham Daily Post* and *The Illustrated London News*, was impressed by the British rubbish on display, enjoying the "festival of super-goonery" in all its chaos and explosions. Trewin commended Ivor's musical contribution, seated at the harmonium in the guise of a "disapproving Dickensian undertaker who had just had a severe fright," and his spoken word pieces, "dialogues of impenetrable obscurity" in which Ivor would "pester himself with question and answer as if his life hung on a well-placed comma."[80] Piers Plowright, who produced Ivor's radio shows in the 1970s and 1980s, was in the audience for one performance:

> There was this man, dressed as an undertaker, with his back to us, sitting at a harmonium, occasionally turning round to give you a baleful look and singing these extraordinary ditties. One I remember went something like "Snip, snip, that's the Duchess cutting the cheese with her nose."[81]

Ivor found the time to indulge in a spot of literary criticism, directing critical comments about an unidentified book to its author, John H. Wallis. Wallis replied, thanking him for his "rude letter," directing him to an upcoming book by Dr Eustace Chesser on the topic and noting that he "will certainly consider your suggestion of writing a much simpler [book] on the same subject."[82] Wallis, the training officer of the National Marriage Guidance Council, wrote books on counselling, marriage, sexual harmony, middle age and retirement. Chesser, a psychiatrist, wrote about dieting, suicide and homosexuality, as well as sharing Wallis's interest in sex and marriage. This suggests that the object of Ivor's ire was *Sexual Harmony in Marriage*, which Wallis published in 1964.[83] Sadly, Ivor's critique is a mystery.

With radio, records, television and live shows now under his belt, Ivor moved on to the last major entertainment medium of the 1960s, the movies, taking a role in *It's All Over Town*, filmed in the closing months of 1963 and released early the following year. It's a B-movie or supporting feature, nothing grander, but it's a jolly, full-colour, low-budget romp that lasts just under an hour and avoids outstaying its welcome. The plot, such as it is, concerns a theatre electrician and his friend, played by Lance Percival and Willie Rushton, out on the town in London's glittering West End and visiting some of the city's most fashionable nightspots. It's hardly a plot at all and the movie ends with the revelation – spoiler alert – that it's all been Percival's dream.

The movie's real aim is to showcase a selection of Britain's best musical acts and some of its "sophisticated" nightlife: it was produced in collaboration with Soho club owner Paul Raymond.[84] Today, it's a historical document of a time when one musical era was coming to an end and another was about to emerge. The nightclubs, with their customers in dinner jackets or evening gowns and the Paul Raymond Bunnies on hand, were already old-fashioned. Singer and all-round entertainer Frankie Vaughan got top billing and the lion's share of the movie: a star in his day, with sixteen Top Twenty hits before the movie's release, he was definitely old school by 1964 with just two Top Twenty hits still to come. The Bachelors and the Springfields were popular, but hardly representative of soon-to-be-swinging London (although Dusty, the Springfields' lead vocalist, was heading for stardom). Clodag Rogers would eventually make it big (as Clodagh Rogers) and represent Britain in the Eurovision Song Contest, but only one act was truly part of the new generation of pop stars: the Hollies, featuring Graham Nash, had just three hits before the movie, but would manage over twenty more in the years that followed.[85]

Mr Acker Bilk and His Paramount Jazz Band were, like Vaughan, past their peak by 1964, but they featured in two scenes that are both, in different ways, oddities. In the first sequence, the band plays Bilk's arrangement of "The Song of the Volga Boatmen" while a depressed-looking brown bear sits in the background with its trainer. The band plays its second number in a mocked-up pub, called the "Charity Alms," where Bilk sings "Sippin' Cider Beside 'er" to the assembled locals (a couple of years before this, Ivor recorded "The Market Place," a song with advice about courtship strategies that include making sure that your date drinks plenty of cider, so that the cider "is now inside her"). There's no depressed brown bear in sight: it's replaced by another dour figure, dressed like an undertaker and giving the distinct impression he'd rather be somewhere else. According to the cast list, Ivor's character is a Salvationist, rather than an undertaker. The Salvationist sits at the corner of the bar, looking miserable and holding a sign that reads "Prepare to Meet Thy Doom" as two female dancers sidle up to him. At first he's irritated, then puzzled, then cheerful as the dancers hand him a glass of beer. Vaughan and a female duo, Jan and Kelly, take over from Bilk to sing an upbeat, gospel-style, number, then the crowd leaves the pub. The Salvationist is the last to go, unsteady on his feet as he staggers across the set and shuts the door.

Ivor's total screen time can be counted in seconds, rather than minutes, but he makes a mark with his distinctive appearance and hammy acting style – his facial expressions hark back to the early days of silent films and his portrayal of the drunken Salvationist exiting the pub is notably over-exaggerated. However, *It's All Over Town* arrived at just the wrong time, and disappeared without trace. Only one bunch of pop artists really counted in early 1964 and the movie missed them completely.[86]

Ivor's next on-screen appearance was far more memorable: he took part in the opening night of BBC Two. This would be the third TV channel available to viewers in the UK, but on opening night it was only broadcast to London and the southeast. According to Kenneth Adam, the BBC's director of television, the channel was "driven by a common excitement to push back the horizon a little," but it would take some time to achieve this laudable if ambitious aim, so he asked viewers "for forbearance when we fall short of our intention."[87] Viewer forbearance was required sooner than expected. Opening night was scheduled to begin at 7.20 p.m. on Monday 20 April, but a major power failure meant that only a few minutes of the news bulletin made it to air: the rest of the evening's entertainment was postponed for twenty-four hours.[88] At 7.30 p.m. on Tuesday night, *The Alberts' Channel Too* was broadcast live, supposedly from the trio's own television centre.[89] Ivor and "Professor" Bruce Lacey joined the Alberts in what *The Times* called "a derisively nostalgic celebration." Ivor's role was to deliver an illustrated talk on the history of electronic communications: he did so "lugubriously ... Not, perhaps, everybody's idea of fun, but clever and in many respects unusual."[90] Twenty-five years later, Ivor remembered that he was cast as Lord Reith, the BBC's founder, a part that involved being covered with cobwebs, while a sound effect made it appear as if he creaked as he moved. The experience made Ivor decide not to be an actor.[91]

Ivor was soon back on stage, with a fortnight residency at the Players' Theatre alongside American actor Mary-Ellen Ray.[92] He ended the year as the composer and sole performer of the soundtrack music for a BBC drama-tisation of George and Weedon Grossmith's comic novel, *Diary of a Nobody*. Ken Russell co-wrote the screenplay and directed the production in the style of a silent movie, with a narration by Bryan Pringle, who played Mr Pooter.[93] Ivor's instrumental soundtrack, performed on harmonium and incorporating classical, jazz and music hall influences, is in keeping with the visual style of the programme. According to Ivor, Russell chose him because he played the harmonium, which he felt fitted the story, telling him "You're the expert in this country."[94] Russell was in the early stages of his career: most of his previous directorial credits were for short films, but he would go on to direct *The Devils*, *Tommy*, *Women in Love* and other major movies. Ivor's career as a soundtrack composer ended here.

In 1964, Ivor and Virginia separated. It seems that despite Ivor's declaration to the *Kensington Post* that Virginia was getting used to his creative talent, their relationship was no longer tenable. Ivor moved to a flat in Fawley Mansions, in Hampstead. It sounds like a grand address, but it was no more than a bedsit.[95] Virginia and the children moved to what Dan describes as "the cheapest accommodation my mother could find, which was in the middle of Notting Hill Gate ... So, she was a single mother for a long time. She never remarried but she certainly had a social life." Virginia became a social worker.[96]

Ivor remained in contact with his sons, but neither Dan nor Jeremy remembers much about their paternal grandparents, uncles or aunts. Jeremy remembered Ivor's relationships with his parents and siblings as somewhat cool and reserved. The brothers were not involved in family events such as weddings, funerals or bar mitzvahs, and Jeremy recalled that Ivor didn't go to Jack or Polly's funerals.[97] Dan remembers meeting Robert Wyatt and Alfie Benge, his father's friends, but he, too, can recall little contact with his father's wider family, either before or after his parents separated:

> On his side, I have almost no memories. I'm sure that we went up to see them at least once, maybe a second time, but that would have been it. I think we may have gone up with my mother. I don't recall much about the visit except the smell of food in the house

was different somehow. It was kosher. Everything was slightly different and therefore odd. But that's about it really.

In London, he occasionally met his Uncle Joseph, who had a medical practice in the city, but Beth was the family member he saw most of, "as much as I've seen anything of any of them."

Ivor was hit hard by the failure of the marriage. According to Phyllis King, "it was very important to him, having the two boys, and when the marriage failed it was a very desperate time for him."[98] He told Michael Watts just how hard he took it and how vital his teaching work was in helping him to deal with its effects: "I had to find a reason for living at all. Then I realised how great it is to be with kids when you work with them and see them smile."[99]

"I thought I was old and ugly because I was forty, and life was over," he told Alastair McKay, "And in fact, life began then, as I discovered."[100] Dan says that Ivor taught at Fox "in part because, as I understand it, he sought out that job because he was no longer living with us. The idea, I don't recall it but the story goes that this was one way in which he stayed in touch." He recalls that to help maintain contact, after lessons "one day a week I would go back with him to his bedsit for the night and on the following morning I'd go back to school," while Jeremy would do the same on another night. Dan describes the bedsit as "smaller and nastier" than the Laurier Road flat that would be Ivor's home for almost forty years. For the time being, it gave Ivor a base, if nothing else.

The early 1960s were a period of intensive work for Ivor: teaching, writing songs and stories, live appearances, radio shows, records, television and cinema. The toll eventually caught up with him. In September 1963 he was receiving treatment in Holloway Sanatorium, an NHS establishment in Surrey (he made it clear to the BBC that he was not being treated for paranoia).[101] Then in 1964 he had a heart attack, perhaps due to the end of the marriage or his intense work schedule, possibly a combination of both. He called it a mild one, but it was enough to frighten him.[102]

His television career was taking off, but Ivor was still on the lookout for further chances at fame. In May 1964 he wrote to Huw Wheldon, suggesting a documentary television programme about his movement and mime teaching technique, which he was using with the children at Paddington Green primary school. His suggestion was not taken up.[103] By October, he had ended his relationship with Box & Cox.[104] At the end of the year, he made his first appearance on BBC Two's new flagship arts show, *Late Night Line-Up*, which was broadcast as the final show of the night, seven nights a week. Ivor performed for the first time on 5 December and in just over a year he appeared on the show at least six times, including a special filmed segment which featured Ivor's "movement to music" class at Fox Primary (a year after Huw Wheldon turned down the idea), and the edition of 31 January 1966 when he took part in a "slapstick panel game."[105]

Ivor made another appearance on BBC Two in February 1965, as the presenter and featured artist on the second of three episodes of the "music depreciation programme" *Off Beat...* He followed this with his debut appearance on BBC One, as a guest on *Musicstand*, a teatime programme from Manchester which promised to explore "the exciting world of music" – the Alberts, Bruce Lacey and Acker Bilk also appeared in the series – then he returned to BBC Two to join Hermione Gingold for the Christmas edition of her variety series *Pure Gingold*.[106] For *Off Beat ...* and *Musicstand*, Ivor was billed as Ivor Cutler of Y'Hup, O.M.P.; for *Pure Gingold* he was plain old Ivor Cutler. Y'Hup, O.M.P. quietly disappeared, never to be seen again, although in 1996 Ivor referred to himself as an "oblique" communicator, and his 2003 collection of poems, *Scots wa' Straw*, credits the artwork as "Illustrated obliquely by the author."[107]

In 1965 Ivor wrote a short script for *This Time of Day*, a midday Home Service show for "listeners with minds of their own." Somewhere in the BBC the script was lost and Ivor received an apologetic letter as well as confirmation that his seven-guinea fee would still be paid.[108] In December, BBC One launched a fifteen-minute, late afternoon story programme for younger children, broadcast each weekday and called *Jackanory*. The first programme went out on Monday 13 December, with actor Lee Montague as the storyteller, and on the following day Ivor wrote to Joy Whitby, *Jackanory*'s producer, telling her that he wished to read a story on the show and emphasising that his pupils thought he was a terrific teller of stories. Whether or not Whitby knew of Ivor as a performer, or as a teacher, the producer was less than excited and Ivor soon received a letter informing him that there was no opening available.[109]

Ivor decided to leave his small and nasty Hampstead bedsit and looked for longer-term accommodation. In April 1966 he placed an advertisement in the *New Statesman*: "Ivor Cutler seeks room near Heath. Cheap!"[110] Joyce Edwards, a photographer with a room to spare in one of her houses, saw a similar advertisement. Joyce and her son, Dylan, were already Ivor Cutler fans, as Dylan remembers: "we listened to his programmes on the Home Service – *Monday Night at Home* – and I recorded them onto a reel-to-reel recorder. My mother said he just put a note in a shop window, a local newsagent: 'Ivor Cutler Wants Flat' or something like that. So she immediately replied."

The house was at 21 Laurier Road. Ivor took a room on the first floor, the largest room in the house, then a little later he moved up to the second floor, retaining the first-floor room where he kept a piano. Joyce and Dylan lived elsewhere, but the house was shared with others, including Alfio Bernabei, a young Italian with ambitions to be a playwright and theatre director. Bernabei had been living temporarily in a shared house in Nassington Road where artists and musicians (including members of Pink Floyd) were regular visitors. The sculptor Ghisha Koenig and her husband Manny Tuckman lived on the top floor and were, as Bernabei puts it, "the most prominent couple in the house." At a house party Bernabei met Ivor, who made an immediate impression on him:

> He was wearing what was then his habitual attire, a kind of rather voluminous shirt /tunic with matching voluminous trousers in an African style in muted colours, all stripes. A cap went with it. He came across to me as a very kind man. His way of talking was unusual, striking. A low voice, a semi-guttural tone, very precise resounding consonants, curiously forensic in tone. He was attracting attention doing very little.

In the course of the evening, Ivor discovered that Bernabei was looking for a room to rent and told him of a spare room in the Laurier Road house. Bernabei moved into a ground floor room in February or March 1967 and stayed until late in 1971. He still has clear memories of the house, including Joyce Edwards's regular visits to clean, collect the rent and empty the meters. When he arrived, the house was heated by paraffin heaters, and there was one shared toilet on the first floor, a shared, coin-operated telephone, and three or four rooms to rent, including the basement, which had a separate entrance. Bernabei's rent was "extremely reasonable" and he remembers the neighbourhood as friendly. Another ground floor room was also rented out: for much of the time during his stay it was occupied by "a mature gentleman with a moustache," quiet and reserved but a keen cricketer. Later, Joyce Edwards told Bernabei that this housemate regularly played cricket with playwright, actor and activist Harold Pinter. Pinter's close friend and collaborator, actor Henry Woolf, was a tenant of 21 Laurier Road during the late 1950s and early 1960s, when he taught young Dylan Edwards to ride a bike, and later got to know Ivor.[111] As for Bernabei's relationship with Ivor, it was congenial but not close: "We didn't have meals together. He never sat down for a chat in my room and vice versa. We spoke in the corridor and sometimes in the street. They were never long chats."

Ivor lived at 21 Laurier Road for almost forty years. Before he moved in, Joyce and Dylan knew Ivor was prone to depression and Dylan believes that the house "became a sort of haven for him, after the breakup of his marriage. He was able to start writing again, and drawing and painting and composing songs. It wasn't all depression of course. A lot of hilarity too." Ivor had periods of depression throughout his adult life. Caroline Richmond, who knew him in the mid-1960s, describes him as "very much a depressive ..." His friend Alfie Benge called him "a very depressive person. He had periods when he'd just totally hibernate ... Something about him was not happy with himself."[112] Bernabei recalls periods when Ivor would isolate himself, telling Bernabei that he felt depressed and did not want to be disturbed, occasionally confiding his state of mind/health by saying "I have to protect myself," without elaborating, but often gesturing, not speaking. "Sometimes," says Bernabei, "he looked like a ghost, positively cadaveric."

A view from Ivor's flat, probably mid-1980s. (Courtesy of John Knutas, photographer unknown.)

"His depressive mood is, I think, most difficult for him," said Phyllis King, "He may put on a false sort of bonhomie but I think one sees through it quite quickly."[113] Ciara Nolan found that at times Ivor "would go to a very dark place, you couldn't get in contact with him. He'd come back fighting fit. He felt everything so intensely." It was a strong contrast with the times when he was happy, when, Nolan recalls, "he was the most wonderful person to be around: he made me look at the world in a completely different way." In the 1990s, Ivor made reference to this state of mind and its negative impact, telling John Knutas that his attempts to teach poetry were among his strategies for avoiding facing reality, an unimportant activity that took his mind off other things: "What a waste! I've never even been drunk!"[114] Ivor did try psychotherapy, but abandoned it having decided that "it was not the way for him."[115]

Around the time he moved to Laurier Road, Ivor and Caroline Richmond began a short-lived relationship. It happened thanks to an innovation imported from the United States: a computer dating process called *Operation Match*. Caroline recalls that "they handed out leaflets outside tube stations: in my case it was Belsize Park tube station. That's how we met. Of course, I recognised his name because I had loved *Monday Night at Home*. He had this wonderful graveyard voice." The pair dated briefly, although, in Caroline's words, "you could hardly call it dating. We met and became friends. What little sex there might have been soon evaporated ... I once left a toothbrush at his place. He handed it back to me and made it very clear that we weren't on those terms." The friendship continued, before fading partly due to

Richmond's new romantic relationship. In the years that followed, Alfio Bernabei saw one or two women with Ivor, but doesn't recall if they were girlfriends or simply visitors. His impression was of "a fairly chaste man."

Ivor's love of jazz, formed during his teens and early twenties, remained strong and he visited jazz clubs around London. The Phoenix, a Cavendish Square pub with a Wednesday night jazz club, was one of his regular haunts and he would often be there to see the Don Rendell/Ian Carr Quintet. He became friendly with the band's bassist and drummer, Dave Green and Trevor Tomkins. Green remembers him as very warm and personable and the three of them often spoke together although, despite a shared love of the music, Ivor never discussed the musicians he loved or admired with these two young professional players. As for Ivor's own musical talent, Green doesn't remember knowing anything about it (Green played with Dudley Moore at the Establishment, but not until Ivor's own residency at the club had ended). So it's surprising to find that when Ivor offered Green and Tomkins a gig, they accepted. "He said he'd played some jazz," says Tomkins, "but we had no idea what it would be like. But we said 'Okay.'"

Perhaps it was the nature of the gig that swayed Green and Tomkins: an appearance on *Late Night Line-Up*. Green still has his gig diary from the period and remembers how the group readied itself for the show:

> It was recorded at the BBC Television Centre on the afternoon of Thursday 13th January [1966], between 2.30 p.m. and 5 p.m. … Trevor and I just turned up, played to the cameras and that was that. We did speak about what to call the piece and I think it was me that suggested "Eastern Feelings". We seemed to get into that sort of sound, a slightly eastern feeling, and Ivor and Trevor agreed to it.

It was fully improvised, according to Green: "It wasn't composed at all, no. We just played. I don't think we even got together with Ivor beforehand. We just turned up, got together and improvised the whole thing."

Green thinks it was probably Ivor who named the band the Three Wise Men. It's an inspired title for an improvising jazz trio, but its use was extremely limited: Cutler, Green and Tomkins never played together again. As for the performance, it's not just an interesting period piece: "Eastern Feelings" is an atmospheric piece of music. Green and Tomkins have the confidence of a rhythm partnership that's played together many times. Ivor is more reticent, his contributions at first tentative compared to those of the bassist and drummer, but becoming a little more confident as the piece progresses.

The Three Wise Men's only performance filled the opening spot of that night's *Late Night Line-Up*. Michael Dean, the presenter, gave Ivor a suitable introduction, calling him a "musician, humorist, eccentric" and explaining that he was appearing for two reasons. First, as a sort of preview of a new show called *Zodiac*, a BBC One series of twelve dance programmes built around the astrological signs. The first of the series was dedicated to Capricorn, and Ivor is a Capricornian. Second, because he'd recently formed the Three Wise Men and, as the trio had never appeared on TV before, it qualified for *Late Night Line-Up*'s "First Time on Television" spot. Once he'd made everything clear, Dean introduced the Three Wise Men performing "Eastern Feelings".

The band's recorded performance begins. Green stands to the left, Tomkins sits behind his drum kit to the right and Ivor sits behind the piano at the centre. The bassist and drummer are dressed smartly, as was the fashion for jazz musicians of the time, in jackets, white shirts and dark ties. The bald and bare-headed Ivor adopts a more casual combination of open-necked check shirt and a light-coloured, cable-knit sweater. All three men are serious and unsmiling, concentrating on the music that's evolving. "Eastern Feelings" lasts for around three-and-a-half minutes, the entire output of the Three Wise Men. As far as Tomkins remembers, Ivor didn't seem interested in playing live gigs with the trio and Tomkins was unconcerned that this was their one and only show, summing up Ivor's musical talent with the comment "He wasn't a great piano player at all."

As Dean promised, Ivor returned to close the show. This time, Dean's introduction touched on the orthopaedic, rather than the astrologic: "most Capricornians live to a ripe old age, but the knees – listed as limb of the month in the *Radio Times* – are supposed to be their weak spot. Well, here is Ivor Cutler's prescribed cure for diseases of the knee … 'Pickle Your Knees'." Ivor performed solo, Green and Tomkins having departed after the afternoon recording of "Eastern Feelings," and this performance, like the rest of the show, was broadcast live. *Zodiac*, with a prime Friday night spot on BBC One, featured three choreographers, ten dancers, four guest artists and the Zodiac Orchestra, but there was no room for Ivor. However, as Dean promised, the Limb of the Month was the knee.[116]

On 9 July, Ivor returned, alone, to *Late Night Line-Up*, with a performance including an unidentified twenty-nine lines of "blank verse" from his latest book, *Cockadoodledon't*.[117] The World Cup, hosted and eventually won by England, would start two days later, but not everyone was going football crazy. Ivor hated competitive sport, and when asked if he was a football fan he said "No. I've avoided competitive situations because I've discovered I'm no good at them, because I'm not a baboon."[118]

BBC Two was happy to cater for those whose interest lay with the arts rather than sport. Ivor's appearances on the channel gave him exposure to an audience that shared this artistic interest: they so impressed a young viewer from a popular beat combo that he found Ivor's phone number and called him up.

7 When Life Was Fab

Once the Beatles finished recording *Sgt Pepper's Lonely Hearts Club Band*, Paul McCartney took a holiday trip to the USA to visit his then partner, Jane Asher, who was in a touring production of *Romeo and Juliet*. In early April 1967 while he was in Denver, he started planning a television special based on a mystery coach tour. It soon developed into a magical mystery tour, which Barry Miles called "a typical Beatles combination of northern working-class culture and taking the fans on an acid trip." Within months, filming was under way.[1]

McCartney explained how Ivor became involved: "I knew Ivor, I'd seen him on telly with his very dour Scottish accent, which I like very much … He had a song I liked called 'I'm Going in a Field', just a lovely little song. I used to want to record that with him." McCartney looked up Ivor's phone number and called:

> I said, "Hello, Mr Cutler. My name's Paul McCartney. I'm one of the Beatles. I'm a great admirer of yours. Would you like to come out to dinner?" "This is very surprising, why are you asking me out?" "Because I like you." "Oh, oh. Oh, very well then. Yes, I wouldn't mind." He's a very precise-spoken Scottish fella, very quiet but real entertaining, real nice bloke. Very sensitive … So in the film he became Buster Bloodvessel and he was very good and very helpful. He made that name up. "Buster, Buster, I could be Buster Bloodvessel."[2]

Although the phone call wasn't the beginning of a long and beautiful friendship, it stayed in McCartney's memory. In a 2021 interview he recalled his life in the mid-1960s and told of how easy he found it "just to ring people up."

Searching for an example, it was Ivor's name that sprang to mind: "Hello, I'm Paul McCartney, you're Ivor Cutler and I really like what you do ... should we go out to dinner?"[3]

As Ivor remembered, McCartney "came along to my place and he said 'Hello' and smiled. He just got on my bed with his shoes and just laid back and started talking."[4] McCartney mapped out a plot on what he called a "scrupt," a pie chart divided into eight segments which, read clockwise, followed the story from boarding the coach to the final song. However, apart from his fellow Beatles, Paul had no particular actors in mind. John Lennon wanted to cast Nat Jackley, a music-hall performer known for "eccentric dancing" and pantomime: he became the first actor to join the film, as the Rubber Man. The scrupt which appears in Miles's biography names Jackley and Ringo, and lists other characters yet to be cast: a courier/driver, a "Busty Hostess," "Fat woman," "Small man" and "lads & lasses." The remaining cast members were found by searching *Spotlight*, the directory of actors, with one exception: in McCartney's words, "We got those people, then we got Ivor Cutler." It seems that Buster Bloodvessel was originally simply called "Small man."[5]

Before *Magical Mystery Tour* started filming, Ivor made one of his rare journeys outside the UK, travelling to Finland to appear in *Billion Dollar Brain*, the movie version of Len Deighton's novel. Michael Caine starred as Harry Palmer, Ken Russell directed and Ivor was cast as a character called Fragoli. Ivor's music for Russell's *Diary of a Nobody* was crucial to the mood and sense of period of that TV drama. Unfortunately for Ivor, his performance as Fragoli proved to be much less vital: it ended up on the cutting room floor.[6] Ivor's trip to Finland did have one happy outcome. In Helsinki's Academic Bookshop, Ivor bought ten small, black notebooks: they proved to be the ideal size for his needs.[7]

As McCartney was busy planning his movie, Ivor was offered the chance to write a new TV series, but *The Ivor Cutler Approximately a Twelfth [sic] of an Hour Show* proved to be another short-lived shot at fame. Ivor was commissioned to write and perform a set of four pilot programmes, intended, according to Humphrey Burton, to lead to a series of five-minute late-night episodes for broadcast on BBC One after the current affairs show *24 Hours*, which Burton hoped would give Ivor cult status. Ivor made the pilot episodes and Paul Fox, controller of BBC One, watched them. "I am afraid they are beyond me," Fox wrote, and refused to commission the show.[8]

Meanwhile, Beatles fans eagerly awaited the band's latest film, their third after *A Hard Day's Night* and *Help!*. Beatles supporter and *Liverpool Echo* columnist "Disker" published an exclusive preview on 16 September, while filming was in progress. "Disker" was the nom de plume of Tony Barrow, who was by this time also the press and public relations officer for Beatles manager Brian Epstein, so he had more of an insider's view of the Beatles' activities than his fellow journalists could manage. As part of his PR role he edited the book that formed part of the *Magical Mystery Tour* album package.[9] Disker explained that the script was being improvised by the Beatles and the actors collaboratively, with a cast including "Jessie Robbins playing Ringo's heavyweight auntie" and "Scotsman Ivor Cutler."[10]

Ivor was following Bruce Lacey, his *British Rubbish* colleague, and Eleanor Bron, his friend from the Establishment, who both appeared in *Help!*.[11] By the time Disker's article appeared, the cast and crew were travelling around the south of England by coach. In amateur film of the coach on its way to Cornwall, Ivor sits on the right side, near the front, dressed conservatively in flat cap, dark coat, light shirt and tie; John Lennon sits behind him, Jessie Robbins sits across the aisle, and McCartney sits behind her.[12] Ivor appears twice in the book that accompanies the album. In the picture of the cast on the coach, with Robbins, Jackley, McCartney, Harrison and Starr all smiling and waving at the camera, Ivor can just be seen on the bottom left, dressed as Buster, not waving, not smiling. In a photo of the cast having dinner, Ivor sits at the front of the shot, dressed once again as Mr Bloodvessel, but he has his back to the camera and his cap obscures his face.

Buster Bloodvessel travelled in uniform, believed himself to be the coach's courier and encouraged the passengers to enjoy themselves "within the limits of British decency." He wasn't really the courier, of course: Jolly Jimmy Johnson (played by Derek Royle) was. Buster provided the film's love interest, along with Ringo's Aunt Jessie, played by Jessie Robbins.[13] Ivor's filming schedule on *Magical Mystery Tour* wasn't onerous, giving him time to observe the cast and crew:

> Sociologically it was extremely interesting to see the way the Beatles behaved towards all the people in the bus and how they behaved back, and what happened on the last night when they said "Well, that's it, folks." You could see the faces dropping all over the bus. It was like being picked up out the primeval slime and then had a wee shot at being up with the gods and then flung back down again … Showbusiness is like that.[14]

Ivor told Douglas T. Stewart of the BMX Bandits about his impressions of the Beatles: Paul was very interested in everyone and what they were doing; Ringo was very interested in the film-making process; George was very interested in India; and John was "very interested in John Lennon and introduced himself as 'I'm John Lennon of the Beatles."

McCartney wanted the BBC to broadcast the film to ensure that it was shown nationwide: commercial television operated as a series of regional stations and it was possible that some stations would choose not to buy or show it. Paul Fox agreed to show the film, but insisted that one scene be removed. McCartney told Miles: "I said, 'What?' thinking, 'Oh, what have we done?' Some drug reference or something a little bit naughty in there?" What Fox objected to was a scene starring Ivor and Jessie:

running around on the beach to the sound of some schmaltzy orchestral version of "All My Loving," which he thought was insulting to old people. I thought it was a very romantic scene: Ivor running in circles around Jessie Robbins so that his footprints drew a heart shape in the sand around her and it was a little love scene. It was a completely innocent little romantic scene ... There was no groping or grappling or anything, but he wanted that out.[15]

For the second time in only a few months, Fox vetoed an Ivor Cutler TV appearance. The BBC reinstated the scene when it showed the film once again, in 1979, and it remained in place when the *Magical Mystery Tour* video became available in 1989.[16] According to Ivor, "[The BBC] cut out my love relationship with Jessie ... They thought it was disgusting. They changed their minds ... and when I saw it I thought it was very sweet."[17] Another of Ivor's contributions failed to make the final cut of either version of the film: his solo performance of "I'm Going in a Field." The scene appears as an added extra in the DVD release of the film: Mr Bloodvessel, in full courier uniform, seated at a keyboard and singing the song, in a field.

BBC One showed *Magical Mystery Tour* on Boxing Day 1967. The film was just under an hour long and went out at 8.35 p.m., peak viewing time for the holiday season. Although members of the Beatles Fan Club thought that it was "lovely," their possibly biased opinion was not shared by the press. "We tried to present something different ...," McCartney said, "but according to the newspapers it did not come off."[18] McCartney's comment suggests that the critics were unanimous in their condemnation, but this was not the case. Douglas A. Grosvenor titled his review "Bravo Beatles!" and couldn't understand why his fellow critics had panned the movie when it was so "fresh, funny, and full of the joi de vie [*sic*] it set out to capture." He felt able to compare some of the direction to the work of Ingmar Bergman, praised its "goonish" style and hailed the Beatles as "modern Marx Brothers." As for the cast of "gorgeous eccentrics," there was none better than Ivor's Mr Bloodvessel.[19]

Unlike most of the critics, Grosvenor based his opinion on the BBC Two showing of *Magical Mystery Tour*, broadcast on 5 January. This differed from the BBC One broadcast in one significant factor: it was in colour, rather than black and white. Grosvenor didn't declare that he'd seen it in colour, but one might expect that a TV critic in 1968 would be equipped with an up-to-the-minute colour telly. In 1968 colour television was a novelty in the UK – the vast majority of the TV audience still had this treat to come – but monochrome images meant that much of the film's visual impact was lost. Colour photographs in the album booklet show the Beatles in brightly coloured outfits, George's custom-painted guitar in pink, green, yellow and white, Ringo's orange and yellow bass drum skin, the bright yellow coach and more. On the front page, the credits declare that *Magical Mystery Tour* is "A colour film for television."

Beatles fans in the USA didn't get the chance to enjoy the film at Christmas and had to rely on reports from others. In the home of the counterculture, the *San Francisco Express Times* published a letter from "Angela," with some thoughts on British life and a Christmas spent in London. Angela was pessimistic about the country's future – "Britain is going down the pan" she wrote – but she had enjoyed the holiday festivities, among them the showing of the latest Beatles project. Her feelings about *Magical Mystery Tour* are mixed, but some of her criticisms are insightful. She declares it a failure, because the Beatles had not thought about its impact on TV rather than on a cinema screen, "And McCartney's rampant middle-class sentimentality turns me off." But there was much to enjoy, including the scene starring the Bonzo Dog Doo-Dah Band, while "Ivor Cutler in dark glasses saying in a voice of infinite sepulchral menace, 'I am your friendly courier'," was "real surreal."[20] According to a footnote, Angela had recently published a novel, *The Magic Toyshop*, which identifies her as Angela Carter, novelist, children's author, journalist and playwright.

In Ivor's opinion, the film was "a sort of curate's egg. Good in bits. I think the film's been proved to be ahead of its time. I don't know – at the time I was too close to it to stand back and appreciate it properly."[21] Ivor's few on-screen minutes are in many people's minds the pinnacle of his career. He was happy to talk about the experience, but didn't usually raise the subject. Lee Freeman was in regular touch with him from 1969, but Ivor never spoke to her about *Magical Mystery Tour* or McCartney's visit to Laurier Road. Back at Fox Primary, Mr Cutler only spoke about the film if one of his young charges mentioned it. Xavier Russell's classmate did mention it, calling Mr Cutler "Mr Bloodvessel": "He said 'Oh yes. I've done the Magical Mystery Tour with my friends the Beatles.'" Kate Williams wasn't aware of her teacher's "other life" as a performer. Her friend, Rebecca Orr-Deas, was similarly unaware until she saw the film in 1979: "He never talked about that, never." Milton Mermikides, at Fox in the late 1970s, didn't know about it either, until he saw the same showing: "and there he was: I don't think I've got over that. Television and fame were different from now, it seemed like an impenetrable barrier: to see this man who was spending time with us appear with the Beatles … was the weirdest and most surreal and disarming thing."

At the time, Ivor told his housemate Alfio Bernabei that McCartney was his favourite member of the Fab Four: "Ivor liked Paul, he told me so. He said he liked Paul more than John. He felt that John kept a bit at a distance. Not as friendly. He also liked Ringo …" However, in interviews Ivor said that Lennon was his favourite. "Actually, I think I got on better with John Lennon than the others," he said four years after filming, and in 1999 he said "Lennon was the one whose personality attracted me. I think he quite enjoyed me too. But he never told me …"[22] Lennon did tell one of his interviewers, however, as Ivor recalled: "George Melly asked him who were the influences in his work. I was one of the four."[23] Beatles biographer Hunter Davies, who was close to the band in the 1960s, wrote of Ivor: "It's often hard to distinguish between authentic behaviour and attention-seeking devices, but if Cutler was artifice he maintained it for the whole of his career … If only the conversations between John and Ivor Cutler had been filmed during the making of *Magical Mystery Tour*."[24]

Ivor told a tale of the Fab Four stealing his music and using it as a base for some of their most successful songs. Three versions of this tale emerged, all of them lacking any firm evidence in their favour, all possibly apocryphal. The first is that Ivor was given the role of Buster Bloodvessel as recompense for having his melodies stolen, while the second is that the chord sequence of "I'm Going in a Field" was used as the foundation of an unidentified song.[25] In the third interpretation, McCartney stole one of Ivor's compositions and turned it into one of the band's most successful songs. At least, that's the story Ivor told to Fred Frith, who collaborated with Ivor on *Velvet Donkey* and recalls that Ivor "played me the song that he claimed Paul McCartney stole from him (as 'We Can Work It Out')." Frith adds that the line about fussing and fighting "does have a very Ivorian ring to it."

If "We Can Work It Out" was borrowed from one of Ivor's compositions, then this happened well before *Magical Mystery Tour*. Ian MacDonald's song-by-song discussion of the Beatles recordings, *Revolution in the Head*, notes that "We Can Work It Out" was recorded on 20 and 29 October 1965.[26] But McCartney and/or Lennon could have been aware of Ivor years before this, through radio, TV or records. Hunter Davies wrote that McCartney "heard Ivor Cutler on the radio and wanted to know more about his harmonium playing" but doesn't say when this happened or name the show. Or it may have been the band's PR, Tony Barrow, who first brought Ivor to their attention: as "Disker," he'd written enthusiastically about Ivor as early as June 1961.[27]

As MacDonald notes, thanks to the influence of people such as film director Dick Lester and his friends Spike Milligan and Peter Sellers, the Beatles became increasingly aware of fringe theatre, the satire of the Establishment and the activities of performers including the Alberts and Ivor.[28] In his biography of McCartney, Miles notes that the Beatle met Ned Sherrin; visited Bertrand Russell, the peace and nuclear disarmament campaigner, philosopher and Ivor Cutler fan, at Russell's home in Chelsea; frequented London nightclubs including the Blue Angel and the Establishment; and was a fan of Lenny Bruce.[29] Another point in favour of Ivor's argument, however tenuous: "We Can Work It Out" features Lennon on harmonium.

Ivor may have honestly felt that the Beatles had "stolen" one of his songs, or he may just have been mischievously spreading a false rumour. He never, as far as I am aware, took his suspicions anywhere near a legal professional. MacDonald states that the song is about McCartney's relationship with Jane Asher and McCartney told Miles that it was originally a "more up-tempo thing, country and western," which Lennon and Harrison helped to refine at the recording session. As for the harmonium (which sounds far more refined and in much better repair than the ones Ivor usually played), McCartney recalled that the group "found an old harmonium hidden away in the studio" and decided to use it to add colour.[30]

Ivor's relationship with the Beatles didn't last for long beyond *Magical Mystery Tour*, but Ivor claimed that it brought the invitation, from one or more of the Beatles, to teach their children: an offer he turned down "on socialist principles," according to journalist Mark Espiner. "What made their kids more special than other kids?" Ivor asked him.[31] The Beatles may not have been as arrogant as Ivor's story makes them seem: one of their plans for their short-lived Apple Corps empire, which included a record label, a boutique and an electronics division, was to establish an Apple School, to provide education for the children of the band's staff as well as the bandmates' own offspring. This part of their plan never came to fruition, but it may have been the place where they envisaged Ivor teaching.[32]

Before the BBC showed *Magical Mystery Tour*, Ivor recorded an album for EMI's Parlophone label, on which the Beatles released their early hits. Called *Ludo*, it was credited to the Ivor Cutler Trio and produced by George Martin.[33] Percussionist Trevor Tomkins, lately of the Three Wise Men, re-joined Ivor. However, Dave Green, now a member of Humphrey Lyttelton's band among others, did not reprise his role from the *Late Night Line-Up* broadcast: "It's quite possible he may have asked me but I was busy at the time and may have been away on tour. I wish I had done it ..." Double bassist Gill Lyons got the job instead – Tomkins had already played with her on a few occasions.

Ivor met Lyons through their mutual friend, Ann Murray. "I think the first thing we did was a pilot for television, for colour," says Lyons, "We were all dressed in green and had our faces and hands coloured green, I'm not sure why! And that's when we played." This is probably the same pilot that involved Ivor and Murray in a bed. Before she recorded with Ivor, Lyons had used her woodworking skills to help Virginia and her sons: "I was doing woodwork for people, trying to make some money, building things, kitchens, furniture ..." Virginia wanted her sons to have "a place to write on with space for books and so on ... I used to heave all this wood up the stairs. ... I made one for each of the boys." Over fifty years later, Dan Cutler confirmed the story.

Lyons is self-effacing about her musical abilities: "I was not the best bass player in London. I was quite amazed that he asked me to do [*Ludo*]. There was a rapport, I would say, and he treasured that more than musical brilliance." The importance of a rapport with collaborators is something that arose frequently in Ivor's projects: Ivor was a friend of many of his fellow actors, book illustrators and musicians before he invited them to collaborate. The trio worked hard to be ready for the recording sessions. "We practised a lot together, up in his tiny top room ... We had to go over everything, very carefully," Lyons recalls. Even those parts of the record that sound spontaneous were carefully plotted, with one exception: "a piece where we had to hum in the background. We didn't know about the humming until we were doing the piece and we had hysterics. I think we must have had about twenty-seven takes and George Martin was absolutely furious! You could see his face behind the glass, absolutely livid …"

Tomkins says he got on "fine" with Martin and recalls that when he and Lyons had hysterics the producer "was falling about as well, then he said 'Come on, we've got to get this done guys'." Lyons, by contrast, found Martin a less than genial presence. "I think he was quite acerbic and bad-tempered generally [throughout the recording] … just a bad-tempered guy in my experience," she said, remembering that Ivor "ignored any unpleasantness and got on with it. He was just interested in what we were doing." Martin had a reputation for producing comedy records, but he was used to exerting at least some control over the process: he was also, according to the Beatles studio engineer Geoff Emerick, "straightlaced."[34] The far-from-straightlaced Ivor's unwillingness to let a producer alter his carefully rehearsed songs and stories was never likely to help form a happy working relationship.

In 2014, Martin was one of Ivor's "famous fans" quoted in an *Observer* article. He was far from effusive in his praise:

> Ivor Cutler was one of a kind – quite the eccentric. Even in his normal speech he sounded as if he was lamenting the passing of a dear friend. I recorded him because he was such a character, and I had always enjoyed making comedy recordings and had some success. These were never significant, sadly [but] the Beatles were amused.[35]

When the Rev-Ola label re-released *Ludo* in 1997, Ivor was thrilled, "Especially to hear my young, strong, voice." But he, like Lyons, remembered that Martin had not enjoyed producing the record: "He said: 'There's no point in my being here'. I suppose I am a bit of a perfectionist. I was more so in those days, when I was less sure of myself."[36]

Cutler, Lyons and Tomkins (with a little help from George Martin) created what is probably Ivor's most accessible album. Douglas T. Stewart names it as his favourite of Ivor's recordings: "I think a lot of the others are less albums, more collections of material. [*Ludo*] has that cohesiveness about it." *Ludo* contains seventeen tracks with Ivor credited as writer, composer and arranger. Just to make this clear, the cover notes added: "I am IVOR CUTLER I wrote all the words and music in this gramophone record I am modest." The cover also includes an odd, apocryphal tale of how he put the group together, which involves violent late-night visits from Tomkins and a trip to the "salon" with Gill Lyons. Ivor plays piano, rather than harmonium, on most of the tracks. Lyons and Tomkins are important collaborators, their instruments used not merely as backing, but as integral to the mood of the songs, accentuating their humour or poignancy. They add backing vocals to a few numbers as well, notably "A Great Grey Grasshopper" and "A Suck of My Thumb."

The album is a mixture of the entertaining, the thoughtful, the absurd and the beautiful. "Mud" and "A Suck of My Thumb" are two engaging ditties, earworms just waiting to be heard. "Mud" was one of Ivor's songs from primary school: Dan Cutler spoke of parents who expected their children "to come back having learned to sing and they'd come back singing of the joys of mud."[37] Gill Lyons took "Mud" and other Ivor Cutler songs into the classroom when she was teaching: "Ivor told me he purposefully made ['Mud'] as if it's about treading in some dog muck. It's actually quite naughty ..." "I'm Happy" is equally jolly, even if Ivor threatens physical violence to any man who disagrees with his appraisal of his emotional state. "Deedle, Deedle, I Pass" is set to a tune that would fit neatly into the repertoire of an English Morris Dance team.

Amid these exercises in cheerfulness are a couple of gentler, more meditative, songs. The pretty, lilting "Last Song" reminds me of the *Andy Pandy* theme Ivor played to his primary school charges. "I'm Going in a Field" is McCartney's favourite and one of Ivor's loveliest songs. It's usually thought of as a romantic ballad: the singer is going to the field to lie down and a line about the colour of his lover's eyes suggests that the singer and his lover are lying down together; but this isn't the only interpretation. The mention of the lover's eyes stands alone, sung with no suggestion that the lover is present. It could instead be heard as a last memory, as the singer lies down next to (not on) the grass and prepares to die. KT Tunstall, the singer and songwriter, favours this interpretation and I'm inclined to agree.[38] Dan Cutler says "I'm Going in a Field" is his favourite of his father's songs: "Yes. I mean, I'm not sure I've heard them all ... There's something about it." He didn't want to discuss interpretation, although he did agree with Tunstall's perspective:

> To me, he creates a mood rather than something interpretable. I prefer the sort of melancholic mood, rather than the cheerful "I'm happy, I'm happy ..." I'd say it's more about death. It's not that he's about to get it on with his girlfriend, it's very different. I think it's ambivalent, like most of his stuff, which I think is a great deal of its charm.

There are four spoken-word tracks on *Ludo*, including two stories, "Mary's Drawer" and "The Shapely Balloon," that appeared in Ivor's second book, *Cockadoodledon't*. Throughout his career, Ivor would produce his works in many forms: a single poem, song or story might appear in print, on the radio, on TV, and on record. The stories are the longest two tracks on the discs – "The Shapely Balloon" lasts four minutes and six seconds as Ivor tells of wanting to buy a balloon but only being able to afford three-quarters of one.

Years later, "Darling, Will You Marry Me Twice" won Ivor a rare accolade.

In response to a request from *The Times* for readers to name the "silliest and most embarrassing" song lyrics, Steve Lowe of Stourbridge submitted five suggestions, including songs from Roxy Music and Devo, and Ivor's request for a double ceremony. It wasn't the only time that people mistook Ivor's humour for seriousness, or seriousness for humour, or just plain didn't understand it: in the USA, Jimmy Fallon, presenter of NBC's *The Tonight Show*, developed his "Do Not Playlist," a regular spot on the show in which he highlighted songs he deemed awful, and awarded Ivor's "Jam," from *A Flat Man*, a coveted spot on the list.[39]

Parlophone released "A Great Grey Grasshopper" as a single (renamed "The Great Grey Grasshopper"), backed with "I Had a Little Boat." It's an odd coupling, when a pair of cheerful, funny, upbeat songs like "Mud" and "Cockadoodledon't" were there for the taking. *Record Mirror* gave four stars to this "Inconsequential, dead-pan, and somehow very funny" record.[40] However, to use a phrase that can be applied to all of Ivor's record releases, it failed to chart.

BBC Two repeated *Diary of a Nobody* on 23 September, shortly after Ivor completed location filming with the Beatles. Then, after the relative intensity of the latter half of 1967 and the premier of *Magical Mystery Tour* at Christmas, it was over a year before Ivor returned to the wireless, making his first appearance on the pop music station, Radio 1, on John Peel's show. The station was barely eighteen months old, still searching for a distinct identity and still combining cosy daytime chat from 48-year-old Jimmy Young with attempts at being with-it and groovy. One of its more successful attempts was the hiring of Peel, a Liverpudlian disc jockey whose broad tastes encompassed top chart bands, folk singers, experimental music and poetry. Peel joined the BBC after working on radio in the United States and on the "pirate" station Radio London. Radio 1 went on air on 30 September and Peel's first programme, called *Top Gear*, went out at 2.00 p.m. on Sunday 1 October. In January 1968 Peel began presenting the midnight to 1 a.m. *Night Ride*, featuring acts from the musical counterculture, few of which would have been candidates for daytime radio play. Some were featured players in the Ivor Cutler story: Fairport Convention, Ron Geesin, the Bonzo Dog Doo-Dah Band and Soft Machine all recorded sessions for Peel in his early years at the BBC.[41]

Ivor was not a fan of the music championed by Radio 1: neither the pop hits on the daytime shows nor the raucous rock acts to be found in the evening schedules were to his taste. He had declared his position regarding modern music on his introduction to "Here's a Health to Simon," back in 1959: "music nowadays is very often distasteful to me, I feel that all the old values have gone ..." It's a viewpoint he reasserted over the years. What would he do if he ruled the world? "I'd dis-invent electricity so that music would be acoustic."[42] He told Gavin Hogg in 1991, "I loathe pop. It has become, for me, a raucous cacophony." Despite these radical views of contemporary popular music, Peel's listeners at the time, fans of Leonard Cohen or Bridget St John as well as rockers like Deep Purple or Free, took Ivor to their hearts, and as time went on and tastes changed he continued to find a fanbase among the followers of new musical genres.

Ivor's first appearance on a Peel show was unusual in that the recorded session was combined with Ivor joining Peel live in the studio. On 5 May he went to Studio S2 in the sub-basement of Broadcasting House, to record three songs – "Trouble, Trouble," "Bounce, Bounce, Bounce" and "In My Room There Sits a Box." Two days later, the session was part of Peel's Wednesday evening show. Bob Cobbing, a poet from a different sphere of practice from Ivor's own, joined the show midway through and Peel's choice of music included tracks from Leonard Cohen, rock-a-boogie artist Merrill E. Moore, and Louis Armstrong and his Hot Five. Ivor's first number was "Trouble Trouble"; a few minutes later Ivor read "An Old Poltroon," then he introduced "Bounce, Bounce, Bounce," which was inspired, he explained, by Princess Berenice from Flaubert's *Salammbô*. Perhaps in fear that Ivor was about to summarise Flaubert's entire body of work, Peel broke in: "Mm, okay, fine. Ivor Cutler and 'Bounce, Bounce, Bounce."

It's a mark of Peel's eclectic taste that the next tracks were Peter Cook and Dudley Moore's "The Leaping Order of Nuns," "Go to the Mirror" by the Who, and a Swedish folk song. Ivor returned, reading "There and Back via Sweden" – either in quick response to the Swedish song, or by pure coincidence, introducing the work as a "miasmic poem" and advising "If there are any children listening, go to bed at once. Now the poem ..." Peel and Ivor then engaged in a short conversation about Ivor's books. Peel's on-air style was always laid-back and relaxed, but he seems hesitant, too, as if unsure how to deal with his guest. "You write children's stories." "Yes, I write children's stories, but I like to send them to bed." "Yeah. I see." Ivor then tells Peel that a book of children's stories might appear in 1970 but isn't yet ready. "What about this one that we've got here, then?" (Peel later says that it's *Cockadoodledon't*) "Well, those aren't children's stories. They're a bit more sophisticated. Children like them a bit, you know."

After "In My Room There Sits a Box," Peel, Cutler and Bob Cobbing chat. Cobbing is there to promote the forthcoming Poetry Marathon at the Roundhouse, which will run without interruption from the following Tuesday until Saturday morning at 6.00 a.m. Ivor is due to perform but lacks Cobbing's enthusiasm, calling the Marathon "a daft idea." He's more enthusiastic about his involvement in Workshop 2, a workshop for amateur poets. Cobbing then talks about his latest recording of sound poems and Peel asks Ivor if he's ever done something similar. "What? Making a noise?" asks Ivor. "Well, sound poems," Peel says, before Cobbing has a chance to respond to Ivor's comment. "Abstract work?" asks Ivor, "Yes, I did and I sent it to *Punch*. And they sent it back." He bursts out laughing and Peel brings the conversation to an end before playing Cobbing and François Dufrêne's "Spontaneous Appealinair

Contemprate Appollinaire." Ivor's final pieces, "Beatrice and Her Dirty Knees" from *Cockadoodledon't* and "An Indirect Love Poem," are separated by Merrill E. Moore's "Rock Rockola" before Peel thanks Ivor for coming on to the show. Ivor replies, with some charm, "And I am also delighted."

One down, twenty-one to go.

Over the next thirty years, Peel regularly played Ivor's records, while his twenty-two Peel sessions are exceeded only by the Fall, one of Peel's favourite bands, and by David Gedge, whose sessions with the Wedding Present and Cinerama match the Fall's total of twenty-four.[43] Surprisingly, none of Ivor's records ever made Peel's annual Festive 50, but his June 1985 session is one of the top 125 John Peel sessions (from around four thousand in total) selected by Peel's friends, family and colleagues.[44]

From the late 1980s Andy Kershaw also broadcast sessions from Ivor, doing so until the early years of the twenty-first century.[45] Kershaw first heard Ivor on Peel's show, this "hilarious, deadpan, Scotsman ... intoning some rather unsettling stories, often to harmonium accompaniment, and usually involving herring, a stern grandfather and unremittingly foul weather. What the fuck was this?"[46] He mentions Ivor only briefly in his autobiography, a decision he regrets, he says, "because I realise now that what he gave me was a love of words. He made me listen to words in a way that I'd not done before ... he taught me about comedy writing, phrasing and timing."

Typically, acts recorded their sessions at the BBC's Maida Vale studios a few weeks before they were broadcast. Most acts would record three or four songs per session: even punk bands, generally known for the brevity of their songs, managed no more than five. Ivor's mix of songs, poems and stories meant that he could record a far higher number of pieces per session, often achieving ten or more, and reaching a record of twenty different pieces at his session of 11 May 1986. The only other act to come close was probably Napalm Death, a band whose average song lasted about as long as an Ivor Cutler poem, enabling them to record ten or more tracks per session.

Ivor was well aware of the impact of his appearances on John Peel's show:

> Every year a new bunch of kids starts on Radio 1 and discovers me in among the other work and knowing it's John Peel and knowing that the other work is stuff that they can enjoy and they come across me they say "Oh, well, if Peel thinks it's good enough to put out, it's good enough for us," and they get hooked on it. And an enormous number of people have come up to me, adults, and said "You know I first heard you on John Peel."[47]

Peel and his producer, John Walters, liked Ivor's sessions because, according to Walters, Ivor was "always reliable, always came up with new stuff, was happy to stand in when some precious artsy-fartsy band cancelled" and, above all, the listeners liked him. Ivor was one of the show's canniest contributors, reading the BBC contract small print and realising that when he brought his harmonium to a session he could charge carriage because it was a "large instrument." When Ivor spoke with Ken Garner in 1992, he was unclear about how he got his first Peel session, but remembered that Peel bought a copy of *Ludo* from Woolworth's in Stowmarket for ten shillings.[48]

Ivor remained grateful to Peel for his new, young, audience and in 1998, when Peel curated that year's Meltdown Festival and invited Ivor to join acts such as Culture, Blur and Sonic Youth, Ivor agreed to appear at the press launch. As Peel reported, Ivor spoke with some warmth, but as a member of the Noise Abatement Society he "was keen to emphasise his commitment to tranquillity." As a result, "Nobody dared to tell him that he was scheduled to appear on the same night as Ipswich's Extreme Noise Terror, and at least three hours of high-pressure sound from a load of Japanese art terrorists."[49] In contrast, *Financial Times* journalist Peter Aspden (a former pupil of Mr Cutler) was at a Meltdown launch and remembered that, rather than speaking warmly, Ivor "glowered and stared ahead of him, answering questions in gruff monosyllables, wondering quite what the game was that he was playing now."[50]

After *Ludo*, Ivor made no records for seven years, his next TV appearance after *Magical Mystery Tour* was not until 1969, and there is no evidence of Ivor on any radio shows, apart from his debut Peel session, between the final episode of *The I.C. Snow*, in January 1964, and *Poetry D-Day*, broadcast on Radio 3 on 23 May 1970. This was a recording of a twelve-hour poetry reading at the Roundhouse, part of the 1970 Camden Festival – barely a sprint, compared to the four-day *Poetry Marathon* of the previous year. Although Ivor was rarely on the airwaves at this time, the *Poetry D-Day* event was just one of many live performances. This was a time of transition for Ivor as a stage performer. His emerging popularity with Peel's listeners not only brought him a new radio audience, it also brought him into a new live arena alongside the musical acts that Peel and his followers also espoused: the university and college circuit beckoned.

Lanchester Polytechnic (later Coventry University) was a leading venue on this circuit and its ambitious student union went beyond the usual weekly dances, gigs and concerts by establishing the Lanchester Arts Festival, where Ivor first appeared in 1970 on a bill with Peel, Ron Geesin and Principal Edwards Magic Theatre. He was back for the following year's festival, this time for an event advertised as "Mixed Media," in the polytechnic's main hall. Ivor shared the bill with his fellow *D-Day* poet, Adrian Henri, in support of the evening's top act, Curved Air. The band, featuring vocalist Sonja Kristina and violinist Darryl Way, was emerging as one of the most popular of the progressive rock acts of the early 1970s, its debut album, *Air Conditioning*, having made the top ten at the end of 1970. The concert is an early example of Ivor's new entertainment milieu: as a support act to top rock bands he was now performing to audiences of one thousand or more.[51]

Ivor began making regular concert appearances in support of rock acts, including Soft Machine and Hatfield & the North, prog-rockers Camel (Phyllis King was also on the bill) and others. In 1976 Ivor and Soft Machine both supported Kevin Ayers (a past member of the Softs) at Edinburgh's Playhouse Theatre.[52] Jeremy recalled seeing his father support Soft Machine, staying on to see the headliners after his father had left the venue.[53] Dan's connection to the band was the only example he could recall of his father using his rock world networks to his son's benefit. As a teenager, Dan started to play drums. It was not the typical teenage drummer story:

> I got into drumming partly because he had been attending an adult education class in hand drumming … It happened to be on the same day of the week that I used to go and spend with him and so he took me as well. He persuaded the guy who was teaching it that I wouldn't be any trouble. I found it very congenial and ultimately he was persuaded that I was serious about it and we bought a second-hand kit from some guy from an advert in a newspaper. I kept it for a very long time. Dad used his contacts. He used to do an interval act for Soft Machine and the guy who took over from Robert Wyatt [John Marshall] was very technically skilled. I used to cycle from Notting Hill over to somewhere in Wimbledon for an hour a week for teaching. That was the only direct benefit of Ivor's connection to that world.

Towards the end of the 1970s, Ivor toured with Van Morrison. Andy Kershaw first saw Ivor on stage when this tour came to Sheffield City Hall: "[Ivor] wasn't billed to appear. Some roadies brought on this tatty old harmonium and out he came, to the bewilderment of a large part of the audience." At the 1986 WOMAD Festival he performed on the day when Siouxsie and the Banshees topped the bill: Ivor's dressing-room tent was next to the headliners' own and, remembers David Jones, "they liked him." His status on the poetry circuit also brought festival bookings, including the 1983 Poetry Olympics at the Young Vic when he was billed to appear alongside Harold Pinter, Fran Landesman, and a musical ensemble featuring organiser Michael Horovitz on saxophone and Scottish psychoanalyst R. D. Laing on piano.[54] By the 1990s, Ivor's appearances as a support act to a headliner were rare. One of his final support gigs was with the Carla Bley trio. A review of their Queen Elizabeth Hall concert commented that "by taking the stage directly after Ivor Cutler, a man for whom the tag 'eccentric' seems pitifully inadequate, Carla Bley managed to appear conventional, almost staid."[55]

Ivor joined in with Peel's Christmas festivities in 1970. It's another incongruous appearance, part of an *ad hoc* group informally named the Top Gear

Carol Singers. As a snapshot of the British rock scene of the time, it's an invaluable historical document: the line-up included Peel, Sonja Kristina, Marc Bolan, every member of the Faces (Rod Stewart, Ronnie Lane, Ronnie Wood, Ian McLagan and Kenney Jones), Soft Machine's Robert Wyatt and Mike Ratledge, and Ivor. In a photograph taken at the session, it's Ivor who stands out among the assembled rockers: he's standing front and left of the group, balding, clad in a tweed jacket with a hankie hanging out of the top pocket, looking as if he could be someone's dad who's joined in by accident (he's not yet forty-eight).[56] Stewart took lead vocals on "Away in a Manger," Kristina sang "Silent Night," the ensemble joined together on "God Rest Ye Merry, Gentlemen" and "Good King Wenceslas" and it sounds like a good time was had by all. Four years later Ivor joined the Faces, Wyatt and DJs Johnnie Walker, Alan Freeman and Terry Wogan at Peel's wedding.[57]

On 8 November 1971 Ivor recorded his second Peel session, at the Playhouse Theatre, for broadcast on 24 November. It included perennial Cutler favourites "Mud" and "I Believe in Bugs," the tale of Y'Hup's finest source of protein, "The Green Rain," and two stories about life in a bizarre and unsettling Scottish household. Ivor's tales of *Life in a Scotch Sitting Room* would beguile, bewilder and befuddle fans for the rest of its creator's life.

8 Life Inside the Sitting Room

Life in a Scotch Sitting Room is a story in many parts. Ivor called them episodes and put them together in a single volume, which he called volume 2: there is no volume 1. Each episode is a self-contained tale and there is no linear narrative to concern the listener or reader, thankfully, because Ivor read episodes in seemingly random order at concerts, or on the radio. It's the story of a Scottish family, a three-generation household of Grandpa, Grandma, Father, Mother and six children (three boys and three girls). Ivor never reveals if the grandparents are paternal or maternal, not that it matters with regard to the narrative. When the stories appeared in a 1984 book titled *Life in a Scotch Sitting Room Vol. 2*, Martin Honeysett's illustrations showed the male members of the family wearing kilts most of the time, with Grandpa and Father completing their outfits with sporrans, and the female members wearing dresses and aprons, with each member of the family looking grim, downtrodden and dour. The final six pages repeat the same drawing of the family, each image smaller than the last, as if the family is slowly disappearing into the distance, or perhaps the past: the children stare out of each page, glum, vacant and hopeless.

The family lives a simple, uncluttered, life untroubled by close relationships with others, but characterised by regular humiliation of the children, an absence of love or even respect between and within the generations, and random acts of violence. One of the children narrates the stories, giving his personal perspective on his relatives and their activities: only in Episode Seven do we discover that he's called Ivor and not until Episode Nine are we told that the family is called Cutler. To a fan, listening to a Peel session, sitting comfortably in the theatre, or reading at home in front of a cosy fire, these tales are funny, a series of ludicrous vignettes ranging from the barely believable to the totally absurd. To the narrator, little Ivor, they are scenes of a domestic life that, with luck, is no more than banal and ordinary, but which threatens at any moment to bruise, physically or psychologically, or draw blood.

Ivor first broadcast an episode of *Life in a Scotch Sitting Room* on the 16 October 1970 edition of *Late Night Line-Up*.[1] However, he presented many more episodes on his Peel sessions between 1971 and 1985. The mysterious Episode Ten was the final episode to be broadcast as part of a Peel session, on 15 July 1985: mysterious, because it doesn't exist or, to be accurate, it consists in total of the words "There is no episode ten."[2]

Life in a Scotch Sitting Room has four lives: broadcast on radio, performed on stage, recorded on albums and published in print. The print version is the most complete, with twenty-one episodes – other episodes could be hidden away in an old notebook, so it may be inaccurate to refer to the book as "the complete" version. Ivor's tales of everyday family adventures were so popular that EMI's Harvest Records, the pre-eminent record label for fans of progressive rock, released a live album titled *Ivor Cutler's Life in a Scotch Sitting-room Vol II*. At least that's what it said on the front cover: the back cover title was *Life in a Scotch Sitting-room Volume 2 – Ivor Cutler* and on the record itself it was *Life in a Scotch Sitting Room, Volume 2*.[3] Ivor recorded the album at Glasgow's Third Eye Centre on 7, 8 and 9 July 1977, interspersing thirteen sitting room stories with four of his renowned "Jungle Tips," brief but useful pieces of advice on what to do if you happen upon an owl, a boa constrictor, a leopard or a lion. The episodes were programmed, as usual, in an apparently random order starting with Episodes Two, Three and Nine and ending with Episodes Six, Four and Thirteen. Eighteen tracks are listed on the back cover, with the final track named as "Episode 0" with a running time of zero minutes and zero seconds.

Ivor was fifty-four, at the height of his powers as an on-stage performer, and sounds confident, if rather rushed in his delivery. Even his harmonium sounds youthful, no rattle from any of the keys. The audiences are onside, sometimes laughing in advance at the upcoming and already familiar jokes. They are especially keen to howl with laughter at the bits where Ivor speaks of physical violence, or bodily functions. Ivor closes the record by thanking his audience and asking "if I may, without being seen to be hypocritical … could you stand another one? It'll be the last one because I'll have run out then." The audience could most assuredly stand another one and so Ivor embarks on Episode Thirteen. He enjoys the story of how his street was home to regular groups of men on galloping horses: at three or four points he's so taken with the humour that he struggles to retain control, fighting, often unsuccessfully, against his desire to collapse in gales of laughter.

Life in a Scotch Sitting Room won Ivor the unofficial title of the Wisest Man in the World, according to Ivor:

> Oh, I thought that was terrific, yeah. In Worcester, Massachusetts, there's a jazz radio station and they came across my *Life in a Scotch*

Sitting Room album and they thought I was the wisest man in the world. They held their annual poll of top albums and I came first and Bruce Springsteen came second and Elvis Costello came third and Joan Armatrading came fourth and I love telling people that because they think I'm telling lies.[4]

"The Wisest Man in the World" may have been an informal award, but topping an Album of the Year poll that also included Springsteen, Costello and Armatrading is surely something worth remembering. Ivor didn't mention the year of the poll, but the October 1979 edition of the Newcastle University student newspaper *The Courier* referred to Ivor as once topping "the best ever album pole [*sic*] at Worcester College Mass.", so it seemed likely that this was the 1978 award. *The Courier* attributed Ivor's informal title of Wisest Man in the World to the *Worcester Mail*, but I can find no evidence that this newspaper ever existed.[5]

Ivor wasn't telling lies, but the story may not be quite as he remembered. There is no Worcester College in Massachusetts, but a radio station called WICN (Worcester Intercollegiate College Network), was established there in 1968.[6] Mark Lynch, who worked on WICN in the 1970s and still broadcasts on the station in the 2020s, gives a slightly different version of Ivor's tale. In the late-1970s Lynch, who describes WICN as mainly a jazz station, was head of the alt-rock department, which played Elvis Costello, didn't play Bruce Springsteen, and played Ivor Cutler "A LOT." Ivor's *Life in a Scotch Sitting Room* was the album which, says Lynch, "we played and loved." The station didn't hold an Album of the Year poll, or have an official Wisest Person in the World award, but Lynch does recall that it produced lists of its favourite albums of the year, so Ivor's album may well have made it onto one of those lists. Not exactly the story that Ivor told, but still an indication of a degree of transatlantic popularity.

The cover of the *Life in a Scotch Sitting Room* album tells its own story. Ivor is photographed on the back, conservatively dressed except for a Tam O'Shanter hat, and seated in front of an upright piano. The photograph is by Joyce Edwards, Ivor's landlady, and was probably taken at his Laurier Road flat. The front cover is dominated by a drawing of a family, sepia-toned and drawn with soft lines. The family surround an upright piano, the paper on the music stand filled by the album's title rather than by staves and notes. It's a happy, smiling, group. There are two kilted boys standing side by side, two slightly older girls, and four others. Mother sits at the piano and plays a tune: she's singing, as are the children. A kilted man, probably Father, stands proprietorially on the left of the instrument, leaning his right arm on its top. The remaining figures are harder to decipher. A figure standing opposite Father may be Grandpa or Grandma: they're bespectacled and smiling but it's impossible to see their clothing and their hairstyle is indistinct. The final figure stands behind the piano and sings, they're also wearing spectacles and only their head is visible. The figure is probably male, perhaps the oldest sibling. It's a very different family from the one that graces the pages of the printed version of *Life in a Scotch Sitting Room*: this cheery bunch are unlikely to have ever micturated in sponges, or spent hours with grains of Troon sand as their only source of fun.

Helen Oxenbury is the artist responsible for this image. She already had a well-established working relationship with Ivor, having illustrated three of his children's books, in which her warm, soft-toned, style was effective in complementing Ivor's writing. There's a personal connection, too: Ivor had taught Oxenbury's husband, John Burningham, at Summerhill and the couple were friends with Ivor before Oxenbury started working with him.[7] It's clear that when this album was released, the Cutler/Oxenbury collaboration was set to continue: a note on the LP's back cover reads "The contents of this album will be published in 1978, illustrated by Helen Oxenbury, as a book." Nineteen-seventy-eight came and went, but no book appeared.

When Methuen eventually published the promised book in 1984, as *Life in a Scotch Sitting Room Vol. 2*, it was filled with Martin Honeysett's images of a grim and downtrodden Cutler family. Honeysett was a *Private Eye* cartoonist, specialising in "fleshy, grotesque, visions of life in suburbia": just the sort of specialisation required to do justice to Ivor's own grotesque imaginings. When the album was rereleased, by Speakout Records in 1987, Honeysett's downbeat family portrait graced the cover.[8] Ivor wrote on the back cover of the book: "This book is me. It is my life. It is your life too – a bit – I expect. I am still reeling from the beauty, the intensity. And the sheer bloody arbitrariness of homo stupidiens." Inside, the dedication reads "To Robert Wyatt with gratitude and to IOU Theatre with gratitude, too."

A dedication to Robert Wyatt is unsurprising, but why would Ivor dedicate the book to a small company which David Wheeler, one of its founders and currently its artistic director, describes as "a collective of musicians and artists putting together ideas into a form that we wanted to define as theatre [and which] helped pioneer the concept of site-specific theatre, or location-based work"? Wheeler's description offers a clue, for a new, innovative, artist collective seeking to advance the idea of performance would surely appeal to an individual artist seeking to carve out his own approach to his art.

Lousie Oliver, another member of IOU Theatre, recalls that the group decided to write to a range of artists whose work they admired, inviting them to see what IOU was doing. Ivor was one of those artists and, Oliver says, he "was very generous. He told us later that he didn't like to go to the theatre but felt intrigued. He liked the tone and sentiment of the letter." Ivor visited an IOU Theatre show at the Oval House in Kennington (which Wheeler thinks was 1979's *Rub-a-Dub-Dub*) where the company designed the space so that it felt "like a cock-fighting ring," with the audience seated in a high semi-circular scaffolding structure, looking down on the action. Wheeler imagines that Ivor was attracted to the pace of the show:

measured and contemplative, with bursts of action mixed with a droll, dark humour … If I remember correctly, the scenes Ivor saw transitioned from a fight between two characters dressed in clanking scrap metal armour … to a sharp monologue delivered by a man in an equally sharp suit; and a dance between a Ford Cortina and a ship.

Oliver remembers that in the show's opening scene she was hidden in a large cardboard box, painted like a cube of water: "Live music was playing. I burst out of the box, dripping wet and proceeded to type a letter on a typewriter. A man and a woman entered and began fighting, really fighting - and eventually fell to the floor exhausted. I pulled the paper from the typewriter and said: 'It's okay. I've made two copies.'"

Ivor enjoyed the event, despite the presence of smoke and loud noise, saw more of IOU's London shows and visited Hebden Bridge, where some of IOU's members lived and which was close to the home of his poetry publisher, Arc Publications. Ivor must have been sufficiently impressed and affected by IOU's aims and intentions to decide that it was worthy of a dedication.

Life in a Scotch Sitting Room presents its episodes in numerical order. Episode Ten gets a page to itself, empty but for the statement "There is no episode ten." The accompanying drawing shows a rustic kitchen containing a wooden dining table, four bentwood chairs, a coal scuttle, an old newspaper and a box of dominoes. There's a pair of slippers on the floor, what seems to be an old sock on one of the chairs, and the head and bones of a fish on the draining board next to the sink – but there are no living beings to be seen. Only one other drawing fails to show at least one Cutler. This drawing accompanies Episode Nine, in which the entire family joins together in singing a medley of Scottish folk songs, and shows a bedraggled bird, looking rather perturbed in contrast to the sentence it illustrates: "The stonechat held its wings over its ears with delight and the rain beat the washing in four-four time."

Coming to these stories for the first time, the absurdity of the life portrayed is striking. This is a world in which the adult Cutlers micturate out of the window while the children have to micturate into a sponge, which Grandma empties out of the same window at regular intervals; where no one ever has a bowel movement; where the pretence of a day trip to the seaside involves staying at home and playing with grains of sand, a lump of salt and spittle; where a surreptitious glance at a second-hand first-aid book brings humiliation and a hard slap; and where a young boy takes offense at something and hides in a kitchen cupboard for a year before disappearing, never to be seen again.[9] There's evidence, too, of the Cutlers' ingenuity. Grandpa puts up notices in the local estuary to ensure that he catches only the most intelligent herring by directing them away from their less intelligent relatives, Ivor's sister makes her own rouge by rubbing two bricks together and the family learn to sing "Loch Lomond" to the accompaniment of a piano with several keys missing.[10]

The absurdities are easy to spot and easy to laugh at: herring can't read, bowels must be moved, a few grains of sand and a scraping of salt don't really replicate a day at the seaside, with or without the spittle from little girls' mouths, and it's unlikely that the children would be woken every Friday at midnight to watch Father re-varnishing the floor.[11] The violence, fear and humiliation are also easy to spot, but less easy to laugh at. At times, the children are hit because they have transgressed a rule, at other times the assaults are arbitrary: Grandpa thumps Ivor in the nose because he cries out "Down the River Clyde!" in excitement, a punishment for a previously unknown crime. Sometimes humiliation replaces the beatings: a kilted Ivor is forced to stand on the table when he's discovered whispering a joke to his siblings, as the rest of the family peer up his kilt and a sister makes a sketch of what she sees. The younger Cutlers are always aware of possible punishment: "ALL the children were busy looking guilty. It was our custom."[12]

Ivor is most upset by another act of violence, committed in the name of hygiene. Mother grabs each child in turn and cleans out their eyes, ears and noses with a handkerchief that grows ever filthier. Ivor is appalled by this act, this removal of his "personal muck" that gives him a unique experience of reality. His response is violent in its own way: "'Damn you to hell, Mother!' I whispered to the sponge."[13] Very occasionally, acts of kindness appear. When Father brings home an orange, it has one segment too few for all the family to have one, so Mother declines her chance of a segment, on the grounds that she's "a little loose ..." When Ivor burns his jacket, his sister attempts to save him from punishment by suggesting that the smell may be from a herring. Small acts, and rare.[14]

It's hard to identify exactly where the Scotch sitting room can be found. It's not in a Govan tenement, or a Pollokshaws Road flat, even though these are the homes the Cutlers lived in during Ivor's pre-teen years. As for the sitting room, it isn't always part of the life that Ivor talks about: the kitchen, the back yard, the front garden, the field at the end of the road, a park, the street and the countryside are all central to one or more of the episodes, while others take place in unidentified parts of the Cutler home. Honeysett's illustrations bring another dimension to the stories: sometimes, once familiar with the book, it can be hard to think of them without thinking of Honeysett's work. The drawings show a rustic, cottage-style, property, comfortable but far from luxurious: the Cutler family, as envisioned by Honeysett, consists of ten people, including six children even though the real Cutler family had five. Ivor's words don't offer such a clear image of the house or its inhabitants, and the information he gives comes in dribs and drabs. The sitting room contains a velvet suite, an onyx clock that no longer functions, and a patterned carpet. There's a sideboard, too, with room for four children, and, of course, there's a very big sponge. The family's prized possession is a black book – or

"THE BLACK BOOK," as it's referred to in print. It's an object of reverence, richly decorated, but Ivor never reveals the words within. There's a griddle and a coal fire, a bureau with a private drawer in which Father keeps the second-hand first-aid book, an upright piano. The houses in the street have gardens, so the people welcome the manure left behind by horses, and the street opens into a round field, accessible to the locals and containing three chimneys, each eighty-feet high. There's a bed in the kitchen, but Ivor doesn't tell us who sleeps in it; there's a wireless set, but it's never switched on. There's no mention of an upstairs, no description of bedrooms, or a bathroom – no Cutler has a bath – or a toilet, inside or outside.

The Cutlers carry out many activities that are recognisably part and parcel of life in the real world: they eat, sleep, get dressed, cook, keep (fairly) clean, knit, and pass urine, it's just that they do so in an exaggerated fashion. On occasions throughout the episodes, Ivor reveals something of his real family's life as well, mixing fact with the dominant fantasy. In Episode Two, the narrator reveals that he is left-handed, in Episode Seven that his name is Ivor, in Episode Nine that the family name is Cutler and that he levered out two of the piano keys with a poker when he was three years old. Then as the saga draws to a close, in Episode Nineteen Ivor mentions that his big brother was going to be a minister. These snippets of information are true, so perhaps Ivor reveals more, now forgotten, truths in these twenty-one episodes.

Ivor never reveals his relatives' first names. The adults have titles – Grandpa, Grandma (aka Grannie), Father and Mother (sometimes Mammy) – and Ivor's siblings are referred to as "brother" or "sister," or occasionally in more precise terms as "big brother" or "kind sister." It's not easy to calculate the exact number of Cutler siblings: it's probably five, including Ivor, assuming that if there is a "kind sister" then there is another one as well, while after one brother disappears forever, the "big brother" is still around. This family setup mirrors the real Cutler family of five siblings, but Episode Two, about an imaginary day at the seaside, suggests an equal number of boys and girls.

The world of *Life in a Scotch Sitting Room* is unique and wonderful, although I doubt it's one where many people would choose to live. Part of its charm lies in the fact that we're not part of it and not likely to be part of it. The misery, strangeness and unpredictability of this life is tempered by the humour Ivor brings to his descriptions, but this humour is outside the experience of those who endure the life. Of course, this is my interpretation of the tales, but it's by no means a common one. Other fans of these stories view them with a less jaundiced eye, celebrating the adventures as barely exaggerated descriptions of day-to-day life, an alternative to the somewhat cosier Scots childhoods of *The Broons* or *Oor Wullie*. Phyllis King felt that the stories, while not literally true, told her much about Ivor's younger years:

> For me, it is Ivor. Now, it's not exactly his family, I mean obviously it didn't happen like that, but to me it did happen like that. I can

see him in these situations, I can see him and his brothers and sisters, mum and dad, and all the various episodes to me are very, very alive and real.[15]

When Karl Dallas suggested that the people in these stories had some basis in reality, Ivor was clear that the families weren't real but he didn't see them as a dream world "because that would be psychotic and I'm not psychotic. They're figments of my imagination but there's something in them that a lot of people are amused by, these kinds of goings on."[16]

Invented worlds such as Ivor's are common in literature, but less common in contemporary rock or pop music. However, one such world does deserve mention alongside *Life in a Scotch Sitting Room*: the world of Rawlinson End. Rawlinson End was invented by Vivian Stanshall, vocalist and trumpet player with the Bonzo Dog Doo-Dah Band. Stanshall's world was, like Ivor's, peopled by strange and unpredictable characters as likely to commit violence as to invite a guest for tea. Unlike the Cutlers, the Rawlinsons were faded minor aristocrats, led by Sir Henry and ensconced in the ancient family seat of Rawlinson End. Stanshall, like Ivor, harboured ambitions to be a full-time painter, appeared on Peel Sessions, displayed an unusual dress sense, enjoyed jazz (trad, rather than modern), and performed with the Alberts and with Bruce Lacey. One of the Bonzos' first TV appearances was on *Late Night Line-Up* and Stanshall was a contributor to Radio 4's *If It's Wednesday ...*, on which Ivor appeared as a guest.[17] Neil Innes, the Bonzos guitarist and songwriter, acknowledged that Ivor's influence on the band was strong.[18] Innes had been a fan since he was a student at Norwich School of Art, when a fellow student, "the late, great, folk singer Peter Bellamy, turned me on to him – he played me 'Gruts.'"[19]

Stanshall's imagined world first appeared on the Bonzo Dog Band's 1972 album *Let's Make Up and Be Friendly*, barely two years after Ivor debuted his Scotch sitting room tales. The album track was followed by Peel sessions, live performances, a book, and a film starring Trevor Howard as Sir Henry. Stanshall's humour is broader than Ivor's: he has a fondness for comedy names like Jeremy Sphincter or, most famously, the family butler known as Old Scrotum the wrinkled retainer, and he wrote and performed the Rawlinson End stories to make his audiences laugh out loud with no threat of pathos to shift the mood. However, Rawlinson End and the Cutler sitting room are both beautifully realised environments, almost but not quite believable, existing parallel to rather than within the audience's own reality.[20]

Many happy hours can be spent teasing out the real from the surreal in *Life in a Scotch Sitting Room*, but Ivor's next series about his early life was more grounded in reality. On 15 July 1985 Peel broadcast the final session to feature a *Life in a Scotch Sitting Room* episode. When Ivor recorded his next Peel session, on 11 May 1986, among its twenty different pieces were episodes 3 and 4 of his new creation, *Glasgow Dreamer*.[21]

None of the *Glasgow Dreamer* episodes are on Ivor's albums, but eventually he read many of them on Peel sessions, on other radio shows including *King Cutler* and *A Stuggy Pren*, and on *Ivor Cutler – by Ivor Cutler*.[22] Ivor is the Glasgow Dreamer of the title.[23] When asked to what extent these childhood stories are autobiographical, Ivor replied:

> None of my work is separate from me, but *Glasgow Dreamer* is much more definitely autobiographical than the others so it's all out in the open. I've monkeyed about with it of course; ordinary autobiography is in the main, I find, fairly boring … Maybe I've been less ashamed of myself, accepting perhaps that what seemed so normal and boring to me might be less so to other people.[24]

Glasgow Dreamer appeared in book form in 1990.[25] The format is similar to *Life in a Scotch Sitting Room*, each of the twenty episodes taking up a couple of pages of text and two full-page monochrome illustrations, once again drawn by Honeysett. The stories tell of the adventures of the Cutler family and are narrated by Ivor: there are parents, grandparents and siblings, as before, and the stories are set in and around Glasgow, but the absurdity and surrealism of *Life in a Scotch Sitting Room* is absent, as are the kilts. Ivor dedicates the book "To vowels, the lubrication that stops consonants from sticking together like boiled sweeties in a paper bag."

Ivor opens and closes every episode of *Glasgow Dreamer* with a brief but useful geography lesson, albeit a Glasgow-centric one. "Glasgow, Glasgow where are you?" is the question. The answers vary but always inform us of the distance between Glasgow and another Scottish town or city: "Forty-four from Edinburgh," or "One two seven from Kingussie," for example. Between these geography lessons, Ivor's stories tell of his childhood, from toddler to seventeen-year-old RAF volunteer, though not in chronological order – in episode 6 he's three years old, in episode 7 he's two-and-a-half, in episode 8 he's six and in episode 13 he's an infant in nappies. Within the stories there are numerous verifiable pieces of information. His father's parents lived in Abbotsford Place; the family moved from Ibrox to Shawlands and sent Ivor to Shawlands Academy; Ivor had an Uncle Sam, his mother's brother, and an Uncle Joe on his father's side; Marie S. Irving was his school music teacher. In his own Proustian moment, Ivor remembers smoking Black Cat cigarettes "to the background of a delightful odour." This odour is *Diorama*, a perfume by Christian Dior, which he doesn't smell again until 1960 when it's worn by the wife of Johnny Mortimer, "ace trombonist" and member of Acker Bilk's Paramount Jazz Band.[26] There are stories, too, that Ivor told to interviewers and friends alike: of his attempted suicide, of signing a pledge never to smoke or drink, or of joining the RAF Volunteer Reserve. To confuse matters, one or two anecdotes don't ring true. If Ivor and his friend Peter discussed Marilyn Monroe's sponge (possibly a bath-time accessory, or perhaps her contraceptive device), this is unlikely to be a childhood or teenage memory as Monroe didn't make her film debut until 1947 – and did the people of Glasgow really celebrate an annual Hypocrisy Day where children could hang their siblings in effigy?[27]

These extremes, from verifiable to unlikely, make the middle ground more intriguing. Did Ivor "catch a disease" when he was three? Did Father take Ivor to watch Rangers play Celtic? Did Emma Walker tell Ivor to go down to the midden, order him to take out his penis and watch as Millie Hamilton dabbed at it with a filthy wad of cotton wool that looked as if it had "come off a sore that was healing"? And was Millie really one of Ivor's ex-girlfriends?[28] The incontrovertible evidence is still to be found.

Honeysett's illustrations for *Glasgow Dreamer* show a smaller family than the one in his sitting-room drawings: grandparents, parents and two small boys, but no sisters. One again, it's never clear if these grandparents are paternal or maternal, although Ivor does reveal that he preferred visiting his father's parents to his mother's, even though his father's parents were desperately poor.[29] An unnamed big brother is mentioned, notably in episode 10, when he tells Ivor a story of a teacher whose penis is fifty yards long, and in episode 18, when Ivor tells of attempting suicide by swallowing six aspirin tablets which big brother, a medical student by this time, has brought home. In the final episode, Ivor reveals that there are four siblings in the Cutler family, including a sister. Other named characters appear: Miss Whyte, the infant school teacher; Donald Macdonald, the boy who rubs snot on his desk; Peter and Alex, Ivor's fellow Gli Horyo Gang members.

To publicise *Glasgow Dreamer*, Ivor appeared on Radio 4's *Loose Ends*. Ned Sherrin presented the show and Emma Freud, one of its regular contributors, interviewed Ivor at London Zoo.[30] Ivor's interview started formally, with Ivor insisting that they refer to each other as Mr Cutler and Miss Freud, but after less than five minutes such formality has been abandoned and the pair have become Ivor and Emma. It's a relaxed, friendly, exchange – it could readily be described as "flirtatious." They begin their tour of the zoo in the children's section. "Want a stroke?" asks Freud. There's a slight pause before Ivor answers, "A rabbit? No, thanks all the same. I've got all these bacteria on my skin and I give them a wee stroke when I feel like it." Later, when Freud asks Ivor to read a poem, he claims that he can only remember one, "Breasts." They move through the zoo, talking cheerfully until the subject of mortality arises, as it often does in Ivor's interviews. This time, the trigger is unusual: Ivor spots a group of Marabou storks. "Oh, hold on. I love them," he says. "When I die I'm gonna be one of them ... Bald, as you see, with a wee bit of fuzz. And it's very bad-tempered and it just stands there with its shoulders up and waits." Freud asks if he thinks about dying. "Sure, all the time," he replies, "Doesn't everybody? I'm bored to death and I've got to do things to stop myself going nuts. I think if I stop working, that'll be it. I'll find a high window to jump out of." The interview returns to happier topics and

Freud attempts to guess Ivor's age. "How old are you? Seventy-five?" Ivor replies as if insulted: "Seventy-five! I'm only eighteen!" There's a brief pause. "I'm sixty-seven." Ivor ends the interview by reading episode 4 of *Glasgow Dreamer*.

The beginnings of *Life in a Scotch Sitting Room* and *Glasgow Dreamer* can be traced in Ivor's early work. "Grass Seed," from *Who Tore Your Trousers?*, is a dialogue between father and son, the latter having requested to grow grass seed on the former's bald head. "Egg Meat," from the same album, is a mother and son tale about the food Ivor is sent to buy so that it can be fed to the eggs. "Gruts for Tea," from *Get Away from the Wall*, finds a son complaining to his father about the family's daily diet of gruts, the same meal he's eaten for tea for the last three years. However, although "Gruts for Tea" is one of Ivor's best-known pieces, it's not about its creator. Instead, it introduces someone who will appear again and again in Ivor's work: the boy in "Gruts for Tea" is not Ivor, but Billy.

Billy, Bill or William is a recurring and often unfortunate character. In "Gruts for Tea" Billy has eaten the mysterious gruts for so long he finally decides to take a stand against his father's insistence that they should continue to be the family's daily meal, but this repetitive diet is a minor problem compared to the difficulties Billy encounters in other tales. In one of Ivor's earliest recordings, "Steady Job," Bill is the father whose son, Sam, plants himself in the garden. It's another precursor of the *Life in a Scotch Sitting Room* style: by the time Bill returns from a work trip, Sam has taken root, his toes now extending beneath the railway lines at the bottom of the garden.[31] In "The Dirty Dinner," Bill's covered in a mound of earth on the dining table, courtesy of his brother Jim, and breathes through a hole he has drilled. Once Jim has collected up the dirt and thrown it out the window, Bill, and the hole, have disappeared.[32] A rather menacing Bill appears in "The Electorate," promoting nepotism, but in "The Spiral Staircase" William is the one being menaced, by his mother who insists he learn a musical instrument so that she can inherit a fortune. In the musical instrument shop, William chooses the spiral staircase and thankfully the shop owner has some sheet music for it.[33] In one of his happier appearances, Bill is the footballer who advises his fellow player to "Pass the Ball Jim." Bill gets the ball and heads for goal, but he falls flat on his face due to loose bootlaces, and although the team wins the cup the glory is mostly Jim's.

In his introduction to "Do You Ever Feel Lonely" on *Who Tore Your Trousers?* Ivor reassures his listeners that "No matter how lonely you are, there is one who is even more lonely than you, Billy." "Her Tissues" finds Bill, an old-timer, dead drunk and lying face down in the snow. The unnamed "She" kicks him in the ribs, "laughing heartily at his predicament as he rolled over onto the pack ice."[34] Bill meets a tragic end in two tales. In "Just in Time" William recovers some forks, stolen from the George Hotel, only to be hit by a careless cyclist as he crosses the road to return them. The car crash that is the subject of "Phonic Poem" causes minor cuts and bruises to the narrator and his friends, with one exception: Bill's injuries are fatal.[35]

There are plenty of other characters in Ivor's work, with names like Jack, Ethel, Harry or Bella, but Ivor usually uses these names no more than once or twice, so why does Bill appear so often and meet with such strange and unpleasant fates? Ivor had an Uncle Willie on his mother's side, but it's unlikely that he's an object of fear or hatred as far as Ivor was concerned. Ivor's early years might have more to do with it, memories of hearing the call of "Are you a Billy or a Dan or an old tin can?" The bullying he experienced may have come mostly from the neighbourhood's Protestants, perhaps from members of one of the most notorious Glasgow gangs, the Billy Boys.[36]

9 A Life on the Page

Ivor's printed output divides broadly into three categories: prose, poetry and children's literature. It's an oversimplification, ignoring his work as an illustrator, his cartoons, and his stickies – few (if any) authors have explored the world of the sticky label like Ivor – but it will do to begin with.

Ivor's career as a writer started in 1962 when he not only drew cartoons for *Private Eye*, but also produced *Gruts*, a compilation of his work published by the Museum Press. The book featured favourites such as "Gruts for Tea," "Egg Meat" and "The Dirty Dinner" as well as lesser-known tales like "Cold Potato" and "Sweet Womanly Talk," alongside some of his drawings and the melodies of three of his songs – "The Shchi," "The Man with the Trembly Nose" and "Do You Ever Feel Lonely?".[1] The contents were copyright not by I. Cutler but by Bocu Music Company, which H. Elton Box had established the previous September.[2]

Cockadoodledon't, the book which John Peel misguidedly suggested might be for children, appeared four years after *Gruts*. According to Susan Hill, the book was "a slim book of off-beat, un-funny, slightly sick stories," from an author who "One either loves or hates ... I doubt if he would grow on a reader." Despite this less-than-enthusiastic review, Hill classed herself as one of the people on Ivor's "own peculiar wavelength."[3] In the rather more countercultural *International Times*, editor Tom McGrath was more enthusiastic, albeit with some chemical assistance: "lets put it this way I'm on a trip right now and this book is groovy to have around ..." he wrote, concluding "Yes, from those 17 million miles high Ivor is the new new testament. Give him your money. He will waste it to great advantage."[4] McGrath's enthusiasm indicates that Ivor was favoured by London's hipper inhabitants before he came to Peel's attention, but neither *Gruts* nor *Cockadoodledon't* grabbed the wider world's interest. However, his output built slowly and steadily over the years, eventually totalling over thirty publications.

Ivor made his debut as a children's author in 1971, with the publication of *Meal One*, the story of a young boy called Helbert.[5] Helen Oxenbury illustrated the story, which she described years later as "a bit sort of way out for most people." Oxenbury was already a friend and well aware of Ivor's work: when he invited her to draw the illustrations, she eagerly accepted.[6] She called the tale "a typical Ivor Cutler story and it's terribly difficult to actually tell you what it is in a sensible way ... I made [the mother] quite a sturdy lady."[7]

Meal One is one of Ivor's most enduring and best loved stories. It was chosen for broadcast on BBC Schools Programmes, appearing on a series for four- and five-year-olds called *Daytime on Two* during the 1980s, and as well as being popular with children and their parents, Oxenbury remembered, it "went down rather well with *Spare Rib*."[8] The feminist *Spare Rib* magazine did approve of *Meal One*, but it wasn't until 1974 that it published a review of the book.[9] At that time, the Children's Books Study Group, a London collective that was assessing the political content of children's books, produced a series of reviews for the magazine. The group felt that Helbert's relationship with his mother was perhaps too good, but praised Ivor's portrayal of Helbert's mum, which dispelled "the picture book stereotype of the aproned mother. Here is a mother capable of having feelings and fun." Oxenbury may have created Helbert's mum as "quite a sturdy" person, but the *Spare Rib* review thought she had illustrated mother's fun-loving persona "richly, even erotically."

Meal One was the first of Ivor's children's books to feature Oxenbury's illustrations. It was followed by 1975's *Balooky Klujypop*, in which a young girl called Balooky finds an elephant, and *The Animal House* a year later. Although they were friends, Ivor could irritate the illustrator:

> Terribly funny one minute and very annoying the next. He used to come round, always, on New Year's Eve, but instead of celebrating at midnight with us he would insist on going at ten to twelve. But we had to give him a lift home, so we all missed it! Typical Ivor.[10]

Oxenbury's annoyance with Ivor might explain why she stopped illustrating his books, but she did provide the cover art for the *Life in a Scotch Sitting Room* album released by Harvest, so there may be another reason for the end of the Cutler/Oxenbury pairing on Ivor's children's stories. It's notable, however, that Ivor worked with a series of illustrators across his children's stories, with most of these artists staying for no more than one or two books.

Although Honeysett collaborated with Ivor on more of his works than any other artist, this partnership was almost exclusively on prose books for adults, with the exception of *One and a Quarter*.[11] Honeysett may not have been first choice for this story. Ivor asked his friend Glen Baxter to illustrate a children's book he was planning and Baxter went to work: "I made a few sample drawings of a sea captain and a crocodile with one boxing glove on its paw. I didn't have a studio space at the time and worked on the floor so the drawings have the texture of the carpet – which I rather liked ..." Ivor took the idea to a publisher which asked for a four-book series but, Baxter remembers, Ivor wasn't keen on this and so the plan was abandoned. He believes that this story became *One and a Quarter*.

A steady stream of illustrators worked with Ivor on the rest of his children's books. His friend Alfie Benge illustrated two of his Herbert stories, but didn't view it as a collaboration:

> Ivor gave me the story ... a page and a half of typing. The pub-lishers then gave me pages of the final layout of the print, around which I had to design the illustrations. We didn't collaborate at all. I did a sample page for the editor to OK, then drawings of the rest of the story which they OK'd and then I did the paintings without any consultation with anyone.

Originally, Benge was expected to illustrate four Herbert stories, but it proved to be more time-consuming than she had expected and she stopped after the first two, describing the job as "a Labour of Hercules":

> My illustrations were very long-winded work... I ended up choosing to do very detailed oil paintings with very fine brushes, often with the help of a magnifying glass ... In the end I really couldn't afford to spend about another year of my life on two more books.... and Robert [Wyatt] persuaded me not to carry on. He was also worried that I was hurting my eyes! I should have chosen a looser way of working, it was my fault, but I had no experience of doing a book ... where as well as all the painting, everyone had to be recognisable from one page to the next etc. It even took a bit of time trying to create a chicken (and an elephant) that looked like a boy before I could even start the story.

The Herbert stories appeared in separate books during 1984 and were then collected together and published as *Herbert: Five Stories* in 1988 with Patrick Benson's illustrations. Ivor's dedication reads "For dreamy girls and boys, the lifeblood of the world." The stories demonstrate many of the qualities of Ivor's children's books: they're funny, surreal, absurd, kind, positive, and tell the reader about the environment in which we live. Herbert Clockfoote wakes up in the morning to find that he's become an animal, has an enjoyable day, goes home and reverts to being a young boy. There's no attempt to explain his met-amorphosis and Mrs Clockfoote takes the change in her stride, as do Herbert, his friend Annie, his schoolmates and his teachers. It's Kafka's *Metamorphosis* without the horror or tragedy, although Herbert's transformations are not without their problems. When Herbert changes back from elephant to boy, he's at the park with Annie and suddenly finds himself naked in public; when he turns into a kangaroo he bumps his head when he bounces too enthusiastically; when one change puzzles Herbert and his mother, they travel to the zoo to discover he's a capybara. In *Herbert the Herbert* it's Annie who changes shape, becoming an anaconda, but after the initial shock no one is worried and the adventure goes well.

Animals, a zoo, an imaginative child and liberal, unfazed parents are common in Ivor's books for children. They all appear in one of his later stories, *Grape Zoo*. Jill Barton illustrated this tale, using warm watercolour images to help tell the story of Belle Grape, an experienced zoo-builder even though she is only four years old. Belle's discovery of "air walls," a result of accidentally squashing some air together, enables her to expand her zoo-making activities and she builds a worm and fly zoo for her friend, the grandmotherly Maisie the Wise. Belle borrows her father's lorry to deliver the new zoo: no one, including her parents and the venerable Maisie, voices any concerns about this pre-school child's lack of driving experience. Next day, the air walls have been washed away and the worms and flies have gone, but Maisie doesn't care and never tells Belle who starts school, forgets about zoos and falls in love with her new teacher, Miss Grimjaw, "whose breath smelled like fruit salad." Once again, Ivor dedicates the book to imaginative children: "For girls and boys who think things nobody has ever thought before."

Doris, Ivor's collaboration with illustrator Claudio Muñoz in which a singing hen finds fame and fortune thanks to her boss, Oliver the parrot, charmed the *Publishers Weekly* reviewer: "Cutler's tale, though somewhat convoluted, is sportively told, and Muñoz's amiable characters are brimming with individuality."[12] Writing in *The Times*, Sarah Johnson was delighted with a later collaboration between Ivor and Muñoz: "I'm in love with Jelly Haystack, the star of *A New Dress* ... a genuinely original picture book for the under fives ... Muñoz's drawings ... are touching and treasurable."[13]

Of all of Ivor's work, his children's stories are perhaps the most universally loved. However, with the notable exception of his appearance on his first Peel Session, Ivor seldom if ever read or talked about these stories, so they remain something of a mystery to many fans.

The period around 1960–1965 saw the brief flowering of a new artistic movement that seems tailor-made for Ivor, or vice versa: "jazz poetry." As the name (sometimes jazzpoetry or jazz/poetry) suggests, this was a fusion of live poetry performance and instrumental jazz. Poet Michael Horovitz, the founder of *New Departures* magazine, was the movement's instigator, taking shows on the road as *Live New Departures*. Some of the UK's leading jazz musicians took part, including Stan Tracey, Bobby Wellins and Ivor's Establishment Club compatriot, Dudley Moore. Jazz poetry poets included Adrian Mitchell and Pete Brown, who would both become friends with Ivor.[14] Ivor was not part of the movement but his absence from the jazz poetry scene, except, perhaps, as an audience member, is easily explained. Ivor was not yet writing poetry.

Although he was an established songwriter, author and storyteller by the mid-1960s, Ivor at first found poetry to be a difficult discipline and it wasn't until the 1970s that he published his first book of poems. He gave more than one explanation of this late flowering, sometimes describing a painless process, at other times claiming it was a long and arduous activity. In one of his final interviews, Ivor claimed the process was simple: "Somebody described my stuff as poetry, so I just became a poet ... it was just a magic word, 'poet'. But it seems that those people who called it poetry were using [the word] in a different way, I think." However, he told Val Hennesy that the process took six years: "I started writing poetry at the age of 42 but wasn't any good until I was 48."[15] When Marc Riley reminded Ivor of this claim, Ivor described the evolution of his poetry over that six-year period:

> I used to listen to jazz, go to concerts and then be busy writing all this rubbish instinctively and after about six years the rubbish started to get fairly sophisticated and I gradually started to introduce English words into these poems and eventually it became all words and then my poetry was good enough. I've been busy shaping it ever since, really.[16]

If Ivor's memory is accurate, then he began trying to become a poet in 1965 and achieved his goal, at least its early stages, in 1971. In another version of the story he claimed that he did not begin writing poetry "seriously" until he was forty-three, taking seven years to achieve poems he felt were of a "professional" level, which suggests that he started the process in 1966 and finished it in 1973.[17] He told Alastair McKay that he was making tentative first steps a few years before this, and retained poems written in his thirties – that is, between 1953 and 1963 – to keep himself "humble."[18]

Other evidence suggests that Ivor's poetry career took off in the 1960s. In 1968 he published three poems in *Ambit* magazine: "A Bird Sits in a Bush," in which he contemplates crushing a bird's head between his fingers, "Cloth" and "Alice."[19] Later that year he was guest editor of *Workshop*, a magazine devoted to new poetry, and published two poems, "An Old Poltroon" and "Vermicular Thinkers," in an issue of *The Poetry Review* that included work by Vernon Scannell, George MacBeth and Cecil Day-Lewis. He was one of the featured poets named on the magazine's cover, another indication that he was not just a raw beginner trying his luck.[20] In February 1969 he took part in a poetry reading at Kentish Town library, chaired by *Ambit*'s editor Martin Bax, then a few months later, during his first Peel session, he read "An Old Poltroon" and "There and Back via Sweden" and spoke about his forthcoming appearance at the Poetry Marathon. Further work appeared in 1970 and 1971, with readings at the 1970 *Poetry D-Day* and the publication of "The Even Keel," in *The Transatlantic Review*.[21] During the summer of 1971 he appeared on London Weekend Television's *Alive and Kicking – British Poets*. Ivor, described as a "poet and teacher," was joined by five children from Fox School, "and showed the sort of spontaneous poetry that children can produce when given encouragement."[22] If he didn't think he was creating "professional" standard poems until at least 1971, plenty of other people were willing and happy to describe him, book him and publish him as a poet before that date.

Ambit Magazine Issue #41 (1969), one of the first issues to feature Ivor's poetry. (By kind permission of Briony Bax at Ambit.)

Ambit was an important outlet for Ivor's poetry: between 1968 and 1985 he contributed to twelve issues. The magazine first appeared in 1959 and by 1968 it was a well-established literary quarterly with a group of editors that included its founder Martin Bax, artist Eduardo Paolozzi and writer J. G. Ballard, and with a circulation of around three thousand copies per issue.[23] Despite sponsorship from the Arts Council and even from Mobil Oil, it was not making anyone rich and other potential sponsors were put off because, according to Martin Bax, its contents could, and did, offend: "The contributors have either been poorly paid, or often not at all ... I thank them. My fellow editors ... will never be paid. I thank them."[24] According to Briony Bax, an editor in the twenty-first century, Martin Bax never had a set rate for contributions and would pay, or not, on an *ad hoc* basis in an apparently random fashion. Martin Bax and Ambit's music editor, trumpeter Henry Lowther, organised Ambit Jazz Events, offering another outlet for contributors at performances that mixed readings with music. On at least one occasion, the band featured Dave Green and Trevor Tomkins, two-thirds of the Three Wise Men.[25] Martin Bax organised poetry readings under the *Ambit* banner, one of which featured Ivor, David Gascoyne and Adrian Henri under the title "Post Surrealist Poets," a description of Ivor that, like "surrealistic folk," never caught on.[26]

Martin Bax and *Ambit* poetry editor Edwin Brock held Ivor's work in high esteem. Bax wrote a brief review of *A Flat Man*, Ivor's second book of poetry, declaring it to be "witty, charming and sometimes even beautiful."[27] When three self-described "far from narrow-minded Library staff" wrote to *Ambit* to complain about the unfunny nature of "the rubbish which you publish as an excuse for poetry" Bax responded politely:

> I am sorry you dislike our poetry so much, but pleased that you feel so strongly about it that you write to us. It is a little difficult to answer specifically as you don't mention which number of Ambit gave you particular offence. If it is the current number, Ambit 57, yes, I do think that Ivor Cutler, who is the first poet in this issue, is a genuinely comic writer, one of the few about.[28]

Brock once submitted for publication a set of poems from Ivor, Jenny Joseph and Brock himself, with the comment "Herewith: Two Brocks, Four Josephs and Seven Cutlers – which seems about right for the talent involved. Actually, I think neither the Cutler nor the Joseph are up to their full potentials, but still think they are better than most at their best – if you see what I mean." Brock's positive comment is at the start of a lengthy letter which criticises *Ambit's* inclusion of prose ("the prose is usually a wank ...") and closes with the postscript "I'm pissed, but that doesn't mean I'm not aware of what I've written."[29]

Ambit 97 dedicated four pages to the publication of a collection called *Odd Old Flora*: seventeen short poems, each around six to ten lines long and telling the tale of a plant, seed or spore, such as the Blool, that lives on sweat; the Oandara(ra) that devours sawdust, lives by a sawmill and breeds during the firm's annual holiday; or the Bèlompèlkey, which "is sometimes called 'Hastener of the dawn.'"[30] There was an eighteenth title, "Kidney Mischief," but there was no text. A final sentence, above a drawing of a flower, declared "This cycle was written in 1970, and lost." In 1971, Ivor had told *Melody Maker* that he was writing a book: "A woman called Rita Parkinson is going to illustrate it. It's called *Odd Old Flora*." The book never appeared, presumably because Ivor misplaced the manuscript.[31]

One of Ivor's longest poems, "Us Men are Only Little Lads at Heart or Take Your Thumb Out, Sailor," appeared in *Ambit* 44, opposite a notable example of the sort of content that exemplifies Martin Bax's claim that the magazine "will offend." J. G. Ballard's "Mae West's Reduction Mammoplasty" imagines, in graphic detail, the surgical procedure that would be necessary if the Hollywood star decided to reduce the size of her breasts. In *Ambit* 62, six of Ivor's poems are followed by eight pictures of women's breasts and one of a woman's pubic hair. These are uncomfortable juxtapositions, given Ivor's later declarations of feminism, but he carried on contributing to the magazine. After all, his feminism was a work in progress: "One of my early poems advised women that if their breasts are too big they will fall over unless they wear a haversack ... I try very hard to be a feminist but I've got a long way to go."[32]

As his poetry career progressed, Ivor contributed work to more publications, including *The New Statesman* ("The Anti-Empiricist" and "The Grass is Greener" appeared together in 1994).[33] He contributed to numerous specialist journals including *Pick: A Magazine of Contemporary Poetry*; *Wheels*; *Kudos: Poetry and Art*; and *Slightly Soiled*, and was the guest editor for an issue of *Doors into and out of Dorset*.[34] His poems appeared in three issues of *New Departures*, edited by Michael Horovitz, and he's one of the cover stars of issue 15, in the company of Gunther Grass, Linton Kwesi Johnson, Kathy Acker and others. He's in the first issue of *Straight Lines*, to which Phyllis King also contributed.[35]

One of the most unusual magazines to publish Ivor's work was *Free Reed: The Concertina Newsletter*, which printed "Birdswing." It's not a concertina-focussed poem, although it is about music, albeit music composed and performed by a thrush, who Ivor advises on the possibility of obtaining a record contract.[36] The appearance of an Ivor Cutler poem in a magazine devoted to the concertina may seem odd, but there are links between Ivor and the instrument that go back to his younger days. Ivor enjoyed folk music, which he explored on trips to Glasgow's Mitchell Library, and was inspired by the sound of the Scottish bagpipes: "Anything folk had a bit of sophistication to it, for me anyway ... The Highland stuff gave me the drone of the bagpipes, a free melodic thing roving in among the drones which I use quite a lot ..."[37] A 1990 interview began with Ivor travelling to a concertina recital, eagerly telling the journalist of the problems associated with keeping the instrument in tune, while a concertina with "flaccid brass reeds" features in Ivor's poem, "Us Men are Only Little Lads at Heart or Take Your Thumb Out, Sailor," as the chosen instrument of an aged sailor who plays slow hornpipes on the deck of a frigate.[38]

In 1973, *Ambit* invited poets to write about a theme which was central to their work. Ivor responded:

> THE THEME is simplicity. How not to know what you are going to say, then let it trickle out a word at a time: to concentrate on the noise that the words are making, together; to let the meaning take care of itself. The unconscious uses the words as a vehicle, and I am astonished/ delighted/amused by what is going on inside. This, at its lowest, is a therapy, and should be private, but when it seems aesthetically good enough and communicable, I make it public.[39]

In the same issue, Ralph Steadman immortalised Ivor in cartoon form.

Ivor's emphasis on simplicity and the unconscious was a consistent element of his approach to poetry, often expressed as the importance of avoiding conscious thought processes: "Creativity communicates best via the unconscious, bypassing the intellect," he wrote.[40] His preference for writing in bed, in the middle of the night, may have helped him to bypass his intellect. He would put on his pyjamas, go to sleep, then wake at about three in the morning, when the fridge started to make a loud noise. If the fridge failed to do this, then gusts of wind blowing through the chimney might do the job: "I quite enjoy that except when it comes down the chimney and into the bedroom."[41]

"The intellect," Ivor said towards the end of his life, "is the thing you get from teachers ... But the intellect doesn't come from the person, it comes from people telling you how to do things."[42] As a reader or listener, according to Ivor, if you avoid the intellect you may not understand the poems, but you may still gain something from them, but try to understand his poetry intellectually, and you'll get nothing.[43] So avoiding the intellect is crucial, even though it can lead to uncertainty about what is going on. Ivor restated his position in conversation with Marc Riley, when he said that his words were simply a vehicle, "rather like radio waves," for a message from his unconscious to the unconscious of the listener.[44] Although he found exceptions, such as his friend John Burnside, Ivor criticised most of his fellow poets for their inability to communicate, and by the late 1990s he'd had enough: "I don't like British poetry, I hate the way I am being communicated with."[45] Ivor's reference to "the listener" raises the question of the role of his distinctive voice in the communication of his work. It's a question he discussed in the student magazine, *Brig*. The reporter revealed "I sometimes find it hard to imagine a different voice reading your poems." Ivor responded self-critically:

Ivor Cutler by Ralph Steadman. (Reproduction courtesy of Ralph Steadman Art Collection Ltd.)

It has been said that the words are not the same without the voice. Sad, isn't it? Because when I'm dead there'll only be the words, and people will say "What was the fuss?" I feel that I'm not much of a poet and that it's only because I have the voice that interprets the words ... That makes me feel sad. I think I'll go and commit suicide now.[46]

Ben Thompson covered similar ground in his 1990 interview, Ivor responding with the same "What was the fuss?" phrase and adding: "I realise that there is a quality of communication in my voice which, if not essential, is certainly important. Once you've heard my voice and you come back to the poetry, when you start to read the poetry you get the voice with it free."[47] According to John Knutas, Ivor was critical of his own writing and suggested that his voice was crucial to the impact of his poems. Ivor told him "People who first read my work on the page often think it's rubbish. Then they hear it, and I catch them ... I wish I could catch them initially on the page, but I'd have to work too hard to be able to do that, and perhaps (perhaps not?) the words would lose their spontaneity."

Fans who first encountered Ivor through his broadcasts or stage shows may well find it impossible to read his work without hearing his voice, the voice, according to one reviewer, "of the weariest human ever to be cursed with existence."[48] As for the voice's origin, most writers ascribed it to Ivor's Scottish-Jewish upbringing, although Karl Dallas referred to it as Scots Presbyterian.[49] Ivor played down the Jewish influence, but combined other elements: "My voice is a bastard. It's composed of Glasgow plus Jordanhill Training College for Teachers plus going out with an Islay girl and picking up the clear 'L.'"[50] As the years went on, Ivor made sure that he looked after that distinctive voice, with a set of exercises. He gave his friend Christine Stark a copy of the exercises for her own use, telling her that he did them every day: sixteen exercises in all, including "Waggle head slightly," "Breathe little and often when reading" and "stick out mid tongue 3 times very gently (no more than twice a day)."

When Val Hennessy interviewed him a decade after the *Brig* article, Ivor referred to himself as a craftsperson: "It's the kind of writing that some people would say wasn't poetry. Heh. Heh. Heh. Let's face it I can't ever imagine being compared with Byron or Wordsworth ... What a laugh!" Hennessy noted that an unidentified critic had called him "one of the most original writers of our time," but in the interests of journalistic balance took pains to point out that another critic, also unnamed, referred to him as "a total headcase churning out unmitigated crap." She became irritated by Ivor's lecture on black rhinos and white rhinos (she was interviewing him at London Zoo) and declared she'd rather be talking to Seamus Heaney or Kathleen Raine, "Some *real* poet who doesn't witter on about rhinos ..." But she still managed to remember the words of Ivor's poem, "Creamy Pumpkins," with which she closed the article.[51]

Ivor's words are not the same without his voice, that's true, but that doesn't make the words on the page a lesser creation. Without Ivor's distinctive voice playing in your head as you read, perhaps your mind is more open to personal interpretation of the poems. As someone who first became aware of his work by reading it, what Ivor sounded like was unimportant, but as soon as I heard him, only a few months later, it became impossible for me to disentangle the sound from the words. By contrast, poet and performer John Hegley heard Ivor on Peel sessions before he read any of his work, but prefers him "on the page." He clarifies his preference, viewing Ivor's drawings in his books of poetry as inseparable from the text: "When one says 'on the page,' one tends to think of just the printed word, but it's not just the printed word, it's images."

Trigram Press published Ivor's first book of poetry, *Many Flies Have Feathers*, in 1973, when Ivor was fifty. He told one concert audience that the title was the publisher's idea: he wanted to call it *A Seal is a Sheep Without Feet*.[52] Four years later, Trigram published Ivor's second poetry book, *A Flat Man*. Then, in the early 1980s, Ivor began a long-term relationship with Arc Publications. Tony Ward, Arc's founder and managing editor, met Ivor at the home of Asa Benveniste, the co-founder of Trigram Press. Benveniste warned him that Ivor could be awkward, and Ward did indeed find Ivor to be "brusque" on first acquaintance, although they developed a closer relationship as the years went on. Arc published ten small books of Ivor's work. These collections are immediately recognisable, each one combining Ivor's poems and artwork in a tiny book of around one hundred pages that measures just eight centimetres wide by twelve centimetres high. According to Ward, size was important. Ivor wanted books that would fit into the pocket of his shirt, a condition most publishers, including Trigram, were unable or unwilling to meet. Ward printed Arc books himself and so, after measuring Ivor's shirt pocket, he agreed to make them in Ivor's desired size: "I said it was possible … He said I could have the job … We did it by word of mouth, a verbal contract. Ivor was an avid contract man, so I felt quite privileged in a way because he trusted us to do the job." Ward took five hundred copies of the first Arc book, *Private Habits*, to Edinburgh where Ivor was appearing at the Fringe and sold them all.

Arc followed this with new books at roughly two-yearly intervals until Ivor's final publication, *Scots Wa' Straw*, in 2003. The books could often be found for sale in record shops as well as bookshops. This was not Ward's deliberate strategy, although sales were good: in his words, "We never pushed them into record shops, they just appeared." The books were often placed on the counter, next to the till, "so they wouldn't get nicked." Initially Ivor's books required little or no editing, but as time progressed Ward found that some of Ivor's pieces were not up to the standard he expected, "so I insisted they were re-written or taken out … One or two books were terribly thin, others were terribly fat by comparison …" Ivor was aware that his work was becoming inconsistent, telling John Knutas that his penultimate Arc publication, *Under the Spigot*, was not good enough, and that he was "embarrassed."[53]

A Stuggy Pren is one of Ivor's most notable Arc books – the title was also used for one of his radio series. At the end of 1992 Ivor visited one of his regular haunts, the Photographers' Gallery, and saw an exhibition by Katrina Lithgow. Ivor described it as an exhibition of nudes, "women in their twenties and thirties. And they were so totally lacking in prurience, I was knocked out …"[54] He tracked down the young photographer, who recalls that Ivor somehow found out where she lived and sent her "an extraordinary letter through my letter-box inviting me round … I have to be honest, I didn't know who he was, but friends knew and were fans. I went round to meet him and it went from there." Lithgow took numerous photographs of Ivor in and around his Laurier Road flat and in a variety of outfits and hats. Some of these photographs were incorporated into the book, published by Arc in 1994 and co-credited to Ivor Cutler & Katrina Lithgow.[55]

On-stage readings were a staple of poets' lives, whether they were in pub back rooms or on more prestigious stages such as the Albert Hall. Ivor was no exception. The 1970 Poetry D-Day, part of Camden Festival, was one of Ivor's earliest readings as part of a major poetry event, with Ivor performing alongside some of the major figures of the British poetry scene including Ted Hughes, Adrian Henri, Stevie Smith and George MacBeth, who were all included in the Radio 3 programme of selections from the event.[56] The following year Ivor performed at the Bedford Square Book Bang, Britain's first literary festival, as did Spike Milligan, Clive James, Lady Antonia Fraser, Coco the Clown, and children's puppet favourites Sooty and Sweep.[57]

During 1971, Ivor went on holiday to Ibiza. Ivor rarely travelled outside Britain and Ireland, so this was an unusual event. Phyllis King, a Canadian now living in London, was also holidaying on the island, staying with her sister who had lived there since the 1950s. In Phyllis's words:

> It was an unusual and extraordinary place to meet him … At that time, in 1971, a friend of Ivor's – I can't remember her name – had invited Ivor down to stay with her for a week. It happened that she knew my sister. She invited my sister for supper one evening and she said "I've got my sister with me." So she said "Bring her along as well." So I went and that's where we met … At the end of the evening, Ivor suggested that we meet in London as we lived fairly near to each other.

Phyllis was particularly attracted by a comment Ivor made that evening: "He said 'Oh, you talk like a poet' and I thought that was probably the best chat-up line I'd ever heard. Anyway, I liked it."[58] This was the beginning of a relationship that would last, on and off, for the rest of Ivor's life. Phyllis began going to Ivor's poetry readings, he encouraged her to write her own poetry, "Then we started writing poetry together … Then when he had a poetry reading he'd ask me if I wanted to read some of my own poetry."

Once back in London, Ivor met Phyllis's daughter, Anna, who was around ten or eleven years old.[59] She often accompanied Ivor and her mother on Sunday outings, visiting Robert Wyatt and Alfie Benge at their home, or going to a museum or gallery. For a year or two, she joined Ivor and Phyllis at Conway Hall for early evening classical concerts on Sundays. As Ivor didn't like symphonies, they went to quartet concerts and Ivor encouraged Anna to take a notebook. Ivor gave Anna "the understanding that you could listen to a quartet and draw whatever you wanted … or write a poem. I guess I wouldn't have done that had Mum not met him." Anna later went to art school, but remembers that Ivor taught her "austerity of word in poetry and austerity of line in drawing."

Despite the length of their relationship, Phyllis and Ivor never lived together. "We always had our own flats," she explains, "I stayed a lot at his and he would stay at mine but we kept our own." There were times when they would separate, the separation made a little easier by the fact that they always kept their own homes. "He wasn't easy – and perhaps I wasn't easy," Phyllis said in 2020. "At times I thought 'Oh, why can't we live together?' but it seemed to work better. He needed his own place …"[60]

These times of separation can perhaps be identified in some of Ivor's interviews, when he speaks about Phyllis without mentioning her by name, or speaks as if their relationship never happened. In 1989 he praised an unnamed woman, probably Phyllis, to Val Hennessy: "I have recently ended a long affair with a woman who had a lot of marvellous negative virtues. She didn't blab. She had a capacity for not being too tidy. She was much more intelligent than I am which isn't saying much. The break up was a great relief to both parties."[61]

After his Ibiza holiday, Ivor returned to teaching, writing, and performing. One of his solo poetry readings, in the mundane setting of a school hall, was both a commercial success and the start of a long-term professional relationship. In the mid-1970s two teenaged Friends of the Earth supporters were promoting events at their school to raise funds for the organisation. The boys, David Jones and Daniel Zeichner, contacted the London Poetry Secretariat which promoted poetry through, for example, the organisation and funding of poetry readings. Jones recalls that for a fee of £30 the Secretariat arranged for Ivor to come to their school where five hundred people paid thirty pence each to attend. Zeichner entered politics, becoming the Labour MP for Cambridge. Jones went on to promote Ivor at various gigs, "for fun, or for different charities where I worked," then Ivor decided he needed someone to organise his live performances and Jones took on the task, doing the job until Ivor retired from the stage. For want of a better word, I'll refer to Jones as Ivor's manager, although, as Jones says, "'Manager' is a very grandiose title for what I did, although I did it for a long time."

Ivor undertook another of the tasks common to authors and musicians: the in-store personal appearance. Bookshops and record stores played host to these events, set up to give fans the opportunity to meet their favourite acts and to give the artists a way of selling more books or records, usually with the perceived added value of the artist's signature. Duglas T. Stewart met Ivor at one such event, in Glasgow's Virgin Megastore in the early 1980s. The meeting "was a massive thing for me," he remembers, but Stewart's excitement wasn't shared by the rest of Glasgow's music fans, perhaps because Ivor was in something of a fallow period as far as records were concerned, and no one else was there: "This is a great man! Where are all the people? ... He did seem genuinely pleased that someone was interested." Hamish Ironside organised a more successful event when he was managing the poetry department of Blackwell's bookshop in Charing Cross Road: "The book signing we did [for *A Flat Man*] was rather informal and unofficial, it was not advertised by Blackwell's, we just sat Ivor at a desk with a pile of books and had one of his records playing, I think." There was a constant stream of buyers, and at the end of the event Ivor told Ironside, "Well, I can't say I've enjoyed it, but my ego has!"

When the chance arose, Ivor's in-store activity was a little more subversive. For a time he would cycle to Blackwell's each week, signing a pile of Arc poetry books on each visit whether or not the staff knew what he was up to. Hamish Ironside enjoyed Ivor's visits, as did Ivor: "I think he just liked mooching around from bookshop to bookshop. He also used to talk to anyone who passed by who took an interest in him, and he handed out his stickers." Fabian Ironside, Hamish's brother, ran the poetry department of Foyles' bookshop, also on the Charing Cross Road, and knew that Ivor would sign books surreptitiously. He never caught Ivor in the act of signing, which demonstrates Ivor's talent for doing so, but remembers the in-shop joke that an unsigned Ivor Cutler book was rarer than a signed one.

Ciara Nolan accompanied Ivor on trips around the city and remembers going into Blackwell's, where he would write little messages in copies of his books, for people to find later when they bought them and started reading them: "I thought that was the sweetest thing." At the South Bank, Ivor made occasional forays into the Royal Festival Hall bookshop to undertake some more unofficial signings. Sometimes he would enjoy being spotted by a staff member: "One of his favourite tricks was to go into the bookshop ... grab one of the books and start writing and drawing in it. If he could find an unsuspecting assistant who didn't know who he was and would look on in alarm ... he'd be thrilled."[62]

Ivor's place in British poetry was further cemented by his presence in two portrait collections. In 1988 Michael Knowles painted Ivor as part of his series devoted to Scottish poets and novelists: the painting is now in the National Galleries of Scotland.[63] Two years later another portrait exhibition placed Ivor alongside the Liverpool Poets, Seamus Heaney, Dannie Abse and others.

The National Portrait Gallery curated a series of full-length portraits by Peter Edwards, titled the exhibition *Contemporary Poets* and chose Edwards's portrayal of Ivor for some of its publicity material. In his portrait, Ivor is seated in an armchair, his legs stretched out and crossed in front of him, his head resting on his right hand which is formed lightly into a fist. He's wearing a red check shirt, a dark blue jacket or cardigan, and a hat with a cat's head badge on its front. He looks pensive and thoughtful. It's an immediately recognisable image, although at first Edwards attempted an abstract and a strip of white and blue paint remains on the right-hand side of the final version. Edwards liked his sitter and thought the feeling was mutual: "I met him and we hit it off, almost like like-minds. I did my drawings, sketches and photographs which were all rather tremulous and we had a nice meal he cooked up in his flat."[64] The gallery's exhibition programme featured a poem from each of the sitters: Ivor selected "An Unhappy Medium," about the ordinariness of the poet.[65]

Anthologies offer another outlet for poets' work, but Ivor's poems appear less frequently in such publications than might be expected. Roger McGough edited numerous poetry anthologies and was always keen to include something by Ivor, but found it impossible: "Ivor was asking for so much money. He always reckoned he was underpaid, the BBC never paid him enough, so he would demand so much money it would often fall through." McGough thinks that Ivor had every right to demand high fees, "but for that reason he didn't have as much of a showing as he might have had. I always thought 'Oh, Ivor, do it. Lots of people are going to read this.'" He did make it into *The Faber Book of Twentieth-Century Scottish Poetry*, however, reviewer Michael Horovitz describing him as one of a group of poets who "deftly versify the uniquely abrasive panache of Glasgow street life and speech rhythms."[66]

Ivor's books and records were widely available, tickets for his live shows could be readily purchased, anyone who wished could watch or listen to his TV and radio programmes, but if Ivor gave you a sticky or two you were part of a more exclusive club. It wasn't completely exclusive, for sticky recipients included complete strangers, unaware of the identity of the odd-looking distributor of the little labels, as well as close friends, family members, correspondents or journalists. But being given a sticky meant that Ivor was, in some way, aware of your existence and that made you a little bit special.

That may sound rather overblown, but almost everyone who told me that Ivor had given them stickies had kept them and spoke of them with warmth. There was one exception: John Burningham, Ivor's former Summerhill pupil, told Piers Plowright that Ivor's stickies made him "rather annoyed." It was much more common to be told that these little labels were precious mementos. Ivor's friend Beverley Crew still has stickies adorning various items "and they always make me think and smile" and as collaborator Steve Beresford put it when speaking about his own collection of Ivor's stickies, "They're treasures, utter treasures."

Ivor's stickies are small but beautifully formed sticky labels, produced to order by Able Labels. He found great pleasure in ordering these stickers from the company, believing that they would brighten the day of the poor person with the otherwise boring job of typesetting nothing but addresses.[67] They are about a quarter to half the size of a credit card, with black text on a white or gold background, although they can sometimes appear with other background colours. Some people refer to the phrases they contain as "Cutlerisms," which is appropriate for the majority, but a small number contain quotations from other sources. "'When I give food to the poor they call me a saint. When I ask why the poor have no food, they call me a communist.' Archbishop Helder Camara," was one example, while another came from the words of Ivor's friend, Craig Murray-Orr: "While looking through a selection over tea I remarked 'Creation requires a certain ignorance' to which he muttered 'Ah ha'. Two weeks later he presented me with a box full of stickies of the remark." The phrases can be memorable or forgettable, funny or moving, puzzling or meaningless, informative or simply strange. To extract the most enjoyment out of them it can help to know something of the man behind their creation, but such knowledge isn't always required. Here is a random selection of stickies:

- "To remove this label take it off"
- "I am very nourishing but – and here is the rub – I taste execrable"
- "made of dust"
- "True Happiness is Knowing That You are a Hypocrite"
- "silent paper"

And two of my personal favourites:

- "Slightly Inperfect"
- "don't tell ME what kind of day to have!"

Journalists often wrote about the stickies when discussing Ivor, but rarely gave them much consideration beyond mentioning that he gave them away or stuck them to envelopes, treating them as little more than a sideshow to his work as a poet, songwriter or storyteller. Ted Harrison took the opposite view, claiming that they were Ivor's "preferred means of communication ... He attaches these labels ... to his correspondence," which somewhat overstates their importance and understates Ivor's forms of distribution. They were certainly an important means of communication, but to credit them with being his preferred means, placing them above conversation, poems, lyrics, letter writing or visual art, is probably a step too far.[68]

The genesis of the Ivor Cutler sticky is lost in the mists of time. He used pre-printed, self-adhesive address labels on some of his correspondence and this may have given him the idea of using such labels for more artistic or subversive reasons. In a 1997 article, Judith Palmer claimed that Ivor "became hooked on sticky labels in 1964," but it's not clear if she heard this from Ivor.[69] Xavier Russell, a Fox pupil from 1968 to 1971, remembered Mr Cutler bringing stickies to school and distributing them in his class: "Sometimes they would just be a word, or a little rhyme. He'd actually put them on your head." Rebecca Orr-Deas, a pupil at the school a year or two later, recalled him bringing sets of gold stickies to the school, two of which read "Nothing" and "Upside Down." Ivor was still using stickies in the last few years of his life, which means that they were part of his work for almost forty years, if not longer. The stickies served multiple functions: Ivor gave them as gifts, stuck them on street furniture, attached them to envelopes, or handed them out to friends, fans and bewildered passers-by. He gave some to the staff of his favourite bicycle shop, included a few with his letters, and carried a selection with him when he was out and about so they were ready to distribute as required.[70] Craig Murray-Orr believes that the stickies "were a serious part of his art, both creating and placing them …" Ivor's fellow poet, Lemn Sissay, agrees, describing Ivor's use of stickies as "a radical act. When I came up in the poetry scene it was all 'Be on stage, articulate your anger, shock the audience'. Ivor was actually doing all of that in such a different way."

Ivor used the stickies in numerous ways, sometimes mischievous, sometimes political and at other times more personal. Out on long walks together, his friend John Burnside saw Ivor placing stickies on walls, signposts and parked bicycles, "wherever he felt they were needed." One acquaintance discovered a sticky on their toilet cistern after Ivor visited.[71] Some stickies encouraged people to join the Noise Abatement Society, another read "THATCHER is an eight-letter word."[72] On a more personal level, Ivor would decide to give someone a sticker and then spend some time deciding which one from the selection he carried was the most appropriate. In a health food restaurant one day he decided to give a sticky to a woman with a newborn baby. He looked through the assortment he had in his wallet then handed her one that said "funny smell." Unsurprisingly, the woman was somewhat bemused by the gift, her confusion no doubt compounded by Ivor's follow-up comments: "Are you still breastfeeding? … Wait 'til he gets on to solids … then you'll certainly know all about it."[73] Sue Edwards knew him when he attended lunchtime gigs at the Royal Festival Hall and recalls that Ivor, a mix of "attention-seeking and shy," would hand out stickies to strangers to initiate a reaction or a conversation:

> He would put a sticker on someone's hat or mug of coffee when they turned round for a second, then stand at a distance to watch the reaction, getting huge amounts of pleasure from a stranger's smile or look of momentary confusion. We spent many lunchtime gigs choosing the right sticker for the right stranger in order to elicit the best reaction. He would often arrive at the gig with a

story of how he had handed a sticker to someone … on a tube train on the way, or to a cashier in the supermarket that morning, and how said person was his new "best friend."

Gifts of stickies often generated confusion in the recipient, unless they already knew Ivor and his ways, but they could create joy, too. Ciara Nolan recalls one unpleasantly hot day in London:

> We were waiting for the number 31 bus. There was a massive queue of mostly older people, waiting and very cross. Ivor didn't mind waiting. The bus arrived and as the people got on they said horrible things to the bus driver … Ivor went up to him and gave him an "I Am Beautiful" sticker … The guy's face changed from tormented to a ray of sunshine. Ivor just grinned his head off.

More than one bus driver received an Ivor Cutler sticky and Ivor enjoyed giving such a gift, even if he viewed drivers as somewhat misanthropic: "I like it when you give one to bus drivers who hate the world and the world hates them and they crease up with laughter. I'm very aware of them sitting in that box all day …"[74] Ivor's stickies became so popular that in 1992 he published *Befriend a Bacterium: Stickies by Ivor Cutler*, a short collection of stickies illustrated by Martin Honeysett. It, too, proved popular, and Foyles Bookshop regularly re-ordered copies of this book, a steady if unspectacular seller.[75]

Ivor often spoke or wrote about other literary figures, sometimes to praise, sometimes to support, occasionally to damn. His opinions about writers started at the top: he was unimpressed by William Shakespeare, telling his friend Craig Murray-Orr that he was "indifferent" to this "over-rated" icon of England. His opinion of Franz Kafka was far more positive, and remained so throughout his life: he was, after all, crucial to the development of Ivor's humour when Ivor first read *The Castle* in his mid-thirties, changing it "quite dramatically from sixth-form humour into proper grown-up humour."[76]

Elaine Morgan was another author whose work affected Ivor. He dedicated one of his poetry books, *Is That Your Flap, Jack?*, "With deep gratitude to Elaine Morgan, author of *The Descent of Woman*, for changing my understanding of man."[77] *The Descent of Woman* was Morgan's first book, although she was already a successful scriptwriter. In it, she discussed and supported Sir Alister Hardy's "Aquatic ape" evolutionary theory, which posited that a key period for human evolution – the loss of body hair, becoming bipedal, beginning to mate face-to-face – occurred through human relations with an aquatic environment, when a group of humans began living on the shore of a large body of water, rather than on the savannah. Her book emphasised the female's importance in human evolution and society, and she went on to expand on her work through a range of later books.[78] It's unclear when Ivor first read Morgan's book, but in a 1988 *New Musical Express* article he listed Morgan and *The Descent of Woman* as one of his "Loves."[79]

Ivor would often praise the talents of friends and acquaintances. On *King Cutler*, he introduced his friend Glen Baxter with the words "Here is a man who is known to you as an artist, but to me his greatest talent is as a poet. He has an immaculate ear."[80] In 1992 Ivor wrote in praise of John Burnside, describing him as the finest poet in the UK, the first poet in almost thirty years who could fully communicate with him.[81] Burnside was already a friend of Ivor's, but was never sure of what attracted him to his poetry:

> Ivor was very critical of the poetry being published at that time. He never really discussed with me why he particularly liked my work, other than to say that he found it more musical than some of the other poets he had been looking at, and I think that was the key for him. A good deal of the work that he was reading seemed to him not only banal, and anecdotal, it also lacked the kind of music that he wanted from poetry.

One journalist wrote that "The results of [Ivor's] tutelage can be seen in the work of ... John Burnside."[82] Burnside strongly disagrees:

> This kind of thing completely mystifies me. There was no tutelage, in terms of the writing [although Ivor did teach him how to perform on-stage to better effect] – and whoever wrote this could have established as much from the most cursory of cross-checks. I would have loved to learn from Ivor – I would have been glad to develop the kind of humorous acumen that informs his work, and I hugely envied his performance skills but, unfortunately, that's not the kind of thing I do.

Ivor's willingness to praise others stems from a generosity of spirit, but may also be an indication of his firm belief that he was unique; a performer, writer, poet, with no competitors, his uniqueness stemming from his unconscious mind, the source of his own brand of humour.[83]

10 A Life on the Stage

For Ivor, the idea of being "on stage" encompasses library corners and book festivals, pub rooms and nightclubs, open-air performances in fields and appearances in thousand-seater concert halls. The nervous and inexperienced songwriter whose debut in a London nightclub was nothing short of a disaster made his final stage appearance in one of London's best-known and most prestigious venues. Along the way, there were triumphs, trials and tribulations, dinosaurs and dusting, sculpture, walk-offs, ejections, critical and celebratory reviews, and a few problems with air conditioners, taxis and lifts.

In the 1960s Ivor's live appearances were mostly in small venues in London and the home counties, but after his early Peel appearances his audiences altered, becoming younger, hipper and larger in number. Ivor credited Peel with bringing him this new audience, which often befuddled his fans from the 1960s: "my older fans ... would find themselves among 16–35s in the theatre and wonder where they came from."[1] For the next thirty years he performed across the UK and Ireland. Posters, reviews, fan sites and diaries reveal the range of venues, including the Royal Northern College of Music, Cambridge Corn Exchange, Battersea Arts Centre, Hackney Empire, Edinburgh Fringe Festival, Aberdeen Arts Centre, the Ulster Museum Belfast, WOMAD, the Gulbenkian Studio Newcastle and the Queen Elizabeth Hall on London's South Bank. At the beginning and end of his career, he usually undertook single dates: he didn't embark on his first multi-date tour until 1977, as he told *Brig* magazine. The interviewer asked, "Do you find touring tiring?" Ivor responded: "Touring tiring? That's nice. Yes. Touring's tiring but this is the first time I've ever done a tour, so it's unique in my experience."[2]

Touring was never a major part of Ivor's work. Even in the early days of his post-Peel fame he wasn't keen on playing multiple dates, another thing that set him apart from the rock world. When he met with a potential new agent,

Ivor found him to be "intelligent, efficient, warm, understanding and straightforward," but there was an obstruction to their partnership: "He boggled a bit at my only wanting to do one gig a week ... Underexposure possesses subtle advantages, like staying alive, like knowing what town you are in, like enjoying what you are doing."[3] Despite this, the agent was prepared to take on Ivor, but whether or not he did is unknown.

Ivor learnt to choose his venues and audiences with care, successfully avoiding the types of audiences that might cause him trouble – he gave Batley Variety Club as an example.[4] There were exceptions in his early career: the *International Times* benefit was one and, at the other end of the socio-political scale, a Masonic Lodge dinner was another. Ivor was booked to provide cabaret for the Masons, but found that the audience, filled with "dreadful people," was hoping for a more comedic performance than he could provide.[5] Ivor enjoyed performing in Ireland, claiming that Irish audiences enjoyed the noise that words make.[6] However, thanks to poorly worded publicity, one Belfast show upset some of his most ardent fans. He was booked to appear at the Ulster Museum for a solo show sponsored by the museum, the Arts Council of Northern Ireland and the Queens University English Society. An advertisement in the *Belfast Telegraph* declared that Ivor Cutler, "entertainer extraordinary and man of many parts," would appear at 8.00 p.m. Friday 28 April. There would be no charge for the event: as the advertisement put it, "adimmsion [*sic*] free." The day following the concert, the *Belfast Telegraph* ran a story under the misleading headline "Anger over free concert that wasn't." The event was, as advertised, free of charge but many of Ivor's fans were unaware that they needed to obtain tickets in advance and after queuing for some time in the "windswept Botanic Park" many were turned away.[7]

Unlike Van Morrison and the other acts he supported, Ivor rarely performed outside Britain and Ireland. David Jones, who managed his live performances for almost thirty years from the early 1980s, remembers only one show overseas, at the Botanique in Brussels: "They worked out that if he got an early flight he could travel over, do a show, and get back to London that evening ... He was wearing a tea cosy on his head, which promoted a lot of discussion as we went through customs." Gill Lyons recalls meeting Ivor in Rotterdam when she was playing with Centipede (a fifty-piece jazz ensemble that also featured Robert Wyatt) at the city's Arts Council and Ivor was there to perform a solo gig, but this would have been around 1970–1971, years before Jones knew Ivor.

Though overseas trips were rare, appearing as support to big-name acts necessitated cross-Britain travel and nights away from home. The gigs brought Ivor to the attention of large audiences, but there was a price to pay. He disliked piped music, air conditioning and the odour of air fresheners and at times one or more of these would make life intolerable. According to Jones, one night on tour with Van Morrison the allocated accommodation proved too much to cope with. Morrison was a fan of Ivor and made sure he stayed in high-quality hotels, but after one concert, says Jones, Ivor apparently ran away from the hotel and stayed in the railway station waiting room: "I heard the story from the tour manager. Van was really upset when Ivor disappeared, wondering where he'd got to, had he been kidnapped." Ivor said that the hotel was the Holiday Inn, Swiss Cottage: "one of those places where they have stags on the doors of the lavvies ...The room was so hot it was definitely not for human beings to be in. So I spent the night balanced precariously on a bench in the station waiting room."[8] It's surprising that the home-loving Ivor even contemplated staying in that hotel, as Swiss Cottage is barely two miles from Laurier Road. Musician Fred Frith told a similar story, this time about a gig with a leading jazz group: "after a gig (I believe he was opening for the Carla Bley band) he refused to check into a hotel at 1 a.m. because there was music playing in the lift, and the entire group were eventually forced to find another hotel where there was no canned music!" One night in an Oxford hotel, Phyllis King recalls, Ivor telephoned reception three times before the staff found him a suitable room.

Troubles with odours or piped music were dwarfed by the troubles caused by noise. In his younger days, Ivor may have enjoyed the sound of aircraft engines or the thrum of factory machines, but as he grew older certain sounds became an almost constant source of discomfort. It's clear to see in the film of his final concert, *Cutler's Last Stand*, when he presses his fingertips to his ears as the audience applaud. "I'm an extremely sensitive man and I'm very sensitive to noise," Ivor said a few weeks before this concert.[9]

The progress of Ivor's noise problem is hard to track. Dave Green, who played bass with Ivor in the Three Wise Men, remembers him as a quietly spoken person, "a very calming influence," but doesn't remember a problem with noise, or Ivor mentioning his dislike of it. When *Melody Maker* invited Ivor to listen to a selection of records for its "Blind Date" feature he listened to tracks by Third World War, the Rolling Stones and Soft Machine without complaining about volume (although he was happy to criticise the quality of much of the music).[10] Jeremy Cutler recalled times when his father was still supporting rock bands, probably around the early 1970s, and would leave a gig immediately after his set "because he couldn't stand the noise."[11] In 1976, Ivor wrote about his intention to go to a concert of African drumming, then in the next paragraph he told of having to "shut the window on radio pop music. The noise comes through so I switch on the Radio 3 – classical piano – kill a nasty noise with a pleasant one, except I really wanted silence." Once the radio pop ceased, he switched off the "boring" classical piano. This didn't give him the silence he craved, but left "Nature's noises," which he was happy to experience: "friendly hammerings, sawing, gear-changing and horn tooting ..."[12]

There's no mention of problems with noise in his 1977 *Brig* interview, and his primary school pupils speak of classes filled with singing, dance and games with no reference to any requests by Mr Cutler to keep the volume down. On the *Life in a Scotch Sitting Room* live album, recorded in July 1977, his arrival on stage is greeted by loud applause and cheers, to which he happily responds "Very good." Seven years later, Ivor made no comment about the audience's loud laughter and applause at a Brighton event. He did make his feelings clear about other irritations, however. He was pleased to see that just a few audience members were smoking, telling the crowd that "my throat doesn't take kindly to smoke, so thank you" and asking people not to use tape recorders or cameras: "It just saves me the trouble of jumping down from the stage and thumping you." There was one sign of sensitivity to noise: he asked the sound engineer to stop a sound emanating from an unknown source and told the audience "It's like being in a lavatory."[13] Graham Duff was on the bill that night but had not heard any unusual sound onstage and when he sat in the audience for Ivor's performance he could still hear nothing untoward. He recalls that after Ivor complained about the noise one of the sound men or promoters apologised profusely, yet it was something no one except Ivor had spotted.

Talking about his love of African drumming, Ivor told *The Wire* that he used to invite groups of friends round to his flat "and give them each something to hit, but very different from one another, so you got a lot of crossing rhythms," which must have created a fair old racket in a small room.[14] In 1985 he said that the sound of electric, rather than acoustic, instruments was "offensive. It hurts my ears …" and three years later when he responded to a Q&A for the *New Musical Express*, Ivor's list of "Hates" was predominantly noise-related: "People who feel they have the God-given right to play music when, where and as loud as they choose. The noise of motorbikes, electric mowers, electric drills, saws, sanders, helicopters, TVs, radios."[15] In the 1990s, journalists regularly referenced his hatred of noise and his active support of the Noise Abatement Society. During one interview, at London Zoo, he inserted earplugs as he spoke and the writer noted his "extreme sensitivity" to noise.[16]

Phyllis King can't remember when noise became a problem for Ivor, but believes that it always affected him to a mild extent. She does, however, recall that the problem got worse as he grew older, affecting his social life and his home life as well as his performances. At home, "He was always aware of not making noise that would be a nuisance to his neighbours and was very aware of noise that came from outside neighbours," but luckily, his neighbours in Laurier Road were generally very quiet. When Ivor and Phyllis went out, he was always concerned about the risk of noise and wouldn't go to cafes or restaurants if they were playing music. "Sometimes," Phyllis recalls, "he would send me in ahead to check it out." Ivor spent much of his time cycling along central London streets, but Phyllis doesn't remember him being affected by traffic noise, believing that "as a cyclist I guess he just accepted it."

John Burnside attended a Philip Glass concert with Ivor and recalls "my most vivid memory is of Ivor curling up in his seat with his hands over his ears whenever the people applauded … he really did hate applause – it wasn't just an affectation to get laughs." Burnside is sensitive to noise and believes that this shared issue "generated some fellow-feeling in him." "My own response to noise at its most extreme," says Burnside, "is a kind of panic, a desire to fight or flee. I think that is how Ivor felt too." Loud noise or poor sound balance on radio shows could also cause Ivor discomfort. He enjoyed listening to Radio 4's *The News Quiz*, but complained that "the studio managers had turned up the volume, they needed to turn it down, the laughter was too loud …"[17] When I discussed the apparent discrepancy between Ivor's love of flying and his hatred of noise with Steve Beresford, co-producer of *Privilege*, he suggested "Maybe Ivor's definition of noise wasn't your definition or my definition. I think that could be it." Ted Harrison suggests that exposure to loud noise in RAF aircraft and the Winsor Engineering factory may have triggered hearing problems which gradually worsened over the years.

The concert requirements for Ivor's 1997 Meltdown Festival appearance at the Queen Elizabeth Hall show just how problematic noise and odours could be. Among the usual requests for microphones, stage monitors and towels there was the instruction "Note: no music or loud noise of any description in Ivor Cutler's presence." Details for his dressing-room read "absolutely no air freshener or polish to be used anywhere backstage." This order was repeated at the bottom of the schedule, in upper case and with an added instruction "PLEASE REMEMBER TO TELL CLEANERS: STRICTLY NO AIR FRESHENER OR POLISH OR SIMILAR SUBSTANCES BACKSTAGE AT ANY TIME THAT DAY!"[18]

Ivor's needs for a good night's sleep, as stated on one of his stickies, were hardly excessive: "1. A Firm Bed 2. Warmth 3. Fresh Air 4. No Central Heating 5. No Noise From: – Traffic, Muzak, Radio, Kitchen Ventilation Etc."[19] Nonetheless, many hotels failed to achieve this and ultimately he found it impossible to stay in one. To compound the issue, Ivor never learned to drive and relied on others acting as drivers, or used public transport. Phyllis, who drove and owned a car, was often called on to transport Ivor, and his harmonium, to gigs. Her daughter Anna calls her "his roadie. She carried everything," but concedes "he might have helped occasionally." Ivor would travel by taxi if necessary, although this could be problematic due to drivers' love of air fresheners and high-volume radio. After one recording, the producer hailed a taxi for Ivor and before he got into the cab, he stuffed cotton wool in both ears and up his nostrils.[20]

If Ivor was often unhappy with accommodation on tour with top musicians, it's unsurprising to find that accommodation at the opposite end of the spectrum would also prove unpopular. With low or non-existent budgets, promoters of poetry readings would often provide visiting poets with a night's stay in their own home. Adrian Mealing was one such promoter: "We put him up in our back bedroom. When I checked it had been warm enough for him, he replied, 'Yes. But the humidity was wrong.'" Ivor didn't reveal what level of humidity would have been "right." Sometimes, if faced with a choice between a hotel or someone's home, Ivor would choose the latter despite the potential drawbacks. When he promoted Ivor's gig at Leeds University in the early 1980s, Andy Kershaw offered to book Ivor into a hotel but Ivor turned him down and gave him an alternative:

> He said "No. I'll stay with you." The shared student house I lived in at the time was a hovel that would have shamed *The Young Ones*. To his credit he didn't blanch when he came up and saw the place. He slept in my room and I slept on someone else's floor. I met him at the train station, of course. Then after that we became pals.

Ivor's brief visit to the Kershaw house came with a frisson of excitement, when he and Kershaw were having tea before the gig and looked out of the window to see two young lads run up the street with a piece of chalk or a spray can and write LUFC (Leeds United Football Club) on the wall of the house over the road. Ivor looked at them, turned to Kershaw and said "Have they not learnt to masturbate yet?"

Ivor's regular failure to find decent overnight accommodation eventually led him to book gigs that allowed him to return to Laurier Road the same night, restricting most of his live shows to within a narrow radius of London. His desire to sleep in his own bed was firmly in place by 1985, when Ivor was fed up of hotels and private homes: "There are very kind caring people who put you in the spare bedroom, which is freezing … I rarely leave London unless I can get back that night."[21] In advance of his show at the Gulbenkian Studio in the following year, the *Newcastle Journal* explained that Ivor would be appearing at 5.30 p.m. so that he could go home that evening, because "he hates hotels." Ivor clarified his position: "I wouldn't say I hate hotels, loathe is better. They have everything possible to offend the five senses."[22]

Ivor played some short residencies, including the three nights at the Third Eye Centre to record *Life in a Scotch Sitting Room*. In 1981 he performed *An Evening with Ivor Cutler* for a week at the Tricycle Theatre on Kilburn High Road, returned for a five-night season the following year, with Phyllis King, and came back in February 1983 for a two-week season of a new show, *Private Habits* (a title shared with his first Arc publication). The preview promised "scientific experiments" as well as the usual songs, poems and stories.[23] However, Mike Gilmore's review made no reference to experiments of any sort, telling instead of Ivor's "whimsical eccentricity and deadpan delivery" in an evening of poems, stories, songs, and a few jungle tips.[24] A season at the Bloomsbury Theatre in 1986 coincided with the release of the *Gruts* album and the *Fresh Carpet* book.[25] Danny Van Emden's positive review of the event is notable for not calling Ivor eccentric: "Perish the word eccentric, Ivor Cutler is a way of life."[26]

"Eccentric is an easy label," says Lemn Sissay, "a way of packaging someone neatly in a box. Given that he was the opposite of a neat package it seems really unfair." However, for most journalists – and many of Ivor's friends and acquaintances – "eccentric" was precisely the word that described Ivor. Ivor disagreed. He took pains to point this out to Karl Dallas, forcefully enough for *Melody Maker* to title the article "Everyone Else is an Eccentric." Dallas gave Ivor enough space to explain why he wasn't eccentric, at least not completely:

> It's more complicated than that, of course … Compared, I suppose, with some people I can be seen to be eccentric. But anyone can be seen to be eccentric if you take him out of his milieu and put him into someone else's. I suppose as an attention-getting person I will be seen as eccentric by those who don't care to draw attention to themselves … But [I am] a fairly aware eccentric. It's almost a mannered eccentricity, but it sits easily on me.

So what is he? "I'm a humorist therefore I'm a preacher."[27]

A year after the Bloomsbury season, the humorist/preacher joined the Cholmondeleys, a quartet of female dancers, for a two-week season at the Shaw Theatre. This show was called *Fremsley*, presumably based on Ivor's book of the same name published that year and consisting of thirty-eight stories first broadcast on *Monday Night at Home*.[28] Pat Rush, writing for *The Stage*, gave a rapturous review to the show, impressed by the Cholmondeleys' "idiosyncratic" dance routines and even more excited by Ivor's performance, which "instantly and totally" captured the audience. Once again, this was an evening of songs, stories and poems, with harmonium or piano accompaniments. Rush wrote of Ivor's lack of animation, his slippers and ill-fitting clothes, his unimposing presence, and his often "dull" keyboard playing, all of which should have created a less than enjoyable evening out, but together, as part of Ivor's persona, their impact was very different.[29]

As a solo performer, Ivor's stage set-up could have been simple: a microphone or two, space for the harmonium and perhaps a piano, a chair to sit in. At times, this might have been sufficient, but Ivor's on-stage requirements could be more complicated. Phyllis King might be on the stage with him, for example, not to read her own poems (she would have a dedicated spot for this) but to do some knitting or some dusting: "That was his idea of course … He said 'Well, just come on and do some knitting' … I think I dusted the harmonium. I probably dusted him as well."[30] David Jones remembers that at one gig, when Ivor was supporting the Roches, he helped to drag a model dinosaur onto the stage, which Phyllis dusted while Ivor performed. A dinosaur was not the only object to grace one of Ivor's sets. He also decorated the stage with Craig Murray-Orr's sculptures, on one occasion giving Murray-Orr a hand-drawn plan of his stage set-up, showing spaces in which the sculptures could be placed. A review of Ivor's 1986 season at the Bloomsbury Theatre

An on-stage plan for an Ivor Cutler concert. (Courtesy of Craig Murray-Orr.)

noted that the stage was strewn with objects "that could be tribal fertility symbols. Or just about anything."[31] At the Derby Hall, Bury, the promoter decorated the stage with antlers, an early Edwardian vacuum cleaner and all manner of props without telling Ivor, who looked into the hall and announced, "It's going to be a very good gig tonight."[32]

Ivor played many different instruments, but he's particularly associated with the harmonium. He played it on his earliest TV appearances and on his first recording, and it's a dominant presence at his final concert and on his final album, *A Flat Man*, which closes with a minute or so of Ivor playing the instrument, with its clattering keys to the fore.[33] Craig Murray-Orr describes Ivor's use of the harmonium as "pragmatic, it was easy to get to gigs. But it also supplied the illusion of simplicity to his words and song. On a large stage it also gave a touching image of vulnerability that added great power to his work."

Ivor played piano in his teens, but only started playing the harmonium in his thirties.[34] Soon after he married, he went to a shop in Camberwell Green to buy a piano. He couldn't find a decent one, but spotted a more unusual instrument which he was told was a harmonium, priced at thirty shillings (£1.50), and he bought it. A few years later, around 1960, Ivor obtained his second harmonium when a fan of his radio shows offered him her late husband's instrument "for a consideration" and delivered it to Ivor's home. Twenty-five years or more later, he still owned it and enjoyed playing it. The instrument was a Mason and Hamlin model 109, with a three-and-a-half octave range, which Ivor described as "ample for my needs."[35]

The harmonium is a type of reed organ, reasonably small and easy to transport and therefore popular with travelling priests or missionaries and with families wanting affordable instruments for the living-room or parlour. Classical composers including Claude Debussy, Franz Liszt and Alban Berg wrote for the instrument, and from the 1960s onwards it's been used in contemporary rock and pop by acts including the Beatles, Nico and Tom Waits.[36] When Ivor started playing the instrument he was probably unique among performers on the cabaret and club scene, blazing a trail that few would follow. Not only was it easily transportable, he believed that it gave him greater freedom when singing, explaining that "The harmonium allows one to use a more free vocal technique. With a piano you'd have to tie more tightly to the voice in the way you were playing."[37]

The harmonium didn't always accompany Ivor on stage. Ron Geesin recalls that early in Ivor's career financial considerations impacted on whether or not the instrument would appear: "He said, 'If they pay me less than £50, I'm not going to take the harmonium: over £50 and I'll take it.'" Two other stories demonstrate a softer attitude to finances. Ivor told Ted Harrison that he contacted the BBC accounts department after one performance to tell them he was "dissatisfied" with the fee and suggesting it should be reduced by 10% because he "hadn't been on form that day."[38] Andy Kershaw tells a similar tale from the 1970s, when Ivor was recording for Virgin Records and Kershaw contacted the label's press office to arrange for Ivor to perform at Leeds University. The press office told him that Ivor handled his own bookings and gave him Ivor's phone number. Kershaw has told this story more than once, the fees varying with each telling. This is the version he related in 2021:

> So I phoned him up. The phone rang for ages and ages and then he said "Hello." I explained what I wanted and he said "I'm sorry I took so long. I was cleaning my bicycle" … I can't remember what I offered him, but let's say it was £1,000. There was a pause at the other end then this little voice says "Offer me less." So I offered £800 or whatever it was: then he said "Done and done".

A harmonium-related problem affected Ivor's appearance at the 1995 Aberdeen Alternative Festival. The *Aberdeen Evening Express* reported that "An off the wall Scots comic" was making an unusual request a few weeks ahead of his performance. Ivor's harmonium was too fragile to transport from London by aircraft, so the festival's director, Duncan Hendry, hoped that a local harmonium enthusiast might be willing to lend an instrument to Ivor for the evening.[39] Ivor's plea was successful: the *Evening Express*'s review of the concert noted his "harmonium-backed songs" as well as his "suspiciously sadistic streak." Sadly, the reviewer didn't credit the harmonium's owner, who must therefore remain anonymous.[40]

As Ivor aged, so, too, did his instruments. In fairness, recorded evidence suggests that they were never young, at least not by the time Ivor acquired them. Ivor acknowledged that his harmoniums creaked, but this was part of their charm: "John Peel has played me since 1969 and John has told me that if I use another harmonium when I'm recording and there's no clicks or bangs, people write to him and complain."[41] He played his 1999 Celtic Connections concert – a late example of a performance far from Laurier Road – using an "ancient" harmonium with, he admitted to his audience, one dud note.[42] Charming though an ancient harmonium with one dud note undoubtedly is, this concert may have been its last. Matthew Lenton, the director of *The Beautiful Cosmos of Ivor Cutler*, told of a bemused Glasgow sound engineer inadvertently hearing Ivor in the wings after an unidentified show, shouting at his inefficient instrument, "Right, that's it. I told you, I warned you, I'm leaving you." Good as his word, Ivor abandoned the instrument backstage, to be rescued by the festival team.[43]

Another of Ivor's instruments, which he used for many years and which appeared in his final concert, sported the word "Sewer" spelt out in tape on its back, facing the audience. I have always pronounced the word as "soo-er," like the system of drains for removing effluent. Phyllis King pronounces it "so-er," because she views the harmonium as resembling a sewing machine. I'm sure Phyllis is right, but it's fun to enjoy the ambiguity of the word.

Audiences at Ivor's concerts expected, and got, a mix of poems, stories, songs and seemingly off-the-cuff comments and jokes. Ivor also played the showbiz game of plugging his work and exhorting the audience to buy it, while at smaller events he would, like many other artists, arrive front of house after performing to sell merchandise himself.[44] There was always the chance of something more: for some audience members, Ivor's concerts offered a test of true love, or its absence. Ivor was proud of the role his work played in his fans' relationships: "People who like my work bring their fiancés along if the fiancé hasn't heard me and if the fiancé doesn't understand or doesn't like what I'm doing they call off the engagement."[45] Judith Palmer wrote that Ivor's work could so "radically polarise" people's feelings that some "have apparently been known to bring their fiancées to concerts, only to cancel the vicar in horror when they discover that their intendeds are immune to his sense of the ridiculous ..."[46] It wasn't all about broken engagements. Ivor claimed that four couples married because of a shared interest in his work: a pair of cucumber gatherers on a kibbutz; a woman laughing away at one of his books in a room full of businessmen, one of whom asked about the reason for her laughter; a couple who married, then divorced, but on good terms; and a woman who took her boyfriend to an Ivor Cutler concert, found he enjoyed it and married him.[47]

For a time Ivor would arrange for other acts to join him when he performed, not in the traditional "support slot" at the start of the evening, but as an interval act. "He'd slightly internalised the idea that somebody else had to be on the bill," says David Jones, "For quite a long time he didn't want to do very long sets but he wanted to give value for money, so he would ask somebody else to be on the bill. He had this idea of a sandwich: he would do a set, then somebody else, then he'd take over again." John Burnside performed as the guest artist at two or three events. He enjoyed the experiences, but acknowledges that he never came close to stealing the evening from the headliner: "I was terrible … Square peg, round hole and, of course, about as funny as toothache. I appreciated the kindness that had prompted him to include me but, to be honest, I was glad when he realised that it wasn't working and, by mutual agreement, we decided not to pursue the partnership."

Ivor's friends and fans have, for the most part, happy memories of seeing Ivor on stage. Burnside's abiding memory is of the way Ivor would sometimes stop when somebody laughed: "He would glare out into the audience, as if disapprovingly, or maybe wounded that he wasn't being taken seriously – and of course, this would only provoke more laughter." When Alasdair Roberts saw Ivor in Scotland at the end of the 1990s, he was struck by how rapturously the crowd received him: "there was a sense of welcoming a Scottish national treasure. Maybe there was also a sense of perhaps this is the last time we'll see him performing." As the years went by, Ivor attracted a younger audience while still retaining his older fans. Douglas T. Stewart saw Ivor live a few times and at the later gigs he noted how the audience "was young, hip, kids – people from nearly every hip band in Glasgow – but also people my age and people from a range of jobs." For Stewart, it's a reflection of people's broadening cultural awareness and willingness to accept "silly stuff" as being of value. Thirty years after coming to John Peel's attention, Ivor was still gathering fans from younger generations: the 1999 Flux Festival saw Ivor joining a bill that starred Orbital and Spiritualized, musicians from the contemporary dance music and electronic scenes.[48] In the same year, Lord Birkett gave Ivor his one and only mention in *Hansard*, in a debate on public service broadcasting when he raised Ivor, unofficially, to the minor nobility: "Like the noble Lord, Lord Bragg, I miss the other elements of radio … like the strange stories of Heinrich Boll, lectures by Sir Isaiah Berlin, talks by Max Beerbohm … and the amazing surreal contributions of Sir Ivor Cutler."[49]

John Knutas knew Ivor for almost twenty years, but saw him on stage only once, on New Year's Eve 1986 at a sold-out concert at the Queen Elizabeth Hall, a "fabulous" night's entertainment for an audience whose mean age was, Knutas estimates, below rather than above thirty: "He was a spellbinding performer … reminding me of the Danish-American Victor Borge, and his inimitable voice and delivery were probably unsurpassed as tools of trade. But a lot of Ivor's appeal lay between the lines, in the poignancy or slightly hidden bottomless melancholy of many of his poems …"

A few concert recordings still exist. In addition to the *Life in a Scotch Sitting Room* live album and the film of his final concert, *Cutler's Last Stand*, one or two amateur recordings can be found on the internet. They demonstrate the adulation of his fans, the uncontrollable bursts of laughter his performances could generate (in the fans and in Ivor) and the quite odd audience responses some of his work received. His reading of "Phonic Poem" at a Brighton gig was received with loud and prolonged laughter despite it being the tale of a car crash, the audience's loudest outburst greeting the shocking news of the crash's worst outcome – "Bill is dead."[50] At Bath Assembly Rooms, he walked on stage, sat at the harmonium and started patting his pockets before walking back to the wings. Sounds of rustling and rummaging could be heard, then Ivor returned, sat down and took out his glasses. "We thought it was a pantomime … his timing was exquisite … it took him just a bit longer than it should have to do anything, up to and including the hand in the pocket to take out his glasses."[51] Was this a genuine episode of forgetfulness, or a practised action?

Backstage, Ivor could be strict in his dealings with fellow performers or stage crew. Comedian Arthur Smith shared the bill with Ivor and although he refers to it as "an honour" his most pervasive memory is that he had to call him Mr Cutler. Graham Duff recalls that while he spoke with Ivor at both the events when they appeared on the same bill, "He was remarkably unfriendly, if I'm honest. Courteous, but I definitely got the impression that he had better things to be doing. Fair enough, he probably had." Duff made the mistake of calling him Ivor and was immediately told "It's Mr Cutler." As for Ivor's approach to the crew, "When he wanted something there were no airs and graces, there was no politeness, even. He definitely had a sense of entitlement to him." Roger McGough recalls that Ivor had a strict pre-show regime: "He'd always arrive and ask, very nicely, if I'd vacate the dressing room for half an hour before the show so he could do his yoga. I'd go out to the foyer, or walk around outside, until he'd finished."

When he was on stage, audience misbehaviour, deliberate or not, could elicit Ivor's immediate response. At the New Year's Eve concert which Knutas attended Ivor walked off stage when an audience member attempted to take a flash photograph, although he returned after a few minutes. Sometimes, audiences reacted to Ivor's displays of displeasure with laughter or delight – after all, wasn't this sort of thing to be expected from an "eccentric" performer? Sometimes, his displeasure was softened by a twinkle in his eye, or a smile: perhaps it was another carefully rehearsed moment, aimed at keeping the crowd on its toes while also raising a laugh. Would Ivor really jump off stage and thump an eager photographer or undercover gig recorder? However, his discomfort when exposed to loud noise was genuine and pleas to audience members to applaud at half volume were not simply attempts to play to their expectations.

On at least two occasions, the noise emanating from a small child produced Ivor's swift and extreme reaction and came close to causing a premature end to the evening's entertainment. When Ivor performed at the Queen Elizabeth Hall as part of the 1998 Meltdown Festival everything was going well, the audience "on-side," as Ivor began the second half of the concert with "Cold Potato," but after twenty-five seconds a young child cried out and Ivor paused for a few seconds. He resumed and less than ten seconds later the child cried out again, a happy cry that caused many in the audience to laugh. Ivor stopped again, then spoke directly to the adult who was with the child: "I think you'd better take your child outside. I'm terribly sorry but, eh, normally it should be said that there is a ..." He paused as the family and child left the auditorium. As they made their way out there was a collective sigh from many in the hall: it seems like a sigh of support for the family. Ivor explained "I had something like this before, and ..." but he was forced to pause again as indistinct male voices rose loudly in complaint and a few audience members walked out. Ivor carried on with his explanation: "This happened some years ago down in Brighton ... a couple of dozen walked out and the papers got hold of it ... There should have been a notice put up saying 'No Children'. I couldn't carry on with the constant noise. I taught children for thirty-one years." There was a smattering of laughter at this comment, but it's clear that Ivor had lost the sympathy of many in the room. "Now to go back to the work in hand ..." he said, and hesitantly resumed "Cold Potato." He sounded distracted and took a couple of minutes to get back on track but by the time "Cold Potato" ended he sounded more confident and the audience's applause was strong.[52] Hamish Ironside, who was at the concert, summed up this episode as "an awkward exchange" and remembers one audience member walking out in protest, shouting "You've lost my vote, Mr Cutler!"

Jeremy Cutler offered another explanation for Ivor's dislike of children at his concerts. In the notes to the re-release of *Privilege* he wrote that it had its roots in Ivor's own childhood and the arrival of his younger brother.

Almost fifty years after his on-stage debut at the Blue Angel, Ivor appeared on stage for the final time, on 1 February 2004. Queen Elizabeth Hall was the place, a fitting venue for his valedictory performance given his many appearances there over the years. *The Guardian*'s Robin Denselow gave a four-star review. He was honest about Ivor's fading abilities, his frailty and his "sometimes-sturdy, sometimes-shaky" singing voice, but saw a unique and talented performer at work: "behind the doddering façade there still lurked a humorist and performer with a magnificent sense of the absurd, acute sense of timing, and – most important of all – a great back catalogue ..."[53] The BBC filmed the concert, broadcasting an edited version as *Cutler's Last Stand* in April 2005. It's an affecting and respectful programme: Ivor is indeed frail and shaky, but his work remains funny, odd, thoughtful and bewildering by turns. The programme opens with an on-stage announcer's plea: "A request from Mr Cutler that you don't eat any noisy sweeties or crisps during the show tonight, and also ... could you applaud at fifty percent of your normal volume." The audience is respectful but enthusiastic, and so by the middle of the show normal volume has been resumed and Ivor makes his own plea: moving his left hand slowly up and down and pleading for things to get "a little quieter."

After the announcement, Ivor walks onto an almost empty stage. One microphone stand is placed centre-stage, upright. Another is next to the "Sewer" harmonium, as is a small table. Ivor wears a gilet, tartan check shirt and a tweed cap with badges and a large sunflower attached. He half-unzips the gilet with an assertive flourish, but his hand is shaking as he holds the book from which he reads at the central microphone. He begins with Episode One of *Life in a Scotch Sitting Room*, but pauses before the final third of the tale to ask "Are there any children here?" "Yes" responds an audience member. "Oh dear," he replies, to audience laughter. There's no sudden demand for the removal of the younger audience members, he's merely apologising for the next line: "The children micturated onto a large sponge ..." The BBC film is a mix of Ivor's "greatest hits" – episodes of *Life in a Scotch Sitting Room*, "Beautiful Cosmos," "Barabadabada," "A Wooden Tree" – and some lesser-known pieces. His introductions are brief, but often musically informative as he identifies which key a song is in. "A Gym Mistress" is in C, "the big one." He introduces "A Bubble or Two" with the words "Watch out for this one. A minor. It's not gonna be a funny one then, is it?"

Despite, or perhaps because of, Ivor's "doddering façade," the audience is warmly appreciative and responds positively to everything he does. At the end of "Beautiful Cosmos" there's a noticeable second or two of silence before the applause begins. It's Ivor's most affecting song of the evening, the point at which he appears at his most reflective and melancholy, a slight error in the lyric (he sings of "cups for tea" instead of "cups of tea") adding to the poignancy. When the applause does come, Ivor gazes down at his notebook, then comments "I bet you when you get home you'll say 'Stupid bugger'," before cracking a smile and briefly shaking with laughter. Ivor closes the concert with "A Wooden Tree," a song that features his father and mother, a sister and a brother. He responds to the applause that follows by sticking his fingers in his ears until the volume recedes. Still seated at the harmonium, he speaks to the audience: "I'd like to thank most of you," he says, then audience and artist laugh together, "Well, what do you expect?" The film cuts to Ivor standing at the central microphone, clutching his notebook and a leather bag as he makes his closing comment: "Most graciously, thank you very much. Good night." He walks off stage slowly, for the final time.

11 A Life on Screen

After his 1960s TV appearances and his role in *Magical Mystery Tour*, Ivor might have expected to become a regular on-screen face, if not a major star, but his screen career is more accurately described as steady rather than spectacular. There was no peak-time *Ivor Cutler Show*, no further big screen acting roles and from 1970 until his death he was most likely to appear as a guest, singing a song or two or perhaps reciting a poem on a range of TV shows, from London Weekend Television's *Alive and Kicking*, where Fox Primary pupils joined him in the studio, to *Turn that Racket Down*, part of a night of BBC Two programmes in celebration of John Peel's sixtieth birthday, when, on a sunny day, he sat on the roof of Broadcasting House with his harmonium and sang "Pass the Ball Jim." In the years between these two shows most of Ivor's TV appearances were on BBC Two, but he sometimes turned up on commercial stations including TV-AM, where he read a story on *Rub-a-Dub-Tub*, an early morning children's show.[1] He also made a couple of appearances away from television, in a movie documentary and a video-only compendium of new music, both of which made the most of his "eccentricity."

Some shows were well suited to Ivor's talents, others less so. In the early 1970s he joined *Six and Seven-Eighths*, a late-night one-off show advertised as "A deadly nightcap of bizarre moments": how deadly or bizarre these moments were is no longer known.[2] A year later, he took part in *Full House*, a Saturday night series that presented a variety of entertainments from rock bands, poets, jazz musicians, playwrights and classical ensembles, appearing alongside Brian Patten and actor Glenda Jackson to read "Gorbals 1930" and "A New Home," from a poetry anthology in aid of St Albans Shelter Group.[3] In a more unusual move, he joined the regular cast of *The End of the Pier Show* for a musical comedy about North Sea oil, titled *Rig O'Doom*, appearing with ex-Establishment Club performer John Fortune and classical actor John Laurie, famous as Private Frazer in *Dad's Army*.[4] Ivor was still making guest appearances on *Late Night Line-Up*: his last appearance on the show was in September 1972, singing "I Believe in Bugs" and "Don't do that to Me," and reading "I Found my Son in the Lavatory." The final edition of *Late Night Line-Up* was broadcast just two months later.[5]

As one long-running show came to an end, another offered Ivor a new opportunity. In early 1973, Joan Hedgecock invited Ivor to write and record an episode of *Jackanory* for broadcast in the week of 28 May. Eight years after he offered his services as a presenter on the show, *Jackanory* had become one of the most popular children's programmes on TV: an invitation to take part was an affirmation of Ivor's talent and popularity, and a chance for him to show that Joy Whitby had made a serious error of judgement in not accepting his offer. However, there was one problem to be overcome: Ivor claimed that the money on offer was "risible." Ivor was very upset by the low fee, but even more upset by Hedgecock's reference to his "jokes." He did not do jokes. His reply to Hedgecock was devoid of humour, a contrast to his usual style of correspondence, and he made his opinion of the BBC's fees clear: in over fifteen years of working for the corporation, he had only been happy with his fee on a single (unidentified) occasion. Three weeks later, an unsigned BBC memo stated that Ivor's appearance on *Jackanory* was not to go ahead.[6] Ivor, so enthusiastic about appearing on the show a few years earlier, had blown his chance. It's unlikely that the show's production team lost any sleep over Ivor's non-appearance: Willie Rushton, Clement Freud, Dudley Moore and Spike Milligan all read stories during that week.[7]

In 1974, with just three television channels on offer, the chance of a TV documentary devoted to a single unusual, but relatively little-known, performer was low. Find an extremely popular stand-up comedian willing to front a documentary about a selection of unusual individuals, however, and a television company could well be interested. Irish comedian Dave Allen, one of the country's most popular TV stars, was willing. Ivor and his old *British Rubbish* collaborator Bruce Lacey were two of the featured individuals, who were all male, white and middle-aged or older. The show was called *Dave Allen in Search of the Great English Eccentric*.[8] No one seemed concerned that Ivor wasn't English.

Lacey opened the programme, sitting in his home-made mock-up of a Lancaster bomber cockpit, flying a "bombing raid" over Germany until Allen interrupted the adventure by knocking on the cockpit canopy. Ivor appeared later in the show, mainly in location footage from London Zoo which showed him and Phyllis King on a day out. They often went on trips to the zoo in the early years of their relationship, to draw or to write poems, so the choice of location was appropriate. Fifty years later, Phyllis has only vague memories of the filming: "It was really early days. I didn't feel I should be part of it but he said 'Oh no, I want you to be in it.' So I just did. I think he said we should take our drawing books and draw something … It didn't matter what animal he was looking at, he would draw what he wanted."

Ivor's section of the programme opens with him standing on a first-floor terrace at his Laurier Road flat and blowing bubbles as Allen stands in the street below attempting to catch them: the scene is soundtracked unimaginatively by "I'm Forever Blowing Bubbles." Although the director might have hoped for suitably eccentric clothing, Ivor is dressed soberly, with frameless spectacles, a brown *faux*-suede hat with peak and earflaps around which appear whisps of curly grey hair, and a brown polyester "car coat" in the style beloved of 1970s football commentators. In later, interior, scenes he's wearing a tweed jacket and waistcoat, orange sweater and dark red shirt. The location soon shifts from the Laurier Road roof to London Zoo, with Ivor and Phyllis wandering past a bird enclosure and a sign marking the gentlemen's toilets before Ivor stops to micturate behind a low wooden panel and Phyllis turns away to keep watch and, perhaps, to minimise embarrassment.

In a voiceover, Ivor explains that he plays games all the time, because the point of life is to have a good time: "I learned that from Rebecca West. She said something about 'If it gives you pleasure, that is your touchstone.' I hope I'm not misquoting her. And I do it with people. I hope I don't hurt them in doing it: I've certainly no intention [to do so]." Next, the scene changes to the interior of Ivor's flat as he plays harmonium and sings "I Think Very Deeply." Allen watches and listens before asking Ivor how he would describe himself. Ivor replies that "humorist" might be appropriate, but decides that being a humorist is a job rather than a personal characteristic. After a pause he decides "I'm a child. Yes, I think that's better." The film returns to the zoo. This time, Ivor and Phyllis sit outside the flamingo pool, behind a rubbish bin, and as Phyllis draws part of the bin Ivor asks why she isn't drawing flamingos. The scene shifts abruptly to Ivor at his harmonium, singing "Old Oak Tree" and corpsing when he reaches the part about a girl with a bra that's too tight. Allen's been listening respectfully, sitting on a sofa with a sign reading "No Dumping Prohibited" over his left shoulder, and he can't resist a smile as Ivor regains his composure. "There's a touch of the anarchist in you, isn't there?" Allen asks once the song ends. Ivor replies, "Em, I must say I like pushing the boat a little, yes. It's my pleasure." He then tells of putting a tape recording in the giraffe house, to replace the "full of good information, but not completely to my taste" descriptive tapes provided by the zoo. Ivor's voice is replaced by the recording, played over shots of crowds looking at various animals. The recording continues as Ivor and Phyllis are shown sitting outside the giraffe and zebra enclosure. Ivor is drawing a defecating elephant.

Ivor stands out from the other participants, even Lacey. He's the only one who seems to have an aim that goes beyond personal enjoyment, the only one with a desire to challenge people's perceptions of life rather than simply to indulge in an odd and fairly extreme hobby. Allen treats all of the characters with respect, even if some of their activities leave him bemused. Of all Ivor's radio and TV appearances up to that point, *Dave Allen in Search of the Great English Eccentric* is the only one that shows something of his day-to-day life, albeit a view that exaggerates certain aspects of it while ignoring other, more mundane, parts such as his teaching career. The programme was shown again in 1976: Ivor's repeat fee was £8.75.[9]

Ivor's 1980s TV appearances include a profile on *South of Watford*, presented by Hugh Laurie; an appearance on *The Innes Book of Records*, starring Ivor Cutler fan Neil Innes, on which he read "Gruts for Tea" while seated in front of what looks like a disused railway tunnel; and a 1986 performance on *Whistle Test*, the BBC's flagship "alternative music" show.[10] For *South of Watford*, Ivor was filmed cycling on Hampstead Heath, and Laurie visited Laurier Road, where Ivor served herbal tea.[11] The anonymous TV critic of the *Liverpool Echo* panned *The Innes Book of Records*, accusing Innes of "serving up 'guests' like dubious 'poet' Ivor Cutler ..."[12] On *Whistle Test* Ivor wore a tartan jacket, yellow trousers and an odd, beige and orange patterned, peaked hat. He performed on a set dressed to look like a small urban back garden, with a brick wall, bushes and bins and a sign saying "Comfy Area." Seated at his "Sewer" harmonium, he read "My Wee Pet" and sang "Shoplifters." A few months later, a week of shows celebrating *Late Night Line-Up* included Ivor as one of the guests: Joan Bakewell was the presenter tasked with introducing him.[13]

Another 1980s show put Ivor back into mainstream family variety, a place he hadn't occupied since his 1960s appearances with Acker Bilk. In the mid-1980s Russell Harty was one of Britain's most popular chat show hosts, attracting millions of viewers each week. On 24 December 1984 he hosted a special edition of his show, as the *Radio Times* explained: "... in a small village in the Yorkshire dales Russell Harty has invited his friends to join him at home. There's plenty going on in this village of Giggleswick ..."[14] Harty's showbiz pals were a mixed bunch, including Ned Sherrin, folk singer and comedian Mike Harding, cricketer Ian Botham, snooker star Alex Higgins, fashion designer Zandra Rhodes and Labour politician Ken Livingstone, as well as Ivor. John Naughton's one-paragraph review opened by calling the show "as bogus a piece of Yuletide programming as we are ever likely to see" and closed by calling it "by any standards, a stupendously artificial event." In between, he namechecked most of the guests but failed to mention Ivor.[15]

Poets Against the Bomb documented the event of the same name at Chelsea Old Town Hall on 15 April 1981 and featured both Ivor and Phyllis.[16] As the title makes plain this was a protest event, organised by the Campaign for Nuclear Disarmament. Performers and audience may have felt that the event was a kick in the teeth for the British establishment, but *The Times* decided that it was sufficiently part of the establishment to publicise it in the "Today's engagements" section of the newspaper, on the page that also included the Court Circular. The day's other engagements included a lecture on "The spirit of the nation: the Church of England" by Enoch Powell, a visit to Bath by Princess Margaret, and the Lord Mayor and Lady Mayoress of London's trip to Cairo and Rome. This was not Ivor's first appearance in

"Today's engagements": he and Phyllis King appeared in the column when they read at the Children's Poetry Festival.[17]

Poets Against the Bomb brought together leading poets including Adrian Henri, Adrian Mitchell, Brian Patten and Pete Brown. In front of a banner that read "No More Hiroshimas," Brown opened proceedings with "There Will Probably Be a Nuclear War in the Next Ten Years." Henri contributed "Death in the Suburbs," and Mitchell added "Requirements in a Shelter." Some poets offered less obvious forms of protest. Nicki Jackowska read "Sometimes Love"; Roy Fisher read "Paraphrases," which he called "a poem about what it is to be a writer," his gentle humour drawing rare laughs from the audience; Phyllis King read "When I Was," a poem about an idyllic childhood; and Harold Pinter recited John Donne's "A Nocturnal Upon St Lucy's Day," dressed like a besuited public accountant in contrast to the scruffiness of most of the poets. In the film, Ivor performs twice. On his first appearance, he sings "Counting Song," which later appeared on *Privilege*: an appropriate song for the event, referring as it does to a woman with six fingers, the result of her enjoyment of radioactive material. He's unaccompanied, standing centre-stage, dressed conservatively in light brown shirt and mid-brown corduroy trousers. There's a piano stage left but no microphone in its vicinity so, Ivor tells the audience, "I could accompany it, but it looks stupid, you know, you run over there to play a few notes then run back here." He looks happy as he sings, smiling and sometimes having to stifle a laugh. After the closing credits, Ivor appears again, in close-up, reciting "Ten Years."

By the mid-1980s the video recorder was becoming commonplace in British homes and people were beginning to buy pre-recorded tapes in the same way that they were buying records, cassettes and the other new entertainment format, the compact disc. Ivor was now a Rough Trade artist and acted as Master of Ceremonies on the label's 1986 video tape, *Not Television*. This was a compilation of songs by Rough Trade acts including the Smiths, Robert Wyatt, and Ivor, who performed "Shoplifters." Ivor first appears looking and sounding stern and schoolmasterly, although this image is softened by his bright red Harpo Marx wig. He introduces himself with "Hello, I'm Ivor Cutler, your friendly link man, linking this Rough Trade compilation. So, sit down and shut up." His job is simple: to offer a brief introduction to each video clip. Each time he does so, he's sporting some different attire: for the Smiths ("The Boy with the Thorn in his Side") he's wearing a top hat. When he introduces himself – "Now it's my shot. Here's a song, 'Shoplifters', from my album *Gruts*" – he's sporting a tartan skull cap and jacket, when he performs the song he's barefoot and wearing a blue cap.

The next decade was a quiet one for Ivor as far as TV was concerned, although he was busy on stage and radio. Then in 1998 Scottish Television [STV] broadcast *Ivor Cutler – by Ivor Cutler*, an episode of its arts programme, *Don't Look Down*, featuring a seventeen-minute interview with and by Ivor, who acts as both interviewee and interviewer, asking and, sometimes, answering questions in his first-floor room at Laurier Road. Ewan Morrison, who directed the programme, was an Ivor Cutler fan thanks to Peel sessions and a gig in Glasgow when, he recalls, "I'd never laughed so much in my life." Morrison suggested that Ivor should interview himself, using split-screen techniques to show two Ivors at once, a suggestion which Ivor found "very, very amusing."

Morrison travelled to London with a small crew and arrived at Laurier Road, energetic and excited. Ivor came to the front door, but wouldn't let the team into the house. "Ivor said 'Oh, no, you can't come in,'" recalls Morrison, "you have all the wrong energy, you're full of negative energy and frustration. I can't have that near me." He offered a few drops of Bach Rescue Remedy to Morrison, who took them and waited outside the door for ten minutes before knocking again: "I said 'Yes, I feel much calmer now'. He said 'Oh, yes. The change in you is quite astounding. You can come in now.'" Once the team were inside, Ivor cleared furniture away. As agreed, Ivor scripted his own questions and answers: the result is "stilted and strange," says Morrison, "You look at it and it's like absurdist theatre." The role of interviewer was tough on Ivor's knees: this Ivor kneels on cushions on the floor throughout the interview, while Ivor the interviewee sits behind his harmonium. Takes were interrupted because the crew couldn't stop laughing, Ivor joined the crew for sandwiches during a break, the filming was completed in the scheduled day, and the crew and the performer parted company. "He didn't like talking about his personal history that much, but he found [the filming] quite cathartic and we parted on good terms," says Morrison.

STV broadcast the programme a week later. After the broadcast, a senior manager came up to Morrison: "He collared me, almost pinned me to the wall and said 'If you ever try a stunt like that again, you're fired!'" Morrison sent Ivor a video of the show, drawing a response in stark contrast to the manager's: "I got a lovely message on my answerphone … It was extraordinary, Ivor Cutler in tears on the phone. He said it was beautiful, he said it looked like a Vermeer. Unfortunately, that was the last time I heard from Ivor."

Ivor's appearance on *Don't Look Down* is unlike any other TV appearances he made. Interviewer Ivor has a childlike voice and remains kneeling throughout as if in supplication. Interviewee Ivor is aggressive, cynical, haughty, although some of his utterances are self-deprecating: "I know nothing and it's taken me a lifetime to get to this stage" he says proudly. This idea was Ivor's, but it wasn't new: in the late 1970s his primary school pupils were acting out an almost identical scenario, one pupil sitting down and acting haughtily as the second knelt at their side and asked questions in an exaggeratedly childish voice.[18] Interviewee Ivor recites poems from *Is That Your Flap, Jack?*, sings a few songs and reads Episode Fifteen of *Glasgow Dreamer*. The interview seems like an ideal situation for Ivor to reveal some of his innermost thoughts, or to proffer insights into his work, but there's little of either. In a typical exchange, interviewer Ivor asks "How do you come to be interviewing yourself?" and interviewee Ivor responds with "I thought it would allow me to explore some of the rich and varied aspects of my personality." In another break from the standard interviewer-interviewee interaction, both Ivors are reading from notebooks, to ensure there is no spontaneity in the exchange, that nothing is accidentally revealed. A lingering close-up of one of the notebooks reveals both questions and answers, word for word as they are spoken. Ivor took his preparation seriously, planning this interview in the same way as he planned a concert: "I've a great fear of not being seen to be professional, so with a concert everything is prepared up to the hilt," he said later.[19]

Ivor speaks about how his younger brother became the focus of the family's attention and of how his Home Service broadcasts made him an object of controversy. "It's much more satisfying than total acceptance, which would turn me into a monster," he says, as the other Ivor stares at his notes. After singing "Lemonade" there's another brief exchange:

> "Did you always want to be a comedian?"
> "I'm not."
> "What are you, then?"
> "A humorist."
> "What's the difference?"
> "Oh, gosh, am I supposed to put up with this ..."
> "Did you always want to be a humorist?"
> "No, a painter."

There's one further exchange, about how it takes bravery to stand alone on a stage and "come out with a funny little poem": "At a crisis, I told the therapist I was a coward. 'What kind?' he asked. And I realised that, on occasion, I was brave and that physically so-called tough men could experience great fear." Before interviewee Ivor reveals any more, interviewer Ivor intervenes to set up a weak joke:

> "You're not a middle-of-the-road person."
> "No, I'm not. I'm a cyclist, I keep to the edge."

Even though *Don't Look Down* didn't offer any new insights into the world of Ivor Cutler, Morrison is to be congratulated for crafting an enjoyable curiosity. After all, when he first proposed the idea Ivor responded with "Oh, I don't like doing television programmes, they're horrible. The questions they ask you are so stupid."

12 Quite a Few Lives on the Wireless

Television may have occasionally taken Ivor to its heart, but radio was far more accepting, offering him what might be called his "spiritual media home," if that's not being too pretentious. By the early 1970s, the Peel sessions had brought him to Radio 1, and he started appearing regularly on Radio 3 and Radio 4, successors to the Third Programme and Home Service. Radio 4 began a series of shows promising a "midweek medley of music, humour and comment." *If It's Wednesday It Must Be …*, was presented by Kenneth Robinson and Kenny Everett, featured Viv Stanshall as a regular performer, and added guest artists including Ron Geesin, journalist Jeffrey Bernard, disc jockey Anne Nightingale and, for two shows, Ivor Cutler. The radio critic of *The Times* was unimpressed by the first few episodes of the show, telling his readers "I am now in a position to complete the puzzle posed in the title, *If It's Wednesday It Must Be …* The concluding words are; …Time to do the Shopping, or Hide in a Cupboard, or Shoot Yourself, or in fact Any Old Thing at all …" A month later, he had changed his mind, deciding that recent shows had displayed "a marked improvement in … tone and content …"[1] By the time Ivor appeared, it seemed that *If It's Wednesday* would become an established feature in the midweek schedule.

Despite the show's potential for collaboration between some of the most creative minds on radio, Ivor performed solo on both his appearances. Geesin, who describes himself as a "semi-regular" on the show, recalls that Ivor was booked separately and emphasises "We certainly did not collaborate." A pity, for a radio collaboration between Cutler, Geeson, Everett and Stanshall is a mouth-watering prospect.[2] But it was not to be. Ivor complained about his fees, feeling that he was being undervalued, and the resulting argument led Richard Gilbert, the show's producer, to write that his booking of Ivor for any future work "in the current circumstances seems quite out of the question."[3]

Then, at the end of June, *If It's Wednesday* came off air for good after just twenty-three episodes.

Ivor made guest appearances on numerous radio shows over the next few years, including reading a Christmas story on Radio 4's *Today*, joining Radio 3's *Poetry Now* and performing on Radio 1's *Saturday Live* presented by Richard Skinner. School programmes including *Music Club* and *Speak* also featured his work and on *Look! Pictures in the Mind* he read "To Giorgio Morandi."[4] As his fame grew, he received a few requests that upset him, as he was strongly against other people editing or reading his work for broadcast. When a World Service show called *Anguish by Radio* asked Ivor for permission to use a forty-eight-second clip of "Birdswing," his reply was brusque. Writing his reply on the back of the letter, he flatly refused to allow an edited version of his work to be broadcast.[5] A few years later, the BBC tried again, this time for Schools Radio's *Word Games*. Carole Blockley sought permission for an actor to read "Fish" on the show. Given Ivor's teaching career, and the fact that actors, rather than guests, usually read poems and stories on the show, it must have seemed like a formality, but Ivor's reply was straight to the point. He was willing to read it himself, but would allow no one else to do so. Janet Whitaker, producer of Schools Radio, wrote back, hoping to change his mind, then Sandy (Sandra) Brownjohn, an educational consultant, spoke to Ivor. Persistence paid off and Ivor agreed to allow an actor to read his poem.[6]

One potentially fascinating recording never made it to air. In May 1983 Ivor was interviewed for a World Service programme, *Who's Afraid of Franz Kafka?*, but whatever he had to say the interview was not used. Even without Ivor's contribution, the *BBC Yearbook* named the show as one of the World Service's "particularly interesting programmes" of the year.[7]

To make the most of Ivor's imagination and inventiveness, the BBC needed to give him a show of his own. A television series, or even a one-off TV special, was probably too great a risk for the corporation, but a radio show could be made with a much smaller financial investment. *The I.C. Snow*, the five-episode series from 1964, was the first show to star Ivor on his own, but it soon disappeared without trace. It took another fifteen years, and a sympathetic and enthusiastic producer, before the BBC trusted Ivor with another show of his own. The show was titled *Silence* and the producer was Piers Plowright.

Plowright had been a radio producer for ten years, joining the BBC as a trainee after working for the British Council in Sudan, and had recently finished producing the Radio 2 drama series *Waggoners' Walk*.[8] He was a long-standing fan of Ivor, having first seen him perform in *An Evening of British Rubbish*. On leaving *Waggoners' Walk*, he thought "I'm free now, I can do something more interesting" and decided to contact Ivor. They met on 19 June 1978, when he visited Laurier Road. Plowright's diary for that day reads:

He opened the door: small, grizzled, boxer's nose, shorts, glasses set firmly forward. In the shadows sat Phyllis King, his partner. Some model pigeons lay on their backs, half-way up the window … Ivor said he was a painter, a singer, and a poet by accident. I said I thought he was one of the funniest men alive. He looked surprised. We talked. We fixed up a recording. Both of them showed me paintings. Very green. I left.

Silence appeared at a time when Ivor was experimenting with drama. In 2019, Scottish actor Bill Paterson gave a reading of a short play, *The Fleas*, which Ivor wrote in the late 1970s.[9] Ivor had passed the manuscript of this work, along with a manuscript of another play, written by Phyllis King and called *Blickets*, to Paterson soon after they were written, when Paterson was a young, up-and-coming, performer. Paterson has described the plays as "surrealist."[10] Although Phyllis recalls that she and Ivor wrote plays "separately, but together" and also remembers drawing a title page, she can no longer recall what either of them were about. It's also no longer clear if Ivor intended *The Fleas* to be performed on stage or on radio.

Six months after they met, the Cutler/Plowright collaboration got under way when they recorded *Silence* on 21 December for broadcast on 4 January. Plowright's diary entry suggests that the recording process was straightforward, but the producer was far from sure about the outcome of the broadcast:

Recorded *Silence* all day with Ivor Cutler. Ivor did all the voices: a phone rings. Ivor answers it. A voice [Ivor] says "Is that Mr Cutler?" "No" says Ivor. "Oh" says the voice [Ivor]. "He's down the road" "Could you call him for me?" [PAUSE] "He's a mile and a half down the road." "Oh" "I'll hit the tray with a spoon." Then begins a series of journeys to a distant window to hit the tray [the spoon flies out of Ivor's hand], distant voices [Ivor], "Hey you, is this your spoon!?" … Ivor worked with Enyd Williams who did all the noises … Are we mad? Will I get the sack? What will Radio 3 listeners say? What will the controller say? Is it a masterpiece? I've no idea.

Plowright's fears were unfounded, as he recalled, when *Silence* "became a sort of mini-hit." The success helped him to cope with Ivor's personality. "I got on with Ivor very well," said Plowright, but "I was a little bit nervous of him because he could be quite moody. I didn't try to control or shape the show: Ivor didn't like changing things …" A mini-hit was a big enough hit for the power-brokers at Radio 3: Ivor went on to create numerous programmes of sketches, plays, songs and poems for radio over the next twenty years, with Plowright and others. Some were one-offs like *Silence*, others were short series of five or six shows, notably *Ivor Cutler and …*, *King Cutler* and *Jelly Mountain*.

In one of their most ambitious collaborations, Ivor and Plowright created *Prince Ivor*, a radio opera (pronounced "Prance Eevor"). This was no three-hour Wagnerian epic, but a twenty-minute show featuring Ivor with Julianne Mason and John Fletcher and broadcast in the interval between Acts 2 and 3 of *Aida*. Once again, Plowright described the recording process in his diary: "Thursday 16th/Friday 17th December 1982. Recorded Ivor's radio opera, Prince Ivor. Ivor arrived in a cloud of badges and plus fours. Playing nearly all the voices. Julianne Mason [other parts] tried valiantly to get a word in edgeways." For an opera, *Prince Ivor* is notable for an almost total absence of music or singing, just a few bars of tuba, played by John Fletcher, and a bar or two of piano from Ivor.[11]

Plowright recorded what he described as "twenty minutes of lunacy." He also remembered an unusual visitor:

> A professor of literature from just north of Frankfurt, who happened to be watching all this (he suddenly appeared in the cubicle, shepherded by someone in a suit), said to Ivor: "This was not strange to me. I have written a book on The Grotesque in European Fiction." Chuckling uproariously, he left for the airport.

Plowright and Ivor worked together for over ten years, even though Plowright confessed to having very little control over these "crazy little stories." They followed *Silence* with two series of short dramas – *Ivor Cutler and ...* and *... Is Approached by Ivor Cutler*. In both series, Ivor meets up with someone and has a conversation and, sometimes, a bit of an adventure. In the first series of *Ivor Cutler and ...* he met with a mermaid, a mole, a princess and his dad. In the second series, broadcast eighteen months later over Christmas and New Year, he met with a barber, a paper seller, a storeman and a small holder: immediately afterwards, he approached a miner and a sheet metal worker (there is no obvious reason for the change in title).[12]

Anyone hoping that *Ivor Cutler and ... His Dad* (featuring Glynis Brooks and Malcolm Hayes, and described by the *Radio Times* as "A man rears a boy") would provide some insight into Ivor's relationship with Jack Cutler will be disappointed. It's a tale dominated by sound effects – birds, a horse, running water, clanking pots – rather than dialogue, telling (if I'm reading it correctly) of a boy who is studying for his A-levels and contemplating killing and eating a caged canary. Father arrives on horseback, asks what his son is up to, then leaves at a gallop. The boy goes back to the cage, ready to eat the bird, which pleads "But I'm only a sweet little canary," then calls for Dad. He returns, the boy invites him to hear his new disc, the disc plays and once Dad is told that the music is from Burundi, man, boy and canary leave on horseback. More birds are heard as the horse gallops away. End.

David Wade, the radio critic whose son refused to go to school when faced with Mr Cutler's teaching, found it hard to explain the initial quartet of shows.

He gave brief summaries of the first three, but gave up trying for number four: "I have not the first idea what it was on about ... All I can say is that I sat very still, more than halfway enchanted and I appeared to be laughing, helicopter fashion, without making any noise. I am not sure that I have ever heard anything quite like [it]."[13] A few years later, Wade's opinion had hardened. He criticised Ivor for being whimsical, pushing a single idea too far, and declared "I think he'll be remembered as a very interesting, I'm inclined to say small, talent."[14] It seems that the judging panel for the Pye Radio Awards were more impressed by the first series of *Ivor Cutler and ...* whether or not they understood it, for Ivor won the comedy section of the 1980 awards or, in the words of the *Marylebone Mercury*, Ivor "forced the judges of the Comedy section of the Pye Radio Awards into creating a new category for him for his Radio 3 series of short plays." *The Stage* put it less dramatically, noting simply that Ivor was "awarded the Pye Radio Award for Humour."[15]

Bat Blues was another one-off production from Ivor and Plowright. Once again, the show was timetabled to surprise the unwary classical music fan, appearing between a violin and piano duo performing music by Hindemith and Strauss and a recital of Liszt's organ music. The premise seemed simple: "Ivor Cutler teaches several bats and one woman how to play jazz piano."[16] The reality was more disturbing. Ivor spends most of his time teaching the unnamed woman how to play a blues, after taking time out to eat various bits of bat. They become flirtatious, although Ivor's request for a kiss is rebuffed until he has chewed some celery: as the woman points out, he has just eaten a bat's head. Eventually, they journey to a nearby cave with the intention of capturing more bats as a post piano lesson treat. One of the bats manages to persuade Ivor to teach him how to play the blues (the long-awaited Bats Waller joke appears at this point), promising that he will pay Ivor by persuading a number of his fellow bats to fly to Ivor's flat, where they can be stored in the fridge and eaten later. Sadly, the bats have tricked Ivor: he is the one who gets eaten, but as he's taken away we hear him singing "Bats of the world, take over ..."

Ivor's working relationship with Plowright ended in 1989 with *Cutler on Education*, in which, according to the *Radio Times*, "Ivor Cutler speaks, for the nation, to a small crowd, an attractive woman, and a petrol pump attendant."[17] The ending was amicable, according to Plowright: "We didn't fall out or anything, it's just that he was wide-ranging by then ..." Years after their collaboration ended, Plowright spoke about his frustration with some of Ivor's work: "Sometimes, he does need an editor to say 'Ivor, I don't think that one works'. I tried that occasionally with the radio. There's that terrible danger for the nonsense merchant, of whimsy ... for a man who's so muscular and sharp, just occasionally the thought is a bit fluffy."[18]

Plowright became aware of another problem when working with Ivor: "getting him to work with anyone else ... He didn't like professional actors ..." This is not to suggest that Ivor was being palmed off with substandard thespians:

on the contrary, he was often joined by leading comedy actors. Natasha Pyne, well known at the time for her starring role in the 1970s comedy series *Father, Dear Father*, joined him for *Bat Blues*; Bill Wallis, a character actor who featured in the *Blackadder* series, notably as Mr Ploppy the jailer, appeared in a number of episodes of *Ivor Cutler and ...* and *... Is Approached by Ivor Cutler*. Talented professionals were not what Ivor wanted, however.

Neil Cargill became Ivor's next producer. They already knew each other, having met in 1984 when Cargill, recently arrived in London from Aberdeen, was recording a documentary for Radio Scotland called *The London–Scottish Connection*. Cargill recalls that the idea was to interview a range of people who had left Scotland to settle in London and discover what had prompted the decision. Cargill had seen Ivor in performance, owned some of his LPs and thought he'd be an ideal person to talk to. Ivor invited Cargill to his flat and the pair bonded through a shared sense of humour, but also, according to Cargill, because "We were both feeling a bit overwhelmed by London – the pace, the noise, the relentless pressure ..." Ivor gave him some books and pamphlets and tiny glass bottles, which provided Cargill with his introduction to Bach flower remedies, and the "Rescue Remedy" in particular.

Cargill kept in touch with Ivor, occasionally discussing the possibility of another radio series, although he found that Ivor was "very cautious, as he revealed that he hadn't particularly enjoyed *Prince Ivor* and felt the end result wasn't what he envisaged." Despite this, just a few months after working with Plowright on *Cutler on Education* Ivor was willing to pitch another idea, this time with Cargill (who was now a Senior Producer in the BBC Radio Light Entertainment Department). They took their idea to the controller of Radio 4, who, according to Cargill, dismissed it with the words "I won't have that man on my network." Undeterred, they went to the controller of Radio 3, John Drummond, who was more positive, telling Cargill "I can't say I understand Ivor's humour, but many people do: how about a series of six half-hours?"

The series was *King Cutler*. The BBC was excited enough, or concerned enough, about the show to give it a couple of previews to boost listener interest. *Radio Times* published an interview with Ivor, which informed readers that "The 'King' is not a reference to the distinctly un-regal Ivor but to his partner, the poet and songwriter Phyllis King. 'For me the most exciting bits of the work are what Phyllis has done,' he said gallantly." It also gave Ivor a chance to namecheck his comedy influences – the Goons, and particularly Spike Milligan. He was asked about classifying his own style: "If I were flip, I could say it was rooted in fear, but I actually think that incongruity is the basis of laughter. Kafka turned me from a sixth-former into an adult as far as humour is concerned." The article noted that there would be a preview of the show on BBC One's behind-the-scenes programme *See for Yourself*, presented by Terry Wogan.[19]

Ivor and Phyllis King had previously collaborated on *King and Cutler*, produced by Piers Plowright and broadcast in 1981. That was a stand-alone show, a thirty-minute two-hander described temptingly by the *Radio Times* as a programme in which Phyllis and Ivor "leave school, inflate the cat, eat porridge by moonlight, run to the edge, and fly off into the wind."[20] If all that was too much, it was followed by an interlude, so listeners could recover before enjoying a concert by the Medici String Quartet. Unlike *King and Cutler*, *King Cutler* featured guests, or "visitors," to join in the fun. *King Cutler* is characterised by episodes filled with short sections: a song, then a sketch, then a poem, and so on. Regular features included Ivor reading episodes of *Glasgow Dreamer*, a weekly drumming lesson, and "Great Races of the World," which discussed the sack race and the three-legged race among others.

Cargill greatly enjoyed working with Phyllis and Ivor. "With Phyllis on board, the title *King Cutler* more or less wrote itself – and provided a wry nod to earlier work ("upping the game from Prince to King ...")," he recalls. "It was always Ivor's intention that this would be the 'definitive' appearance by Phyllis ..." By contrast, Cargill has the impression that Phyllis wanted the focus to be on Ivor: "she was always very skilled in pitching her performance in the supporting role very sensitively. Putting Ivor in his place in some of the dialogue was very convincing, however! He had great respect for her work and said she was the better poet."

Cargill recalls that preparation took a long time, with meetings in his office and at Ivor's flat. Improvisation was still possible, however, and much of the dialogue was developed during recording. The editing process was, by contrast, very tightly controlled, with Cargill making a rough copy of each show before he and Ivor listened together and made the final editing decision, at times through a rather unorthodox process:

> The duration of the silence between each scene or song was decided by us both closing our eyes and saying "now" when we felt it was right: only when we both said "now" at the same moment would the splice be made and the next scene would begin. Much the same process was used for deciding how long a particular effect should last: we had great fun letting (e.g.) the wrapping of a bridge in paper go on, and on, and on and on ... And on, and on and on ...

Once editing was complete, Ivor was eager to protect the finished shows to ensure that they were not altered for future broadcasts. Cargill recalls that "he had many tussles with the copyright department over the clause in his contract regarding assertion of moral rights, ensuring that the programmes were 'untouchable.'" He wanted *King Cutler*'s impact to be retained, its ability to confuse or bewilder its audience to continue: according to Cargill "he was delighted by the beautifully ambivalent BBC Audience Feedback comment regarding *King Cutler* which was simply 'This is unbelievable!'"

Ivor told Cargill that working on *King Cutler* was the first time he felt he'd truly collaborated on a broadcast. "I just worked with him exactly how any drama production would be produced," Cargill says, "but more often than not in the past he had been left on his own to record material for use in programmes with neither producer nor presenter coming to the studio." He told Cargill that the experience "would make him doubt whether his songs or poems were any good after all. These sorts of feelings hit Ivor hard." It's unclear to which programmes Ivor was referring. Lucy Armitage, who produced the Andy Kershaw radio shows, recalls that producers often did not meet guest performers when they arrived to record sessions, which supports Ivor's memory, although she always met Ivor, "because I was such a fan." Her own memory of the Ivor Cutler sessions she produced for Kershaw, from 1994 on, is of a more collaborative and friendly atmosphere. The usual Radio 1 session set-up for daytime shows involved the studio manager and producer in the booth, with the DJ and guests in the studio itself. On a typical session, therefore,

> [Ivor] would perform directly in front of Andy. It was live and direct, and Andy's reactions were always spontaneous. Every now and then Andy would request something but for the most part Ivor would decide what he was going to do ... I'm sure he had some pieces planned, because he had some markers in his books. He would converse with Andy in a very relaxed manner, he knew what was coming next ... no matter what he did, it was always spectacular and because his pieces are so short he could do twelve or fifteen items when other acts could only do two or three.

On one occasion, for now-forgotten reasons, Kershaw was in the studio at Egdon House and Ivor was in a basement studio in Broadcasting House: "I introduced Ivor's first number and said 'Ivor's live with us tonight, in a basement studio in Broadcasting House. Are you there Ivor?' There was a pause and then a little voice said 'No'."

King Cutler was the first of Ivor's radio shows to tackle his dislike of working with professional actors. From now on, Ivor's fellow actors came from outside the profession, but inside his social circle, including Ted Harrison who recalls performing as "the BBC straight voice." Dylan Edwards was another guest: the son of Joyce Edwards, who owned 21 Laurier Road, he was living in the house and working as a professional translator, so Ivor invited him onto the show to translate phrases in Czech, Russian and Greek. He went on to join the cast of *A Stuggy Pren*, *Jelly Mountain* and *A Wet Handle*. Craig Murray-Orr was another cast member for *King Cutler* who returned for the three later series.

Artist Glen Baxter was a guest on the first episode of *King Cutler*: he had been a fan of Ivor's work since the mid-1960s and first met him in the 1970s.

Baxter's contribution was a story about a party he attended, given in honour of Salman Rushdie and where, as Baxter says, "I had the honour of being mistaken for myself!" Dylan Edwards, Murray-Orr and Baxter all knew Ivor for many years before joining him on the radio. Other guest performers had much shorter relationships with Ivor. Alison O'Kill appeared in three series, *A Stuggy Pren*, *Jelly Mountain* and *A Wet Handle*. She was joined in *Jelly Mountain* and *A Wet Handle* by another newcomer to Ivor's "repertory company," Beverley Crew. O'Kill was Neil Cargill's production assistant and, later, his broadcast assistant. Like the others, she had no background in drama: "I think that was the point," she said, "Ivor liked to find people that weren't trained, that had a natural feel." Ivor invited her to join *A Stuggy Pren*:

> I joined Neil just after he'd recorded *King Cutler* … Ivor came into the office … we got on really well and then when we had the next series, *A Stuggy Pren*, Ivor said he'd like me to take part, read some poems. That was how I got involved. When I did the first recording I was a little bit anxious. He was always lovely … I was really fond of him, but he liked things done a certain way … it was very much his programme.

Beverley Crew met Ivor in the 1990s, when she was organising events at the South Bank Centre. He invited her to take part in *Jelly Mountain*, which was recorded in Ivor's flat: "We were a completely disparate bunch: none of us was chosen for their acting skills. The worse we were, the happier he was …" She describes *Jelly Mountain* as "just funny, improbable, weird."

Ivor continued to appear on other radio shows, reading poems on *Poetry Now*, talking about his life and career to Ted Harrison on *Profile*, or speaking to his friend Craig Murray-Orr about "neighbours, art and English inhibitions" on *Ivor Meets Craig*, for example.[21] In 1996 Ivor joined presenter Paul Boateng M.P. on *Looking Forward to the Past*, engaging in "a light-hearted chat about history" with comedian Lee Hurst, writer and critic Sheridan Morley, and author Colin Dexter, the creator of Inspector Morse.[22]

For two series, *Ivor Cutler Has 15 Minutes in the Archives* and *Cutler the Lax*, Ivor created programmes using selections from the BBC radio archives. He did so with obvious relish, explaining "When I enter the archives I just send out my vibes and all the best stuff starts inching its way towards me, moving its hips like an octopus on a fishmonger's slab and whispering 'Take me, take me' …"[23] Ivor's archive selections encompassed classical music, education, rock and roll, jazz, charity and cheese. There's also the occasional personal insight, biographical detail or opinion – "my great-uncle was a crossing sweeper" he revealed (or made up) in *Cutler the Lax*; "From Rebecca West, to whom I am ever grateful, I culled the idea that religion is irrelevant to my spiritual life," he told listeners to *Ivor Cutler Has 15 Minutes in the Archives*. He also reminded listeners about noise reduction: "I should like to thank you

Ivor in Craig Murray-Orr's studio. (Courtesy of Craig Murray-Orr, photograph by Craig Murray-Orr.)

on behalf of your neighbours if, out of common decency, you played your radio so that no one could hear it but yourself. Here's a kiss."[24]

Ivor's selections were varied and esoteric. He played the national anthem of Kenya, followed it with a song from a group of Malaysian singers, then moved on to Shakespeare: "To the Bard, not a man I get along with but undoubtedly popular. Here is his famous speech about soft pencils, 2B or not 2B," he said, before playing an Esperanto version of the speech.[25] Sometimes there's a clear link between selections, at other times there's none. Ivor opens episode one of *Cutler the Lax* by telling listeners that he will begin with "Mozart's Moonlight Sonata" then plays "Shout for Joy" by boogie-woogie pianist Albert Ammons, claiming afterwards that he couldn't find the Mozart. Then Edna Peterman of Philadelphia speaks about a series of clubs which support a "home for the aged in Akron, Ohio." As soon as Edna Peterman has informed us that there are forty-eight of these clubs, "which doesn't necessarily follow that we have one in each state …" the interview clip ends and Ivor introduces his next selection. This time, it's a recording from the 1950s of a young man who "made a gramophone record. It sank like a stone and the man disappeared with it. He's probably now selling clothes in Shaftesbury Avenue." Who is this lost genius of British music? It turns out to be Ivor Cutler, performing "Mary is a Cow," although Ivor is self-effacing enough not to reveal the singer's identity and anyway, he's already moving on to a recorded interview with Professor Julian Huxley.

When Ivor was interviewed on radio, he could be guarded, open, cooperative, funny or tetchy. Much depended on the interviewer. A 1983 interview with John Walters, Peel's long-term producer, was generally good-natured, but halfway through Ivor accused Walters of being "very good at taking and twisting what I say. I don't mean in a nasty sense … Using the information I've given you, you put it together and it sounds slightly different from what I gave out." Bonhomie was quickly restored, however, and Ivor pointed out that he had "a great deal of respect and warmth" for Walters. When Walters asks "Is the Scotch Sitting Room a kind of parable about Scotch – or Scottish I better say," Ivor replies sharply, "No, it's Scotch actually."

"But a rather repressed, rather dour, childhood."

"No. I think it's a synthesis of a lot of things half-remembered from childhood or actual memories transmogrified."

Despite his declared respect and warmth, Ivor sounds cross and irritable for much of this interview, partly perhaps in response to Walters, or maybe because he's talking about his childhood and his relationship with his parents.[26] Elsewhere, Ivor took exception to a comment by Ned Sherrin about their first meeting in the offices of Box & Cox, when Sherrin referred to Ivor's clothes as being "vivid and eccentric." "No, they weren't," Ivor responded, "No, I don't think they're vivid and eccentric anyway."[27]

Ivor's friendliest radio interview is probably his 1995 meeting with Brian Morton, for Radio Scotland's *Sweet Inspiration*, a show which, according to Morton, aimed "to talk to people in many different walks of life who were united by music as a quite particular inspiration, which might be anything from the scientific to the spiritual." Morton and Ivor first met in the early 1970s and knew each other well. Although Morton feels that this friendship didn't come across in the programme, it may explain the relaxed interaction between them, which overcame Ivor's initial concerns about the studio environment. Morton remembers the interview as "hilarious, perhaps in a slightly 'you had to be there' way" – his description of the recording emphasises the unorthodox interviewer/interviewee relationship that Ivor engineered:

> We got into the studio, a tiny studio inside the technical area. The air conditioning was on quite high and Ivor immediately started to fuss: "Oh, I don't think I can stay in here. I've got a skin condition, it brings me out in a rash." So the interview was conducted with Ivor wearing two technician's brown dustcoats, and his legs up across mine. We were basically sitting as though we were a couple. And I've never known to this day … how much of it was done just to unsettle people.

Despite their friendship Ivor proved reluctant to respond to direct personal questions, but the experienced Morton managed to persuade him to do so: "I remember talking about my own background and my relationship with my father, and Ivor then talked about his own upbringing, how cold it was, how little interest anyone had shown in him and how he had retreated into himself quite early on." Morton describes Ivor as "a mischievous old bugger" and that sense of playfulness emerged once more as the interview ended:

> As we were leaving, one of the techies said "Take care" and Ivor had one of those carefully staged meltdowns. "I *hate* it when people say 'Take care'. It makes it sound as if I can't look after myself!" The guy couldn't quite work out whether it was a gag and kept a rather uneasy smile on his face as Ivor ranted a bit. Also I've no idea whether the "skin condition" that required protection from draughts was real or not. I do remember that when we went back out onto Langham Place, the wind was coming pretty much horizontally from Siberia and he seemed untroubled.

Ivor recorded his final session for John Peel, in Laurier Road, on 12 June 1998.[28] Andy Kershaw broadcast a session from Ivor on 2 November 2001, then broadcast some recordings from his recent show at the Lyric, Hammersmith, on 22 March 2002. A few months later, on 6 December, Kershaw broadcast a further selection of recordings from that concert, then a few days after his eightieth birthday Ivor appeared on *Poetry Please*, a Radio 4 programme of listeners' poetry requests. Roger McGough, Ivor's fellow poet and performer, presented. It was Ivor's final radio show.[29]

13 Long Players

By the time Ivor was becoming a regular and much-loved session guest on John Peel's radio shows, his early recording career was becoming something of a distant memory. Ivor may not have become the young man whose gramophone record "sank like a stone," as he told listeners to *Cutler the Lax*, but neither was he causing queues outside the country's record retailers. It had been over a decade since the release of *Ivor Cutler of Y'Hup* and even the Ivor Cutler Trio's *Ludo* was four years old. Peel's influence was strong, however, and the rock music press took notice.

After his brief relationship with *International Times*, Ivor's first major appearance in the rock press was Michael Watts's 1971 *Melody Maker* interview. It's an impressive mix of hyperbole, confusion and inaccuracy. Watts began by introducing his interviewee, who's pictured in his "Gospel Oak flat," as "a little scrubby-haired old man" – Ivor was forty-eight – originally from "the industrial area of Paisley." Despite his seemingly advanced age, he meets Watts's approval: "an ordinarily extraordinary man ... he never ceases to amaze. He is an original. He is a painter who is a film actor, an actor who is a musician, a musician who is a writer, a writer who is a poet, and a poet who is a teacher." According to Watts, he'd also released an album called *Life in a Scots [sic] Sitting Room*. It's a positive article, despite the inaccuracies, an insight into an artist who's becoming popular on the rock scene.[1] Ivor told Watts that he was busy recording an album for Dandelion, the record label which John Peel co-founded and which could have been an ideal home for Ivor's recordings, with a more than sympathetic Peel at the helm, a ready market among Peel's fans and the chance to be a labelmate of acts such as Bridget St John, Medicine Head and Stackwaddy. Whether or not it was recorded, the album never emerged.[2]

Virgin Records, not Dandelion, became Ivor's next label. A new label devoted to recording some of the more intriguing of the emerging rock talents

– Mike Oldfield's *Tubular Bells*, German bands Tangerine Dream and Faust, singer-songwriter Kevin Coyne – it was soon one of the hippest and most commercially successful labels in Britain. *Tubular Bells* sold millions of copies worldwide, becoming, in future label executive Jon Webster's phrase, "like a cash cow forever." It offered a level of financial security that allowed Virgin to sign acts that would never achieve huge sales, including Ivor, who released three albums on the label: *Dandruff*, *Velvet Donkey* and *Jammy Smears*. All three feature cover designs by Phyllis King, are credited solely to Ivor (although Phyllis performed her own stories and poems on them), feature episodes from *Life in a Scotch Sitting Room*, advertise Compendium Books in Camden as an outlet for Ivor's books and records, and contain over thirty tracks at a time when top-selling albums typically contained eleven or twelve songs at most.

Virgin released *Dandruff* in 1974. Ivor recorded the album at the Manor, Virgin's Oxfordshire recording studio, with engineer Tom Newman and was credited as producer as well as performer. Newman was an experienced producer and engineer, and had been involved in building and equipping the studio.[3] *Dandruff* includes "The Aimless Dawnrunner," from the 1966 book *Cockadoodledon't*, and eleven poems from *Many Flies Have Feathers*, as well as new work such as a short opening instrumental, "Solo on Mbira."[4] Apart from this track and a few on which Ivor plays harmonium, it's predominantly a spoken-word album. Phyllis wrote and performed seven poems as well as designing the cover, a medieval scene of a servant, broom in hand, sweeping up a pile of dandruff flakes from beneath the feet of a man who shakes his fist at the sky as an older man and a young girl look on, mystified. At least, that's my interpretation.

The back cover features two photographs. In one, Ivor sits and stares at the camera, his right hand resting upon his left, the legend beneath the picture reading "burned hand." In the second, Ivor and Phyllis sit side by side on a bench, neutral expressions on their faces. This time, the legend reads "oops." A sentence appears on the back cover and on both the labels on the record. It's a statement of a quandary and perhaps a subtitle as well: "What to do about dandruff: save it up, play it or give it away."

Dandruff contains forty-five tracks and has a running time of around forty-five minutes. This means the average track duration is just under sixty seconds, but there is a wide variation: "Face Like a Lemon," a love song from Ivor to someone who resembles a citrus fruit, lasts for three minutes and twenty seconds, while "If Everybody" is over in eight seconds. The timings given for other tracks overstate Ivor's activity: for example, "When I Entered" lasts for thirteen seconds, but Ivor stops talking after six seconds and the remaining seven offer nothing but silence. The two episodes from *Life in a Scotch Sitting Room* are the first to appear on record, four years after Ivor debuted the first episode on *Late Night Line-Up*. Ian MacDonald gave the album a brief but generally positive review in *New Musical Express*:

The subjects here are many, but the unifying mood is that of the summer. The undertow of menace or the overtow of comic cosmicity present in earlier Cutlerama … has been replaced by a sunny straightforwardness and a quicker, less dour delivery.[5]

"I Believe in Bugs" remains a favourite with Ivor's fans almost fifty years after *Dandruff*'s release, as do "I'm Walkin' to a Farm," "Trouble Trouble" and "Fremsley."

Two years later, Ivor released *Velvet Donkey*, an album with a mere thirty-one tracks squeezed into a running time of just under forty-seven minutes. Phyllis King's front cover design is a jolly, colourful, affair: brown and gold, with a bright red donkey in the centre. "He was calling it *Velvet Donkey* so I thought if that's the name of it I'd better draw a donkey," Phyllis recalls. Her back cover design, featuring the same red donkey only this time facing to the right rather than the left, declared the album's title to be *Velvey Donket* and included a Popularity Chart. The instructions were clear: "Play 'Velvet Donkey' to your friends, then write their names and ask them what they now think of you, out of 10. You will soon have a useful chart. E.g. Anna 8." *Velvet Donkey* contains some poems that had appeared elsewhere, notably "The Even Keel," published in *Transatlantic Review*, and "Birdswing," which appeared in *Free Reed: the concertina newsletter*.[6] As for Ivor's adventures in his sitting room, *Velvet Donkey* contains Episodes Two and Seven.

Velvet Donkey is one of Ivor's most popular albums (and my personal favourite) but it is at the centre of another of Ivor's arguments with the BBC about who could read his work on air. Alannah Hensler of the Copyright Department wrote to Ivor seeking permission to use "the words of the song Velvey Donket," to be read by an unnamed performer on BBC Scotland's *The Scotched Earth Show*. Oops. Ivor replied immediately, absolutely refusing to give permission for any other person to read his work and explaining to Hensler that there was no song or poem titled "Velvey Donket." The request was swiftly withdrawn.[7]

Ivor moved from the rural splendour of the Manor to the top floor of a house on Camden High Street, a short bike ride from Laurier Road, to record *Velvet Donkey* at Kaleidophon Studio with engineer David Vorhaus. Vorhaus's expertise was in electronic music – as part of White Noise he had already released two albums, *An Electric Storm* and *Concerto for Synthesizer* – but Ivor kept faith with acoustic instrumentation.[8] *Velvet Donkey* is more musical than *Dandruff*, with more songs and more harmonium, plus the added attraction of Fred Frith on viola. Frith is a long-standing Ivor Cutler fan, having first heard him when, as a young teenager, he "listened raptly" to *Monday Night at Home* and enjoyed his "eccentric radio presence." He first met Ivor in 1973, when he was a member of Henry Cow and Ivor supported the band at the London School of Economics. He remembers little of Ivor's performance that night, as he was busy getting ready for his own set, but one thing has stayed in his mind, talking with Ivor about his time in the RAF and discovering that he knew Morse code: "I asked him to make me a Morse code chart that I used to experiment with in a composition I was writing for the Ottawa Company. I still have the chart ... But nothing remains of the composition alas!"

A few months after the Henry Cow gig, Ivor and Frith made guest appearances on Robert Wyatt's *Rock Bottom*. Frith's contribution to the album was directly responsible for Ivor's invitation to him to contribute to *Velvet Donkey*. As Frith remembers, his was one of the final contributions to Wyatt's record: "By the time I was involved it was pretty much finished ... As far as I remember Ivor had already recorded his part and I came in and overdubbed the viola after he was done." However, "When Ivor heard my viola on *Rock Bottom* he was excited, it seemed to strike a chord, and he suggested we get together and try out some songs. I was of course equally excited to play with one of my childhood heroes."

Frith went for dinner at Ivor's flat, where Ivor showed him some of the songs he was working on. Frith was familiar with Kaleidophon, having recorded his own solo guitar album there in the previous year: he returned to the studio to play viola on "I Got No Common Sense," "Yellow Fly," "Nobody Knows," "Gee, Amn't I Lucky" and "Sleepy Old Snake":

> We recorded as much as possible in one take as far as I remember, it just fell into place. I think we agreed that the viola should not be hamming it up, it needed to sound more like someone who was trying their best and wasn't very good. Which was pretty much true of course! But this was more intuitive than planned ... Ivor gave me free rein to try it how I felt it. These so-called arrangements were spontaneous and improvised, and the "first take feeling" was critical to their success. Whether they were done together or with me overdubbing afterwards I can no longer clearly remember, probably both. I'm pretty sure "Common Sense" was overdubbed, but the others I'm not sure. I do remember both of us laughing quite a bit when we were done. And him unfailingly sending me a cut of whatever the songs earned from the PRS [the Performing Rights Society] for quite a few years afterwards, which was touching.

That conversation about Morse code and RAF service may have been the trigger for Ivor to write "Little Black Buzzer," a song based around a short passage of Morse code. The lyrics refer to Ivor being on top of the world, white-faced and cold-bummed, playing a message for an unidentified "you" on his little black buzzer. Phyllis King learnt Morse code as a child: "When we discovered we both knew it and really liked it he went to his cupboard and found these buzzers ... He'd sit on one side of the room and I'd be on the other side and we'd tap out messages."[9] This shared interest may be another starting point for the song.

One of Ivor's loveliest songs, "Yellow Fly," is a Cutler/Frith collaboration, the viola mimicking the erratic flight of the fly as it sings of its life, its hollow legs and its duties towards its queen. Ivor's delivery almost makes life as a yellow fly seem like a desirable way to spend your time on Earth. The album also includes Phyllis King's reading of her own poem, "Uneventful Day." It's a favourite of mine, a paean to the simple pleasures to be had from life:

> An uneventful day,
> no beauty
> touched my eyes.
> I didn't gaze on blossomed boughs
> against March skies,
> nor feel the warmth
> of winter sun,
> nor even talk to anyone.
> But, late that evening
> As I sat reading,
> I heard a daffodil
> Break its skin.

King's tale of "The Stranger" is the longest track on the album by far, at six minutes in length. It's also one of the oddest tracks on the record, which is saying something when the album is full of songs sung by flies, poems about a car crash or turning a cat into a hot water bottle, and strange tales of a Scottish childhood. *Music Week* recommended *Velvet Donkey* to "confirmed Cutlerists ... also to those who have never heard him," describing the album as "Cutler in good form." As a trade paper, *Music Week* marked each record out of three stars for sales potential rather than artistic merit. It gave *Velvet Donkey* one star.[10]

Jammy Smears was Ivor's final release for Virgin. Once again, David Vorhaus recorded the album at Kaleidophon. The front cover is wholly occupied by a photograph of Ivor in a pugilistic stance: hands raised and formed loosely into fists, naked from the waist up and sporting what might be pyjama bottoms, he stares straight at the camera as a speech bubble bearing the legend "Yours & oblig Ivor Cutler" emerges from his mouth. Prior to the album's release, Ivor was concerned about his choice of cover image: he referred to the photograph as "personal beefcake" and was not sure if it was "still in vogue."[11] The back cover, which Phyllis designed, includes an image of Ivor and Phyllis, arms around each other, sitting in his flat. Joyce Edwards took the photographs, or, to give her the credit as it appears on the sleeve, "Ivor Cutler's landlady, JOYCE EDWARDS, took the photographs." As with its predecessor, *Jammy Smears* has thirty-one tracks and lasts for around forty-five minutes. Phyllis King contributes six tracks: "Wasted Call" is another bizarre story in the vein of "The Stranger" while "Filcombe Cottage Dorset" and "Red Admiral" are linked, the butterfly of the second poem's title having flown to Wiltshire from the titular cottage of the first poem.

The harmonium makes regular appearances on *Jammy Smears* but Ivor's piano playing is an emphatic presence on a few songs, notably "Bicarbonate of Chicken," on which Ivor displays a fiercely attacking style of boogie-woogie, the punchy "Barabadabada," "Wooden Tree" and "Rubber Toy." The album contains another of Ivor's loveliest compositions, "Beautiful Cosmos," a song encapsulating a world in which two people live quietly but contentedly, meeting from time to time to talk of nothing, drink tea, eat sandwiches and, in the case of the singer, stare at a roll. The obvious interpretation for anyone familiar with Ivor and Phyllis's personal relationship at the time is that it's a love song from Ivor to Phyllis. It's highly likely, but as Phyllis says, it was never definite:

> Now about "Beautiful Cosmos". I too thought the song was about our relationship. That's about all I can say as Ivor didn't ever say, or I don't remember him saying, "This is a song about us". But he was writing it at a time when the relationship was good. Of course there were times when it wasn't a very "Beautiful Cosmos".

Jammy Smears brought Ivor one of his rare accolades, when it achieved a prize in the 1976 *Music Week* Awards. The trade magazine's major awards categories included Best Selling Album, Top Male Artist (Albums) and Top Songwriters: all three were suitable categories for Ivor and his work, but these awards went to *ABBA's Greatest Hits*, Demis Roussos, and the ABBA songwriting team of Björn Ulvaeus, Benny Andersson and Stig Anderson respectively. Ivor's award was less prestigious: the cover of *Jammy Smears* was highly commended in the Full Price Pop section of the Sleeve Design Awards, won by Deaf School's *2nd Honeymoon*.[12] Curiously, the award (an unassuming certificate) fails to credit Joyce Edwards or Phyllis King, crediting Robor, the company that printed the sleeve, instead. But it does justify Ivor's decision to go with the "personal beefcake."

Phyllis's involvement with Ivor's albums ended with *Jammy Smears*. Although she enjoyed designing the album covers, the act of recording didn't appeal: "I did enjoy the poetry readings. I didn't enjoy the recording sessions as much, I couldn't get used to the sound of my own voice. When I had to record LPs or on the radio I never felt I was very good and so I didn't feel very confident."

Such was Ivor's fame by this point that he was given an entry in the prestigious *International Who's Who in Music, and Musicians' Directory*. The reference work created some debate: Ivor, Joan Baez and George Melly were included among the ten thousand entries, but Thelonious Monk, John Lennon, Paul McCartney and Bob Dylan were absent. The directory doesn't give any information about its selection policy, but does note that each

John Knutas, Phyllis King and Ivor at Kew Gardens, mid-1980s. (Courtesy of John Knutas, photographer unknown.)

person listed was sent a copy of their entry for correction and approval. Ivor's entry notes that he has two sons and describes him as "Composer; Singer; Musician; Poet; Illustrator; Writer; Humorist; Teacher." It summarises his TV and radio appearances, lists some of his books and notes that he is a contributor to various journals and a member of Equity, the actors' union. Oddly, given the directory's focus on music, it only mentions Ivor's three Virgin albums, ignoring his Fontana and Decca releases. Many entries include hobbies (Melly's were trout fishing, and collecting old blues records and modern art) but Ivor's does not.[13]

An entry in a prestigious directory isn't everything, though: Virgin Records dropped Ivor from its roster after *Jammy Smears*. By 1976 the label was attempting to revamp, to ensure it remained relevant in a changing musical climate, which meant that some of its current artists had to go: "they were great, but they were never going to sell any records," according to Ken Berry, a Virgin executive at the time. Ivor was firmly within this great but not profit-making group and out he went. Within months, Virgin signed the Sex Pistols.[14]

Both of Ivor's parents died in the mid-1970s: Polly Cutler died in 1973 and her husband Jack died three years later. As Ivor explained, neither Polly nor Jack was too impressed with his achievements, giving him no more than a "lowland Scots" type of approval: "When I was starting on radio they'd say 'Why aren't you on the telly?' You know. I don't know what they wanted but I didn't have it."[15] Despite their lack of appreciation of their son's artistic achievements, he claimed that he kept in touch by holding imagined conversations with them: "I occasionally talk to [my parents] in Heaven, but they're usually busy playing cards." He gave Mark Espiner a taste of such a conversation: "'Dad, I'm doing a gig at the Festival Hall tonight.' 'Ivor, is that you?', he says. 'Just a minute, I'm in the middle of a hand' – he played bridge, you see." Cutler then puts on a falsetto voice: "'Oh, that's nice, Ivor. I hope you sell all the seats.'"[16]

After Virgin released him, Ivor was signed by EMI's progressive rock label, Harvest. Like Virgin, Harvest was one of the hippest record labels of the 1970s and, like Virgin, it had its own multi-million selling album, Pink Floyd's *Dark Side of the Moon*. Harvest played host to a couple of artists who can be seen as kindred spirits to Ivor, Kevin Ayers (ex-Soft Machine) and Syd Barrett (ex-Pink Floyd), but released just one Ivor Cutler album, *Life in a Scotch Sitting Room*. For anyone familiar with the stories from Ivor's concerts, Virgin albums or Peel sessions, the record held no surprises but *Music Week*'s anonymous reviewer gave the album two out of three for saleability. Ivor, wrote the reviewer, "is blessed with that curious style of black humour beloved by Glaswegians and Liverpudlians and even the Welsh." Acknowledging that Ivor was already well known, the review suggested that the album could be stocked anywhere, but especially "where the market is Scots/student/folk/comedy."[17]

Record Mirror's Robin Smith was a tougher judge. Giving the album just one star out of five (a rating of "Unbearable"), Smith claimed that Cutler was "more decipherable than Billy Connolly ...": a reference to their humour or their accents, a compliment or a criticism? The review went on "... his humour is lost on me. Cutler's one of those intellectual humorists, a clever person who you're meant to like." Smith was unimpressed by the audience's "forced laughter" and was clearly too savvy to be fooled by Ivor's "Wacky lines about Scottish life." Opening the review with a sporting comparison, he made it plain that neither Scottish humour nor Scottish tennis had much to offer the world, "Good Scots comedians are about as rare as good Scots tennis players ..." Smith wrote, which must make Ivor Cutler the Andy Murray of the stage. Given his many references to himself as a non-intellectual, Ivor would probably be wryly amused by Smith's insistence that he's an "intellectual humorist." Smith reviewed two other albums that week: Samantha Sang's *Emotion* (one star) and Marianne Faithfull's *Faithless* (one star).[18]

Ivor made no more records until 1983 when he signed to Rough Trade, releasing three albums for the label – *Privilege*, *Prince Ivor* and *Gruts* – over the next three years. Once again, Ivor was signed by one of the most important labels of its time, home to the Smiths, Aztec Camera and Ivor's old friend Robert Wyatt. In his role as presenter of Rough Trade's *Not Television* video, Ivor held the cover of the *Privilege* LP to the camera, tapped the cover image of himself as a small boy and asked, a touch inaccurately, "Who would have thought that this little fellow would have grown up to become a TV link man for HMV?"

Privilege is credited to Ivor Cutler and Linda Hirst and follows the pattern of Ivor's Virgin releases by programming lots of short tracks (thirty-eight in this case) in a running time of around forty-five minutes, including a couple of *Life in a Scotch Sitting Room* episodes. There are tracks that last less than thirty seconds, others that last more than three minutes, and a couple of "Jungle Tips," on dealing with killer bees and piranhas. There's also "Pass the Ball Jim," a song about playing football that Ivor dedicated to John Peel and which sounds like a song written by someone who's never played football. Ivor was singing this song with his pupils in the late 1970s, telling them that he'd been inspired to write it by watching some of the boys playing football on the school playground.[19] The title of the Cutler/Hirst duet, "I Love You but I Don't Know What I Mean," echoes Prince Charles's famous response in a TV interview on his 1981 engagement, "Whatever 'in love' means." Probably a co-incidence, but perhaps the Goon-loving Prince of Wales inspired Ivor's writing. The album closes with what would become Ivor's most-covered song, "Women of the World."

The cover design for *Privilege* is co-credited to Ivor and Martyn Lambert. The overall idea is simple: the front cover is dominated by the Cutler family photo, on a white background with a simple edging pattern; the rear cover uses the same edging, with black text on a white background, and features the by now routine list of Ivor's available books and the address of Compendium, which can supply them "in case of difficulty." It's further enlivened by Ivor's cartoon figures and a straightforward political statement contained in two speech bubbles. "Join the Ecology Party!" one figure exhorts, "Porritt for P.M.!" cries the second. The Ecology Party formed in 1975 and would become the Green Party ten years later.[20] Jonathon Porritt was one of its leading figures, co-chair of the party when *Privilege* was released, and, in the mid-1980s, another inhabitant of Laurier Road who became friends with Ivor. It seems that Ivor was a fan before becoming a friend: as Porritt remembers "I don't think he did tell me about the cover for his Privilege LP, which came out while I was still Co-Chair of the Green Party – or Ecology Party as it was then called! I'm not even sure I'd met him by then!" Ivor's support of environmental campaigns didn't stop him seeing some of the campaigners with a jaundiced eye: "Whale Badge" tells of a young hiker who cares deeply about the environment and her fellow creatures and wears a Save the Whale badge, but she still carries a leather satchel and micturates in a ditch with no thought for the millions of microscopic creatures she has destroyed with her urine.

Linda Hirst trained as a singer at the Guildhall School of Music and Drama and went on to become head of vocal studies at Trinity Laban Conservatoire.[21] By the time she joined Ivor for *Privilege* she had been a member of the Swingle Singers and had recorded with Pink Floyd (on *Atom Heart Mother*) and Frank Zappa (*200 Motels*), however, like many of Ivor's collaborators, she was a friend before she worked with him. In the early 1970s Hirst lived in a flat in Laurier Road and would often see Ivor in the area, meeting on the street or chatting about produce in local shops. One day, the flat she shared was broken into: "Ivor happened to be passing and I told him. He said 'Maybe I can help you'. He was fantastically good about insurance ... He helped me to fill in the forms, he was really concerned, he invited me up for tea. We became friends."

Hirst joined Ivor for tea at his flat on a few occasions, but the shift from friends to collaborators took ten years:

> He knew I was a singer ... Towards the end of my time in Laurier Road, around 1975 or maybe a year or two later, he said "Linda, would you like to make a record?" Of course, I said yes. I was singing Bach and Handel then, but I'd had other experience too ... It took us a while to get it going. My daughter was born in 1982 and I remember she was just a baby – or maybe not even born – when we recorded *Privilege*. I really had no idea what it was going to be like. I'd heard him a couple of times but really hardly at all. I was certainly not an Ivor Cutler devotee!

Hirst's words about being asked to record *Privilege* echo those Gill Lyons used about her invitation to play bass on *Ludo*: "He didn't look for a good singer to get on his record. He knew me and he knew I could sing and he knew my personality a bit, so he asked me. I love the way that happened. There was nothing hierarchical ..." She enjoyed the recording process, remembering it as efficient, professional and fun, with her tracks taking just two days to record: "I think we only did a few takes. I was pretty much a one-take person back then ... It was a joy." Although Hirst found Ivor to be funny, with "a wicked sense of humour as well as a multi-faceted one," once in the studio he was professional in his approach. "He took the recording process very, very seriously. He didn't muck about. He didn't make me feel subordinate. He left me room to think and to appreciate what he was doing and to respond to that. I was very much a co-artist, I was never just a supporting singer." As a co-artist, rather than a session performer, Hirst was paid royalties, but says she never earned much.

Privilege is a unique Ivor Cutler album in its involvement of two producers who also contribute musically. Steve Beresford and David Toop were experienced musicians and producers, and added a variety of sounds to the album – Toop is credited with alto flute, banjo, singing, percussion, effects and recordings of night insects from Amazonas, Venezuela; Beresford with euphonium, piano, trumpet, singing, percussion and effects. They recorded the album at London's Studio 80 with engineer Dave Hunt, having been invited to take on the task by Geoff Travis, the head of Rough Trade Records. "David and I were, at that point, production partners," Beresford recalls,

"We'd produced the Frank Chickens [a Japanese band that recorded six Peel sessions], worked with some African musicians, produced some hip-hop ... We worked together all the time: a production duo who also played instruments. When Geoff said 'Would you like to do an Ivor Cutler album?' we said 'Yeh! Absolutely." Beresford and Toop had also worked with Ivor's friend Lol Coxhill, the jazz musician, and Beresford believes that he already knew Linda Hirst through his sister Anna. Toop first encountered Ivor in 1968 or 1969, at Watford College of Art: "They had a very good programme of invited speakers and performers ... Ivor was one of them and [I have a] really strong memory of Ivor sitting at the harmonium, playing and singing."

Although they were enthusiastic about producing *Privilege*, they were aware that it would be no easy task. Toop's experience of Ivor's Watford appearance gave him an insight into potential problems:

> Two students came in late ... he just stopped and looked at them with this really terrifying expression. He said something intimidating. They both looked as if they wanted the floor to open and scuttled to their seats. It was really shocking ... and it gave me a strong sense of Ivor's personality, that lack of compromise. He was a small man, but he could be intimidating and severe.

Toop and Beresford were in a band called Alterations, which Toop describes as "a pretty noisy improvising quartet using amplified instruments" although Beresford says it was "discordant, but not that loud." Because he would be working with the pair, Ivor went to an Alterations gig: "Afterwards," says Toop, "we spoke with him and he had bouquets of toilet paper sticking out of his ears. He more or less said to us that he didn't hear anything because as soon as it started he'd stuffed his ears."

Toop began the recording sessions with the image of Ivor at the Watford gig in his mind: "It was quite useful, because I knew he could do that. He was tricky to work with because he didn't want anything changed, anything added. The question for me and Steve was 'Why are we here?' particularly with the two of us working together." His memory of the sessions, despite Travis's support, is that they were "difficult." As George Martin, Piers Plowright and others had discovered, once Ivor was clear about what he wanted, there was little chance of changing his mind. This was difficult for a pair of producers who were used to experimenting. "We used to get excited in the studio, trying different things, different sounds," Toop says, "With Ivor it was Puritanism. You couldn't do anything ... I wouldn't say it was an unhappy experience. It was difficult."

Prior to entering the studio, the producers decided that while they had no intention of altering Ivor's words, they were keen to change previous albums' reliance on numerous short tracks. Beresford remembers:

We were quite keen on doing something that was a little bit longer … by perhaps repeating a chorus or doing a little instrumental. We got tiny concessions – he would maybe play four bars more at the end, but no repeating of choruses. We did point out that choruses were repeated on many nice pop songs, Hoagy Carmichael, the Beatles. That didn't have any effect at all.

Eventually, Beresford and Toop managed to gain a few small concessions from Ivor. Beresford added a piano overdub to one song: "I think I played maybe three notes, and Ivor said it was 'virtuoso minimalism' or something. So there were tiny, tiny, things that we were allowed to add. But all those were hard-won." In what was possibly their major victory, they managed to persuade Ivor to perform one song in a laid-back, Hoagy Carmichael style. On "Old Black Dog," as Toop recalls, "I played banjo, Ivor played piano and Steve played drums, I think. The idea was that Southern, back porch, lazy feel and we managed to get Ivor to go along with it."

The recording sessions were over in three or four days: Toop calls the project "a low-budget record. There was no need for it to be anything else." It was enough time for Toop to get annoyed occasionally, but once recording was over the post-production phase was more straightforward. Rough Trade decided to release a single: on 13 August, *Music Week* announced that it would be "Women of the World," with "Counting Song," about the six-fingered woman with a liking for radioactive material, on the B-side. The article explained that the A-side was "a plea for the reins of world power to be put in safe hands – female hands." The following week, the magazine's Tony Jasper briefly reviewed the A-side, referring to "Simplistic lyrics about women saving the world … but a certain lady is not for consideration as pithy end comment makes clear."[22] Years later, Graeme Virtue helpfully described "Women of the World" as "a strident song about overturning the patriarchy to subvert a global apocalypse," which perhaps underplays its singalong quality.[23]

Toop calls "Women of the World" "a strange sort of song in relation to Thatcherism. [Ivor] hated Thatcher: it depended what kind of women would take over … It had a peculiar atmosphere, slightly pious. It seemed to exist out of time … like a throwback, but also something new." Neither Beresford nor Toop expected a chart hit, as Beresford remembers, "but we thought it might sell OK. I suppose it's more anthemic than the other tracks." Hirst still remembers the song fondly: "I like it a lot, I've sung it to a lot of people."

A few months before the release of *Privilege*, Ivor revealed that the Greenham Common women's protest was the inspiration behind "Women of the World," describing the protest as politically the most exciting thing he'd ever known, an event which "made me realise that the sooner men were put to one side and women took over the better." A few days after the protest came to his notice, Ivor woke in the night and wrote a song: "I discovered it was a song about the Greenham Common women …"[24] Between April and June

1982, Britain and Argentina fought each other in the Falklands War, giving Ivor another reason to hate Thatcher. Introducing "Home is the Sailor" Ivor says, with reference to the conflict, "Anent the nonsense in the South Atlantic in '82, here's a useful song." It's not a useful song, it's a daft song. Is this the dying sailor home from the sea, as Robert Louis Stevenson wrote?[25] No, this sailor is merely home from the shops, carrying groceries. There's no romance or heroism in Ivor's lyrics, just the mundane day-to-day of shopping, going to the pub and eating crisps.

From its back cover exhortation to join the Ecology Party, to songs and poems about the environment, conflict, the by-products of the nuclear industry and the failure of men to rule the world wisely, *Privilege* is Ivor's most obviously political album. Ivor puts his messages across directly in some cases, more discretely in others, but it's clear that these are issues he cares about.

Before any further Rough Trade albums could appear, Virgin Records made its own trio of Ivor Cutler LPs available as part of a mid-priced set of re-releases. Jon Webster had worked in Virgin's record shops when the label deleted Ivor's albums and by the early 1980s he was its head of marketing. He asked the head of production why Ivor's records were no longer available and was told "They don't sell." "Well," Webster replied, "they don't sell because you're not making any!" Webster decided that they were worth re-releasing, as did his boss, label head Simon Draper. "I'll be perfectly honest," Webster admits, "I was not a big fan. I knew him from Peel but I hadn't really listened to lots of it." However, the re-issue process was relatively inexpensive and Ivor, as Webster puts it, "was gigging all the time and he was in the media. He was always popping up in different places," so it made good economic sense to include his albums in the mid-price series.

Jammy Smears appeared first, followed by *Dandruff*. *Velvet Donkey* was scheduled to appear along with *Dandruff*, but Webster was unable to find the sleeve films, the artwork from the original release that was necessary to print new copies of the sleeve, and so the album's release was delayed. One day, the receptionist called Webster, who was now the label's general manager. As Webster recalls, the receptionist said "Jon, there's a man to see you."

"Who is he?"

"I don't know, but he's got a bike."

"What's his name?"

"Ivor something."

"Oh, God! It must be Ivor Cutler!"

Ivor arrived with an invoice for royalties from the reissues of the first two LPs – at that time, artists were informed about royalties then had to supply an invoice to claim them. Webster explained to him that sleeve films were missing: "That's okay," said Ivor, "I'll ask Phyllis to do another one." Phyllis painted a new version of the sleeve and the LP was reissued.

Ivor's remaining two albums on Rough Trade deviate markedly from the pattern he followed on *Privilege* and his three Virgin albums. For *Gruts*, released in May 1986, Ivor re-recorded a mix of stories and songs from his first decade as a performer. The album was released to coincide with the re-publication of the book of the same name, which had itself first appeared in 1962, and could be considered as a "Best Of" compilation, revisiting songs such as "Mud," "I'm Happy" and "Darling, Will You Marry Me Twice" along with favourite stories like "Egg Meat," "The Dirty Dinner" and "Gruts for Tea." *Music Week* was enthusiastic about the album, awarding it a red tick and advising dealers to stock it. The age of the works "matters not a jot, operating as they do independently of everything outside his wantonly charismatic imagination."[26]

Prince Ivor, released in November 1986, is Ivor's only double album. Previous form would suggest a record of at least sixty tracks, but the four sides offer just twelve. What's more, none of them is less than four minutes long and two of them exceed seventeen minutes. All of them had already been broadcast on BBC radio, for *Prince Ivor* is a compilation of Ivor's work with Piers Plowright. It opens with *Silence*, from 1979, goes on to *Ivor Cutler and ...*, then *... Is Approached by Ivor Cutler*, and closes with 1983's *Prince Ivor*. Ivor's dedication reads, "For Piers Plowright, but for whom ..." The front cover features another of Joyce Edwards's photographs of Ivor, the back cover features a joke in Hebrew (with helpful notes from Ivor regarding Ashkenazi pronunciation). When *Music Week* announced the album's release at the beginning of November it referred to Ivor as "That strange bare chested person," a reference, presumably, to the beefcake cover of *Jammy Smears*.[27] Jane Wilkes reviewed the album positively, recommending its "riotously amusing mind puzzles" but noting that Radio 3 may have reigned-in some of Ivor's ideas, for his "grotesque observations are strangely absent."[28] By the end of November, *Music Week* reported that *Prince Ivor*, *Stupidity Maketh the Man* by Depraved and *Free Dirt* by Died Pretty were "bubbling under" the independent album chart.[29] Sadly, *Prince Ivor* never bubbled any higher.

Rough Trade released no more Ivor Cutler recordings, but a set of his Peel session tracks appeared on Strange Fruit in 1989. *The Peel Sessions: Ivor Cutler* was an EP, Ivor's first since 1961's *Get Away from the Wall*, and consisted of the pieces Ivor recorded in Maida Vale on 10 August 1977. It was one of Ivor's busier sessions, with fourteen pieces including four "Jungle Tips" and two episodes from *Life in a Scotch Sitting Room*.

A new decade brought Ivor to Creation Records, the home of Oasis and Primal Scream. Ivor joined Creation towards the end of the 1990s and released *A Wet Handle* and *A Flat Man*, his first albums on compact disc. The albums were named after two of Ivor's poetry collections: Arc Publications had published *A Wet Handle* just a year before the album of the same name appeared, but *A Flat Man* dated from 1977, so Arc reissued the collection to coincide with the release of this album. Ivor hadn't released an album of new material for ten years and when Ted Harrison interviewed him for *The Times*

Magazine he referred to the Creation signing as a "relaunch" which would introduce Ivor to a new generation.[30]

Alan McGee, the head of Creation, compared Ivor to Noel Gallagher of Oasis, seeing them both as "maverick, eccentric characters." After ten years without a recording contract, Ivor was something of an unknown to the new bands on the label and McGee recalled that no one at Creation knew who he was, apart from Glasgow rockers Primal Scream. Some people, McGee said, thought he was the cleaner. Ivor met Noel and Liam Gallagher, and decided to pin badges on both of them: according to McGee, the rock stars "were looking at this old age pensioner" and wondering what he was up to.[31] Ivor was equally bemused by the music Oasis was making, deciding that what he heard "wasn't for me at all. When it comes to that kind of music, I'll stick to the Beatles."[32]

Compact disc technology increased the potential length of an album from the LP's average twenty minutes per side to over seventy minutes total running time. *A Wet Handle* made the most of the extended running time as Ivor reverted to the short pieces of *Dandruff* and *Jammy Smears*: the new recording contained eighty-three tracks. *A Wet Handle* and the book of the same name have almost identical contents and to confuse matters further, *A Wet Handle* is the name of Ivor's five-part radio series broadcast on Radio 3 in June of 1997. *A Wet Handle* is a solo album: the cover notes declare "Poetry & music sung, played on harmonium, spoken, composed & drawings drawn by Ivor Cutler."

A year later, Creation released *A Flat Man*. Once again, it's a solo album, with Ivor credited with all poems, compositions, vocals, instruments (harmonium, mbira and "sundry other Nigerian ones" according to the notes) and drawings. The cover is dominated by Katrina Lithgow's portrait of Ivor wearing a white vest and a flat cap, with the title written below, the "F" printed in reverse. The album features forty-eight tracks, lasting for between nineteen seconds and two minutes, with the exception of the lengthier "Ep. 1. Doing the Bathroom."

In *The Times*, Veena Virdi gave *A Flat Man* eight out of ten, calling it "superb … [with] quirky, Edward Lear-like ditties that veer from the dotty and bizarre to the absolutely horrific."[33] Reviewing the re-release in 2008, Graham Bent of *Record Collector* was equally complimentary, writing that the album was "stamped with Ivor's trademark obsessions. As ever mixing the banal and the fantastical with the supreme free-association skills of a master surrealist."[34] Ivor opens the album by stating its title, then begins "A Bubble or Two," a sombre tale of a mother's suicide and a father's abandonment of his son (also, perhaps, by suicide) that still manages to fit in a few laugh-out-loud jokes. Elsewhere, Ivor blows some fine raspberries on "What Have You Got?," mentions raspberries and other fruit on "Jam" and tells the cautionary tale of what happened when "I Ate a Lady's Bun." The material on *A Flat Man* covers almost all of Ivor's career: "Shoes" was the poem that first alerted me to Ivor's existence back in 1971.

"Ep. 1. Doing the Bathroom" is a *Life in a Scotch Sitting Room* type of tale. Father, mother, young Ivor, a big sister, middens, mince, pineapple chunks, juice, sudden violence and unhygienic activity all come together in a story of everyday family goings-on. The track begs the question: if this is episode one, did Ivor plan a series of episodes, or give the series a title, or even write a few? Further episodes did not arrive, despite a report in 2000 that Ivor was signing to McGee's new label, Poptones. "Ep. 1 Doing the Bathroom" is the final track on the final album to appear during Ivor's life.[35]

14 Ivor for Hire

Was it possible to hire Ivor Cutler? It was certainly possible to invite him to do something – an interview, a radio show, a charity event or a recording – and he might accept the invitation, but Ivor was never a "celebrity for hire." With his immediately recognisable voice and distinctive visual presence, he was an obvious candidate to front an advertising campaign, but he wasn't interested. Chat shows seem like another obvious environment for Ivor, with his way with words and his extensive collection of poems and stories, but he never became a chat show regular like Kenneth Williams or Billy Connolly. On his own records, radio shows or gigs – even when he was performing as a supporting artist – he had a high degree of control, but being a guest in someone else's creation, a part of someone else's artistic vision, was a different matter.

"Cutler could bring pleasure to millions as another talking head on the endless round of chat shows, but you can be sure he rather relishes his obscurity," wrote John Best in *Music Week*.[1] John Knutas was present at the Laurier Road flat one Thursday afternoon in the mid-1990s when Ivor received a phone call: "Ivor answered with his customary 'Yes', listened for a moment, then said 'No, I'm sorry, but ...', listened some more, said 'I'm afraid I can't do that' or something of similar content, and hung up." Ivor explained that a BBC TV producer was inviting him to appear on a talk show on the following Saturday night. Knutas watched the show when it was broadcast and recalls, "when Ivor had backed out, the next celebrity the BBC had called (and gotten to the studio) was Rod Stewart." For Knutas, this story said something about Ivor's "celebrity status": if you can't get Ivor Cutler, get Rod Stewart!

Ivor's refusal to appear might be taken to support Best's contention that he enjoyed his obscurity, but Ivor's willingness to accept other invitations suggests otherwise: and can someone who recorded so many radio sessions and shows, and sold out the Queen Elizabeth Hall more than once, really be labelled "obscure"? Ned Sherrin proposed that describing Ivor as a "cult" was more appropriate: "Ivor was highly individual and highly creative, but he was an oddball, possibly unique. And unique doesn't get a lot of followers. Unique is something special ... Ivor fans are the ultimate cult. That's the best word to apply to Ivor, I think, cult."[2] It may be a suitable description, but it's not one Ivor was happy with: "The first time I heard it I thought 'Wow! Cult!' but I have since realised that in the business 'cult figure' means a failure, unable to reach the dizzy heights to which big stars belong."[3]

Whether he was a cult, a celebrity or something in between, Ivor's level of fame, coupled with his distinct personality, voice and image, made him a popular guest columnist in magazines and newspapers. In an early guest appearance, Ivor contributed a "Blind Date" column to *Melody Maker*.[4] The premise is simple: take a musician, put them in a room, play them a selection of music without revealing who is performing, and ask them for comments. Some musicians will play it safe, not wishing to upset their peers, but no one asked Ivor in the expectation of bland ideas and faint praise. Ivor gave praise where he felt it was due – to John Cale and Terry Riley's "Hall of Mirrors in the Palace of Versailles," which he called great, fantastic, a tour-de-force, and to Soft Machine's "Fletcher's Blemish," a "very respectable sound." He was less enamoured of Third World War's "MI5's Alive," which he listened to with his head in his hands: nice music to dance to, but "You can hear the gimmicks ... why don't they bring his voice forward over the noise? Oops! Sorry, I didn't mean that. Instruments, I should have said." He was not happy with "The Falconer" by Nico, a fellow harmonium player. The harmonium was amplified, which made him "very irritated" although he liked her voice and felt that the track was "not the one to do her justice." He reserved his most vitriolic comments for "Sister Morphine" by the Rolling Stones: "Oh it's such crap after [Cale and Riley]! This is so corny, so commercial, so empty and so insincere ... The BBC make such a big thing when the Rolling Stones are on television. I saw it with my kids and they were so excited. I couldn't see why."

The Wire called its blind date column "Invisible Jukebox," but the premise was the same. When Ivor was the column's guest contributor he had the chance to comment on jazz and contemporary artists that might be more to his taste than the selection of music offered by *Melody Maker*. He was pleased with Thelonious Monk's "Crepuscule with Nellie" – "I love him dearly," he said of Monk and declared that the music "gives you hope for the world" – but a spoken word track by Cecil Taylor left him unimpressed, telling his interviewer "There's nothing there for me."[5]

Ivor was a reliably original contributor to "Questions & Answers" columns of one sort or another. One of the most unusual of these was the weekly "My Top Ten" published in Newcastle's *The Journal*, where invited contributors offered a top ten and discussed the reasons for their choices. The newspaper invited Ivor to contribute a top ten and journalist Tony Jones truthfully, if naively, confessed that "We didn't know what to expect." Ivor submitted his list, but refused to be drawn on his reasons for selecting his top ten and so the newspaper felt unable to print his contribution in the usual Saturday slot. Instead, it printed the list in Jones's "Midweek" column. Ivor chose to submit his top ten animals, hoping that it would prove "of interest and pert":

1. Kiwi
2. Echidna
3. Slender loris
4. Boatbill
5. Springhaas
6. Armadillo
7. Rock hyrax
8. Stilt
9. Gannet
10. Degu.[6]

In the *New Musical Express* Ivor offered a few more lists. His list of favourite books included works by Toni Morrison and Asa Benveniste, as well as both of Phyllis King's poetry books, *Dust* and *Close Views*. His "Likes" included fresh air, natural courtesy, and silence. His "Hates" included commercials, parasites, PR, and racists. Under "TV Programmes" he stated "Threw my telly out years ago." His list of "Sex Symbols" consisted of Karl Malden, Oscar Homolka, Oliver Hardy and Albert Einstein: Homolka and Malden both appear in *Billion Dollar Brain*, so Ivor may well have awarded them sex symbol status after meeting them on set.[7]

Ivor made few guest appearances on recordings, but each was memorable in its own way. When he was beginning to acquire new fans through his Peel sessions, Ivor guested on Neil Ardley's 1972 album, *A Symphony of Amaranths*. Ardley gathered together a large jazz orchestra for the record, including Stan Tracey on piano, Karl Jenkins (later a member of Soft Machine), on electric piano and *Ambit's* music director, Henry Lowther, on trumpet.[8] Ivor's contribution was not to the title track, but to the track that opened side two of the original vinyl LP, Edward Lear's "The Dong with a Luminous Nose." Accompanied by what neilardley.com describes as "an unusual chamber orchestra," Ivor intones the words in a dull monotone but with utmost seriousness: after all, this is the tale of a love lost, a lover ditched by a fickle other, a Dong forced to develop a luminous nose in an effort to trace the Jumbly Girl who's up and left him. *A Symphony of Amaranths* received mixed reviews on release and on its re-issue in 2012, with Ivor's contribution dividing critics' opinions. Chris Parker called Ivor's "eccentric recital … maddeningly arch."[9] Dave Gelly, a jazz journalist as well as the album's glockenspiel player, called Ardley's decision to offer Ivor his guest spot "brilliant" and described Ivor's sound as a "solemn, lugubrious, McGonagall voice." To Jonathan Coe, Ivor narrated with "lugubrious glee."[10] Listening to the recording fifty years after its first release, it strikes me as one of Ivor's more mundane recordings, with hardly a jot of "eccentricity" to be seen. It's rather a forgotten corner of Ivor's career: obituaries didn't mention it, interviewers rarely if ever asked about it and I could find no evidence of Ivor ever speaking about it.

In sharp contrast, Ivor's guest appearance on *Rock Bottom*, his friend Robert Wyatt's 1974 album, is often and happily remembered.[11] Ivor was extremely fond of Wyatt: he spoke of him as "my chum ... the most intelligent man I've ever met. After I've had a session with him I have to wait a fortnight before I can go back again because my brain has to digest all that took place."[12] Ivor appears on "Little Red Riding Hood Hit the Road" and "Little Red Robin Hood Hit the Road." He's in good company. As well as Wyatt and bassist Richard Sinclair, who play on both tracks, he's joined by trumpeter Mongezi Feza on "Little Red Riding Hood Hit the Road" and by drummer Laurie Allen, viola player Fred Frith and guitarist Mike Oldfield on "Little Red Robin Hood Hit the Road." Ivor recites Wyatt's words on both songs. His contribution to "Little Red Riding Hood Hit the Road" is brief and buried beneath Feza's frenetic trumpet playing. It consists of five lines which Ivor delivers with a staccato attack, almost spitting out the words. On "Little Red Robin Hood Hit the Road" Ivor's vocal is upfront, his delivery slower and more considered, each of the dozen lines spoken crisply, with a sense of menace and violence. It begins

> I fight with the handle of my little brown broom
> I pull out the wires of the telephone
> I hurt in the head, and I hurt in the aching bone
> Now I smash up the telly with remains of the broken phone ...

Although they were already friends, when Wyatt invited Ivor to be on *Rock Bottom* he wasn't aware of how rare an Ivor Cutler guest appearance was: "I didn't realise at the time that Ivor did not, as a rule, do stuff by other people, and that it was therefore an even greater honour that he accepted my invitation," he recalls, "Thank heavens that he did – his contribution gave me the PERFECT 'finale' for that record."

In 1980, an act called Vogel released a single. On one side was "Guten Morgen," on the other was "Arschloch," featuring Ivor's vocal.[13] Even a cursory knowledge of German can enable the curious listener to translate the title. Robert Vogel, credited as the sole songwriter, was a studio engineer at Sunrise Studio in Kirchberg, Switzerland, and the song was first released on the studio's Sunrise label. Chris Cutler (no relation to Ivor) met Vogel when he was recording at Sunrise with the Art Bears, a band that also included Fred Frith. He heard the track, liked it and released it on his own label, Recommended Records. Sunrise Studio's founder, Etienne Conod, calls Vogel "a very gifted sound person and musician," and believes that Vogel recorded the basic backing track at home, before joining Sunrise: "He told me he was fascinated with

Ivor Cutler's voice," Conod recalls, "The sound of it and perhaps the aura. So one day he went to England, met up with Ivor, and had him say the words." Over a droning, repetitive, electronic riff Ivor intones a downbeat lyric bereft of hope, only his brief cackle in the closing seconds lifting the mood above despair. The Vogel/Ivor Cutler partnership is an unlikely one, but it works: Ivor's doom-laden narration has the drama that his Dong narration lacks, even if his voice is sometimes overwhelmed by Vogel's backing.

In the same year, Ivor contributed to a compilation of tracks known as *Miniatures: A Sequence of Fifty-one Tiny Masterpieces Edited by Morgan Fisher*. In his sleeve notes, Fisher, a musician who had been a member of Love Affair and Mott the Hoople among others, described how he invited "a highly personal selection of creative artistes" to contribute pieces with a maximum length of sixty seconds.[14] The artists included Robert Wyatt, Neil Innes, Fred Frith, Lol Coxhill and Bob Cobbing. Ivor contributed "Brooch Boat," a part-spoken, part-sung, sixty-second story with harmonium accompaniment.

Some performers make a career out of covering other people's songs, but a discussion of Ivor's recorded cover versions is by necessity brief as I am only aware of one: on the 1993 album *The World is a Wonderful Place*, Ivor intones Richard Thompson's "Wheely Down" from Thompson's first solo album, *Henry the Human Fly*.[15] *The World is a Wonderful Place* is a charity album on which a range of performers – Tom Robinson, Victoria Williams and Peter Blegvad among them – cover Thompson's compositions. "Wheely Down" is a duo performance, with Ivor reciting the lyrics and Ian Kearey (previously with The Oyster Band) playing bass, banjimer (a banjo/dulcimer hybrid) and harmonium. Once again, there's a link to Bruce Lacey: Fairport Convention recorded "Mr Lacey," a song about him written by bassist Ashley Hutchings, in late 1968 when Thompson was the band's lead guitarist. Lacey was present in the studio, "kneeling in the corner surrounded by his pieces of equipment, saying 'now' at the appropriate moment."[16]

It was just as unusual to find Ivor performing the work of other poets, but he did so in 1996 at his favourite bookshop, Compendium, as part of a celebration of the poetry of A. C. Jacobs.[17] Jacobs grew up in Glasgow's Jewish community: in its review of Jacobs's *A Bit of Dialect*, the *Jewish Chronicle* described his poetry as "[continuing] its exploratory probes in that Scots-Jewish accent one also finds in the zany poems of Ivor Cutler" and referred to Jacobs and Ivor as "kindred spirits."[18]

Ivor put his readily identifiable voice to another use, as the narrator of animated films created by students. The British Film Institute credits Ivor with narrating two films, *Woodpecker and the Acorn Tree*, directed by Lisa Cousins in 1988, and a 1986 animation by Ronald Macrae.[19] During his animation course at West Surrey College of Art and Design, Macrae was given the brief to produce a film on "The Family." As a fan of Ivor's, he decided that an episode of *Life in a Scotch Sitting Room* would be an ideal fit for the brief. His tutor knew Ivor and put animator and artist in touch with each other (according to Macrae, previous students had already worked with Ivor). Macrae phoned Ivor and asked if he would agree to being recorded reading an episode.

Macrae decided to base his animation on Episode Eighteen, in which Ivor burns his jacket pocket lining and receives a slap from his mother "that banged my head against my kind sister's." In Macrae's four-and-a-half-minute animation the background is monochrome, with simple, line-drawn furnishings and kitchen utensils. The family members – dour, hard-faced and angry adults, worried-looking children, and a dog – are rendered in colour. "Ivor" wears a dark grey jacket and sports a crewcut: his kind sister wears a blue dress and ties her hair in pigtails. Ivor reads the story to the accompaniment of his harmonium (Macrae's original intention was to use music by Robert Wyatt and Viv Stanshall, but cost and copyright issues prevented this). Macrae was worried that Ivor might be difficult to work with, but found him "very entertaining" and Ivor gave him some stickies, including one that read "Patella Hammers Where Are You?" As for the narration, Macrae remembers Ivor's timing as being "so exact. I realised when I recorded him that I couldn't edit." In the end, Macrae added one short pause to the recording to ensure an exact fit with the visuals.

Ivor may have been denied a university education, but Oxbridge students invited him to their unions to join in with a few debates. In 1962, Ivor took part in a Cambridge Union debate. Three minutes of his speech were broadcast on the BBC Home Service show, *Don't Look Now*, and Ivor thought that there was enough material in his speech for a special programme, suggesting this to the BBC and noting that his speech had elicited "11 rounds of applause, 153 laughs and 2 boos." Perhaps that was two boos too many: his suggestion was ignored.[20] For Easter Term 1970, Cambridge Union Society invited Ivor to join in the "Funny Debate" titled "Don't Let the Bastards Grind You Down" and credited him as "Mr Ivor Cutler of 'Y'Hup'." He took part along with satirist and *Private Eye* contributor John Wells, and jazz musician and composer John Dankworth. He returned for the 1975 Michaelmas Term Presidential Debate, billed as "An Evening of Reactionary Humour" and titled "Fings Ain't Wot They Used to Be." The debate featured Peter Bazalgette, the Union's retiring president and later a television executive, TV presenter Esther Rantzen, and Ivor's friend and fellow musician Ron Geesin.[21] Oxford Union followed suit a year later, inviting Ivor to speak in a debate titled "This House Would Rather be Good Looking than Good." Revealing the invitation in "8 Days a Week," Ivor wondered on which side he would be asked to speak.[22]

"8 Days a Week" – named after the Beatles song – was a popular *Melody Maker* column in which a well-known musician wrote about a week in their life. For the most part, Ivor reported on a mundane week: he sent some stickies to Robert Wyatt, discussed an idea for new shows with Phyllis King, and travelled by bus to an exhibition. Thursday was the most eventful day:

Tried a new shampoo, heavily advertised. My poached egg fell into the sink as I drained off the water ... I gingerly rinsed the hot egg and ate it with burned toast. I hope I shall not die. Injured – whiplash – in a bus crash, I wrote to London Transport suggesting how much compensation I ought to receive, as the pain is in my hands and I am a keyboard man.

Thursday was also the day when he received the proofs of *The Animal House*, his new book for children. His reaction was a mixture of pleasure and a hint of tetchiness: "It's a fine book, but they have made Helen Oxenbury the illustrator's name twice the size of mine. I know why but I wonder whether it is valid, and whether I'm angry or enjoying the sensation." On Saturday, Ivor went to a performance by Brazilian dancers. It featured plenty of nakedness, "which I was obliged to enjoy hypocritically, as I prefer nakedness in private." He spent time on Sunday with his nineteen-year-old son, Dan, watching teenage girls racing on Parliament Hill: "The vibes were sweet ..." Dan went home wearing his father's "posh" watch. "I'll bet the bugger is laughing his head off at my discomfiture," wrote Ivor.

When Ivor took over the *Weekend Guardian*'s "Diary" column, he took the chance to vent his anger at Camden council and to discuss, as the column's title revealed, "Trouble with Marmalade."[23] Ivor was attending a ceramics class – "I've spent my life going to evening classes" – but it was in danger of being closed because it attracted too few students: "How the hell are we supposed to be creative, waiting for the counter? ... If it were a Tory council I could understand. But Socialists!" Ivor made many objects in the class, often giving them to friends. He also enjoyed the class for another reason, telling Neil Cargill that "the women – and they were all women – found his presence there bewildering, but exciting." Ivor enjoyed generating such a response, real or imagined, in life or in works such as "The Specific Sundry," in which, after annoying a shopkeeper with his desire to browse the shop's sundries collection, he leaves the premises and jumps on a bus, "for women to admire my agility."[24]

Ivor's marmalade problems seem insignificant in comparison to the council's threat to his ceramics class. A lover of good marmalade, he declared himself "spoiled by a woman who made a thick, chunky, one." The unnamed woman was "no longer available" and so Ivor was on the search for a suitable replacement. His search ended in triumph when he discovered a new, three-fruit, marmalade somewhere in Camden Town. As to the identity of the mystery woman, Phyllis King is the likeliest candidate. Phyllis recalls "I did make a thick chunky marmalade (with demerara sugar and very good) and Ivor did like it. However he did have a few friends who also made marmalade. He may have told them he liked theirs too BUT I'm sure he liked mine best!" Ivor ended the column with a homage to "my best correspondent," John Knutas.

In 1992 *Scotland on Sunday* offered Ivor a regular column in its magazine. Alastair McKay was working for *Scotland on Sunday* at the time and Ivor contacted him in response to the idea, expressing some concern about his ability to produce work to a deadline as well as outlining his plans for the column, which included combining poems and drawings.[25] Ivor attached an address label to the bottom of the postcard. It read "iuop cvtlep, opsimath." *Scotland on Sunday* appeared each week but the magazine supplement was only published on a monthly basis, which meant that Ivor wasn't put under pressure to produce a new article every few days. In each column Ivor's name was clearly displayed in large uppercase print, accompanied by a title, but otherwise the format varied. Ivor's photograph – a head and shoulders, looking directly and unsmilingly at the camera – might appear or it might not; some columns were printed in the magazine's standard typeface, some were reproduced in Ivor's handwriting, occasionally with corrections or crossings-out; some included a drawing or cartoon. Content varied from the absurd to the surreal to the possibly autobiographical.

McKay recalls that Ivor posted the columns to the newspaper's Edinburgh office in envelopes decorated in his usual distinctive style. Ivor allowed no editing or corrections to be made and was well paid for his contributions: McKay believes he was paid "a couple of hundred pounds or so" for each one and the column lasted for about a year, until the decision was made to stop the magazine's publication. He remembers that Ivor was "wounded" when the magazine ended and demanded to know what the person who had made the decision looked like. He explained that the individual wore glasses and parted his hair. Ivor wanted further details of the decision-maker's physical appearance: "Parting? Side, or on his head? Does he put Brylcreem on his head? A tie? Shorts or longs?" Even with those details, Ivor was powerless to recover his position as a columnist and his suggestion to McKay that the column could move to *Scotland on Sunday*'s daily equivalent, *The Scotsman*, came to nothing.

The unpredictable nature of Ivor's contributions, coupled with their bizarre and challenging stories, make it easy to see why a conservative Sunday newspaper would be glad to end the relationship. In "Doing the Bathroom," which also appears on *A Flat Man*, young Ivor dives into the middens to find useable bottles of wine and sauce to accompany the family meal and is beaten "like an old rug" by Mother for his pains. "Steaming Pancake" is harmless, a story of the renaming of butter which Ivor claims is due to a European directive, but the accompanying illustration is of a fresh cowpat. "Not for Hens," which appears on *A Wet Handle*, begins as a whimsical tale of chickens playing football, a jolly drawing of a hen kicking a ball taking up half of the column, but it soon degenerates into violence as Ivor kills the striker "before its muscles got too tough to eat." "My Hip" opens with the sentence "My son is at the gun stage – he's 4 – so I bought him a pistol ..." and quickly moves on to the point where Ivor gives him "a bloody good thrashing."[26]

Ivor's love of poetry and support of environmental activism came together in the mid-1990s when Alex Mermikides, one of Ivor's former pupils, invited him to participate in *Poems on the Buses – Moving Poems*, which was linked with *Going Places*, an art initiative featuring work from Peter Blake, Sophie Morrish and others, in celebration of the twenty-fifth anniversary of Friends of the Earth. Mermikides arranged for poems to be posted inside buses on routes through central London, Stoke Newington and Hackney: some were selected through an open competition for local people, others were drawn from invited poets including Lemn Sissay, Simon Armitage, Benjamin Zephaniah and Ivor.[27] Ivor attended the launch event in Covent Garden on 23 May 1996 and was photographed posing on and around a London bus.

Two guest appearances gave Ivor a chance to share some of his favourite music with listeners, one on radio and one on record. The first was on Radio Scotland's *Sweet Inspiration*. As well as talking about his early love of music by Schubert, Dvořák and J. S. Bach, Ivor talked about his love of more contemporary music, speaking particularly fondly of "Shout for Joy" by Albert Ammons, which he first heard when he was still living in Scotland. In so doing he gives a rare insight into his relationship with Bernard, recalling that he bought the record when he was twenty-seven, took it to Bernard's house when he went to babysit for him that night and "[played] it the whole evening, again and again. I utterly loved it ..." The record leads on to a discussion about later jazz, when Ivor reveals his love of another musician, Lennie Tristano.

Presenter Brian Morton, aware of Ivor's record choices, asked him if he admired any contemporary songwriters. Ivor's response may seem surprising, although according to Phyllis King he was a fan of Joni Mitchell when they first met, so his liking for another North American singer-songwriter is in keeping with his enjoyment of Mitchell's work. "That leads to the next record," said Ivor, "Randy Newman is the man and 'Goodbye Old Man' is the song ... I can't remember who it was that died, but he chose that to be played at the funeral and it just choked me up. Just empathy, I suppose."[28] Newman went on to write award-winning songs for Walt Disney movies, including the *Toy Story* series.[29] "Old Man" comes from a much earlier period, when Newman was writing and singing songs with strong, and usually unremittingly downbeat, views of human nature. The old man is dying, but only the singer stays, everyone else has left. Why does the singer stay? Should we be applauding his altruism, his kindness, his humanity? Probably not. The lyric suggests the singer is there not to comfort the man in his final hours, but to remind him that no one cares, that he is alone and that there is no God.

Sweet Inspiration was recorded in the mid-1990s, but Ivor's love of Newman's work went back to at least 1971, when he took part in *Melody Maker*'s Blind Date and declared his love for the work of Alan Price, a singer and pianist who first came to notice in the Animals: "I like Alan Price ... He once sang a song which made me cry. It was a Randy Newman thing. Beautiful."[30] Price was an early fan of Newman's work and recorded many of

Ivor at the launch of *Moving Poems*, 23 May 1996. (Courtesy of Alex Mermikides, photographer unknown.)

his songs in the 1960s, so it's not easy to identify which song so affected Ivor, although "Living Without You" seems like a decent bet.[31]

Ivor's final choice was from one of his favourite contemporary composers, Arvo Pärt's "Fratres (for 12 celli)."[32] Ivor called Pärt a giant who created "chords for dissonances that make your hair stand on end ..." His love of Pärt's work wasn't total, however: "Not all of his work is of this calibre, as I discovered to my disappointment. It's nice that people should be imperfect, it's a way of showing up the potential for perfection that they have."

Twenty years after leaving EMI's Harvest label, Ivor returned to the company to take part in the Songbook series of compilation albums. To celebrate EMI's centenary Ciara Nolan was tasked with developing an idea that would involve material from the company's archive and decided, she says, "to bring character back to CD artwork as well as the music so I set up a series called the Songbook Series." Nolan invited artists she admired to select some of their favourite recordings. Novelist Iain Banks (whose selection included Ivor's "Unexpected Join") and artist Ralph Steadman were among those Nolan invited to take part. "The two people I was most scared of ringing were Hunter Thompson, of course, and Ivor Cutler," Nolan says. Ivor "was so wonderful. I think he was quite charmed and delighted ..." Ivor said that he took part because "I thought it would be a bit of a giggle. And anyway, I thought, 'Why not earn a few quid?'"[33] Nolan negotiated a contract, but then asked to use some of his art. "He turned up at the office with examples of his work and a little receipt book: it was like 'Oh, if you want to use my artwork you'll have to pay me extra." Ivor painted a brightly striped horse (or donkey, or mule, or zebra) for the cover of the CD, which was called *Cute, (H)ey?*. "As soon as we put the [CD] booklet together," Nolan recalls, "he said 'Oh, it's cute, hey.' So that was the title."[34]

Ivor took thoughtfully to the task of selecting the music and Nolan thought his choices were "beautiful. He introduced me to music I'd never heard before." The selection process "happened kinda one by one," as Nolan puts it, with Ivor bringing pieces of music to the EMI offices:

> He would sashay – that's the only word for it – into the building. He charmed everyone he met, although some people were really confused by him. We would listen to the music he'd brought. We would have some moments when we were both in tears listening to the music, or he would get up and dance around the office. I'd be howling with laughter.

On the album contemporary classical music is represented by four movements from Arvo Pärt's Beatus "7 Magnificat-Antiphonen" performed by the Estonian Philharmonic Chamber Choir, and Béla Bartók's "6 Romanian Folk Dances." "Shout for Joy" is included, as is Lennie Tristano's "Turkish Mambo." There's no room for Randy Newman's "Old Man" but there are Nina Simone's

"I Wish I Knew How it Would Feel to be Free" and Mahalia Jackson's "Didn't It Rain," which Ivor once called his "second best song."[35] Traditional music from Mozambique, Japan and South Africa is included, as are three Ivor Cutler compositions: his own recordings of "I'm Walkin' to a Farm" – Ivor's favourite of his own songs[36] – and "I Believe in Bugs," plus Robert Wyatt's "Grass." Nolan launched the Songbook album series in Abbey Road Studio 2. Most of the compilers attended, but as she was about to make a speech Ivor had still not been seen. "I was in the control room," she recalls, "[I] turned around and there was Ivor sitting in the corner. He'd been there all the time. He loved doing stuff like that, he really was quite naughty and playful."

Cute (H)ey? represents Ivor's favourite music at one particular time in his life, but, like his opinions of poets and visual artists, his musical tastes changed over the years. Ivor included two songs by the Hungarian singer Márta Sebestyén in his selection, having been a fan of Sebestyén for many years, and declaring in an episode of *Cutler the Lax* that her work "makes me drunk with pleasure and it is cheaper than liquor." He used similar words about Irish singer and harpist Mary O'Hara: "I am a bit of a cold fish, but Mary O'Hara singing, with her clarsach, lowers my drawbridge and lifts my portcullis."[37] Ivor's love of Sebestyén's music ended in the early 2000s when she performed in London and "went for a heavy sound and completely killed the thing that I was once desperate for." His love for Pärt ended at the same time: "I've stopped getting my kicks from Arvo Pärt, too." Now aged eighty, he was losing his love of music in general, telling Will Hodgkinson a fortnight before his final live performance that "my capacity for listening to music has become very sluggish."[38]

15 Covering Ivor Cutler

Ivor Cutler may be noted for many things, but performing cover versions of other people's songs is not one of them. Look in the opposite direction and the picture is rather different. Ivor's output can't compete with Lennon and McCartney's, but there are more than forty cover versions of Ivor's songs on disc and there are many other artists who've covered Ivor's work on stage or online. Admittedly, over twenty of the recorded covers are on the tribute album *Return to Y'Hup*. "Covers" of Ivor's work go beyond bands and musicians making new recordings of his songs, however: artists from the worlds of theatre and dance have brought new approaches to his output. Some of these seem likely to have met with his approval, had he the chance to experience them: one, at least, is more likely to have inspired his anger.

As *Return to Y'Hup* shows, Ivor's songs, poems and even album sleeve notes are ripe for re-interpretation, and, despite his voice and words seeming so central to his work, there are instrumental covers around. Ivor made few comments about covers of his work, probably because only a small number of them appeared during his lifetime and those that did were often the work of obscure artists – Out of the Compost and Brown Tower are two examples of bands that have long faded from the collective memory.

One of the earliest Ivor Cutler covers (possibly the first) is also one of the most unusual and one of the most enjoyable. It came, as one might expect, from a Finnish ska band. The group was called SE and "Riitaa, Riitaa, Riitaa" is a one minute and thirty-two second dash through Ivor's "Trouble Trouble," a rare non-English-language cover and one of the few Ivor covers that you can dance to. It formed the B-side of a single, released in 1980, which John Knutas remembers as a radio hit in Finland. Knutas doesn't think Ivor ever heard the song: "We never discussed it. I don't even remember if I ever told Ivor there WAS a Finnish version of 'Trouble Trouble.'"[1] Spanish band

Kiev Cuando Nieva recorded a Spanish language "Step It Out Lively, Boys" on *Parece Doble*, an album of covers of Nick Drake, Syd Barrett and others of their favourite "outsider artists." It's a rather sweet interpretation of the *Privilege* track, played with a gentle swing.[2]

Given their close friendship, it's not surprising that Robert Wyatt recorded one of Ivor's songs. Wyatt released his cover of "Go and Sit Upon the Grass" – which he re-titled simply as "Grass" – in August 1981 as part of a double A-side single with "Trade Union," by Dishari, occupying the other side.[3] Both songs were included on *Nothing Can Stop Us*, a collection of singles Wyatt released the following year.[4] Wyatt's recording of "Grass" features two members of Dishari, Kadir Durvesh on shehnai and Esmail Shek on tabla: the result is a rhythmic, propulsive, rendition of the song and, in my opinion, one of the finest of all the Ivor Cutler covers. Ivor selected it for *Cute (H)ey?*, so he was clearly a fan.

Most of Ivor's works have been covered by just one, or perhaps two, artists. More artists have been attracted to "Go and Sit Upon the Grass" and "Women of the World," which, at the time of writing, have attracted at least four covers each. Out of the Compost, a New Zealand quartet, recorded "Go and Sit Upon the Grass" as "Go and Sit" on their 1987 self-released cassette *Scrapings & Peelings*. Eddi Reader, the Scottish ex-Fairground Attraction vocalist, covered it on a limited-edition CD single seven years later.[5] More recently, Max Andrzejewski's Hütte & Guests recorded their version on their Wyatt tribute album *Hütte & Guests Play the Music of Robert Wyatt*, an album that also includes versions of "Little Red Riding Hood Hit the Road" and "Little Red Robin Hood Hit the Road." Jerome Wilson described drummer Andrzejewski and vocalist Cansu Tanrikulu on Cutler's song "cheerily singing in call-and-response as synthesizer and guitar squeak and flash on a raga-like melody which eventually pulls and distorts into an old-fashioned psychedelic freakout." It seems unlikely that Ivor would have been keen.[6]

Jim O'Rourke recorded "Women of the World" on *Eureka* as part of an eight minute and forty-five second track called "Prelude to 110 or 220/ Women of the World," omitting the spoken word line about men having had their shot which Linda Hirst contributed to the original.[7] Yacht recorded a hardcore version, a guaranteed mosh pit filler, on their 2007 album *I Believe in You. Your Magic is Real*. This version omits the spoken word line, but it's only two minutes long.[8] Scottish singer and songwriter Karine Polwart included her version of the song on her 2019 album, *Karine Polwart's Scottish Songbook*, with Louis Abbott on lead vocal.[9] This rendition omits the spoken word line. There's a definite pattern emerging here. Maybe one of the world's biggest rock bands can break that pattern.

In 2018 there were few if any rock bands bigger than U2. During their U2 Experience and Innocence tour, which ran from May to November at venues across North America and Europe, the band used "Women of the World" in each performance to help in publicising the movement to "close the gender gap for women living in poverty." Rather than U2 performing the song live, a video with a soundtrack based on O'Rourke's version of the song was played at each concert. The band invited fans to upload clips of themselves singing the song to social media platforms, using the hashtag #womenoftheworld, and these clips were added to the video soundtrack to create a large-scale choir. U2 vocalist Bono appeared on *The Ellen Degeneres Show* on American TV and persuaded Degeneres and her audience to sing along.[10] The result, as seen on a number of online videos, created a strong message to the fans in each arena. However, U2's choral singalong omits the spoken line.

For those despairing of ever hearing Hirst's spoken words in a cover version, *Return to Y'Hup* is the place to go. This version includes all of the words to be found in the original recording, whether they were spoken or sung. Tracyanne Campbell was lead vocalist on the track, although this was not the original intention. As she remembers, "I think I was quite late to the project … 'last man in' or something. I went in just to sing on 'Women of the World' as part of the chorus and after we'd finished they decided my vocal should be the lead."

Alasdair Roberts has covered two of Ivor's songs: "I Had a Little Boat" and "OK, I'll Count to 8." He's another fan who first encountered Ivor on a Peel session and *Ludo* is his favourite of Ivor's recordings because, he believes, "the quality of the songs, the humour, the very minimalist approach to the arrangements, they don't detract from the narrative." When he saw Ivor in concert in the late 1990s, Roberts "warmed to him, this inner shining force from his eyes. It makes it seem like I'm talking about some sort of cult leader!" He covered Ivor for the first time when Rough Trade asked him to record "I Had a Little Boat" for its twenty-fifth anniversary album, *Stop Me if You Think You've Heard this One Before.*[11] A few years later Roberts was asked to record "OK, I'll Count to 8" with Olivia Cheney, for a project that resulted in *Revenge of the Folksingers*, an album that mixed traditional songs and tunes, classical pieces and contemporary compositions, performed by various musicians.[12] The arrangement is slower than Ivor and Hirst's version, but faithful to the original's light-hearted jollity, with the addition of a few introductory piano chords from the opening of Benjamin Britten's arrangement of the traditional song "O Waly, Waly."[13]

Return to Y'Hup is not the only album dedicated to Ivor Cutler cover versions. The Parenthetical Girls from Portland, Oregon, devoted the entirety of their 2009 mini-album, *The Scottish Play*, to seven of Ivor's pieces plus Phyllis King's "The Best Thing": an entirety that totals a mere eleven and a half minutes. The record's cover is a drawing by David Shrigley, based on the cover photo from *Jammy Smears* but with the addition of a third eye on Ivor's forehead. Rather than the original's "Yours and oblig," the speech bubble offers a subtitle for the record: "Wherein the group Parenthetical Girls pay well-intentioned (if occasionally mis-guided) tribute to the works of Ivor Cutler."[14] The band pays tribute on a mix of songs and poems. "Whale

Badge" is recited over the sound of a torrential rainstorm; "I Need Nothing (Doughnut Song)" is Ivor's "A Doughnut in My Hand" retitled; "A Nuance" comes across like John Cale's "The Gift," from his Velvet Underground days; "I'm Going in a Field" has an ethereal beauty, respectful of Ivor's original recording, although the arrangement may be a bit over-complicated. Once the initial shock of hearing the works delivered in American accents is overcome, this is a fine tribute that never strays too far from the sound of the original recordings.

Jazz musicians have paid tribute, too, for example *Tomato Brain* by the Golden Age of Steam.[15] The title track is yet another cover of a *Privilege* song, a dense and disruptive reading of the tale of a man who becomes a sandwich, full of worrying electronica. James Allsopp, the band's saxophonist and leader, describes Ivor's music as having "something absurd but not funny about it. It really somehow made a lot of sense." As for "Tomato Brain" itself: "I don't know if it's something about the harmonium or the way he sings it, but there's something incantatory or prayerful about it, in a totally irreligious way." The track closes with a sample of Ivor's voice, intoning the final phrase of "Phonic Poem," "Twenty-nine Redburn Avenue": "I wanted to put him in," says Allsopp, "I thought it would be nice to have him saying something completely removed and out of context." He was unaware at the time that this had been Ivor's family home.

Picture the scene. A smartly dressed, avuncular-looking chap, spectacles, white suit, grey hair, neatly trimmed grey beard, walks along with the light support of a walking cane. He's wandering through a traffic jam, by the side of a deserted outdoor swimming pool and on a major league baseball field. He's a cheery soul, content with his lot. He has everything he needs, because he's holding a large bucket of fried chicken pieces. He's Colonel Sanders, and as he walks along he sings a familiar song.[16] When Ivor had everything necessary for a contented existence, he sang of having "A Doughnut in my Hand." The Colonel was clearly not a fan of the doughnut, but he was as happy as Ivor, because he was carrying a bucket full of chicken pieces and singing a slightly altered version of one of Ivor's songs.[17]

Ivor resisted lending himself or his work to advertising campaigns, so when David Toop saw the advertisement for fried chicken "It kind of scandalised me a bit. I used to see Ivor around Bumblebee health food shop, near to his flat – he was so 'allergic' to all that stuff in a very militant way that I can't imagine him approving any bit of that." David Jones remembered spending "a considerable amount of time saying 'No' in many different ways to people who wanted him to do adverts." Eventually, he asked Ivor if he would consider doing advertisements of any sort. "Well, I would do an advert for the Co-op Bank," Ivor told him, and then, "Almost the next week a request came for him to do an advert for the Co-op Bank! But he found a way out of it." To Jones's knowledge, Ivor never took part in any commercial advertisement apart from campaigns for his own recordings or performances: he's highly unlikely to have responded favourably to his song being used to sell fried chicken, even if bicarbonate of chicken, according to his song of the same title, was one of his favourite meals.

In the twenty-first century, the worlds of dance and theatre have become attracted to Ivor's work and life. In 2009 Morag Deyes, the artistic director of Dance Base, was working on a new show called *Off Kilter*, which she describes as "a whole other way of looking at Scotland." She invited Ashley Page, the then artistic director of Scottish Ballet, to contribute a short piece and sent him a selection of music: within that selection were some of Ivor's pieces which, she recalls, "completely bewitched" him. As Page recalls:

> I knew he had been in *Magical Mystery Tour* and he was talked about quite a lot in the circles in which I moved in the '70s ... but I didn't really do a thorough investigation until Morag suggested him, along with other composers ... So, I was listening to all of this music and the kids [then aged fifteen and thirteen] just loved it so I thought "Maybe I should do this."

Page created an eleven-minute piece based on some of Ivor's songs, which Deyes titled *Paisley Patter*. He designed the piece to combine dance, performed by three members of the Errol White Company, with Ivor's songs and a backdrop of photographs of the Gorbals in the 1950s taken by Oscar Marzaroli. Page no longer has his production notes and no recording was made, but he believes that he used around eight songs including "Good Morning! How Are You? Shut Up!," "A Great Grey Grasshopper," "Cockadoodledon't," "I'm Going in a Field" and "Mud," with "Last Song" as the final piece. Page designed *Paisley Patter* to make full use of the trio of dancers: "I had pieces with all three of them, 'Going in a Field' was a duet, and then a trio thing at the end. So, it had some variation in terms of tempo, dynamics and so on."

Mark Morris, the American dancer and choreographer, was another contributor to *Off Kilter*. He saw and enjoyed *Paisley Patter* and Deyes sent him some of Ivor's recordings, "thinking that he would enjoy it but not thinking for a minute that he would set anything to it." Morris is well known for only working with live music, but in this case he made an exception and, in Deyes's words, "up popped *A Wooden Tree*." Morris's interpretation of Ivor's songs involved eight dancers and ran for twenty-four minutes. *A Wooden Tree* premiered at the Merrill Wright Mainstage Theatre in Seattle, on 4 October 2012 and over the next four years the Mark Morris Dance Group performed it in venues across the USA, as well as in the Teatro Ristori in Verona, Sydney Opera House, Sadler's Wells in London and His Majesty's Theatre in Aberdeen.[18] Robert Gottlieb referred to Ivor as "the obscure (to us in Brooklyn) British songwriter," and he wasn't overly impressed by the songs, calling them "a little Gertrude Stein, a little Edith Sitwell, a lot self-conscious," but he was impressed by one of the dancers: Mikhail Baryshnikov, then aged sixty-five but still able to transfix the audience.[19] Susan Saccoccia's review was more positive:

> Morris responds to the oddity and droll humor of the songs with choreography to match … Wearing outfits that could have come from a thrift shop … the dancers appear to be having a ball as they execute frolicking but precise movements in tune with Cutler's slightly surreal tales.[20]

One of Ivor's most popular children's books, *Meal One*, has also found its way to the theatre. 509 Arts, a Bradford-based arts organisation, has adapted the book for the stage in partnership with Hull Truck Theatre and with the support of Mind the Gap, and has taken the production on tour. Alan Dix, the artistic director of 509 Arts, is the show's director. Dix's father was an early Ivor Cutler fan, bringing him to his son's attention in the 1960s. Mr Dix senior "absolutely loved Ivor Cutler. Every now and then he'd just go 'Gruts for tea'. He loved the absurdity of Ivor's work." Alan Dix became a fan, then passed his love of Ivor's work on to his own daughters. When his oldest daughter gave him a copy of *Meal One* for Christmas, he started to think about developing a stage version and planning began in 2019 with the production, which 509 Arts describes as "an immersive and playful family show," touring in 2022.[21]

All of these stage productions take Ivor's work as their starting point. *The Beautiful Cosmos of Ivor Cutler* includes many of his works, but focuses on his life. The play, a joint production by Vanishing Point and the National Theatre of Scotland, toured Scotland in 2014, then played Brighton Festival the following year.[22] Sandy Grierson, who played Ivor, describes him as "a kind of symbol of musical kudos in Scotland. You were aware of him … I was aware that people who had a deep knowledge and love of music, Ivor Cutler would always be in their record collection."

Director Matthew Lenton suggested writing a play about Ivor, but didn't initially follow the idea up. According to Grierson:

> The idea sat there for ages. Then in 2012, when I was at the Royal Shakespeare Company and my daughter had just been born, Matt told me they were going to do a development of the Ivor Cutler idea. I just remember feeling that I really was desperate to be involved. He had a previous working relationship with James Fortune and we all went to Inverness to work on developing the show.

Lenton became the play's director, Fortune its musical director, and Grierson its lead actor. Elicia Daly, who played Phyllis King, and performers and musicians Jo Apps, Ed Gaughan, Magnus Mehta and Nick Pynn completed the company. Grierson arranged to meet Phyllis at Laurier Road: "Her explanation of how to get there was almost identical to Ivor's explanation ..." Phyllis loaned Ivor's "Sewer" harmonium to the production team, but it was too out of tune to be played on stage. Elicia Daly also met Phyllis, who saw the show at the Traverse Theatre in Edinburgh.

The critics were generally positive about the play. Mark Fisher of *The Guardian* called it "A big grin of a show" and a "marvellous production," and awarded four stars.[23] Lorna Irvine previewed the play, telling readers that "it's sure to be a real labour of love, as touching as it is hilarious."[24] For Joyce McMillan of *The Scotsman* it was "almost irresistible, both in the loving strength of its central performances and in the sheer beauty of the cosmos it sometimes conjures up, thanks to exquisite set and lighting design by Kai Fischer."[25] Despite its popularity, the Brighton performances of *The Beautiful Cosmos of Ivor Cutler* were its last ones at the time of writing. The play did make it onto radio, however. Grierson and Matt Thompson adapted the play and the production, which Thompson directed and which featured the original cast, was broadcast on Radio 3.[26] As for Phyllis's opinion of Grierson's on-stage performance, she told me "He does a lovely Ivor."

16 A Life Outside the Limelight

Where did Ivor Cutler live? For forty years he lived at 21 Laurier Road, but where was that? Some journalists were no more specific than London, others narrowed it down to north London, others placed his home in Denmark Hill, Tufnell Park, Parliament Hill, Kentish Town, Gospel Oak or Camden. To Jonathon Porritt, another Laurier Road resident, the location became a source of entertainment: "Laurier Road is actually in Dartmouth Park. Ivor was always very amused at the difference between those who insisted on calling it Dartmouth Park (out of straight snobbery, in his opinion!) and those who felt more comfortable with Camden." Thankfully, Ivor gave clear directions to his flat during his Radio 3 show, *Silence*, when he declared that the flat was in Parliament Hill Fields and could be reached by taking the tube to Tufnell Park, on the Northern Line. Emerging from the station, there were five roads "like the fingers of a hand." The middle finger was Dartmouth Park Hill. Going up the hill, taking the fifth turn left at the church, then forking right after thirty yards brought you to Laurier Road, where Ivor's flat was "number one, two one, top bell."

The directions are accurate, the only possible confusion that might arise coming from Ivor's phrasing of "one, two one," which could be taken to mean that he lived at one hundred and twenty-one. Given Ivor's attention to detail, this ambiguity may be deliberate.

Ivor's visitors arrived by tube, car or taxi, or by Ivor's preferred method, the bicycle. They usually left with clear impressions of what they found, whether they visited once or many times. Over Ivor's forty-year occupation of the flat alterations were made to the property, so these impressions can appear contradictory, but they all describe a distinctive home in a large corner house. Joe Coles, who visited on just one occasion, recalls a bird cage occupied by a "pretend bird"; Zoe Hood, who was with him at the time, remembers numerous bird cages, all empty, and textiles in Scottish weaves of dark colours – décor she calls "maximalist." Neil Cargill remembers "the most extraordinary artwork, curios and the paraphernalia he'd introduce into his performances … on string and pegs were all the original Martin Honeysett drawings for one of the *Life in a Scotch Sitting Room* books." Ivor owned a record player, but once it broke he didn't have it repaired and so it sat, unused.[1] There had been a television too, but in 1988 Ivor told the *New Musical Express* that he had thrown it out years before.[2] Everything was covered, according to David Jones, in a rich patina of dust.

On his first visit to Ivor's flat, John Knutas thought that it seemed

> almost indecently untidy, his only explanation for the chaos being "I love bacteria!", which implied he didn't want to disturb the minuscule organisms by cleaning or any similar activity … Ivor's [flat] was never dirty, it was just overcrowded with stuff he loved. Overcrowded, now weighing the word, actually is an understatement.

Journalists, too, felt moved to comment on what they saw. Alastair McKay visited in 1994, finding "surprises everywhere … a display of organised chaos." Among the wooden birds and plastic flies was a photograph of a younger Ivor, bald on top but with black hair around the side of his head. McKay saw a resemblance to the six-foot seven-inch tall comic actor Bernard Bresslaw.[3] Five years later, Mark Espiner came to see Ivor and described his home as a "humble hermitage," with paintings drying on the indoor washing line and objects including stuffed birds, ceramics, and a wax ear illustrating acupuncture points nailed to the wall. Espiner spotted some items of ivory cutlery – "a deliberate pun" – on the mantlepiece.[4] He assumed that the pun was Ivor's idea, but Dan and Fraser Geesin remember that their father added the y's to Ivor's name and sent him some of the cutlery as, in Ron Geesin's words, a "surrealist in-joke."

In 1985 the *Observer Magazine* invited Ivor to take part in its "A Room of My Own" series and despatched Ena Kendall to his flat.[5] Despite the title, half of Kendall's article is taken up by a discussion about Ivor's work and life. Five years after giving up teaching, he told Kendall that the only children now of interest to him were his sons: "it's a cool interest, only as individuals and not blood. Parents have a habit of creeping out of the woodwork at the least opportunity so I think – let them be. We have a good relationship. I think they quite like me." The room of the title is, in Ivor's case, his bedroom. Posters of Chinese and Japanese characters, a bronze head of Artemis bought from the British Museum, sculptures by Ghisha Koenig and Lucy Meikle, his own pottery bull's head, bottles of vitamin tablets, and a shoe-bag filled with postcards and tourist literature are among the things Kendall decided were worthy of comment.

Guglielmo Galvin's photograph dominates the article: Ivor sits on the arm of a leather chair in front of a fireplace, the back of his head reflected in the black-framed mirror that stands over a small brown side-table. Next to the table, the edge of what looks like an abacus can just be seen. A case at Ivor's feet might contain a portable typewriter, or a tape recorder, or an accordion. The head of Artemis, the sculptures, the bull's head and the pill bottles are all visible. The foot of the bed can be seen, a bentwood dining chair standing next to it, a coil of wire lying on its seat. Anna Morshead recalls that she painted this room in the early 1980s when working as a decorator, so the paintwork is likely to be hers. However, the window frame is bare wood, knots clearly showing, a narrow strip of what appears to be fresh plaster along its left-hand side. Ivor referred to it as his "Polish window" because it's been made by a Polish carpenter, so this is probably a recent addition to the room, a replacement frame with finishing touches still to be made. An electric panel radiator sits in the fireplace, a magnetic checkers game and three pool balls lie on the floor, a copy of *Life in a Scotch Sitting Room* can be seen on the overstuffed bookshelf and a card with Bruce Lacey's name on it has been placed on the mantle-piece. Below the bull's head is the "No Dumping Prohibited" sign which was in the flat when Dave Allen came in search of English eccentrics a decade earlier. It's certainly a cluttered space: a record, at the time, of twenty years of Ivor's occupancy, a collection of objects that Ted Harrison described as "the trophies of a lifetime spent in the melancholic contemplation of the human mind and its humorous potential."[6]

Will Hodgkinson and John Lewis were probably the last journalists Ivor welcomed to his home. Twenty years after Galvin's photograph, Hodgkinson found a flat "which redefines conventional concepts of untidiness and enters into the realm of the bomb-shattered": a living room crammed with photographs, books, other bits and pieces, a harmonium and an electric bar heater. On the toilet wall was a photograph of teenage girls at a finishing school. Ivor told him, "After relieving myself I turn and look at the girls ... There's 18 of them, and I've never been able to decide which one I'd really like to know."[7] Lewis described the flat as "cheerfully ramshackle ... like the kind of house that a small child would establish," with heaps of newspapers and a bath full of books.[8] The flat had been Ivor's home for almost forty years by then, and the eighty-year-old was finding it increasingly hard to cope with.

In most properties, a well-designed kitchen, a stunning sitting room or a grand entrance hall might leave the biggest impressions on a visitor. Ivor's bathroom had a similar impact. Dylan Edwards, whose mother was Ivor's landlord, has lived in the house since the mid-1970s. When Ivor moved in there was only one bathroom for the entire property and this situation stayed unchanged for many years until, as he remembers, a bathroom, with a toilet, was fitted in Ivor's flat in what had originally been Joyce Edwards's darkroom. Phyllis King, who probably visited the flat more than anyone else, has a slightly different memory:

He was on the top of the house, on the second floor. There was a shared toilet on the landing, shared with the person who lived on the ground floor. Ivor had his flat on the second floor but he also had a big room on the first floor where he had his piano and things like that. In his flat upstairs he had a sitting room and a bedroom and a bathroom and a kitchen. After a while Dylan put a loo in the flat: there was a bath there but not a loo.

Whatever the fine details of Ivor's bath and toilet facilities may be, the bathrooms were oft-remembered. Elicia Daly, who met Phyllis in the house, recalls the shared toilet clearly: "I remember it being really, really cold, it almost had the feeling of an outside loo. A beautiful old porcelain bowl with a really long chain." Frances Geesin went to dinner with Ivor in 1969, when the shared toilet was the only one in the house, and remembers "The loo rolls were mounted on the door and they each had the owner's name above the roll." In the mid-1980s, Neil Cargill became a regular visitor. He recalls the shared toilet and its wildlife:

> One odd memory I have of the place is the toilet, found tenement-style on the landing of the stairs up to his flat. The small window had a bird feeder hanging from the top, above a plant pot full of earth. Ivor explained that birds from all over London would perch on the feeder, crap into the plant pot, and the deposited seeds would grow into completely unpredictable flowers – always a surprise.

John Knutas, who visited the flat every three years or so over a twenty-year period, was a fan of Ivor's "largeish" bathroom, describing it as "a piece of art" with its pictures of the Avro Anson airplane from his RAF training, "a harem picture so innocent it went over the other edge and turned out hilariously frivolous," joke shop toilet rolls and art reproductions, among them Finnish painter Hugo Simberg's late 1800s picture *Frost*, which, says Knutas "I had nothing to do with - Ivor was a fan of Simberg's already before we first met." At first glance, *Frost* appears to show a naked figure sitting on a toilet, but closer inspection reveals a more disconcerting image, of a figure sitting on a small haystack, or possibly being engulfed by some sort of agricultural monster. As for where this "piece of art" should have ended up, Knutas believes that "it's a crime against humanity that it wasn't possible to lift out Ivor's bathroom after his death, and recreate it at Tate Modern."

Sometimes Ivor would mention his flat or its contents to interviewers, enlightening readers still further about life in Laurier Road. In one personal insight, Ivor informed his interviewer that "after two years half the weight of your pillow is mite shit ... I've got one pillow that I've had for twenty-odd years and it weighs a ton."[9] In the house, Ivor arranged a system for mail delivery so that he didn't need to go down stairs to pick up his post. It's a system many of his friends remember. Dylan Edwards describes it as a bulldog clip suspended by a length of typewriter ribbon: "When letters came for him I'd put them on this bulldog clip and later he'd pull them up." It sounds like something Bruce Lacey might have invented, a simple but practical solution to what most people wouldn't see as a problem.

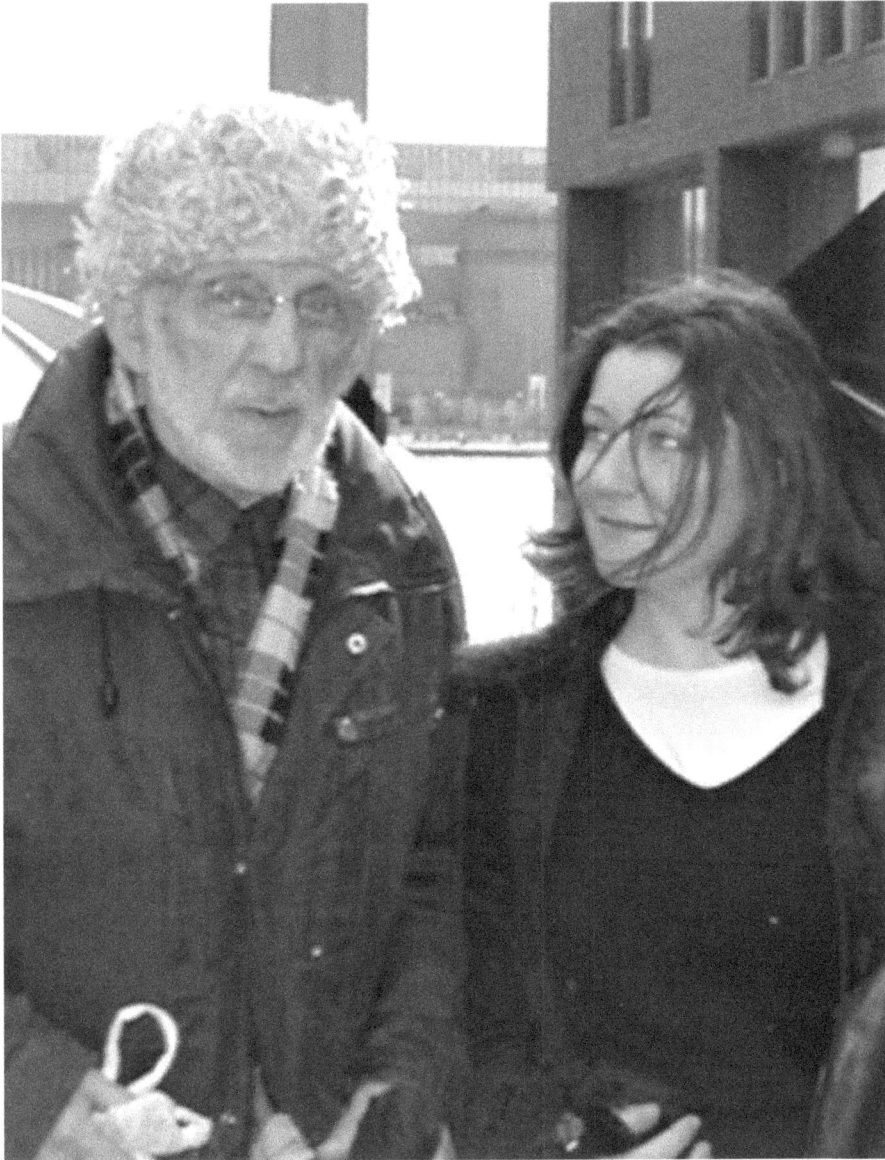

Ivor and Christine Stark outside Tate Modern, c.2000. (Courtesy of Christine Stark, photograph by Amanda Rodgers.)

In the early years, Ivor entertained groups of friends in the first-floor room, as well as using it as a rehearsal room.[10] Although Ivor lived alone, he frequently invited people to visit for a cup of tea and a chat, for a meal, to learn how to write poetry, to interview him for a newspaper or magazine article, or to record a radio session or programme. Ivor kept a selection of teas and enjoyed asking which one you would like, but according to Beverley Crew, "Even if you chose the second one he mentioned he'd still talk you through the entire selection." In the kitchen, Ivor had a collection of stickers from different varieties of apple, which he stuck to his fridge: "He would point to them and say 'The Cox, the Russet,' you know."[11] Christine Stark saw a list of dates, from the 1970s on, recording when he had defrosted the fridge: in contrast, she says, "he never cleaned his grill pan."

Ivor provided a range of meals to those lucky enough to join him for lunch or dinner. Dylan Edwards was an occasional dinner guest: "I enjoyed that (for the conversation), but it wasn't my idea of a full meal. It was a bit minimal, a slice of salami in the middle of the plate." Trevor Tomkins visited Ivor's flat once, in 1966, and received a "quite spartan" meal of "Scottish neeps, whatever they are." Neeps are boiled turnips or swede, usually accompanied by potatoes to form neeps and tatties, but it seems that Ivor omitted fifty per cent of the recipe. Other guests recall a range of meals: fried Polish sausage, vegetarian sausages, meals of chicken or fish, or the choice of a kipper or a Greek sausage.[12] Zoe Hood and Joe Coles received what Hood describes as "a very traditional tea, I think there were probably Eccles cakes," and Nicola Barker received an extensive menu of "two small, vaguely obscene, boiled vegetarian sausages" and a packet of crisps as a first course, followed by a mug of tapioca.[13] Ivor presented Alex Mermikides with eggs and bacon: as part of his preparation, he rinsed the bacon under the tap to get rid of the salt. Ivor didn't drink alcohol very much. Dylan Edwards says that he kept some in the flat for visitors, but Beverley Crew recalls that "He hated being in the company of people who drank, he didn't like that kind of looseness."

In the late 1970s Ivor invited all the members of IOU Theatre to tea. They were delighted to accept the invitation, as Louise Oliver recalls: "He seemed a bit surprised that we'd come. There were seven of us and it must have been a bit daunting to have us all crowding in. I think maybe Phyllis was there and I remember him speaking about her leaving hairgrips in the bed." Sadly, Oliver no longer recalls the menu.

By the late 1980s portable recording equipment was good enough to produce broadcast-quality radio programmes and BBC teams began recording Ivor at home, a relief from the studio air conditioning.[14] His session of 8 January 1994, broadcast by both Peel and Andy Kershaw, was recorded at the flat in the previous November and he recorded his final Peel session there in 1998.[15] James Birtwistle engineered these sessions, which became known as the "but and ben sessions" in reference to the Scottish term for a small cottage, and would cycle to Laurier Road with the equipment in a rucksack. Birtwistle wanted to add reverb to the recordings but Ivor would have none of it, asking for him to leave it out because with added reverb the recordings didn't "sound miserable enough."[16] Ivor also recorded *A Stuggy Pren* and *Jelly Mountain* in his flat and there were at least two failed attempts at home recordings. In the first, Glen Baxter and Ivor got together to work on a radio play, using a small tape recorder that Ivor placed on the table. "Unfortunately or perhaps fortunately," Baxter recalls, "Ivor forgot to turn it on, so that project never got off the ground." The second occasion arose when Ivor suggested to the BBC that they might like to record an improvised dialogue between him and his friend John Burnside. A young producer arrived at the flat and set up her equipment. The two men started to chat, launching into what Burnside describes as an "odd, surreal, actually very funny number, completely unrehearsed." The conversation had been going well for fifteen minutes when the producer realised that the machine was not recording. She informed them of the problem, apologised and asked if they could start again. Burnside was happy to do so:

> he was in great form, and I was really just along for the ride as straight man – but Ivor simply looked at her, pursed his lips in that odd way he had and said: "No." Nothing else, just no. He then called for a taxicab and the poor producer was sent on her way. And that was that. I made a few attempts at mollifying conversation, but he wasn't interested. He could be quite ruthless at times.

The flat suited Ivor: it was well situated, large enough for his needs and, eventually, self-contained. However, there was a period when a fellow resident made his life difficult. Dylan Edwards experienced the tension between Ivor and this second tenant:

> For a long stretch of time it seemed to be just Ivor and [the second tenant]. [He] was a long-term tenant … He lived in a room just below Ivor's flat. He was friendly enough at the start, then he seemed to get more and more hostile towards Ivor. I think he made Ivor feel quite uneasy sometimes … [One day] I didn't notice his usual activity and found him dead in the little kitchen. It was an unpleasant situation to have these two people in the house.

When the man died, Kate Lithgow received a telephone call from Ivor, who was laughing with relief.[17]

Ivor would sometimes travel by public transport, or persuade someone to drive him to different places, but the bicycle was his favourite mode of transport and he was always keen to promote cycling to others. In *Silence*, Ivor advised the unnamed BBC producer (also played by Ivor) to travel to Laurier Road by bicycle. He was enthusiastic about cycling's health benefits and the pleasure of passing queues of traffic, but admitted "I have been knocked down, in Regent's Park, and lots of narrow misses." The Regent's Park incident occurred less than a year before Ivor recorded *Silence* and such was Ivor's fame that the story made the gossip column of *Record Mirror*. The paper's "Juicy Lucy" column printed stories, anecdotes, scurrilous tales and unsubstantiated rumour to delight rock fans across the country: its lead story on 18 February 1979 told of how Rod Stewart's limousine had burst into flames on the M4 motorway; there was a plea on behalf of a member of the Damned who was desperately looking for a new flat; a story about Elizabeth Taylor's Cartier diamond; a report that Sid Vicious and his "delightfully amusing belle" Nancy Spungen had appeared at Marylebone Magistrates Court; and a "punks aren't all bad" good news item about a concert by the Fall, Buzzcocks and other Manchester acts that raised money for cancer research. There was a report of a car crash involving another punk band, the Adverts, and then came the report of Ivor's own road traffic incident:

> Last Thursday, Ivor Cutler, humorist, was knocked down on his Bickerton folding bike by a large yellow saloon at the southeast corner of Regent's Park's Outer Circle. Cutler had the right of way, but the other man had a yellow car. Having knocked him down, he zoomed off to Camden Town, not checking to see whether or not he had killed the unfortunate Cutler.
>
> "He didn't have enough time to get up the speed to do the job properly," said Cutler, "I thought it was only the drivers of red cars who had inferiority problems. I shall have to watch out for the yellow ones, too."[18]

Even though the drivers of yellow and red cars posed a genuine threat to his road safety, Ivor remained a keen cyclist and enthusiastic promoter of cycling for most of his life. Many of the people interviewed for this book remember Ivor's cycling activities and many interviews mentioned Ivor arriving at appointments by bike. Ivor kept his bike in the hall of the Laurier Road house and took it to his favourite bicycle repair shop, the Whizzer on Mornington Crescent, for repairs and maintenance.[19] He was often seen cycling around London. Andy Kershaw would be "roaring up Dartmouth Park Hill on my motorcycle and ahead of me I'd see Ivor wobbling dangerously as he cycled up the hill." He was also spotted cycling near Hyde Park clad in a yellow sou'wester and cape.[20] Lucy Armitage, Kershaw's producer, went on cycling trips with Ivor. On one trip, to the Museum of London, Armitage's bike had a puncture. He "was so organised, had the entire puncture repair kit and really wanted to have a go at fixing it. But there was no way that Ivor was going to be able to mend it, so we had to go home on the train."

There are occasional glimpses into Ivor's other activities on London's streets, some no doubt genuine examples, others perhaps more spurious: once someone has been labelled an "eccentric" often and long enough, it becomes easier to believe any tale of strange behaviour that turns up. One activity Ivor undertook over many years was the identification and highlighting of dog faeces in Camden. This was a particular problem on Laurier Road, a favourite "doggie-run" through to Hampstead Heath.[21] He described the activity as his "hobby ... drawing flowers with coloured chalk around mess made by dogs on the pavement," and explained to Emma Freud that "I get a set of coloured chalks and I do faces round ... and mid-coloured flowers round them to give them sweetness and dignity ... It did cut it down, I think it made [dog owners] a little ashamed."[22] The care Ivor took over these functional and temporary designs led Craig Murray-Orr to describe them as "works of art created to shame." Caitlin Moran told of Ivor, aged eighty, travelling around the London Underground "improving posters for the new Sheryl Crow album by affixing tiny stickers that read 'Funny Smell' between her legs."[23] According to Craig Murray-Orr, Ivor enjoyed using his bus pass and also aimed to visit every station on the London Underground, an aim that Murray-Orr thinks he came close to achieving. Murray-Orr went on many day trips with Ivor and the pair would often behave like mischievous children. "Our visits out into the world would best be described as adventures," said Murray-Orr, "asking for a wheel-chair at museums and public galleries, taking turns at sitting and pushing was always good for conversations with strangers." Dana Purvis, Murray-Orr's wife, used to take Ivor to the supermarket, where he enjoyed pointing out any product's shortcomings. Often, he would only buy two or three things, returning them the following week for a refund.[24]

Ivor didn't always need a partner-in-crime. One solo adventure took place in Kensington, beginning with a trip to the Science Museum. He was sitting and staring at an engine when "Two Frenchmen of 35," as he described them, asked if he had built the engine. Ivor told them that he had built it that morning, having brought the parts to the museum himself, and was checking that the engine worked. They went away, any plans they may have had for making fun of Ivor now foiled. Ivor wandered the short distance to the Victoria & Albert Museum and engaged with a member of the security staff, telling her that he had some chocolate in his bag. She couldn't find it, for the simple reason that there was none. Ivor went to look at some statues and found a homeless man asleep on a bench: he quietly placed a "Kindly Disregard" label beside him, then moved off to the shop.[25]

Less controversially, he enjoyed flying his kite on Primrose Hill.[26]

Despite the fame gleaned from Peel shows and support spots with big-name bands, Ivor was rarely to be found socialising with rock stars. No newspaper published photos of Ivor crawling out of the Speakeasy at four in the morning, no gossip column wrote of him appearing "tired and emotional" after a night on the town with Led Zeppelin. However, he did merit a mention in the *Melody Maker* gossip column, "The Raver," when it reported on a party at The Manor, a year or so after he recorded *Dandruff* at the studio, to celebrate the studio's relaunch. It was a star-studded affair, with suitably rock-star behaviour directed at music journalist Karl Dallas, who was thrown into the studio swimming pool: "There was quite a crew of celebrities joining in the festivities – Robert Wyatt in straw hat and clutching a flask of tea, Ivor Cutler, Henry Cow [clearly, the band's members weren't well known enough to be named] ... John Cale, Chris Spedding, Lady June, Mike Oldfield, and Roy Harper."[27]

Ivor attended at least one BBC Light Entertainment Christmas Party in the early 1990s. Held at the Paris Theatre in Lower Regent Street, it was regarded as the major BBC party, filled with current and past stars of entertainment. It was very unusual for Ivor to attend anything like this, but he seemed to enjoy the attention from admirers.[28] Ivor's social life was usually a more relaxed affair: dinners with friends, trips out, holidays in England. Joyce Edwards occasionally invited Ivor and others to dinner at her Hampstead house. For one of these events, Joyce invited her son Dylan, Ivor and Henry Woolf, the actor who lived in 21 Laurier Road a few years before Ivor. The evening was not a great success, as Dylan recalls, due to what he describes as a "clash of personalities." Joyce felt that both Woolf and Ivor were used to being the centre of attention and thought, after the event, that it had not been a good idea to bring the pair together. Dylan believes that Woolf was irritated by what he calls "Ivor's 'self-display': the badges, the unusual clothes. 'You get that out of your system on stage,' was Henry's comment." In the final years of Ivor's life, says Dylan, they did find some common ground, with Woolf describing Ivor and himself as "lugubrious Jews."

Friends and relatives interviewed for this book often spoke about Ivor's daytime social activities, but seldom mentioned evenings out – never mind late night socialising. Glen Baxter, for example, recalls meeting Ivor in Covent Garden for tea and cakes in the courtyard behind Neals Yard cheese shop. When he was in his mid-70s Ivor summarised his social life: "I go to second hand bookshops, I go to museums and the zoo ... I don't go to the theatre, cinema or go on holiday."[29] His last trip to the cinema was probably around 1980. "Ears can't stand loud sound," he wrote, "which is the only sound available, cos everybody's ½ deaf (except me) from heavy metal."[30] Ben Thompson mentioned Ivor's love of blowing bubbles from his balcony "to gladden the hearts of returning commuters" – Ivor's first appearance on *Dave Allen in Search of the Great English Eccentric* shows him blowing bubbles, although there are no commuters to be seen.[31] Nicola Barker remembered him carrying a small bird noise machine in his pocket, so that it seemed as if small birds were hiding in his clothes: as the imaginary birds tweeted, his face would remain "as straight as a ruler."[32]

"Little Bedwyn" was a favoured holiday spot during the 1970s. It was a cottage in the Wiltshire village of the same name, which Alfie Benge describes as a small, wheelchair-friendly property, part of a farm owned by a friend. Benge and Wyatt stayed there after Wyatt's accident, which left him unable to walk, while they were buying an accessible flat in London.[33] Wyatt recorded some of *Rock Bottom* there and after moving into their new flat they continued to use the cottage for holidays. Ivor and Phyllis were able to use the cottage at other times and Benge remembers that they went down "quite a lot … I think they really enjoyed it down there." Ivor immortalised the place in "Empty Road at Little Bedwyn" on *A Flat Man*.

Ivor and Phyllis also took advantage of an offer from Helen Oxenbury and John Burningham, who owned Filcombe Cottage in Dorset. "They were happy to let us go there for a week or two in the summer holidays," Phyllis recalls, "It was a little cottage in the woods with a long walk through the woods and a meadow down to the sea. We loved the cottage and the walk and the sea. [We spent] hours at the seaside with picnic and paintbrushes and choosing stones to carry back to set up our separate displays." Ivor immortalised this holiday venue on "Garden Path at Filcombe" and "Filcombe Cottage Brook," while Phyllis did the same on "Filcombe Cottage Dorset."[34]

After Ivor retired from teaching, he offered singing and poetry lessons to selected individuals, free of charge. John Burnside received a lesson or two on performing poetry after they first met when Ivor saw him at a South Bank Centre poetry reading. It was one of Burnside's first public readings and took place after a day filled with business meetings, hence Burnside was "on a massive coffee buzz" when he took to the stage, reading far too quickly. Afterwards, in the bar, Ivor emerged from the crowd with a "serious, almost threatening look in his eyes." Without introducing himself or making small talk, Ivor said "in that soft voice of his: 'You write beautiful poetry.' [This] was immediately undercut by what he said next – with just enough of a pause for effect. 'But you're a terrible reader.'" Ivor gave Burnside his name and address, told him to get in touch if he wanted to improve his on-stage reading ability and walked away. Burnside was tempted to laugh the encounter off, but curiosity got the better of him and he made contact. He arrived at the flat, where Ivor cooked lunch (sausages from, Burnside thinks, a local Greek delicatessen), then announced that he would teach Burnside to sing. Ivor ignored Burnside's declaration that he was a terrible singer, because learning to sing would improve breath, timing and control. The lessons worked: "though I have to say that I'm still by no means a great performer of poetry, he did make a difference. At the very least, he slowed me down, which gave the audience a sporting chance of at least partly understanding what I was saying."

Craig Murray-Orr was another beneficiary of Ivor's singing lessons. He recalls having at least three and thinks Ivor taught quite a few other people. For the most part, however, Ivor spent time teaching the writing of poetry, using a technique centred on his often-stated belief in bypassing the intellect. He referred to it as "the Cutler Method," which required the student to write a poem in no more than three minutes:

> Once they've done it, I read the poem aloud in my posh voice and their jaw just drops. They can't believe they've written it … You

have to get past the intellect which is why I only give people three minutes to write a poem. It gets people to listen to words rather than their meanings and rubbish words make more noise.[35]

The Cutler Method incorporated relaxation techniques, voice exercises and the use of an egg-timer to ensure the student's adherence to the three-minute time limit.[36] Ivor claimed that his first few attempts to teach the method caused him physical distress: "I taught 17 people then my brain started to hurt – I had a headache for months and months."[37] He carried on, however, but not always successfully. Sue Edwards remembers Ivor meeting people in the South Bank Centre and taking them to a quiet spot – the National Poetry Library, at the Festival Hall, was one such place – to give them poetry lessons. The library was quiet and there was somewhere to sit, and, she believes, he came to see the venue as his "office." Ivor offered her the chance to experience the Cutler Method, but the experience was short-lived:

> I never did get on with the Ivor poetry method which seemed to consist of getting into a kind of relaxed hypnotic state whereby your subconscious would produce noises and nonsense words. My tendency to lapse into Keatsian verse frustrated him immensely, and he soon gave up on me as a disciple …

Ivor once asked Christine Stark to recite a poem, possibly in advance of offering her a lesson in the Cutler Method, but due to her choice of poem things did not progress. She recited John Hegley's "Miserable Malcolm from Morecambe," but soon became aware that Ivor "couldn't stand Hegley. I said 'Why is that?' and he said that he'd blanked him at some event or other." If Hegley did blank Ivor, he can no longer recall the event, but remembers that his last meeting with Ivor, outside the Poetry Library in the early 2000s, was "a cheery meeting." It was also a valuable meeting. Ivor suggested that Hegley should go into the library and find poetry by the American poet and author Grace Paley, which he did, "and I was very grateful to him for introducing me to her ..." He still reads Paley's *Responsibility* at some of his own performances.

Zoe Hood's poetry education was happy, though brief. She met Ivor during work experience at the South Bank, arranged by Sue Edwards who was a family friend. He told her that he gave poetry lessons "with a strategy that by-passed logic" and her initial lesson took place on the first floor above the foyer. "I tried to write some things. He looked slightly disappointed, then said kindly 'I think you are too conscious to write from the subconscious." Despite her apparent lack of talent, Ivor invited her to his flat for tea. As she was only sixteen, her mother told her not to go alone and so she took her then-boyfriend, Joe Coles. When Ivor saw Coles, she recalls, "his face just fell." However, he invited them both in and an afternoon of songs, stories and poems followed. He played "Jam" on the harmonium, gave them both a poetry lesson and,

Coles recalls, tutored them in creative writing, giving them ten minutes to write a story then asking them to read them aloud. After his initial disappointment, Ivor warmed to Coles and complimented his work: "He liked my stuff and said that when he died I should take over from him as the King of Nonsense. So I guess I'm now the King of Nonsense."

"What is your most unappealing habit?" asked *The Guardian*. "My inability to accept a gift graciously, as it puts a weight on me" Ivor replied.[38] Those who tried to give him presents gained first-hand experience of this habit. Ciara Nolan accidentally lost his kite one day and bought him a new one: "it was like I'd slapped him in the face. He would not accept a gift to save his life." Christine Stark also found that Ivor never accepted presents, but she did persuade him to accept one gift, a battery-operated lighter for his kitchen gas rings. John Burnside, who suggests that Ivor's reluctance to accept gifts stemmed from his concern that "people would try to get things out of him, and he was on guard all the time on that front," gave him gifts of home-made jam. "One of the most generous people I knew," Burnside wrote, "he delighted in playing the skinflint, and his main pleasure in accepting this gift, he claimed, was in knowing that it was free. He knew, of course, the labour that had gone into its making but the truest compliment he could offer was to pretend to take all that for granted."[39]

Burnside and Ivor went on long rambles, visiting Kew Gardens, Wisley (the gardens of the Royal Horticultural Society), and various other public parks and gardens, both of them particularly enjoying their autumn walks among the fallen leaves and fruits.[40] Ivor took great pleasure from his visits, alone or with friends, to places such as this and many of his friends spoke fondly about trips with Ivor. London Zoo, in Regent's Park, was one of Ivor's favourite places: it's where he and Phyllis were filmed for the Dave Allen programme in the early 1970s. Ivor told Val Hennessy that he used to visit London Zoo with his descant recorder to play soothing melodies to the animals: "I played Arabic melodies to the camel hoping to get the odd tear out of his eye as he remembered the old days of taking tourists round the pyramids." He could be flippant about his relationship with the zoo – when Hennessy asked him why he wrote there, he replied "Because I've got a season ticket" – but this relationship seems to have developed over the years.[41] In 1990, Emma Freud described him on *Loose Ends* as "an associate of London Zoo." By 1992, he had become a Fellow of the Zoological Society of London (ZSL), an award which the *Radio Times* mentioned when he appeared on *The Afternoon Shift* to discuss "man aping the animals at Regent's Park Zoo."[42] Anyone could apply to become a Fellow – the society has been awarding fellowships for almost two hundred years – but an applicant had to meet the society's criteria, pay the necessary fees and ensure that they behaved according to the rules of the ZSL. Criteria for election as a Fellow have varied over time, but the society's 1988 byelaws stated that any applicant for a fellowship must either be proposed and seconded by existing fellows, or have been an Associate for at least seven years. In either case, each proposal was considered by the Zoological Society's Council before the fellowship gained approval. Charles Darwin and Sir David Attenborough are among Ivor's fellow Fellows.[43] In 1995 the society received a Royal Charter and associate membership was abolished. Associates automatically became Fellows at that point.[44]

Ivor was a regular visitor to the ZSL library in Regent's Park, often several times a week. Ann Sylph, a ZSL librarian, recalls enjoyable conversations with Ivor and still has a collection of stickies. Ivor presented copies of *Fly Sandwich and Other Menu* and *South American Bookworms* to the library, which also obtained a copy of *The Animal House*. All three books are still available in the library.[45] At London Zoo, the aquarium was one of Ivor's favourite places for writing, despite its environmental challenges. Ivor liked its warmth and darkness and came prepared: "I have a torch pen, rather like the critics, and I can see well enough to write by. I like writing in the dark, it's satisfying." Val Hennessy put it rather more poetically: "On chilly days, Cutler does his writing in the thermostat-controlled fug of the aquarium … His illuminated, battery-operated pen darts like a neon tetra in the gloom." On warmer days, she noted, Ivor preferred working at a wooden seat "up-wind of the rhino enclosure."[46] Neil Cargill believes that the zoo was the venue that most inspired Ivor, in particular the aquarium, "where the tranquillity seemed to suit him. It was as if he knew all the fish personally – especially the more exotic or bizarre ones – and felt he needed to reconnect with them to boost his (and probably their) batteries."

Don Watson met Ivor at the aquarium, then walked with him to the giraffe house. Ivor was polite and informative throughout Watson's interview, but only became enthusiastic when they walked past an enclosure of long-nosed pigs: "Tapirs! … Tapirs are my favourite animals." He added, enigmatically, "If I were to re-design the urban landscape of Britain I would use tapirs."[47] Ivor's affection for different species developed over the years. When he met Emma Freud at the zoo he told her about his love of Marabou storks, while Jeremy Cutler recalled that the capybara was one of his father's favourites.[48] He had a love of insects and built up a collection of books about them, often visiting second-hand bookshops to add to the collection.[49] Phyllis King remembers trips to London Zoo with Ivor in the early years of their relationship, then trips to Kew Gardens with a drawing book, a picnic and a notebook for writing poetry. Kew Gardens is ten miles from Laurier Road, a more demanding cycle ride than the short two-and-a-half-mile journey from the flat to the zoo, but it soon became another of Ivor's favoured venues for a day out.

Popular people are often described as having "a wide circle of friends." Ivor's many friends are better imagined as a series of circles, occasionally overlapping like a Venn diagram, but more often sitting apart from each other. Friends of many years knew few, if any, of Ivor's other friends and remembered that they would usually meet Ivor with no one else present. Even if someone else was there, Ivor did not always introduce them, giving some the impression of a compartmentalised life. Linda Hirst believes "You don't really get to know Ivor. You get to know layers of him …" Beverley Crew met other friends of Ivor's when she appeared on his radio shows, but for the rest of the time she knew him, "He kept us all quite separate. He seemed to like keeping each person for himself." Brian Morton remembers meeting in "these odd little cafes. There was a cafe near the Post Office Tower that he liked, and a famous salt beef bar near the National Portrait Gallery, called Gaby's … The owner had a photograph of Ivor on the wall." Despite their lengthy friendship, Morton never met Phyllis King, or Dan or Jeremy, and never visited Ivor's flat. He did remember Ivor's friendship with Scottish painter Craigie Aitchison, also a friend of Morton's: a friendship which, although it lasted some years, was not mentioned by any other person I interviewed. Morton feels that Ivor preferred to meet people one-to-one: "That's very nice, having Ivor to yourself rather than round a table full of people who knew him better. I remember meeting him at a photographic gallery: he was with someone but we weren't introduced to each other." Ted Harrison doesn't think that Ivor compartmentalised his friends, "But he would never have dreamt of organising a party."

Ivor particularly enjoyed women's company. When he was in his seventies, Nicola Barker described him as "an amazing lothario."[50] Ron Geesin believes that he "would play the 'frail old fellow' to surround himself with admirers, mainly females." Phyllis King thought that his interest stemmed from his childhood: "Well, he always said he liked women. One of the things he always said was 'I'd like to know what women are thinking'. When he was a child he'd always sit under the table when his mum and his aunties were talking and he loved to hear that chatter."[51] Frances Geesin recalls joining Ivor in a quick-step during a dinner party in around 1970 and describes him as "a nifty dancer." Others recall Ivor's flirtatious side, which was not always welcomed. Anna Morshead recalls that when she was in her early twenties Ivor would flirt with her girlfriends, behaviour she describes as "just appalling." He flirted with journalists, too, as Val Hennessy discovered. He took Hennessy to task for wearing high heels, telling her that if a woman wears such footwear "she goes down a couple of notches in my estimation." Soon after, when she asked if he had a "girlfriend" he responded: "Really! … It's the sort of question I'd expect from *Woman's Weekly*. Hmmm. On second thoughts are you by any chance making me an offer? I could easily disregard your high heels. Heh. Heh. Heh. Only joking."[52]

Some of Ivor's relationships, as he described them, were rather mysterious. In an undated interview he spoke about two women.[53] One of them was, he said, the first woman he'd been in love with: "She came to live with me and we sat down to lunch and I couldn't believe it – she made a real racket with her mouth when she was eating … after a few days she decided to go back to her husband and they made off to Australia." Ivor met the second woman a couple of months before the interview. She looked very similar to the first woman and he asked her to come to his flat because he was keen to teach her the

Cutler poetry method: "not only did she look like the previous woman but she ate like the previous woman as well." The descriptions give no clue as to the identities of these mysterious women, or when the first of these relationships occurred. At some time in the early 1990s, Ivor told Gavin Hogg, a "teaching nun" from Liverpool became a fan. Ivor explained that the nun seemed to be very pleasant, but when he discovered that she wanted to use him as a "psychological aid" he stopped their letter-writing activity. He suggested to Hogg that if he met a very intelligent and attractive nun, "it's her."[54] When journalist Karen Grant informed readers that "the broad spectrum of his interests … include women," Ivor told her "I enjoy women but if they haven't got anything up in the top storey, I would feel embarrassed because it would be a fairly physical thing."[55]

Olwen Ellis found that Ivor's attitude to her altered quite suddenly, thanks to a protest. She first met Ivor when she was involved with the London Poetry Secretariat in the early 1980s, around the time David Jones booked Ivor to give a reading at his school. Because of her role as an administrator, she thinks that Ivor initially saw her as somewhat officious, but this opinion changed one day outside Holloway Prison. In March 1984 Sarah Tisdall was gaoled for passing secret government documents to *The Guardian*. Ellis, like many others, was incensed about this and when a demonstration was called to protest outside the prison, she went along to take part:

> I toddled along and there was no one there, so there was only me with my placard outside and who should come cycling along the road but Ivor. He recognised me and that's sort of how we got to know one another. He was quite a political person, so we sort of made a friendship around that: he realised I had views similar to his.

Outside the prison, as Ellis continued her lone protest, "He gave me the support I needed, with his little CND hat on." Ellis doesn't believe that they had a great friendship, but she would join Ivor for trips to the zoo, go to Laurier Road for dinner, or visit just to stand in the kitchen and chat. She, too, speaks of Ivor as a private person, but doesn't view him as odd or eccentric and thinks that her perception of Ivor may also have helped their friendship: "I remember telling him he was a very ordinary person. He thought that was extraordinary, that I should think that, because most people thought of him as very weird and strange and to me he just seemed like a very normal guy … a nice guy, and very funny."

By the late 1980s Ivor started to propose marriage, sometimes something more, to some of his female friends and it was not always clear just how serious these proposals were. According to Beverley Crew "He kept on asking me to marry him: I've spoken to other friends of his who said the same thing." When he first proposed, she told him that she was still married to someone who lived in France, "and he got very excited about the idea of my being a bigamist." Alison O'Kill recalls that Ivor "would make the odd comment but not an inappropriate comment … nothing you could be offended by at all." Kate Lithgow believes that Ivor became slightly obsessed with her: "apparently quite a few women had that. I was in my early 20s then … He constantly used to ask me to take my clothes off and I'd just say 'Don't be ridiculous, Ivor.' He did ask me to marry him … He didn't mean it, it was just Ivor being Ivor." Once he got to know Lucy Armitage he began to telephone her regularly, often on a daily basis, and asked her to join him on days out. "I do remember one of our trips to London Zoo," she says, "We were sitting on a bench. He'd written this really funny poem about a cow and I was laughing out loud. He got off the bench, got down on one knee, and asked me to marry him. I just said 'No.' He was quite affronted, I think. I still don't know if he meant it seriously …"

Being Ivor's friend could be difficult, however fond of him you were. Ciara Nolan and John Knutas both believe that Ivor could "wear out" his friendships. "He was a very intense person and as a friend he could call you and be on the phone for two or three hours," says Nolan, "which was wonderful but if you had any people in your life that could be really difficult." Some of Ivor's relationships lasted until his death, but some slowly fizzled out, over months or even years: "We sort of drifted apart" is how Piers Plowright described the end of his friendship with Ivor. Alfie Benge and Robert Wyatt remained friends with Ivor throughout his life, but they saw him less often when they moved to Lincolnshire in 1988. Ivor never visited their new home, but they did meet when Benge and Wyatt visited London. Andy Kershaw attributes his long friendship with Ivor to physical distance: "That really was helped by me moving to north London. We never fell out." John Knutas's friendship continued throughout Ivor's life, a longevity which he, like Kershaw, attributes to the geographical distance between them. They would typically meet every three years, the rest of the time relying on letter-writing to keep in touch: after a few years of corresponding, Knutas recalls, Ivor could write in Finnish, "astonishingly well and at his best for two whole pages."

Other friendships ended more abruptly. Ron Geesin recorded the exact date, place and time his thirty-year friendship with Ivor came to its end: during a party for Piers Plowright, at 6.30 p.m. on 10 December 1997 in Broadcasting House.

> Following a speech, I was holding a wine glass and couldn't clap, so I whistled with a fingerless whistle that will stop a taxi at 100 metres. Ivor, who was some 20 metres away, leaning on a wall, screwed up his face and put his hands to his ears. I went over and said, "Are you all right, Ivor?" He said, with suitable grimace, "Who wus that whustlin'? It's completely spoilt my evening." "That was me, Ivor – bye bye." I never saw him again.

After Lucy Armitage refused Ivor's London Zoo proposal he asked her why she had turned him down. "I told him 'Because you're seventy-three.' I was thirty-one at the time. He was really offended and that was the cut-off point: the letters stopped, communication ended."

Some friends found that Ivor's attitude to them changed after they gave birth. Beverley Crew's relationship with him continued until she had a baby:

> He wasn't mad about babies, he actively despised the noise they make and thought women became too sensible for his liking once they'd had children. I met him a few months after I'd had my daughter, he came over and whispered in my ear that I didn't look anything like a mother. That was obviously a massive compliment.

Ciara Nolan stayed friends with Ivor after she married in 2000, although "Ivor was really pissed off at me for doing that," but their relationship altered when she had a baby:

> When I became pregnant Ivor was not impressed. After my son was born we did meet a few times but my son was quite poorly and I just couldn't spend ages on the phone. It sounds awful but I had to fade him out so I could concentrate on my son and we lost touch.

Christine Stark's friendship could have ended more than once. She recalls that Ivor always expected her undivided attention when they were together, but one Christmas, when she was getting ready to go to her parents' house, Ivor arrived and began chatting: "I was doing other stuff. He was so cross. He said, 'That's it. I don't need your friendship anymore. I'm going.' So I said 'Why do you come here anyway?' He said 'Toilet stop.' He did come back ... There were a few times when he got cross but he always came back."

For most of his life, Ivor was involved in political and social campaigns. David Jones describes him as very willing to speak up for causes, happy to sign a letter or give a benefit performance, and with a strong belief in noise abatement and voluntary euthanasia. In day-to-day relationships he promoted the benefits of Bach flower remedies, or extolled the virtues of cycling. In interviews, or through lending his name to petitions, he would spread the word for causes in which he believed and occasionally he would make his beliefs known in his songs or poems. Like many performers, Ivor gave his services to charities and causes with a wide range of aims.

Ivor's first known public appearance in aid of charity was his performance in aid of Ealing's Questors Theatre in 1960.[56] A few years later he appeared in aid of a much more radical cause, performing at the *International Times* Uncommon Market in the Roundhouse. The Sunday afternoon event took place just a couple of weeks after *IT*, the newspaper of the emerging counter-culture, printed its favourable review of *Cockadoodledon't*. However counter-cultural *IT* may have been, it still needed money and the Uncommon Market was a money-raising venture, a combined bazaar and auction, with a promised appearance by Pete Townshend of the Who. The *Get Away from the Wall* cover photo of Ivor was the centrepiece of the advertisement for the event, even though the photo was already six or more years old.[57] The market proved popular, with around eight hundred people of all ages enjoying the numerous "spontaneous happenings," including artist Mike Lesser basking naked in jelly and paint, but its fundraising activities fell short and "didn't raise all the bread that IT people were dreaming of ..." Ivor didn't have the best of days, either. He failed to enrapture the crowd and had to be "shuffled off the stage because of noise and re-established in a booth round the back..."[58]

Ivor gave high-profile charity performances, such as the CND-organised *Poets Against the Bomb* at Chelsea Town Hall in 1981, but there were lower-profile activities, too. For example, he signed a petition, published in *The Times*, in support of Action Bangladesh at a time when the country, then known as East Pakistan, was seeking independence from West Pakistan: fellow signatories included Melvyn Bragg, Willie Rushton, V. S. Naipaul and Diana Athill.[59] In September 1975, Ivor and Phyllis King joined Soft Machine, Kevin Coyne and others at the National Abortion Campaign Benefit Festival: the review in *Spare Rib* noted that singer-songwriter Joan Armatrading "loved by feminists, didn't turn up."[60] In the 1980s and 1990s he joined the campaign against the abolition of the Greater London Council and appeared on the bill of the GLC's "Jobs Year Roadshow"; joined the GLC-funded Apples & Snakes Arts in Danger Week events; performed at the Purcell Room for an Apples & Snakes anti-apartheid benefit; and performed at the Queen Elizabeth Hall in aid of Shelter, on a bill that also featured the Balanescu Quartet, jazz vibraphonist Orphy Robinson and the Penguin Cafe Orchestra's Simon Jeffes.[61] When comedian and activist Mark Thomas organised an "evening for peace" at Hackney Empire, for the National Peace Council and the Campaign Against the Arms Trade, *The Stage* urged readers to attend, reporting that Thomas was to be joined by "an impeccable line up of socialists, flower wavers and bona fide peaceniks, such as Jeremy Hardy, Arthur Smith and Ivor Cutler."[62]

John Knutas says that Ivor was tired of politics by the time the pair met in the mid-1980s, preferring to explore languages or his love of fauna. However, it's clear that he never stopped supporting causes in which he believed, even if he became a less active campaigner as time passed. He claimed membership of the Noise Abatement Society and the Voluntary Euthanasia Society, and life membership of Friends of the Earth, three organisations devoted to causes which he supported to the end of his life.[63]

"What would you do if you ruled the world?" the *New Musical Express* asked Ivor in 1988. The ninth of Ivor's ten answers was "Euthanasia would be legal."[64] This was no attempt at causing a stir, or being provocative, in the way that many celebrities might wax lyrical on a controversial subject for effect and a bit more publicity, but a genuine and strongly held belief. "Death is a very good friend," he said in 1997.[65] Over a decade earlier he told Ted Harrison, "I'm over fifty. I've had my life," and when Harrison spoke with him about contemplating suicide, Ivor replied cheerfully "Och, I've made a hobby of it," and described suicide as "a good friend to me."[66] It was comforting because it was always available, yet "extremely difficult without doing yourself an injury." He thought about ways of killing himself, but was conscious that "The options are really not very pleasant." Jumping from a high building was his preferred method at one point, but when he was on the eighth floor of a building, when jumping would have been easy, he decided against it, "Because I have discovered at times of great despair it's usually a preamble to exciting things happening. So I've hung on."[67]

Ivor's aversion to noise in its many forms led him to actively campaign for noise abatement and to join the Noise Abatement Society. One article claimed that he regularly donated his royalties to the society, although this claim was not backed up by any other evidence I could find.[68] One of his stickies exhorted readers to "Save the Eardrum: join the Noise Abatement Socy" and gave the society's phone number.[69] He illustrated the sticky with a drawing of *Cutleria multifida*, a species of marine algae. One journalist described the eighty-year-old Ivor as a man "on an eternal if ultimately fruitless quest for silence."[70] This seems an overstatement given Ivor's love of conversation, singing, drums and music. His quest seems more like a quest for peace and quiet, for a society in which no person's noise should intrude into the lives and well-being of others. He enjoyed silence, "the music of the cognoscenti" as he described it, but a world without sound was not something he campaigned for.[71] When unwanted noise did intrude into his life, Ivor could be quick to anger. On a tube train with an interviewer one day, he was disturbed by a fellow passenger's personal stereo (presumably a portable cassette or CD player, popular in the days before mobile phones could stream an entire world of music): "With an ill-muffled curse of shocking intensity, he pointedly inserts a yellow Noise Abatement Society earplug, having offered spares to those with whom he is conversing." As the annoying passenger leaves the train, Ivor "makes as if to poke him."[72] Sometimes, however, the situation could be resolved on friendlier terms. On one occasion, there was noise coming from a house across Laurier Road and, said Ivor, "it was hell." He went over to complain and found that "the man was very nice. There are a lot of nice people around. Have you noticed?"[73]

As a man who hated loud noise produced by others, Ivor was conscious of the possible impact of noises he produced himself. When one interviewer asked "Do you want the window open or closed?" Ivor replied "Open, though shut when listening to the radio, to avoid irritating the neighbours."[74]

Ivor was physically active for most of his life, cycling or walking around London regularly, but in the late 1980s his heart once again caused him problems. In November 1989 he told John Knutas that he had recently had another "tiny" heart attack and investigations showed that he needed a triple bypass operation, which was scheduled for October of the following year. Ivor looked forward to his recovery, after which, he told Knutas, no woman or farm animal would be safe from him, except hedgehogs.[75] At seventy years of age he wrote his will, describing himself in one word, "humorist," dividing his worldly goods and chattels between Phyllis King, Jeremy and Dan, stating that "I have no religious beliefs and I do not want any mourning at my death" and declaring that his body could be donated for anatomical research.[76]

In his seventies, Ivor spoke of spending his days "filling in the time between getting up in the morning and going to bed at night ..."[77] It sounds like Ivor found this to be something of a struggle, but he had plenty to do. Shopping was a necessary activity, but one he enjoyed from time to time. In his search for a new marmalade he went from his favourite health food store of the time, Bumblebee, to a shop in Marble Arch and then to another in Camden, comparing the taste, texture and prices of a range of products.[78] One journalist claimed that he bought his plus-twos from Harrods and goat's cheese from Selfridges.[79] According to Neil Cargill, Ivor's favourite store was Laurence Corner army surplus, slightly less upmarket but probably offering goods at lower prices. It's here that Cargill remembers Ivor buying a magnetic door stop ("You never know when you might want to stop a door," Ivor told him) and a roll of two hundred stickers advising "Keep Away from Children." In more general terms, as Ivor wrote for John Burningham's book about getting old, "After a long life of being stupid, I have decided to continue being, being stupid for the remainder ... I wrote 'being' twice in mistake, but I refused to start again, & anyway it's an extra meaning."[80]

When Ivor reached his eightieth birthday, the BBC celebrated with a radio documentary, *Glasgow Dreamer*, presented by Arnold Brown. Adrian Mitchell's birthday present to Ivor was his poem, "The Granite Gift," telling of Mitchell's plan to give Ivor a bicycle made of granite, and why that plan failed to reach fruition.[81] In his ninth decade Ivor continued to offer people stickies, to write poems, to highlight dog mess on Camden's streets and to cycle around his home city. As his performance schedule reduced, his social visits to various venues across London became more frequent. David Jones referred to these places as Ivor's "haunts": BBC buildings, the Photographer's Gallery, the offices of Serious and the South Bank complex were all on Ivor's list of places to visit, places where he enjoyed meeting younger people in particular and often formed close relationships with them. Ivor's visits, for the most part, increased the general jollity of the day, but at other times he could puzzle, irritate or annoy those whose working hours he interrupted. Jones remembers Ivor in the Serious office, checking if there were any new staff he could unsettle, but is keen to emphasise the benign nature of Ivor's intentions:

> Ivor was very friendly to most people. He would sometimes disconcert them and occasionally he just broke people because they

couldn't cope. He would make some complicated joke which they couldn't see through and they'd take it personally. He never intended to be cruel or malicious: his intent was always to reach out to people.

It wasn't always easy to tell when Ivor was being funny: as Ted Harrison puts it, "You never knew when he was being a deadly serious Ivor Cutler and at what point he was taking the mickey." A deadpan look might indicate seriousness, but might have been followed immediately by a cackle of laughter and a broad grin displaying what Harrison described as a "mischievous gap" between his two front teeth.[82]

In Christine Stark's office, her fellow staff members loved Ivor's visits, although those in charge were less welcoming: "Of course, they had no idea who he was … there were a lot of raised eyebrows!" When Ivor came to see Neil Cargill at his Langham Street office his visits always caused a stir. Ivor enjoyed using an assumed name when he arrived, leading the BBC commissionaire to announce that "someone" was at reception and should he just make his own way up. Eventually Ivor would appear at Cargill's door: "I'm not sure where he went in between, but it was often quite a while before he'd appear … complete with hiking boots, plus fours, bicycle clips and hat covered in fishing flies – probably stopped en route by many admirers."

For some years, the Royal Festival Hall foyer at the South Bank became the centre of Ivor's little world. Free lunchtime events were a daily occurrence, featuring classical, folk or jazz musicians, all of which might appeal to the music-loving Ivor, and he soon became a familiar figure and a friend to the organisers. As he told *Time Out*, "I see music at the South Bank Centre foyer a lot – largely because it's for nothing!"[83] Sue Edwards became an events programmer at the South Bank in 1990 and first came into contact with Ivor when he telephoned to complain about the volume of a performance he had attended. According to Edwards, "When I agreed with him, he seemed a little confused, and we started talking about other things. Approximately ten minutes later it was like we were the best of friends." They soon met at a foyer event and developed their friendship. A few years after Edwards met Ivor, Beverley Crew joined the team at the South Bank and helped to manage the lunchtime events. She, too, soon became Ivor's friend and recalls that on a typical day Ivor cycled to the venue, arrived just before the music was about to start, and settled in at the bar, sitting or standing and often remaining silent for some time. Spying a likely stranger, Edwards says, he would leave the bar, follow them around and hand them a sticky: "He had one that said 'I am Beautiful' and he loved giving that to someone: just seeing them smile would make his day." Zoe Hood enjoyed Ivor's visits, recalling that he was "a creature of habit," dressed in what she calls "an amazing Ivor outfit" of woollens and pom-pom hats. Once in position, he would tell a story about the day's journey to the venue and begin handing out snacks: "He always used to bring these giant pretzels, as snacks," recalls Hood, "big chewy ones. He used to feed everybody. He'd also have some kind of object to show." Sometimes he'd give out confectionary from an old tin: "the kind of sweets and herbal tablets only found in the dustiest of village sweet shops or apothecaries …" as Edwards describes them. Such behaviour often confused the lucky recipients of stickies or sweeties, who were obviously unaware of who Ivor was. Edwards recalls "random crazy dance routines" which he performed when the music was particularly to his taste: again, to the confusion of many of the assembled music lovers.

Beverley Crew enjoyed Ivor's company in the foyer, but not everyone was so pleased. Some older members of the audience who came, as she put it, "with their sandwiches and thermos flasks to enjoy the free music," regarded Ivor with incomprehension and a degree of suspicion. Other audience members were cheered by Ivor's appearance, which, Crew recalls, varied from string vests and nylon shorts to plus fours, checked shirts and tweeds. Crew was impressed by his headgear, which ranged from a fez or a flat cap adorned with a big plastic sunflower, to wigs and a floppy sunhat. One of her favourite items was a 1960s style blond wig, but she also enjoyed the plastic flies that adorned his jackets and emphasised that "there weren't signs of any major failings in the personal hygiene department. Ivor actually smelt rather pleasantly of paper bags, books and potatoes, despite the fact that he didn't believe in soap and water." Ivor is usually thought of as a man with a distinctive style and Crew feels that this style was at its best in the 1990s:

> I think he definitely got better as he got older. The period I knew him he was a really beautiful man. The Summerhill era he was wearing brown corduroy trousers and Jesus sandals, he hadn't developed his sartorial style at that stage. I think he had a really fantastic sartorial style so it's always been interesting to see photographs of him from the 1950s and 60s because he looked a bit of a nobody, while later he expanded his persona in every respect. Maybe being in the public eye gave him the confidence to do that.

When the musicians were not performing, Ivor and Sue Edwards would hold long conversations, speaking seriously about very silly things and lightheartedly about very serious things. There were days when he would look to be the centre of attention and other days when he avoided contact with people he didn't know. As Edwards described it, "He was a strange mix of attention-seeking and shy, not quite understanding why the large sunflower on his hat was attracting quite so much attention, and often, when feeling unsociable, hiding behind me at the bar when anyone looked like they were approaching …"

The music was important to Ivor, the chance for social interaction perhaps secondary to the opportunity to hear new performers and new compositions.

Noise was an important consideration, however, so Edwards would often sit with him and go through the forthcoming programme of events, marking those concerts which she thought would be suitable with regard to volume. Ivor didn't always plan his visits around this advice: he was sufficiently impressed by at least one band that he endured the high volume at which it played. This was the Honky Hep Cats, later known as the Big Buzzard Boogie Band. "He loved them," Edwards recalls, "They were very madcap, but they were way too loud for him so he'd go up to the sound desk and moan about it and put his fingers in his ears, but he still watched them." At other concerts, she says, Ivor would wander down to the stage to see how many microphones were set up and would decide whether to stay or not based on his assessment of the band's likely volume level.

At one lunchtime concert, the pianist was introducing her bandmates to the crowd when she recognised Mr Cutler from her days at Fox Primary. Kate Williams was the pianist:

> I remember … seeing this figure standing by the bar. He hadn't changed a bit. I went up to him and the first thing he said was "You probably won't remember me." I just said "How could I forget, you look exactly the same." We sat down and had a really nice chat and a cup of tea. He told me he'd enjoyed the gig and went on to say that he liked my band partly because it wasn't too loud, then proceeded to tell me how he was a member of the Noise Abatement Society. I think he gave me a few stickers and we exchanged phone numbers.

Ivor recalled the meeting in a 2004 interview:

> One day there was a girl called Kate Williams playing with a jazz trio. She was brilliant. When she came for the bow, she saw me in the audience. And she was a little girl who I once taught! And she saw me and gave me a big hug and said, "if it hadn't been for you, doing those wee classes during playtime, I would never have done a thing like this!" You can see the tears are coming now …[84]

Williams recalls two phone conversations in particular. In the first, "He rang me up … and he was really sweet. He said he'd love to give me a quote for my next album: it was 'Kate Williams attacks the piano as if she will stand no nonsense from it.'" On the second occasion, "he rang up – I don't think he even said who he was – and just said 'Have you got an interest in natural history? Because you remind me of an insect.' I don't think many people could say that without sounding at all rude."

17 "I Will Become a Hermes"

Death and dying are commonplace in Ivor's work, from Bill's demise in the car crash of "Phonic Poem" to the deaths in "A Bubble or Two," the killing of Fremsley so the bird could be eaten with chips, the cheery verse in "I Believe in Bugs" when he sings of lying in the ground as the bugs gradually eat his remains, and the lines from "A Doughnut in my Hand," in which Ivor sings about climbing into a silver coffin. They were also regularly referenced in Ivor's interviews, when he spoke to journalists about his hopes and fears, expressing preferences for how or when to die. "Holding my breath while reading a book of jokes," he told one journalist.[1] One of his few published references to his father included another preference: "I remember my dad when he was in intensive care. 'Hey, Ivor,' he whispered … 'I want to tell you something. I've left you bugger all in my will'; and I thought, 'How marvellous.' I want to die like Dad, making a joke."[2] Then again, perhaps going out with a bang, or at least a punch, was more Ivor's thing, a chance to exact some revenge on a noise-maker on the way out. "When I do a gig, quite often you'll get one person whistling instead of clapping. It drives me nuts. It'd be worth going to prison for if I attacked them … And halfway on the way down to punch this guy up I get a heart attack like Tommy Cooper. That's the way I'd like to go."[3]

The possibility of a "slow degeneration" was Ivor's particular fear, the chance that his final years would see him having to live with dementia, as both his father and one of his brothers had apparently done.[4] For many years, Ivor spoke to friends and journalists about this fear, concerned that any hint of forgetfulness might be a sign of incipient dementia. When Alastair McKay interviewed him in 1994, Ivor spoke about "spasms" of absent-mindedness but emphasised that "it's not Alzheimer's." A few years later, walking near his flat with Ciara Nolan, Ivor "was chatting away and lost his train of thought: he looked at me with absolute terror and said 'Oh, God. I think it's happening.

I'm beginning to forget things.' He'd always been terrified that this is how it would go."

Ivor's final letter to John Knutas was brief, just five lines below a couple of recognisably Cutlerian drawings. The final words were "You takes a great load off my shoulder. At last it moves silence." Those final five words still puzzle Knutas: "The line had nothing to do with anything else in that letter. I still don't know what he meant."[5] Neil Cargill heard from Ivor a few months after Ivor wrote this final letter and remembers the phone call as a "very poignant" occasion:

> I didn't fully realise the significance of it at the time. He phoned me one evening and chatted as normal, then became a little sub-dued and I remember him talking about how people's paths cross and then diverge for a reason – something along the lines of how their connection has great meaning for a long time, and then its essential nature changes and they should feel no sadness in the fact they no longer have the chance to share the same path. He ended by saying, with a laugh, he just wanted to let me hear his lovely voice once more – and also he wanted to hear my voice "one last time". He just said "bye-bye" then rang off. These last few words shook me a little ... it was only later that I learned these phone calls he'd been making were just before he left his flat for good and moved into the home.

Dylan Edwards became concerned when Ivor, always meticulous about paying the rent and his share of the water bill, became unreliable for the first time since moving to Laurier Road. "He couldn't cope with figures, so I just thought I'd let it go," Edwards said, "I was worried about him in the last few months he was in this house. He got very disorientated, lost his sense of direction. I was worried about him going out." In late September 2004, according to Piers Plowright's diary, Ivor "wandered out of his house ... in a daze" and was admitted to the Royal Free Hospital. Plowright visited him at the hospital on 5 October and Ivor told him "My head's been broken into." By November, Ivor was in a care home, coincidentally the home where Plowright's step-mother was living. Plowright's diary entry for 28 December reads, "I think Ivor just wants company and followed him upstairs to his room to talk about Matisse and music. He's been doing some drawing in the hall. 'Art is about the secret heart' he said."

The care home wasn't ideal. Plowright recalled that Ivor would sometimes go into a communal area to play the piano, "but he wasn't popular. They all wanted Vera Lynn, they didn't want Ivor Cutler!"[6] Jeremy looked for another, more suitable place for his father. Eventually, he found Osmond House, a home near Hampstead Heath managed by a Jewish charity. "My brother spent a great deal of time trying to find places," Dan remembers, "It was really great that he was in there, the nurses managed to make him happy." David Jones visited and found that Ivor was often lucid and talkative: "we would chat and he would tell funny stories ... He seemed very happy to be within a Jewish identity and to be in a part of London he knew and liked." More old friends came to visit, but as time passed Ivor's memory failed him. Andy Kershaw recalls that when he and Glen Baxter visited Ivor in Osmond House "It was really sad, he didn't really recognise either of us." Baxter has a happier memory of this final visit, however:

> I remember trying to get him to reveal just a little of the magic spark that had entranced us all for years. At one point I pulled out my copy of *Gruts*, told him it was one of my favourite books – and asked him if he could read something from it. He declined and so I asked if it would be OK if I read something. Ivor looked me straight in the eye and said "I'd rather you didn't." Which was, of course, PERFECT IVOR – the Ivor of Old, the Ivor we all loved.

Ivor collapsed one morning at Osmond House and was admitted once again to the Royal Free Hospital. Jeremy, Dan and Phyllis were all able to be with him in the hospital, where he died the following day, on 3 March 2006. His death was recorded as due to an intracerebral haemorrhage, but a post-mortem examination showed, in Dan's words, "classic signs of Alzheimer's." His father's brain was preserved to be used in medical research.[7]

Ivor's funeral took place at Golders Green crematorium five days later. Piers Plowright was there, and noted in his diary that Adrian Mitchell and his wife, Celia Hewitt, attended, Phyllis and Jeremy both said a few words, and the rabbi "spoke in a warm ordinary voice as if the words had just occurred to him and this seemed right." As the funeral ended, wrote Plowright, "We went out to Ivor singing 'I'm Going in a Field'." He was introduced to Ivor's ex-wife, Virginia, who he described as "a tall woman in black."

The funeral was a relatively low-key event; the memorial was much larger. Plowright noted the wording of the invitation: "The family and friends of Mr Ivor Cutler invite you to an afternoon of reminiscence and celebration of his life and work. Doors 2.30 p.m., event 3 p.m. at Cecil Sharp House." Plowright estimated that around one hundred people attended, including Robert Wyatt, Andy Kershaw and John Knutas. Cecil Sharp House is the headquarters of the English Folk Dance and Song Society and sits in an imposing detached property on Regent's Park Road, a short walk from Camden Town tube station, in a part of London very familiar to Ivor. The memorial was a light-hearted affair, at the end of which, Plowright wrote in his diary, "we all sat in the sun, as if waiting for a man in knickerbockers with a mask-studded cap to pedal into the garden."

Each guest received a souvenir package labelled "*Genuine* IVOR CUTLER 'lucky' BAG," a pink and white striped paper bag containing stickies, plastic insects, rubber bands and paper clips.[8] According to Dan the bag was Jeremy's idea:

> I thought it was a fabulous idea. I remember going with him to a joke shop … Ivor had a fondness for joke shops. When I was a kid there used to be a department store, Gamages, and they had a joke department. When it was my turn to stay with him we would go there and he would look for things to amuse himself with, fake flies to scatter in sugar bowls, that kind of thing.

Ivor's impact on British culture was big enough for major publications to note his passing with an obituary. *The Independent*, *The Times*, *The Guardian* and *The Stage* all remembered him and retold many of the stories and anecdotes that had come to be associated with him over his lifetime. The Westminster Parliament ignored Ivor's death, but the Scottish Parliament didn't forget one of the country's favourite sons and two MSPs tabled motions, praising his talents and his influence on later generations of Scottish comedians and musicians.[9] Pauline McNeill of Scottish Labour proposed the first, on 7 March. In memory of Ivor's role in *Magical Mystery Tour* it was titled "I am concerned for you to enjoy yourself within the limits of British decency – Death of Ivor Cutler":

> That the Parliament expresses its deep sadness and regret at the death of poet, singer, songwriter and storyteller, Ivor Cutler, who was born and bred in Glasgow; extends its condolences to his surviving family and friends; notes the profound influence that Cutler had on his fellow Scots, Billy Connolly and members of the band Franz Ferdinand, as well as Bertrand Russell, the Beatles and John Peel, and recognises the outstanding contribution which he made to his art and Scottish culture through his unique insight and wit.

McNeill's motion attracted the support of thirty-eight of her fellow Members of the Scottish Parliament, including Scottish Green Party MSP Patrick Harvie. The following day, Harvie proposed his own motion, with the more prosaic title of "The End of Ivor Cutler," attracting sixteen supporters including McNeill:

> That the Parliament celebrates the life of Ivor Cutler, poet, musician, and artist, who sadly died this week after entertaining and occasionally perplexing audiences for half a century; hopes that Ivor Cutler's passing will not stop new generations from discovering his work and delighting in it as so many have before, and, now that the coffin is closed, hopes that he enjoys the doughnut.

The coffin was closed but Ivor carried on, his voice, words and music available through re-released recordings, repeats of his radio shows, various tribute programmes and a few less predictable events. Few, if any, years have passed since 2006 without at least one notable tribute, appraisal of or addition to his body of work. In 2007, Jeremy and Dan established Hoorgi House Limited and its record label, Hoorgi House Records (named after "The Hoorgi House" on *Gruts*). Since then, the label has re-released three albums; *A Flat Man*, *Privilege* and *A Wet Handle*; and released *Singing While Dead*, a download-only EP of previously unreleased recordings of "The Man with the Trembly Nose," "There's a Hole in my Head," "Rolling Pins and Rolling Pins" and "Wooden Stew."[10] Among other notable Ivor-related events, *The Old Guys*, the BBC television comedy series starring Roger Lloyd-Pack, Clive Swift and Jane Asher (McCartney's girlfriend around the time when he and Ivor first met), used "I'm Happy" and "Barabadabada" as its theme songs.[11]

One unusual but appropriate tribute appeared in 2018, when Charles S. Eiseman and Owen Lonsdale named a newly discovered species of North American leaf miner fly as *Liriomyza ivorcutleri*, immortalising Ivor in the entomological record. The note on the Bug Life website reads, "This species is named for Ivor Cutler (1923–2006), Scottish recording artist, whose several entomologically themed compositions include one that begins 'I am a yellow fly.'"[12] Eiseman is a twenty-year fan of Ivor's work: when he and Lonsdale began identifying new species of leaf-mining flies, he says, "I started hoping one of the yellow ones would turn out to be new so I could name it after Ivor."

Liriomyza ivorcutleri, a yellow fly. (Courtesy of Charley Eiseman, photograph by Charley Eiseman.)

Ivor's "Yellow Fly" (from *Velvet Donkey*) inhabits its own unique world, captured in a mere one minute and thirty-six seconds:

> I am a yellow fly
> I fly high up the sky
> You cannot see me when the sun shines
> For I am the colour of the sunshine
> I am the colour of the sunshine
>
> My legs are long and green
> But they're hollow so they can't be seen
> I often fill them with liquid
> Go back and feed them to my queen
> Go back and feed them to my queen
>
> I am a yellow fly
> I fly high up the sky
> You cannot see me when the sun shines
> For I am the colour of the sunshine
> I am the colour of the sunshine
> I am the colour of the sunshine.

It's unlikely that *Liriomyza ivorcutleri* leads such a romantic existence.

Although Radio 4's *Desert Island Discs* has been broadcast since the 1940s, Ivor was never invited to imagine life on a desert island, not that he would have needed to imagine, having experienced life on Y'Hup. In each edition of the show a guest selects recordings, a book and a luxury to take to the island, but for many years no one asked for anything by Ivor. It was 2020 before a guest asked to take some of his work to the island and then, like buses, two arrived in quick succession. On 24 May the conductor and broadcaster Charles Hazlewood chose as his book an unspecified collection of poetry "by the great Glaswegian Bard, Ivor Cutler. A man always found sweating over a wheezy harmonium ... He's a bit like a Shakespearian Fool, there's a kind of a surreal nonsense to his language and his message but of course there's always a deep, human, truth enshrined in it." Six months later, Helen Oxenbury chose episode one of *Life in a Scotch Sitting Room* as one of her recordings, taken from the live album.[13]

Ivor continues to appear on radio, with repeats of his shows on Radio 4 Extra and regular re-broadcasts of his Peel and Kershaw session tracks on 6 Music. He also pops up in less obvious places, such as another long-standing Radio 4 show, *Round Britain Quiz*. On an edition that included broadcaster and Ivor Cutler fan Stuart Maconie on the North of England team, contestants were asked why a piece of music might bring to mind "a type of recharge-able battery, a seventeenth-century plotter and Prufrock's life measures." The music was Ivor's "Beautiful Cosmos," from what sounds like a late-period session performance. The tenuous link is cutlery: a nickel/iron battery offers the chemical symbols NiFe, the plotter is Guy Fawkes, T. S. Eliot's Prufrock measured life in coffee spoons, and a cutler makes cutlery.[14]

Round Britain Quiz represents a style of radio show that would be familiar to listeners from the 1940s: comfortable, amusing and profoundly old-fashioned. After all, it's been a fixture on BBC radio since 1947, a decade or more before Ivor appeared on the wireless. Back in the 1960s, it may have been supposed that a new generation of artists and programmes – the Goons, the Beatles, *Round the Horne*, Peter Cook, Ivor Cutler – would consign *Round Britain Quiz* and equally venerable shows such as *Desert Island Discs* to oblivion. But it hasn't worked out that way, and *Round Britain Quiz* happily co-exists with the work of Noel Fielding, Matt Berry and others, in much the same way that progressive rockers and punk rockers still co-exist after the mid-1970s arrival of the latter was supposed to eliminate the former. Ivor Cutler created some of the most distinctive, idiosyncratic and original recordings and broadcasts of the late twentieth century, was feted by Lennon and McCartney, played support spots with prog rockers and punks, but still makes an appearance on *Round Britain Quiz* and continues, as Patrick Harvie hoped, to attract new fans and admirers.

His poems, songs and plays are popular with lovers of quirky, left-field flights of fancy, but Ivor himself is also attractive to those who value individuality and distinctiveness, the idea of Ivor as an "outsider." But what makes Ivor an outsider, what is he outside of? After all, in many respects he spent his life inside established society, paying his rent on time, living quietly in the middle of London, working as a teacher and spending thirty years gainfully employed by the Inner London Education Authority. David Bramwell views Ivor as an outsider "In terms of the work and the way he went about the work, those awkward pauses he honoured whether on radio or records, for an artist to embrace that and love it, that's what I associate with him as an outsider." Graham Duff sees Ivor's outsider status as arising from his ability to resonate with fans from alternative cultures without ever being part of those cultures himself:

> I think [it's] about operating just outside the prevailing culture, so that during the Beatles psychedelic hippy era, or an era where you've got Peel reading Tolkien and Marc Bolan talking about pixies and elves ... it was easy to see him as part of that for the hippy generation, and yet he's outside that because of the violence [in his work], because of the spikiness, because of the very parochial and distinctly Scottish feel of what he's doing. Later, in the punk and post-punk era, he's got the spikiness but there's that remnant of the sixties about him as well ... He resonates with various cultures but I don't think he ever entirely fitted in.

Lemn Sissay has a similar opinion, describing Ivor as "an important, rebellious, spirit in the world of poetry" and "quite possibly an outsider wherever he was":

> All poets, definitely, feel like they're outsiders, that is a prerequisite for a poet. It's at the core of who they are ... The power of recognising and relating in a very big way to yourself as an outsider is in recognising that you have a unique experience that you want to share ... I am an outsider and I'm seeing things and I want you to see things in the way that I see them. I do believe we are all outsiders but the artist has to have a real urgency about communicating what they're seeing as an outsider.

In 2003, Ivor summed up his own contribution to humanity in generally positive terms, with a hint to an "outsider" approach to life:

> I think I've been a useful member of the human race, in particular, getting the backs up of authority ... creating trouble wherever I go ... to come along and stir things up a bit. It comes over like I'm really some sort of a hellion, doesn't it? It's not that, it's just shaking people up and they suddenly realise that their brain has been asleep.[15]

If there was going to be a life after death, Ivor offered a few ideas about what it might entail. He may have wished to return as a Marabou stork, as he told Emma Freud.[16] He may once have thought about returning to Earth in the guise of an adjutant bird – "Very bad tempered," he told Eve Kendall.[17] Then again, he expressed an interest in returning as *Cutleria multifida*, marine algae that would serve as animal feed.[18] But he also responded to "Do you believe in life after death?" with "What the hell would I want to live for? I've done that." Perhaps he might find a job. Returning as an adjutant bird was a short-lived ambition and when Kendall visited he had a new idea: "My latest idea is that when I die I will become a Hermes and run around doing messages for God." There was something he would miss: "I shall be glad to get away from loud pop music and motor cars, but I shall miss – insofar as when one is dead one can miss anything – the beautiful kindnesses of those people to whom courtesy comes naturally."[19]

So what might Ivor be up to these days? Try as I might, I can't imagine him paddling around in the guise of a Marabou stork, or grumpily flying across the skies as an adjutant bird. Perhaps he'd be better suited to a reappearance as a *Liriomyza ivorcutleri*, or even *Cutleria multifida*. However, there is one form that might suit a man who spent his life communicating with the world in novel and fascinating ways, one he suggested to Eve Kendall – the guise of a Hermes. Sit quietly (as he would wish you to do), stare at the sky

Ivor and his bicycle, on York Rise. (Courtesy of Dylan Edwards, photograph by Joyce Edwards.)

and listen, and on a still, clear, night you might hear the occasional "squeak, squeak" of an aging bicycle as the octogenarian Messenger of the Gods travels at a steady pace around Mount Olympus, chewing on a doughnut, delivering sticky notes to selected deities, checking that Cerberus hasn't left any unpleasant deposits on the road down to Hades, asking Dionysus to keep the noise down a bit, and leaping nonchalantly onto a passing chariot to impress Aphrodite with his agility.

Notes

All websites were accessed in January 2022 and all interviews were with the author (face to face, phone, online or email) between October 2019 and February 2022. All quotations in the text are taken from these interviews unless otherwise noted. Books and journals are referenced in full in the bibliography; other sources are referenced in full in the notes, on first appearance. The following abbreviations are used in the notes (dates of TV or radio programmes are dates of first broadcast):

BBC WAC	BBC Written Archives Centre
CR	*Cult Radio*, BBC Radio 5 Live, 20 July 1993
GD	*Glasgow Dreamer*, BBC Radio 4, 4 February 2003
GLIC	*Great Lives: Ivor Cutler*, BBC Radio 4, 27 April 2021
IC90	*Ivor Cutler at 90*, BBC Radio 4, 10 August 2013
ICKT	*Ivor Cutler by KT Tunstall*, Sky Arts, 13 October 2020
ICLSC	*Ivor Cutler's Little Squeaks and Creaks*, BBC Radio Scotland, 24 April 2010 (broadcast as part of the *Comedy Zone* series; the date of the original interview is not known)
ICS	*The Ivor Cutler Story: Life in a Scotch Sitting Room Volume 2*, Radio Scotland, 13 April 2002
LFTWP	*Ivor Cutler: Looking for Truth with a Pin*, BBC Four, 15 April 2005
P	*Profile*, BBC Radio 4, 17 November 1984
SI	*Sweet Inspiration*, BBC Radio Scotland, *c*.1995 (precise date of transmission unknown)

Details of national BBC television and radio shows can be found in the BBC Programme Index at genome.ch.bbc.co.uk.

Acknowledgements

1. Hussey, M. (2021) *Clive Bell and the Making of Modernism*, 426.

1 An Introduction

1. *Ivor Cutler – by Ivor Cutler* (1998) Scottish Television. Broadcast as part of STV's weekly arts programme, *Don't Look Down*. Date of first broadcast unknown.
2. As told to me by Beth Marcuson, Brian Morton, Craig Murray-Orr, Alfie Benge, Alison O'Kill, Beverley Crew, Charlotte Steel, Ciara Nolan, David Toop, Dylan Edwards, Jonathon Porritt, Kate Lithgow, Kate Williams, Linda Hirst, Milton Mermikides, Olwen Ellis, Rebecca Orr-Dees, Ron Geesin, Ronald Macrae, Sue Edwards, Zoe Hood, John Knutas, Anna Morshead, Ted Harrison, Tony Ward.
3. Levin, B. (1974) "A Festival of Sweetness and Light." *The Times*, 28 June; Anonymous (1994) "Highlights." *The List*, 20 May, 81; Williamson, N. (2002) "Choice: Ivor Cutler." *The Times*, 2 March.
4. Thompson, B. (1990) "Off the Wall." *New Statesman and Society*, 27 April, 44.

2 Return to Y'Hup

1. Chemikal Underground Records (2020) CHEM255.
2. Shepherd, F. (2020) Concert review. *The Scotsman*, 31 January; Virtue, G. (2020) Concert review. *The Guardian*, 30 January.
3. Cover notes to *Ivor Cutler of Y'Hup* (1959) Fontana TFE 17144.
4. nms.ac.uk/press-office/first-major-exhibition-on-scottish-pop-music-opens-in-edinburgh/.
5. Doncaster, P. (1959) "On the Record: New Faces!" *Daily Mirror*, 9 April.
6. britannica.com/event/Great-Smog-of-London.

3 Early Life

1. Moris was the son of Berky, a cap maker, and Risha. He was twenty-two and Shipre was twenty when they married. See Joseph Cutler's birth certificate.
2. By 1911 Glasgow's Jewish population had grown to around nine thousand, much larger than Edinburgh's Jewish population of around two thousand. See Collins, K. E. (2008) *Scotland's Jews*, 16; Collins, K. E. (2016) *The Jewish Experience in Scotland*, 1.
3. Frank, F. (2012) *An Outsider Wherever I Am?*, 103–104.
4. Kendall, E. (1985) "A Room of my Own: Ivor Cutler." *The Observer Magazine*, 2 June, 78–79.
5. *LFTWP*.
6. Many migrants would have been in touch with family members who already lived in Scotland, or planned to make the country their destination in the knowledge that it already offered Jewish communities, synagogues, Yiddish-language newspapers and support groups. As for mistaking Scotland for the USA, this myth may have a place in stereotyping the migrants as uneducated, easily fooled or stupid but this was not the case. Certainly, some migrants saw Scotland as a temporary destination before heading further west and others may have decided to remain because they were too ill to travel further, or too poor to afford the additional tickets, but many people intended to head for Scotland and, like the Kushners, were happy to stay. (Information from Fiona Brodie, Scottish Jewish Archives Centre.)

   The Cutlers were living in Greenock when Joseph was born on 26 June 1900. Moris's death certificate notes that he was "formerly Kushner" and Caroline

Richmond, Ivor's girlfriend in the mid-1960s, recalls that Ivor told her of the change of name, but the reason for the change is unclear. Names vary across official documents: Moris is sometimes spelt with two r's, Shipre is sometimes referred to as Sophie or Sophia, while Dushditz is also spelt Duozezic or Dushtiz. Many members of Scotland's Jewish community retained their original surnames for their entire lives. Those that changed their names did so for a variety of reasons: some wanted to assimilate into the new country's culture by taking on a less obviously "immigrant" name, some changed for professional or business reasons. Some families changed their names at the outbreak of World War I, afraid that they sounded not too Jewish, but too German. Importantly, as Brodie puts it: "It was rare if ever for people's names to be changed on entering a new country ... It was almost always a matter of choice." It's no longer clear why the Kushners made that choice. See Moris Cutler's death certificate; Shipre Cutler's death registration (recorded as Sophia Cutler); Joseph Cutler's birth certificate; 1901 Census; Frank, F. (2012) *An Outsider Wherever I Am?*, 115.

7. The couple married at South Portland Street synagogue on 21 November 1893, when Fishel was twenty-four and Tilla seventeen. See 1901 census.

8. The family home was at 35 Hutcheson Street, across the Clyde from the Gorbals, with another Goldberg family headed by Philip, a tailor and a Russian citizen. Philip and Fishel may have been brothers. See 1901 census.

9. The family was living at 66 South Portland Street in the Gorbals when Eva was born, close to the synagogue where Fishel and Tilla had married. Of the Goldbergs' children, six died at birth or in infancy with nine surviving into adulthood. Lee Freeman; Eva Goldberg's birth certificate.

10. Soon after arriving in Scotland, Moris Cutler became a "picture traveller." A decade later Moris (recorded in the 1911 census return as Max) was a canvasser and collector in the drapery industry and Jacob was working in an ironmongery. There were two more children by 1911: six-year-old Lazarus and four-year-old Annie. Lazarus was never a fit and healthy child: born with patent ductus arteriosus, a then-incurable cardiac anomaly, he died of cardiac failure on 4 November 1914, aged ten. The 1911 census recorded the number of windowed rooms in a household, as an indicator of economic status: the Cutler home had just two such rooms, the Goldberg household had four. See 1901 and 1911 census returns; Lazarus Cutler's death certificate.

11. Frank, F. (2012) *An Outsider Wherever I Am?*, 70–71.

12. Lloyd, A. L. (1948) "The forgotten Gorbals." *Picture Post*, 31 January.

13. Glasser, R. (1987) *Growing Up in the Gorbals*, 2–16.

14. Jack Cutler and Polly Goldberg's marriage certificate; Taylor, A. (2014) "Are You a Billy, or a Dan, or an Old Tin Can?"

15. Glasgow Valuation Roll, 1925; Moris Cutler's death certificate; Shipre Cutler's death registration (recorded as Sophia Cutler).

16. Jack Cutler and Paulina Goldberg's marriage certificate.

17. The street was redeveloped and renamed Rhynie Drive. See glasgowguide.co.uk/info-streetschanged3.html; Glasgow Valuation Roll, 1920.

18. Espiner, M. (2006) Obituary. *The Guardian*, 7 March; Isadore Cutler's birth certificate.

19. As told to Ronald Macrae. For the hypothetical phone call, see Love, D. (2015) "A Message from Ivor Cutler." Reprinted at glasgowmusiccitytours.com/blog/a-message-from-ivor-cutler/.

20. Episode 6; episode 16.

21. "Gorbals, 1930" is on *A Flat Man*, Creation Records CRECD 236. Uncle Joe, Jack's younger brother, worked as a fishmonger's assistant and lived with his parents until 1932 when he married Jeannie Yaffy, a fishmonger and possibly his boss. See Joseph Cutler and Jeannie Yaffy's marriage certificate.

22. *ICS*. In *GD*, episode 8, he claimed the move occurred when he was six.

23. Love, D. (2015) "A Message from Ivor Cutler."

24. Watson, D. (1986) "Grut Cutlet." *New Musical Express*, 10 May, 6–7.

25. Bernard and Joseph became doctors, in Glasgow and London respectively, and Bernard later became a noted Hebrew scholar. Rita married Isodor Cohen in 1947 and moved to Cheshire. Beth married the artist Lawrence Marcuson and moved to Israel in the 1960s. The Cutler brothers went by a variety of first names over the years. By his early twenties, Ivor was no longer known by his registered name of Isadore, socially, professionally or on official documents. Beth refers to her oldest brother as Bernard and her youngest as Jo, while Lee Freeman, their cousin, recalls that the family usually referred to Bernard as Berl, the name by which he was known in the field of Hebrew scholarship (Anonymous (1997) "Dr Bernard Cutler." *The Herald*, 27 December). Phyllis King remembers that Ivor called his brothers Berl and Josie.

26. Bruce, K. (1995) "Playing on Words with Ivor the Poetry Engine." *Herald Scotland*, 13 July.

27. Anonymous (1938) "Driver's Front Wheel Skid: Can it Be Corrected?" *Jedburgh Gazette*, 4 November.

28. *P*.

29. *Privilege* (1983) Rough Trade ROUGH 59.

30. Cutler, J. (2009) Notes to *Privilege*, Hoorgi House Records HHCD02.

31. Harrison, T. (1997) "The Comeback Kid." *The Times Magazine*, 5 April, 25–27.

32. *LFTWP*.

33. Lee Freeman, interview.

34. *LFTWP*.

35. *Cutler's Last Stand* (2005) BBC Four, 15 April. This is a recording of a performance at Queen Elizabeth Hall, London, on 1 February 2004.

36. *ICS*.

37. Glasser, R. (1987) *Growing Up in the Gorbals*, 2–3.

38. Taylor, A. (2014) "Are You a Billy, or a Dan, or an Old Tin Can?"

39. *SI*.

40. Dallas, K. (1974) "Everyone Else is an Eccentric." *Melody Maker*, 16 November, 54; Rae, I. (1977) "Ivor Cutler." *Brig* 8: 5: 8.

41. *SI*.

42. *LFTWP*.

43. Barnes, M. (1997) "Invisible Jukebox." *The Wire*, June, 50; as told to John Knutas.

44. Lewis, J. (2004) "Quiet Riot." *Time Out*, February. Accessed at johnlewisjournalist.co.uk/ivor-cutler.

45. *SI*.

46. *LFTWP*.

47. Barnes, M. (1997) "Invisible Jukebox," 51.

48. Thomson, G. (2020) *Small Hours: The Long Night of John Martyn*, 15.

49. *SI*.

50. Barnes, M. (1997) "Invisible Jukebox," 51.

51. *SI*.; Rae, I. (1977) "Ivor Cutler." 8.

52. Thompson, B. (1990) "Off the Wall"; *ICS*.

53. *ICLSC.*
54. *SI.*
55. Ivor Cutler to Gavin Hogg, 11 February 1991.
56. Hoare, N. (ed.) (2018) *Y'Hup: Ivor Cutler*, 10.
57. Frank, F. (2012) *An Outsider Wherever I Am?*, 126.
58. Love, D. (2015) "A Message from Ivor Cutler."
59. McKay, A. (1994) "Ivor Cutler, Absurdist Poet, Teacher, Songwriter, Magical Mystery Tourist, Survivor of a Scotch Childhood." Published to accompany an exhibition of Katrina Lithgow's photographs at the Stills Gallery, Edinburgh, 5 June. Accessed at alternativestovalium.blogspot.com.
60. Kendall, E. (1985) "A Room of my Own: Ivor Cutler." *The Observer Magazine*, 2 June, 78.
61. Frank, F. (2012) *An Outsider Wherever I Am?*, 109.
62. Anonymous (1945) "Medical Examinations." *Scotsman*, 27 January.
63. McKay, A. (1994) "Ivor Cutler, Absurdist Poet ..."
64. *P.*
65. Lewis, J. (2004) "Quiet Riot." In Lewis's interview Ivor says he was thirteen.
66. Flintoff, J-P. (1992) "The Great Scottish Eccentric." *Jewish Chronicle*, 24 July, 24.
67. McKay, A. (1994) "Ivor Cutler, Absurdist Poet ..."

4   A Life in the Clouds

1. *SI.*
2. Calvin et al. (2014) "Childhood Evacuation During World War II," 229–230.
3. Beth Marcuson, interview.
4. Beth Marcuson, interview.
5. Donald, A. (1997) "The Write Stuff." *The List*, 25 July, 98.
6. McKay, A. (1994) "Ivor Cutler, Absurdist Poet ..."
7. Ivor Cutler to Gavin Hogg and Hamish Ironside, 11 February 1991. Cited in Hogg, G. (2011) "Signed, Sealed, Diverted." *The Word*, August, 33.
8. Pattinson, J. (2016) "'Shirkers', 'Scrimjacks' and 'Scrimshanks'?" 715–718.
9. Lee Freeman, interview.
10. Bridge, M. (2020) "Fitting Memorial for RAF Lancaster Hero, 75 Years on." *The Times*, 26 December.
11. McKay, A. (1994) "Ivor Cutler, Absurdist Poet ..."
12. Forces War Records, forces-war-records.co.uk/; National Archives AIR 78/41/4.
13. Sugarman, M. (2002) "More than Just a Few," 185.
14. Donald, A. (1997) "The Write Stuff," 98.
15. "Wingtip" (2014) bbc.co.uk/history/ww2peopleswar/user/22/u521522.shtml; iwm.org.uk/memorials/item/memorial/11566. As the RAF's training programmes changed regularly it's not possible to be accurate about the programme Ivor followed.
16. Saxon, P. (1997) "The Second World War," 52–62.
17. *ICLSC.*
18. Carroll, J. J. (2014) *Physiological Problems of Bomber Crews in the Eighth Air Force During WWII*, ch. 2, 6; ch. 3, 2ff.
19. McKay, A. (1994) "Ivor Cutler, Absurdist Poet ..."; Donald, A. (1997) "The Write Stuff," 98.
20. *SI.*
21. Rae, I. (1977) "Ivor Cutler."

22. *A Stuggy Pren* (1994) series 1, episode 4, BBC Radio 3, 2 June.
23. Ivor Cutler to John Knutas, 1 January 1993.
24. *ICLSC*.
25. Post Office Glasgow Directory for 1941–1942, 633.
26. *Ivor Cutler: Life in A Scotch Sitting Room Volume 2* (2002) BBC Scotland. The institution was later known as Jordanhill College of Education.
27. Anonymous. (2006) "Ivor Cutler." *The Times*, 7 March.
28. *LFTWP*.
29. Cruickshank, M. (1970) *A History of the Training of Teachers in Scotland*, 208.
30. Blane, D. (2012) "We Were Made into Real Teachers." *Times Educational Supplement*, 21 December. Accessed at tes.com/news/we-were-made-real-teachers.
31. Cruickshank, M. (1970) *A History of the Training of Teachers in Scotland*, 33, 35–38, 165.
32. Moris Cutler's death certificate.
33. *SI*.
34. *LFTWP*.
35. McKay, A. (1994) "Ivor Cutler, Absurdist Poet ..."
36. Anonymous (2018) "Remembering the Lochgelly Tawse." *The Scotsman*, 5 September.
37. McKay, A. (1994) "Ivor Cutler, Absurdist Poet ..."
38. Hodgkinson, W. (2004) "Cutler's Drawers." *The Guardian*, 16 January.
39. McKay, A. (1994) "Ivor Cutler, Absurdist Poet ..."
40. Grant, K. (1996) "Three-Minute Poet." *Aberdeen Evening Express*, 20 June.

5   Back to School

1. summerhillschool.co.uk/history.
2. Espiner, M. (1999) "The Wizard of Odd." *The Guardian*, 12 August; Wilby, P. (2013) "Summerhill School: These Days Surprisingly Strict." *The Guardian*, 27 May.
3. *LFTWP*.
4. *LFTWP*.
5. Lindsay, B. (2020) *Two Bold Singermen*, 69–71.
6. Croall, J. (2013) *Neill of Summerhill*, 11–12.
7. Croall, J. (2013) *Neill of Summerhill*, 205.
8. McLean, C. (1994) "Cutler's Crusade." *The List*, 1 July, 81.
9. Zoë Readhead, interview.
10. John Knutas as told to Sandy Grierson; Irwin, C. and Richmond, C. (2006) "Ivor Cutler." *The Independent*, 9 March.
11. Ivor told the story to John-Paul Flintoff, during an interview for "The Great Scottish Eccentric."
12. *LFTWP*; McKay, A. (1994) "Ivor Cutler, Absurdist Poet ..."
13. Watts, M. (1971) "Ivor." *Melody Maker*, 27 February, 35.
14. Watts, M. (1971) "Ivor," 35.
15. Flintoff, J-P. (1992) "The Great Scottish Eccentric."
16. McLean, C. (1994) "Cutler's Crusade," 81.
17. Clark, A. (1973) "Have You Heard the One about the Two Scotsmen?" *Cream*, July, 18–21.
18. *LFTWP*.
19. John-Paul Flintoff, interview.

20. *ICKT*.
21. Alex Mermikides; Kate Williams; Charlotte Steel; Milton Mermikides.
22. Wade, D. (1980) "General Uncertainty All Round." *The Times Saturday Review*, 5 July, 7.
23. Charlotte Steel, interview.
24. Charlotte Steel, interview.
25. Kate Williams, interview.
26. John-Paul Flintoff, interview.
27. Kate Williams, interview.
28. Milton Mermikides, interview.
29. Murray's acting credits include *Dixon of Dock Green*, *Armchair Theatre* and an uncredited appearance as an A-Wing pilot in *Star Wars: Return of the Jedi*. See imdb.com/name/nm0614832/.
30. Irwin, C. and Richmond, C. (2006) "Ivor Cutler." *The Independent*, 9 March.
31. Charlotte Steel, interview; Kate Williams, interview.
32. Xavier Russell, interview.
33. Alex Mermikides, interview; John-Paul Flintoff, interview.
34. Rebecca Orr-Deas, interview.
35. Kendall, E. (1985) "A Room of My Own: Ivor Cutler." 78.
36. Ivor Cutler to Gavin Hogg, 1 September 1999.
37. Cutler, I. (1988) "The Material World of Ivor Cutler." *New Musical Express*, 16 July, 8.
38. Ivor Cutler to Gavin Hogg, 1 September 1999.
39. Gayford, M (2019) *Modernists & Mavericks*, 43.
40. Gayford, M (2019) *Modernists & Mavericks*, 50.
41. Ron Lawrence (2013) "Ron Lawrence on Ivor Cutler," discussion with Ceri Thomas, University of South Wales. Accessed at vimeo.com/126266306.
42. Concert at Sallis Benney Hall, Brighton, 27 September 1984; Cutler, I. (1988) "The Material World of Ivor Cutler." *New Musical Express*, 16 July, 8.
43. Ivor Cutler to Gavin Hogg, c.1997.
44. Sandy Grierson, interview.
45. Beth Marcuson, interview; Anna Morshead, interview.
46. Ivor Cutler and Virginia Pearson's marriage certificate.
47. Jeremy Simon Cutler's birth certificate.
48. Daniel Franklin Cutler's birth certificate.
49. *LFTWP*.
50. *GLIC*.
51. Rae, I. (1977) "Ivor Cutler," 8.
52. Rae, I. (1977) "Ivor Cutler."

6   A Life of Whimsical Fantasies

1. "Coconuts" was written by the pair along with Lewis Ilda, under the pseudonym of Fred Heatherington.
2. Hoare, N. (ed.) (2018) *Y'Hup: Ivor Cutler*, 73.
3. Hayward, K. (2013) *Tin Pan Alley*, 35–36.
4. Rae, I. (1977) "Ivor Cutler." 8.
5. *Ivor Cutler – by Ivor Cutler*.
6. Flyer for *Gruts* at the Bloomsbury Theatre, 12–17 May 1986.

7. It became the Blue Angel in the 1980s. See pubwiki.co.uk/LondonPubs/Islington/BlueCoatBoy.shtml.
8. Willetts, P. (2013) *The Look of Love: The Life and Times of Paul Raymond*, 226.
9. MacQueen, A. (2011) *Private Eye: The First 50 Years*, 278.
10. Ivor Cutler to BBC, 13 August 1957. Brian Mulliner to Ivor Cutler, 28 August 1957. Both in BBC Written Archives Centre RCONT1 Cutler, Ivor (Artists File 1) 1957–1962.
11. Sherrin, N. (2005) *Ned Sherrin*, 80.
12. *LFTWP*.
13. Sherrin, N. (2005) *Ned Sherrin*, 80.
14. Anonymous (1957) "Tonight." *Radio Times*, 15 February, 15.
15. Sherrin, N. (2005) *Ned Sherrin*, 80.
16. *CR*.
17. McKay, A. (1994) Unpublished section of his interview for "Ivor Cutler, Absurdist Poet …"
18. H. Elton Box to Kenneth Corden, 12 August 1958; Contract dated 1 April 1958. Both at BBC WAC TVART1 Cutler, Ivor 1958–1962.
19. H. Elton Box to Donald Baverstock, 27 March 1958. BBC WAC TVART1 Cutler, Ivor 1958–1962.
20. Ned Sherrin to Ivor Cutler, 2 June 1958. Ivor Cutler to Ned Sherrin, 1 June 1958. BBC WAC TVART1 Cutler, Ivor 1958–1962.
21. H. Elton Box to Ned Sherrin, 10 July 1958. BBC WAC TVART 1 Cutler, Ivor (Artists File 1) 1958–1962. A note on the letter states that Box was telephoned a few days later, but the nature of this call is not revealed.
22. Sherrin, N. (2005) *Ned Sherrin*, 89–90.
23. Ivor Cutler to Kenneth Corden, 22 September 1959; Kenneth Corden to Ivor Cutler, 29 September 1959. BBC WAC TVART1 Cutler, Ivor, 1959–1962.
24. Barbara Scott to Ivor Cutler, 20 October 1959; BBC audition notes, 23 October 1959; Barbara Scott to Ivor Cutler, 23 October 1959. BBC WAC TVART1 Cutler, Ivor 1958–1962.
25. Doncaster, P. (1959) "On the Record: New Faces!" *Daily Mirror*, 9 April.
26. Bridges, J. (1959) "Monday Night at Home." *Radio Times*, 8 May, 9.
27. Talks Booking Requisition, 15 September 1959. BBC WAC RCONT1 Cutler, Ivor (Artists File 1) 1957–1962; Anonymous (1959) *Radio Times*, 16 October, 32.
28. *IC90*.
29. *CR*.
30. Anonymous (1960) "BBC's Witty Causeries du Lundi." *The Times*, 17 February.
31. *Ivor Cutler – by Ivor Cutler*.
32. Ilic, D. (1986) "Passing the Time." *City Limits*, 8–15 May, 18.
33. Palmer, J. (1997) "Manic Street Preacher." *The Independent*, 1 June.
34. thegoonshow.net/history.asp.
35. Carpenter, H. (2004) *Spike Milligan*, 11, 42–43, 71, 163–164.
36. Gillard, D. (1990) Preview of *King Cutler*, *Radio Times*, 11 January, 86–87.
37. *P*.
38. See Adamson, J. (1974) *Groucho, Harpo, Chico and Sometimes Zeppo*.
39. *GD*.
40. See Brod, M. (1960) *Franz Kafka*, 3, 92–93, 173. Kafka died of tuberculosis, aged forty.
41. Undated handwritten note. In Hoare, N. (ed.) (2018) *Y'Hup: Ivor Cutler*, 7.
42. Hodgkinson, W. (2004) "Cutler's Drawers."

43. Anonymous (1960) "Variety in Aid of New Theatre." *Middlesex County Times*, 24 September.
44. "A.P.S." (1961) "This Off-beat Has a Message." *Kensington Post*, 22 September.
45. Jenny Miller to Variety Bookings, 29 June 1961. BBC WAC RCONT1 Cutler, Ivor (Artists File 1) 1957–1962.
46. "A.P.S." (1961) "This Off-beat Has a Message."
47. "A.P.S." (1961).
48. "Disker" (1961) "Off the Record." *Liverpool Echo and Evening Express,* 3 June.
49. Bentley, J. (1961) "Old Timers are on Parade for Otto." *Sunday Pictorial*, 1 October.
50. Reeves, A. (1961) "Record Review." *Coventry Evening Telegraph*, 15 August.
51. "R.B.M." (1961) "A Good Night at the Players." *The Stage*, 16 November, 13.
52. *P.*
53. MacQueen, A. (2011) *Private Eye: The First 50 Years*, 69. MacQueen provides a detailed history of the magazine.
54. "Cutler" (1966) Cartoon. *International Times*, 28 November–11 December, 5.
55. Cook, W. (2006) *So Farewell Then*, 124–145.
56. Dave Green.
57. Hepple, P. (1962) "A Cure for the Grumps." *The Stage and Television Today*, 8 March, 7.
58. Cover notes to *The Establishment* LP, Parlophone PMC1198, released 1963.
59. Anonymous (1962) "Exciting Innovations at the Establishment." *The Stage and Television Today*, 22 February, 6.
60. Bruce, L. (2016) *How to Talk Dirty and Influence People*, 158.
61. Bruce, L. (2016) *How to Talk Dirty*, 104–128.
62. Cook, W. (2006) *So Farewell Then*, 143–144.
63. Tynan, K. In Bruce, L. (2016) *How to Talk Dirty*, xi–xiii.
64. Tynan, K. In Bruce, L. (2016) *How to Talk Dirty*, xiii.
65. See Bruce, L. (2016) *How to Talk Dirty*.
66. Watts, M. (1971) "Ivor." *Melody Maker*, 35.
67. "G.S." (1962) Review of *Get Up and Gruts*. *The Stage and Television Today*, 6 September, 14.
68. *Let's Imagine: A Judgement on Our Time*: see contract at BBC WAC TVART1 Cutler, Ivor 1958–1962. *A World of One's Own*: see BBC Genome. The shows were broadcast on 15 December 1961 and 2 February 1962.
69. officialcharts.com/artist/30120/mr-acker-bilk/.
70. Dallas, K. (1974) "Everyone Else is an Eccentric," 54.
71. Anonymous (1962) "Writers' and Producers' Conference." *The Times*, 2 November. It's not known if Ivor accepted the invitation.
72. Anonymous (1963) "Whittling Free Dancer." *The Tatler*, 9 January, 90.
73. *The I.C. Snow* (1964) BBC Home Service, 6–10 January.
74. Correspondence regarding fees can be found in BBC WAC RCONT1 Cutler, Ivor (Artists File 1) 1957–1962; RCONT12 Ivor Cutler File II, III and IV, among others.
75. Note added to the copy of a letter from Patrick Newman to Ivor Cutler, February 1960. BBC WAC RCONT19, Cutler, Ivor.
76. Ivor Cutler to Patrick Newman, 22 January 1961. This correspondence is in BBC WAC RCONT1 Cutler, Ivor (Artists File 1) 1957–1962.
77. Ivor Cutler to Miss Alexander, 9 December 1965. BBC Payment Form, 17 December 1964. BBC WAC RCONT19, Cutler, Ivor.
78. Ivor Cutler to Heather Dean, 24 June 1967. BBC WAC RCONT19, Cutler, Ivor.
79. Anonymous (1963) "Misfires in New Revue." *The Times*, 25 January.

80. Trewin, J. C. (1963) "An Evening of British Rubbish." *Birmingham Post*, 25 January; Trewin, J. C. (1963) "The World of the Theatre." *The Illustrated London News*, 9 February, 206.
81. *GD*.
82. J. H. Wallis to Ivor Cutler, 24 March 1964. In Hoare, N. (ed.) (2018) *Y'Hup: Ivor Cutler*, 29.
83. Wallis, J. H. (1964) *Sexual Harmony in Marriage*, Routledge and Kegan Paul.
84. Willetts, P. (2013) *The Look of Love*, 185.
85. All information from officialcharts.com.
86. See imdb.com and filmography.bfi.org.uk/film/150064400.
87. Adam, K. (1964) "A Stretch Towards Happiness." *Radio Times*, 16 April, 4.
88. Youngs, I. (2014) "BBC Two's 50th Anniversary: Disastrous Launch Remembered." bbc.co.uk/news/entertainment-arts-27033129.
89. Anonymous (1964) *Radio Times*, 16 April, 29.
90. Anonymous (1964) "No Anti-climax for BBC2." *The Times*, 22 April.
91. Ivor Cutler to Gavin Hogg, 6 March 1991.
92. Anonymous (1964) "Chit Chat." *The Stage*, 2 July, 8.
93. *Diary of a Nobody* (1964) BBC Two, 12 December.
94. Cutler, I. (undated cutting) "Where Did You Get That?" Source unknown. The accompanying photograph is by Katrina Lithgow, which dates the article to post-1994.
95. Ivor gave his address as Flat 1, Fawley Mansions, Fawley Road on a letter to the BBC: Ivor Cutler to Heather Dean, 29 May 1964. BBC WAC RCONT19, Ivor Cutler. Dan Cutler remembers it as a bedsit.
96. Dan Cutler, interview.
97. *IC90*.
98. *LFTWP*.
99. Watts, M. (1971) "Ivor." *Melody Maker*, 35.
100. McKay, A. (1994) "Ivor Cutler, Absurdist Poet …"
101. Ivor Cutler to Miss Heritage, 14 September 1963. BBC WAC RCONT12 Ivor Cutler File II, 1963–1967. The address on the postcard is Dale Ward, Holloway Sanatorium, Virginia Water, Surrey. For information about the sanatorium, see exploringsurreyspast.org.uk/themes/subjects/living/1-2/.
102. John Knutas.
103. Ivor Cutler to Huw Wheldon, 14 May 1964. BBC WAC TVART3 Cutler, Ivor, Artists 2: 1963–1970.
104. Ivor Cutler to BBC, 1 October 1964. BBC WAC TVART3.
105. See contracts in BBC WAC TVART3 Cutler, Ivor Artists 2: 1963–1970.
106. *Off Beat …* was broadcast on 5 February 1965; *Musicstand* was broadcast on 15 June; *Pure Gingold* was shown on 27 December.
107. Ivor Cutler to Ms Warley, 28 February 1996; Cutler, I. (2003) *Scots wa' Straw*, Arc Publications.
108. Copyright Department to Ivor Cutler, 1 December 1965. BBC WAC RCONT19 Ivor Cutler. The programme's final edition was broadcast on 1 October 1965: see BBC Genome for programme details.
109. Ivor Cutler to Joy Whitby, 14 December 1965. Joy Whitby to Ivor Cutler, 4 January 1966. BBC WAC TVART3.
110. *LFTWP*.
111. Dylan Edwards, interview. Woolf's credits include *The Rocky Horror Picture Show*, *Rutland Weekend Television* and *The Lion in Winter*. He also acted with The Alberts. See imdb.com/name/nm0941146/.

112. *ICKT.*
113. *P.*
114. John Knutas, from letters of 18 February 1995 and 17 October 1996.
115. Harrison, T. (1997) "The Comeback Kid." 27.
116. *Radio Times* (1966) Programme details for *Zodiac*, 14 January. See BBC Genome.
117. Heather Dean to Ivor Cutler, 12 July 1966. BBC WAC RCONT19 Cutler, Ivor 1963–1969.
118. *A Stuggy Pren* (1994) episode 2, 31 May; *CR.*

7 When Life Was Fab

1. Miles, B. (1997) *Paul McCartney: Many Years from Now*, 349–350.
2. Miles, B. (1997) *Paul McCartney*, 359.
3. Paul McCartney in conversation with James Daunt. First shown 19 November 2021 at youtube.com/watch?v=oQjXT2wwkVI.
4. *ICKT.*
5. Miles, B. (1997) *Paul McCartney*, 356, illustration between 336 and 337, 359.
6. collections-search.bfi.org.uk/web/search/simple. *Billion Dollar Brain* was released on 16 November 1967.
7. John Knutas.
8. Agreement Form, 24 June 1967. BBC WAC RCONT19. Humphrey Burton to Controller, BBC One, 15 May 1967; Memo from Paul Fox, 26 September 1967. BBC WAC TVART3 Cutler, Ivor Artists 2: 1963–1970.
9. Laing, D. (2016) "Tony Barrow Obituary." *The Guardian*, 18 May; *Magical Mystery Tour* (1967) Parlophone PCTC 255.
10. "Disker" (1967) "On a Magical Mystery Tour." *Liverpool Echo*, 16 September.
11. See imdb.com/title/tt0059260/.
12. *The Beatles: Magical Mystery Tour Memories* (2008) Arthouse Pictures DVD.
13. The cast list shown in the film and the album omitted one of the b's from her name.
14. *ICS.*
15. Miles, B. (1997) *Paul McCartney*, 367.
16. Miles, B. (1997) *Paul McCartney*, 36.
17. *ICS.*
18. Anonymous (1967) "Beatle Reply to TV Film Critics." *The Times*, 28 December.
19. Grosvenor, D.A. (1968) "Bravo Beatles!" *Coventry Standard*, 11 January.
20. "Angela" (1968) Letter. *San Francisco Express Times*, 8 February, 9.
21. Watts, M. (1971) "Ivor." *Melody Maker*, 35.
22. Watts, M. (1971) "Ivor." *Melody Maker*, 35; Evans, R. (1999) "Ivor Cutler." *The List*, 12-19 August, 91.
23. Carnahan, P. (1997) "An Interview with Ivor Cutler." reversedpolarity.co/ivor-cutler/.
24. Davies, H. (2016) *The Beatles Book*, 46–47.
25. Piers Plowright, interview; Sandy Grierson, interview.
26. MacDonald, I. (2005) *Revolution in the Head*, 171.
27. Davies, H. (2016) *The Beatles Book*, 46; "Disker" (1961) "Off the Record." *Liverpool Echo and Evening Express*, 3 June.
28. MacDonald (2005) *Revolution in the Head*, xvii–xviii.
29. Miles, B. (1997) *Paul McCartney*, 125–136, 293. The story of Lord Russell's being a fan of Ivor's is told in articles including Espiner, M. (2006) Obituary. *The Guardian*, 7 March, and Flintoff, J-P. (1992) "The Great Scottish Eccentric."

30. MacDonald (2005) *Revolution in the Head*, 171; Miles, B. (1997) *Paul McCartney*, 210.
31. Espiner, M. (1999) "The Wizard of Odd."
32. Brown, C. (2021) *One, Two, Three, Four*, 480.
33. Parlophone PMC7040.
34. Brown, C. (2021) *One, Two, Three, Four*, 343.
35. Rogers, J. (2014) "Ivor Cutler: 'He Didn't Live by the Same Rules as Everyone Else.'" *The Observer*, 16 March.
36. Carnahan, P. (1997) "An Interview with Ivor Cutler." The rerelease is on Rev-Ola CREV049CD.
37. *ICKT*.
38. *GLIC*.
39. Lowe, S. (2002) Letter. *The Times*, 26 August; Sullivan, S. (2017) "The Tonight Show Just Found the Most Hilariously (Literally, Can't Breathe Laughing) Awful Songs Ever." 26 September. news.onecountry.com/entertainment/so-not-play-these-songs/.
40. Jones, P. (1967) "Singles Reviews." *Record Mirror*, w/e 19 August, 12.
41. See bbc.co.uk/radio1/johnpeel/.
42. Cutler, I. (1988) "The Material World of Ivor Cutler."
43. Garner, K. (2007) *The Peel Sessions*, 272.
44. See bbc.co.uk/radio1/johnpeel/.
45. See valentine.me.uk/ivor/sessions.html.
46. Kershaw, A. (2012) *No Off Switch*, 64.
47. *Turn that Racket Down* (1999) BBC2, 29 August.
48. Garner, K. (2007) *The Peel Sessions*, 272.
49. Peel, J. (1998) "John Peel's Meltdown Diary." *The Times*, 20 June.
50. Aspden, P. (2006) "Surreal-Life Story." *Financial Times Magazine*, 18/19 March, 46. Aspden remembered the press launch as being around five years earlier, so this may be the 2001 Meltdown, curated by Robert Wyatt, rather than the 1998 festival.
51. Lanchester Arts Festival 1971 programme; officialcharts.com/.
52. See edinburghgigarchive.com/.
53. *GLIC*.
54. Jacobs, G. (1983) "In View." *Jewish Chronicle*, 25 November, 13.
55. Parker, C. (1995) "Notes for the Whole Story." *The Times*, 7 March.
56. See peel.fandom.com/wiki/Carol_Concert.
57. Peel, J. and Ravenscroft, S. (2005) *Margrave of the Marshes*, 286.

8   Life Inside the Sitting Room

1. On 13 October 1970 he recorded episodes one and two, but only episode one was broadcast. See Enid Musson to Sandra Coombs, 14 October 1970. BBC WAC RCONT20 Cutler, Ivor 1970–1974.
2. Ivor's Peel Sessions are listed at bbc.co.uk/radio1/johnpeel/artists/i/ivorcutler/.
3. Cutler, I. (1978) *Ivor Cutler's Life in a Scotch Sitting-room Vol II*. Harvest SHSP 4084. For the sake of simplicity, I will generally refer to this work as '*Life in a Scotch Sitting Room*' and will only be more precise when discussing the title of a specific edition of it.
4. *CR*.
5. Jarvis, K. and Challoner, P. (1979) "Ivory Cutlery." *The Courier*, 31 October, 3.
6. See wicn.org/history-of-wicn/.

7. *Culture File* (2011) RTE Lyric FM, October.
8. MacQueen, A. (2011) *Private Eye: The First 50 Years*, 139; Speakout Records SPOUT2001.
9. Episodes 1, 2, 7, 15.
10. Episodes 6, 19, 9.
11. Episode Four.
12. Episodes 2, 3, 18.
13. Episode 5.
14. Episodes 8, 18.
15. *LFTWP*.
16. Dallas, K. (1974) "Everyone Else is an Eccentric," 54.
17. Randall, L. and Welch, C. (2001) *Ginger Geezer*, 27–28, 39, 146.
18. *LFTWP*.
19. *Arthur Smith and Neil Innes Discuss Ivor: Comedy Club Interviews* (2016) Radio 4 Extra, 3 March.
20. Randall, L. and Welch, C. (2001) *Ginger Geezer*, 164–171.
21. See bbc.co.uk/radio1/johnpeel/artists/i/ivorcutler/.
22. See bbc.co.uk/radio1/johnpeel/artists/i/ivorcutler/; *King Cutler* (1990) Radio 3, 11 January–15 February; *A Stuggy Pren* (1994) 30 May–3 June; *Ivor Cutler – by Ivor Cutler*.
23. *SI*.
24. Thompson, B. (1990) "Off the Wall."
25. Cutler, I. and Honeysett, M. (1990) *Glasgow Dreamer*.
26. Episode 11.
27. Episodes 11, 3.
28. Episodes 6, 1, 15.
29. Episode 16.
30. *Loose Ends* (1990) BBC Radio 4, 21 April.
31. On *Who Tore Your Trousers?*
32. On *Velvet Donkey*.
33. Both are in *Fremsley*.
34. *A Wet Handle*, episode 3.
35. *A Wet Handle*; *Velvet Donkey*.
36. See glasgowlive.co.uk/news/history/ikiped-gang-brigton-billy-boys-12243020.

9 A Life on the Page

1. Cutler, I. (1962) *Gruts*.
2. See find-and-update.company-information.service.gov.uk.
3. Hill, S. (1966) *Coventry Evening Telegraph*, 23 June.
4. McGrath, T. (1967) "The New Scriptures Contd." *International Times*, 16–29 January, 15.
5. Cutler, I. and Oxenbury, H. (1971) *Meal One*.
6. *Culture File* (2011) RTE Lyric FM, October.
7. *Desert Island Discs* (2020) BBC Radio 4, 29 November.
8. The episode featuring *Meal One* was first broadcast on 1 November 1983; Oxenbury, *Desert Island Discs*.
9. Children's Books Study Group (1974) "Review of *Meal One*." *Spare Rib* 27, September, 43.

10. *Desert Island Discs* (2020) BBC Radio 4, 29 November.
11. Cutler, I. and Honeysett, M. (illus.) (1987) *One and a Quarter*.
12. Anonymous (1992) "Doris," *Publishers Weekly*, 9 November, 85.
13. Johnson, S. (1995) "Spell of a Witch Report," *The Times Weekend*, 22 April.
14. See the sleeve notes to *Blues for the Hitchhiking Dead (Jazz Poetry Superjam #1)* (2013) Gearbox Records GB1518, 1–3.
15. *LFTWP*; Hennessy, V. (1989) *A Little Light Friction*, 158.
16. *CR*.
17. Hoare, N. (ed.) (2018) *Y'Hup: Ivor Cutler*, 10.
18. Alastair McKay, interview notes.
19. *Ambit* (1968) 36: 37.
20. *Workshop* (1968) no. 4; *The Poetry Review* (1968/9) 59(4): 240.
21. *Ambit* (1970) 43: 45; *Transatlantic Review* (1971) 39: 58–59.
22. *Alive and Kicking – British Poets* (1971) London Weekend Television, broadcast on 18 July; Anonymous (1971) "Poetry is Alive and Well …" *Kensington Post-Mercury*, 23 July.
23. Briony Bax.
24. Bax, M. (1985) *Ambit*, 101: 3–4.
25. Advertisement (1975) *Ambit*, 62: 61.
26. *Ambit* (1984) 98: 62.
27. Bax, M. (1977) Review. *Ambit*, 70: 88
28. Bax, M. Letter to Mrs J. Nichols, Miss A. Grimshaw and Mrs E. Somerville, 19 February 1974. Cited in Vowles, C. J. (2006) *The Little Become Big?*, 322.
29. Brock, E. Letter to Martin Bax, 30 March 1976. Cited in Vowles, C. J. (2006), 322–323.
30. *Ambit* (1984) 97: 92–95.
31. Watts, M. (1971) "Ivor." *Melody Maker*.
32. Hennessy, V. (1989) *A Little Light Friction*, 157.
33. *The New Statesman* (1994) 7(313): 41.
34. Miller, D. and Price, R. (2006) *British Poetry Magazines 1914–2000*, 183ff.
35. *New Departures* (1975) 7/8 and 10/11, (1983) 13 and 15; *Straight Lines #1* (1978) Spring.
36. *Free Reed* 4: January/February 1974.
37. Dallas, K. (1974) "Everyone Else is an Eccentric," 54.
38. Thompson, B. (1990) "Off the Wall"; *Ambit* (1970) 44: 8.
39. *Ambit* (1973) 54: 9.
40. Greenstreet, R. (2000) "The Questionnaire: Ivor Cutler." *The Guardian*, 5 February.
41. *ICLSC*.
42. Hodgkinson, W. (2004) "Cutler's Drawers."
43. *A Stuggy Pren*, episode 3.
44. *CR*.
45. Carnahan, P. (1997) "An Interview with Ivor Cutler."
46. Rae, I. (1977) "Ivor Cutler," 8.
47. Thompson, B. (1990) "Off the Wall."
48. Best, J. (1984) "Ivor Cutler." *Music Week*, 11 August, 26.
49. Dallas, K. (1974) "Everyone Else is an Eccentric." 54.
50. *ICS*.
51. Hennessy, V. (1989) *A Little Light Friction*, 155–158.
52. Concert at Sallis Benney Hall, Brighton, 27 September 1984.
53. Ivor Cutler to John Knutas, 3 February 2002.

54. McLean, C. (1994) "Cutler's Crusade." 81.
55. One photograph is now in the collection of the National Galleries of Scotland. See nationalgalleries.org/.
56. *Ambit* 43: 45. Ivor's work was absent from the limited-edition book of poems from the show, Couzyn, J. (1970) *Twelve to Twelve*.
57. Grove, V. (2021) "Olden Life: What Was the Bedford Square Book Bang?" *The Oldie*, June, 12.
58. *GLIC*.
59. Now Anna Morshead.
60. *ICKT*.
61. Hennessy, V. (1989) *A Little Light Friction*, 158.
62. Beverley Crew, interview.
63. See nationalgalleries.org.
64. Edwards, P. (1990) *The Artist's and Illustrator's Magazine*, October. Accessed at peteredwards.net/articles.htm.
65. Cutler, I. (1981) *Private Habits*.
66. Horovitz, M. (1992) "Mapping the Gaelic Landscape." *The Times Saturday Review*, 25 July, 39.
67. Neil Cargill, interview.
68. Harrison, T. (1997) "The Comeback Kid." 25.
69. Palmer, J. (1997) "Manic Street Preacher."
70. Dylan Edwards, interview; Andy Kershaw, interview; Lucy Armitage, interview; *Comedy Club Interviews* (2016) BBC Radio 4 Extra, 3 March.
71. Burnside, J. (2016) "Season of Mists … and Foraging with Ivor." *New Statesman*, 30 September, 83; Sandra Brownjohn, interview.
72. John Burnside, interview; Neil Cargill, interview.
73. Barker, N. (1995) "Heroes & Villains." *The Independent*, 25 March.
74. Espiner, M. (1999) "The Wizard of Odd."
75. Fabian Ironside, interview.
76. Kendall, E. (1985) "A Room of my Own," 78.
77. Cutler, I. (1992) *Is That Your Flap, Jack?*, 5.
78. Morgan, E. (1972) *The Descent of Woman*, Souvenir Press; Brooks, L. (2003) "Come on in, the Water's Lovely." *The Guardian*, 1 May.
79. Cutler, I. (1988) "The Material World of Ivor Cutler."
80. *King Cutler* (1990) episode 1, Radio 3, 11 January.
81. Ivor Cutler to Alastair McKay, 21 February 1992.
82. Bruce, K. (1995) "Playing on Words."
83. *CR*.

10 A Life on the Stage

1. Garner, K. (2007) *The Peel Sessions*, 272.
2. Rae, I. (1977) "Ivor Cutler," 8.
3. Cutler, I. (1976) "8 Days a Week." *Melody Maker*, 14 August, 10.
4. *P*.
5. *P*.
6. *CR*.
7. Advertisement (1978) *Belfast Telegraph*, 20 April; Anonymous (1978) "Anger Over Free Concert that Wasn't." *Belfast Telegraph*, 29 April.
8. Watson, D. (1986) "Grut Cutlet."

9. Hodgkinson, W. (2004) "Cutler's Drawers."
10. Cutler, I. (1971) "Blind Date." *Melody Maker*, 1 May, 14.
11. *GLIC*.
12. Cutler, I. (1976) "8 Days a Week," 10.
13. Concert at Sallis Benney Hall, Brighton, 27 September 1984.
14. Barnes, M. (1997) "Invisible Jukebox," 51.
15. Hunter, S. (1985) "Ivor Cutler." *Texas Hotel Burning* 3: 12; Cutler, I (1988) "The Material World of Ivor Cutler."
16. Palmer, J. (1997) "Manic Street Preacher."
17. Alison Harbert, interview.
18. Provisional schedule, dated 18 June 1997, for concert on 23 June 1997.
19. Courtesy of Craig Murray-Orr.
20. Beverley Crew, interview.
21. Kendall, E. (1985) "A Room of My Own." 78.
22. Heeps, D. (1986) "Flavour of Humour." *Newcastle Journal*, 31 October.
23. Entertainment Guide (1981) *The Times*, 5 June; Advertisement (1982) *The Times Preview*, 8–14 January, v; Anonymous (1983) "Out to Grab the Audiences." *Reading Evening Post*, 12 February.
24. Gilmore, M. (1983) "Cutler's Weird World." *The Stage*, 17 March, 5.
25. *Fresh Carpet* (1986) Arc Publications; *Gruts* (1986) Rough Trade ROUGH98.
26. Van Emden, D. (1986) "Gruts with Everything." *Music Week*, 24 May, 20.
27. Dallas, K. (1974) "Everyone Else is an Eccentric." 54.
28. *The Stage*, 4 June 1987, 16; Cutler, I. and Honeysett, M. (illus.) (1987) *Fremsley*, Methuen.
29. Rush, P. (1987) "Nitty Gritties and Deadpan Ditties." *The Stage*, 18 June, 7.
30. *IC90*.
31. Van Emden, D. (1986) "Gruts with Everything." 20.
32. Adrian Mealing, interview.
33. *A Flat Man* (1998) Creation Records CRECD236.
34. Rae, I. (1977) "Ivor Cutler," 8.
35. Cutler, I. (undated cutting, post-1994) "Where Did You Get That?"
36. See collections.nmc.ca/.
37. Dallas, K. (1974) "Everyone Else is an Eccentric." 54.
38. Harrison can't recall the performance to which this story relates.
39. Anonymous (1995) "Festival Comic Needs an Alternative." *Aberdeen Evening Express*, 21 September.
40. Riddell, A. (1995) "Ivor Big Laugh." *Aberdeen Evening Express*, 16 October.
41. *ICLSC*.
42. Anonymous (1999) "Celtic Connections, Ivor Cutler, Glasgow Royal Concert Hall." *The Herald*, 25 January.
43. Rogers, J. (2014) "Ivor Cutler: He Didn't Live by the Same Rules as Everyone Else." *The Observer*, 16 March.
44. Concert at Sallis Benney Hall, Brighton, 27 September 1984.
45. *CR*.
46. Palmer, J. (1997) "Manic Street Preacher."
47. Ivor Cutler to Gavin Hogg, undated postcard but probably 1996–1998.
48. Woolfson, A. (1999) "Bridge-Building Brothers Get Back in the Loop." *The Times*, 13 August.
49. *Hansard* (1999) Lords Chamber volume 597, column 1700.
50. Concert at Sallis Benney Hall, Brighton, 27 September 1984.

51. Morag Deyes.
52. Ivor Cutler at the Queen Elizabeth Hall, 2 July 1998.
53. Denselow, R. (2004) "Ivor Cutler." *The Guardian* 3 February.

11 A Life on Screen

1. Davalle, P. (1983) "Television and Radio Programmes." *The Times*, 14 May.
2. *Six and Seven-Eights* (1972) BBC Two, 17 September.
3. *Full House* (1973) BBC Two, 17 March. The BFI Archive lists Ivor as one of the poets and names the poems he read: see collections-search.bfi.org.uk/web/Details/ChoiceFilmWorks/150446983.
4. *The End of the Pier Show* (1974) BBC Two, 1 December.
5. Enid Musson to Brian Turner, 17 September 1972: BBC WAC RCONT20 Ivor Cutler. Contract, 31 August 1972: BBC WAC TVARTS Cutler, Ivor 1971–1980. Both documents give 17 September as the date of Ivor's contribution. This was a Sunday, so this is probably the date of recording as *Late Night Line-Up* was not broadcast at weekends.
6. Joan Hedgecock to Ivor Cutler, 30 January 1973; Ivor Cutler to Joan Hedgecock; memo from Joan Hedgecock, 23 February 1973: BBC WAC RCONT20 Ivor Cutler.
7. There was no *Jackanory* on Monday 28 May as it was a Bank Holiday.
8. *Dave Allen in Search of the Great English Eccentric* (1974) ATV, 8 October.
9. Cutler, I. (1976) "8 Days a Week," 10.
10. *South of Watford* (1986) LWT, 9 May; *The Innes Book of Records* (1981) BBC Two, 12 October; *Whistle Test* (1986) BBC Two, 3 June.
11. As recalled by John-Paul Flintoff.
12. Anonymous (1981) "TV Guide." *Liverpool Echo*, 12 October.
13. *Late Night Line-Up* (1986) BBC Two, 3 November. The BFI archive credits Ivor with appearing on 3 and 6 November: see bfi.org.uk/films-tv-people/4ce2ba4ad5680.
14. *Harty's Christmas Party* (1984) BBC Two, 24 December.
15. Naughton, J. (1985) "Someone Else's Christmas." *The Listener*, 1 January, 31.
16. See player.bfi.org.uk/free/film/watch-poets-against-the-bomb-1981-online.
17. Anonymous (1981) "Today's Engagements." *The Times*, 15 April; Anonymous (1976) "Today's engagements." *The Times*, 5 November.
18. John-Paul Flintoff, interview.
19. Ilic, D. (1986) "Passing the Time," 18.

12 Quite a Few Lives on the Wireless

1. Wade. D. (1972) "Wallpaper Listeners." *The Times*, 15 July and 5 August.
2. Ivor appeared on 4 and 11 April 1973.
3. Memo from Richard Gilbert to Brian Batchelor, 9 May 1973: BBC WAC RCONT15 Ivor Cutler File IV, 1973–1982.
4. Contracts for *Today* dated 11 January 1977, *Poetry Now* dated 26 February 1980, *Music Club* dated 19 January 1979: BBC WAC RCONT15 Ivor Cutler File IV. Contract, *Saturday Live*, dated 6 July 1983: RCONT26 Cutler, Ivor 1983–1987. Contract, *Speak*, dated 1 March 1980: RCONT22/358/1 Cutler, Ivor 1980–1984. Contract, *Look! Pictures in the Mind*, dated 1 December 1978: RCONT21 Cutler, Ivor 1975–1979.
5. David Gower to Ivor Cutler, 31 August 1977: BBC WAC RCONT21 Cutler, Ivor 1975–1979.

6. Correspondence, dated 13 June, 15 June and 11 July 1983, in BBC WAC RCONT22/358/1 Cutler, Ivor 1980–1984.
7. BBC (1984) *BBC Annual Report and Handbook*, 71.
8. Plowright died on 23 July 2021, a few weeks after he spoke to me by phone. Melvyn Bragg wrote his obituary, calling him "a rare and good man" and quoting a brief passage from *Ivor Cutler and ... a Mermaid*. See Bragg, M. (2021) "Piers Plowright Obituary." *The Guardian*, 6 August.
9. Carrier, D. (2019) "Word Play." *Camden New Journal*, 5 September.
10. "The Scotsman Sessions" #255: Bill Paterson, 17 June 2021 at dailymotion.com/video/x81zszy.
11. The *Radio Times* credited Ivor as "Composer/Tenor," Mason as "Contralto" and Fletcher as "bass."
12. *Ivor Cutler and ...* Series 1 was broadcast on BBC Radio 3, 21-24 June 1980; series 2 was broadcast on Radio 3 on 22, 24, 26, 28 December 1981. ... *Is Approached by Ivor Cutler* was broadcast on Radio 3 on 30 December 1981 and 1 January 1982.
13. Wade, D. (1980) "General Uncertainty All Round." *The Times*, 5 July.
14. *P*.
15. Anonymous (1981) "The Music Column." *Marylebone Mercury*, 22 May, 2; Anonymous (2006) "Obituary: Ivor Cutler." *The Stage*, 15 March. Accessed at thestage.co.uk.
16. *Bat Blues* (1987) BBC Radio 3, 5 March.
17. *Cutler on Education* (1989) BBC Radio 3, 30 March.
18. *GD*.
19. Gillard, D. (1990) "King Cutler I." *Radio Times*, 4 January, 22; *See for Yourself* (1990) BBC One, 7 January.
20. *King and Cutler* was broadcast on Radio 3 on 22 May. The *Radio Times* quote is taken from genome.ch.bbc.co.uk/.
21. *Poetry Now* (1980) BBC Radio 3, 8 February; *P*; *Ivor Meets Craig* (1993) BBC Radio 4, 12 June.
22. *Looking Forward to the Past* (1996) BBC Radio 4, 16 May.
23. *Cutler the Lax* (1991) episode 2, BBC Radio 4, 9 August.
24. *Cutler the Lax* (1991) episode 3, BBC Radio 4, 16 August.
25. *Ivor Cutler Has 15 Minutes in the Archives* (1990) episode 2, BBC Radio 4, 3 August.
26. *Walters' Weekly* (1983) BBC Radio 1, 26 February.
27. *Loose Ends* (1986) Radio 4, 10 May.
28. bbc.co.uk/radio1/johnpeel/sessions/1990s/1998/Jun12ivorcutler/.
29. *Poetry Please* (2003) BBC Radio 4, 9 February.

13 Long Players

1. Watts, M. (1971) "Ivor." *Melody Maker*, 27 February, 35.
2. The Dandelion label is discussed in Peel, J. and Ravenscroft, S. (2005) *Margrave of the Marshes*.
3. Prendergast, M. (1987) "Tubular Bells, Bayou Moon and Other Stories: Tom Newman." *Sound on Sound*, March 1987. Accessed at muzines.co.uk/articles/tom-newman/1534.
4. The Mbira is also known as a thumb piano and is an instrument that can be found across Africa.
5. MacDonald, I. (1974) Review. *New Musical Express*, 26 October, 23.

6. *Transatlantic Review* (1971) 39: 58; *Free Reed* (1974) 4: January/February, 9.
7. Alannah Hensler to Ivor Cutler, 26 October 1976; Ivor Cutler to Alannah Hensler, 31 October 1976: BBC WAC RCONT21 Ivor Cutler.
8. Ellis, D. (1981) "David Vorhaus and Kaleidophon Studio." *Electronics and Music Maker*, June. Accessed at muzines.co.uk/articles/ikip-vorhaus-and-kaleidophon-studio/2670.
9. *IC90*.
10. Anonymous (1975) Review. *Music Week*, 1 November, 46.
11. Cutler, I. (1976) "8 Days A Week," 10.
12. Anonymous (1977) "Music Week 1976 Awards." *Music Week*, 19 February, 43, 48.
13. Anonymous (1977) "Who's Who?" *The Stage and Television Today*, 25 August, 17; Gaster, A. (ed.) (1977) *International Who's Who in Music, and Musicians' Directory*, 8th edition. International Biographical Centre. Information is taken from the 9th edition (1980), 155.
14. White, A. (1998) "Ken Berry: The Billboard Interview." *Billboard* 110(36): 30.
15. *Last Words* (2006) BBC Radio 4, 10 March.
16. *P*; Espiner, M. (1999) "The Wizard of Odd."
17. Anonymous (1978) Review. *Music Week*, 22 April, 57.
18. Smith, R. (1978) Review. *Record Mirror*, 18 March, 16.
19. John-Paul Flintoff, interview.
20. See green-history.uk/.
21. See trinitylaban.ac.uk/study/teaching-staff/linda-hirst/.
22. *Music Week* (1983) 13 August, 12; Jasper, T. (1983) Review. *Music Week*, 20 August, 17.
23. Shepherd, F. (2020) Concert review, *The Scotsman*, 31 January; Virtue, G. (2020) Concert review. *The Guardian*, 30 January.
24. *Walters' Weekly* (1983) Radio 1, 26 February. The Greenham Common camp was established in 1981 as part of a protest against American nuclear missiles being based in the UK and became a women-only camp a year later. It closed in 2000. See Bindel, J. (2021) "Greenham Common at 40: We Came to Fight War, and Stayed for the Feminism." *Observer*, 29 August.
25. "Requiem" by Robert Louis Stevenson (1850–1894).
26. Anonymous (1986) Review. *Music Week*, 17 May, 16.
27. *Music Week* (1986) 1 November, 10.
28. Wilkes, J. (1986) Review. *Record Mirror*, 1 November, 16.
29. Henderson, D. (1986) "A&R Indies." *Music Week*, 22 November, 32.
30. Harrison, T. (1997) "The Comeback Kid," 25–27.
31. *GD*.
32. Carnahan, P. (1997) "An Interview with Ivor Cutler."
33. Virdi, V. (1998) Review. Supplement to *The Times*, 4 July, 11.
34. Bent, G. (2008) "A Flat Man, Ivor Cutler." *Record Collector*, 8 May, 11. The re-release is on Hoorgi House Records HHCD01.
35. Howarth, A. (2000) "McGee Seeks European Distributors for Poptones." *Music & Media*, 3 June, 4.

14   Ivor for Hire

1. Best, J. (1984) "Ivor Cutler." 26.
2. *LFTWP*.

3. *P.*
4. Cutler, I. (1971) "Blind Date." *Melody Maker*, 14.
5. Barnes, M. (1997) "Invisible Jukebox," 51–52.
6. Jones, T. (1986) "Midweek: Animal Cracker," 30 October, 7.
7. Cutler, I. (1988) "The Material World of Ivor Cutler." See imdb.com.
8. Neil Ardley (1972) *A Symphony of Amaranths*, Regal Zonophone SLRZ.1028. See neilardley.com/symphony-of-amaranths/. The album was rereleased in 2012 on Dusk Fire DUSKCD107.
9. Parker, C. (2013) Review. *London Jazz News*, 11 January (londonjazznews.com/).
10. Gelly, D. (2012) "A Symphony of Amaranths by Neil Ardley," singsongmusic.com/feature-dave-gelly-discusses-neil-ardleys-symphony-of-amaranths/; Coe, J. (2017) "Jonathan Coe on A Symphony of Amaranths by Neil Ardley." *New Statesman*, 17 December, newstatesman.com/.
11. *Rock Bottom* (1974) Virgin V2017.
12. Barnes, M. (1997) "Invisible Jukebox," 51–52.
13. Vogel (1980) "Arschloch." Sunrise Records 080/1972 and Recommended Records RR7.5.
14. Various Artists (1980) *Miniatures: A Sequence of Fifty-One Tiny Masterpieces Edited by Morgan Fisher*, Pipe Records Pipe 2.
15. Various Artists (1993) *The World is a Wonderful Place*, Hokey Pokey Records HPR 2003; Richard Thompson (1972) *Henry the Human Fly*, Island Records ILPS 9197.
16. "Mr Lacey" is on *What We Did on Our Holidays*. See Wood, J. (1972) Sleeve notes to *History of Fairport Convention*, Island ICD4.
17. Advertisement (1996) *Jewish Chronicle*, 22 November, 49.
18. Rudolph, A. (1992) "Voices that Cry Out to Be Heard." *Jewish Chronicle*, 28 February, 23.
19. Cousins, L. (director) (1988) *Woodpecker and the Acorn Tree*, Royal College of Art; Macrae, R. (director) (1986) *Life in a Scotch Sitting Room*, West Surrey College of Art and Design.
20. Ivor Cutler to Mr Newby, 28 November 1962: BBC WAC RCONT1 Cutler, Ivor (Artists File 1) 1957–1962.
21. Information on both debates taken from advertising handouts.
22. Cutler, I. (1976) "8 Days a Week." 10.
23. Cutler, I. (1991) "Trouble with Marmalade." *Weekend Guardian*, 23 March.
24. Cutler, I. (1996) *A Wet Handle*, 14.
25. Ivor Cutler to Alastair McKay, 21 February 1992.
26. Undated *Scotland on Sunday Magazine* cuttings, *c.*1992, courtesy of Alastair McKay.
27. Alex Mermikides, interview; sophiemorrish.net/friends-of-the-earth.
28. The song is "Old Man," from *Sail Away* (1972) Reprise Records K 44185. Sandy Grierson told me that Phyllis remembered Ivor's love of Joni Mitchell.
29. See imdb.com/name/nm0005271/awards.
30. Cutler, I. (1971) "Blind Date." *Melody Maker*.
31. The song appears on the Alan Price Set's 1967 album, *A Price on his Head*, Decca LK4907.
32. From *Tabula Rasa*, (1984) ECM 1275.
33. Bradley, M. (1999) "Pet Sounds." *The Times* (music supplement), 27 February, 15.
34. Ivor Cutler (1999) *Cute (H)ey?* EMI Songbook Series 4966 102.
35. Hodgkinson, W. (2004) "Cutler's Drawers."
36. Ivor Cutler to Gavin Hogg, April–May 1990

37. *Cutler the Lax* (1991) episode 1, BBC Radio 4, 2 August; *Ivor Cutler has 15 Minutes in the Archives* (1990) Episode Two, BBC Radio 4, 3 August.
38. Hodgkinson, W. (2004) "Cutler's Drawers."

15   Covering Ivor Cutler

1. SE (1980) "Riitaa, Riitaa, Riitaa." Johanna Records JHNS140B.
2. The album, released in 2012, is on En Vez de Nada EVDN#01.
3. Rough Trade press release, dated 7 August 1981; "Grass" by Robert Wyatt and "Trade Union" by Dishari (1981) Rough Trade RT 081.
4. Robert Wyatt (1982) *Nothing Can Stop Us*, Rough Trade Rough 35.
5. *Scrapings & Peelings* was released as an LP in 1989, Ode Records SODE314; Eddi Reader (1994) "Joke (I'm Laughing)." Blanco Y Negro NEG72CDX.
6. Max Andrzejewski's Hütte & Guests (2019) *Hütte & Guests Play the Music of Robert Wyatt*, WhyPlayJazz WPJ052; Wilson, J. (2020) Review. allaboutjazz. com/hutte-and-guests-play-the-music-of-robert-wyatt-max-andrzejewski-whyplayjazz.
7. Drag City (1999) DC162CD.
8. Marriage Records MAR040.
9. Hegri Music HEGRILP11.
10. See u2.com/news/title/womenoftheworldtakeover/news/
11. Various Artists (2003) *Stop Me if You Think You've Heard this One Before*, Rough Trade RTRADECD100.
12. Various Artists (2011) *Revenge of the Folksingers*, Delphian DCD34108.
13. See concal.org/albums.
14. Parenthetical Girls (2009) *The Scottish Play*, Tomlab 130LP.
15. The Golden Age of Steam (2020) *Tomato Brain,* limitedNOISE LTDN013.
16. See youtube.com/watch?v=1uBmxigazPY.
17. "A Doughnut in my Hand" is on *Privilege*.
18. The full list of songs Morris used is as follows: "Here's a Health to Simon," "Stick Out Your Chest," "The Market Place," "Rubber Toy," "Trouble, Trouble," "Little Black Buzzer," "I Got No Common Sense," "Deedle, Deedle, I Pass," "A Wooden Tree," "Phonic Poem," "I'm Going in a Field," "I Love You but I Don't Know What I Mean," "Beautiful Cosmos" and "Cockadoodledon't"; see markmorrisdancegroup.org/work/a-wooden-tree/.
19. Gottlieb, R. (2013) "Four by Morris." *New York Observer*, 9 April.
20. Saccoccia, S. (2015) "Mark Morris Dance Group performs at Institute of Contemporary Art." *The Bay State Banner*, 28 January.
21. See 509arts.co.uk/project/meal-one/.
22. See vanishing-point.org/our-work/the-beautiful-cosmos-of-ivor-cutler/# for details of the production.
23. Fisher, M. (2014) "The Beautiful Cosmos of Ivor Cutler Review." *The Guardian*, 21 April.
24. Irvine, L. (2014) "The Beautiful Cosmos of Ivor Cutler." *The List*, 20 March, 95.
25. McMillan, J. (2014) "Theatre Review: Beautiful Cosmos of Ivor Cutler." *The Scotsman*, 12 April.
26. The play was part of the *Drama on 3* series and was broadcast on 3 July 2016. See bbc.co.uk/programmes/b07j3m50.

16 A Life Outside the Limelight

1. Irwin, C. and Richmond, C. (2006) "Ivor Cutler."
2. Cutler, I. (1988) "The Material World of Ivor Cutler."
3. McKay, A. (1994) "Ivor Cutler, Absurdist Poet ..."
4. Espiner (1999) "The Wizard of Odd."
5. Kendall, E. (1985) "A Room of My Own: Ivor Cutler," 78–79.
6. Harrison, T. (1997) "The Comeback Kid," 25.
7. Hodgkinson, W. (2004) "Cutler's Drawers."
8. Lewis, J. (2004) "Quiet Riot."
9. McLean, C. (1994) "Cutler's Crusade," 81.
10. Alfio Bernabei, interview.
11. Lucy Armitage, interview.
12. Glen Baxter, interview; Lucy Armitage, interview; John Knutas, interview; Kate Lithgow, interview.
13. Barker, N. (1995) "Heroes & Villains."
14. Garner, K. (2007) *The Peel Sessions*, 272.
15. See bbc.co.uk/radio1/johnpeel/artists/i/ivorcutler/. Three other Peel sessions don't have a recording venue listed: they, too, may have been recorded at Laurier Road.
16. Garner, K. *(2007) The Peel Sessions*, 272.
17. Lithgow remembers this occurring in the mid-1990s.
18. "Juicy Lucy" (1979) *Record Mirror*, 18 February, 3.
19. Dylan Edwards, interview.
20. Adrian Mealing, interview.
21. Jonathon Porritt, interview.
22. Kendall, E. (1985) "A Room of my Own: Ivor Cutler." 78; *Loose Ends* (1990) BBC Radio 4, 21 April.
23. Moran, C. (2003) "Strange Ways." *The Times*, 6 June, arts supplement, 13. Craig Murray-Orr, interview.
25. Postcard to Lucy Armitage, undated but *c.*1996.
26. Ciara Nolan, interview.
27. "The Raver" (1975) *Melody Maker*, 16 August, 10.
28. Neil Cargill, interview.
29. Donald, A. (1997) "The Write Stuff," 98.
30. Ivor Cutler to Mark Ritchie (1991), probably August. Courtesy of Gavin Hogg.
31. Thompson, B (1990) "Off the Wall."
32. Barker, N. (1995) "Heroes & Villains."
33. In the early 1970s Robert broke his back in an accident.
34. On *Dandruff, A Flat Man* and *Dandruff* respectively.
35. Grant, K. (1996) "Three-Minute Poet."
36. McKay, A. (1994) "Ivor Cutler, Absurdist Poet ..."
37. Bruce, K. (1995) "Playing on Words."
38. Greenstreet, R. (2000) "The Questionnaire: Ivor Cutler."
39. Burnside, J. (2016) "Season of Mists ... and Foraging with Ivor."
40. Burnside, J. (2016) "Season of Mists ... and Foraging with Ivor."
41. Hennessy, V. (1989) *A Little Light Friction*, 155–156.
42. *Loose Ends* (1990) BBC Radio 4, 21 April; Ann Sylph, ZSL librarian, interview; Anonymous (1996) "The Afternoon Shift." *Radio Times*, 7 September.
43. Byelaws of the Zoological Society of London, 1988 (details provided by Emma Milnes, ZSL librarian).

44. Information from Ann Sylph.
45. See library.zsl.org/. He presented *Fly Sandwich* in November 1996 and *South American Bookworms* in October 2000. Ann Sylph recalls that he signed the copy of *Fly Sandwich*.
46. Heeps, D. (1986) "Flavour of Humour"; Hennessy, V. (1989) *A Little Light Friction*, 155.
47. Watson, D. (1986) "Grut Cutlet."
48. *Loose Ends* (1990) BBC Radio 4, 21 April; Cutler, J. (2008) Notes to *A Flat Man*.
49. *LFTWP*.
50. Barker, N. (1995) "Heroes and Villains."
51. *IC90*.
52. Hennessy, V. (1989) *A Little Light Friction*, 157–158.
53. *ICLSC*.
54. Ivor Cutler to Gavin Hogg, *c*.1996–1998.
55. Grant, K. (1996) "Three-Minute Poet."
56. Anon (1960) "Variety in Aid of New Theatre." *Middlesex County Times*, 24 September.
57. Advertisement (1967) *International Times*, 30 January, 16. The event took place on 29 January. Barry Miles, Paul McCartney's biographer, was on the *International Times* editorial board and Adrian Mitchell contributed to the first issue, published on 14 October 1966.
58. Anonymous (1967) "Strip It." *International Times*, 13 February, 3.
59. Advertisement (1971) *The Times*, 13 May.
60. Wandor, M. (1973) "Review of Patten, B and Krett, P (eds) (1973) *The House that Jack Built: Poems for Shelter*." *Spare Rib*, 12 June, 32; Anonymous (1975) News report, *Spare Rib*, November, 21.
61. See spokenwordarchive.org.uk/content/artist/ivor-cutler; Advertisement (1993) *The Times*, 11 December.
62. *The Stage* (1996) 11 July, 17.
63. Garner, K. (2007) *The Peel Sessions*, 272; Ivor Cutler to Ms Warley, 28 February 1996. The Noise Abatement Society was established in 1959. See noiseabatementsociety. org/. The Voluntary Euthanasia Society was formed in 1935 and changed its name to Dignity in Dying in 2006. It advocates for the right to "a good death." See dignityindying.org.uk/.
64. Cutler, I. (1988) "The Material World of Ivor Cutler."
65. Harrison, T. (1997) "The Comeback Kid," 25.
66. *P*.
67. McKay, A. (1994) "Ivor Cutler, Absurdist Poet …"
68. Palmer, J. (1997) "Manic Street Preacher."
69. Burningham, J. (2003) *The Time of Your Life*, 203.
70. Hodgkinson, W. (2004) "Cutler's Drawers."
71. Mulvey, J. (2005) "Peel's Poet." *The Times*, 26 March, supplement, 20.
72. Thompson, B. (1990) "Off the Wall."
73. Hodgkinson, W. (2004) "Cutler's Drawers."
74. Love, D. (2015) "A Message from Ivor Cutler."
75. Ivor Cutler to John Knutas, 27 September 1990.
76. Last will and testament of Ivor Cutler, 8 December 1993.
77. Palmer, J. (1997) "Manic Street Preacher."
78. Cutler, I. (1991) "Trouble with Marmalade."
79. Palmer, J. (1997) "Manic Street Preacher."

80. Burningham, J. (2003) *The Time of Your Life*, 202.
81. Mitchell, A. (2004) *The Shadow Knows*, 124–125.
82. *P.*
83. Lewis, J. (2004) "Quiet Riot."
84. Lewis, J. (2004) "Quiet Riot."

17 "I Will Become a Hermes"

1. Greenstreet, R. (2000) "The Questionnaire: Ivor Cutler."
2. Harrison, T. (1997) "The Comeback Kid."
3. Evans, R (1999) "Ivor Cutler."
4. Espiner, M. (2011) "Cutler, Ivor." *Oxford Dictionary of National Biography*.
5. Ivor Cutler to John Knutas, 17 May 2004. The letter can be seen on *ICKT*.
6. *ICKT.*
7. Ivor Cutler's death certificate; Dan Cutler, interview.
8. The memorial took place on 2 July 2006, according to the label on the Lucky Bags.
9. Motions S2M-04072 and S2M-04082. See parliament.scot/chamber-and-committees/votes-and-motions/votes-and-motions-search.
10. Hoorgi House Limited: information at find-and-update.company-information.service.gov.uk/company/06279071.
11. See en.wikipedia.org/wiki/The_Old_Guys.
12. Eiseman, C. S. and Lonsdale, O. (2018) "New State and Host Records for Agromyzidae." The fly was discovered in Iowa. See bugguide.net/node/view/1591017.
13. *Desert Island Discs*, Radio 4, first broadcast 24 May 2020 and 29 November 2020. If Oxenbury explained the reason for her choice, this didn't make the programme as broadcast.
14. *Round Britain Quiz* (2021) BBC Radio 4, 10 May. I'm grateful to Lee Freeman for alerting me to this programme.
15. *P.*
16. *Loose Ends* (1990) BBC Radio 4, 21 April.
17. *Loose Ends*; Kendall, E. (1985) "A Room of My Own: Ivor Cutler," 78.
18. Cutler, I. (1992) "My Farm." In *Is That Your Flap, Jack?*, 16.
19. Greenstreet, R. (2000) "The Questionnaire: Ivor Cutler"; Harrison, T. (1997) "The Comeback Kid." This quote appeared in at least three of Ivor's obituaries.

Discography

The following are all original recordings, credited to Ivor Cutler unless noted. The list excludes reissues and compilations.

Ivor Cutler of Y'Hup (1959) Fontana TFE17144 [EP]
Who Tore Your Trousers? (1961) Decca LK4405
Get Away from the Wall (1961) Decca DFE6677 [EP]
Ludo (1967) Parlophone PMC 7040 [credited to The Ivor Cutler Trio]
Dandruff (1974) Virgin Records V2021
Velvet Donkey (1975) Virgin Records V2037
Jammy Smears (1976) Virgin Records V2065
Ivor Cutler's Life in a Scotch Sitting-room Vol. II (1978) Harvest SHSP 4084
Privilege (1983) Rough Trade Records ROUGH 59 [credited to Ivor Cutler and Linda Hirst]
Prince Ivor (1986) Rough Trade Records ROUGH 89
Gruts (1986) Rough Trade ROUGH 98
The Peel Sessions (1989) Strange Fruit SFPS 068 [EP; 1969 recordings]
A Wet Handle (1997) Creation Records CRECD 217
A Flat Man (1998) Creation Records CRECD 236
Singing While Dead (2019) Hoorgi House Records CATNO004 [EP download; 1950s recordings]

Bibliography

Adamson, J. (1974) *Groucho, Harpo, Chico and Sometimes Zeppo*. Coronet Books.

BBC (1984) *BBC Annual Report and Handbook, Incorporating the Annual Report and Accounts 1983-84*. British Broadcasting Corporation.

Braber, B. (1992) "Integration of Jewish Immigrants in Glasgow, 1880–1939." Unpublished PhD thesis, University of Glasgow.

Brod, M. (1960) *Franz Kafka: A Biography*. Schocken Books. (First published in 1937.)

Brown, C. (2021) *One, Two, Three, Four: The Beatles in Time*. 4th Estate.

Bruce, L. (2016) *How to Talk Dirty and Influence People*. Da Capo Press. (First published in 1965.)

Burningham, J. (2003) *The Time of Your Life: Getting on with Getting on*. Bloomsbury Paperbacks.

Calvin, C. M., Crang, J. A., Paterson, L. and Deary, I. J. (2014) "Childhood Evacuation During World War II and Subsequent Cognitive Ability: The Scottish Mental Survey 1947." *Longitudinal and Life Course Studies* 5(2): 227–244.

Carpenter, H. (2004) *Spike Milligan: The Biography*. Coronet Books.

Carroll, J. J. (2014) *Physiological Problems of Bomber Crews in the Eighth Air Force During WWII* (e-book). Pickle Partners Publishing.

Collins, K. E. (2008) *Scotland's Jews: A Guide to the History and Community of the Jews in Scotland*. Second edition. Scottish Council of Jewish Communities.

Collins, K. E. (2016) *The Jewish Experience in Scotland: from Immigration to Integration*. Scottish Jewish Archives Centre.

Cook, W. E. (2006) *So Farewell Then: The Untold Life of Peter Cook*. HarperCollins.

Couzyn, J. (ed.) (1970) *Twelve to Twelve*. Poets Trust.

Croal, Jonathan (2013) *Neill of Summerhill: The Permanent Rebel*. Routledge Revivals. (First published in 1983.)

Cruickshank, M. (1970) *A History of the Training of Teachers in Scotland*. University of London Press.

Cutler, I. (1962) *Gruts*. Museum Press.

Cutler, I. (1966) *Cockadoodledon't*. Dobson Books.

Cutler, I. (1973) *Many Flies Have Feathers*. Trigram Press.

Cutler, I. (1977) *A Flat Man*. Trigram Press.

Cutler, I. (1981) *Private Habits*. Arc Publications.

Cutler, I. (1984) *Large et Puffy*. Arc Publications.

Cutler, I. (1986) *Fresh Carpet*. Arc Publications.

Cutler, I. (1988) *A Nice Wee Present from Scotland*. Arc Publications.

Cutler, I. (1992) *Is That Your Flap, Jack?* Arc Publications.

Cutler, I. (1996) *A Wet Handle*. Arc Publications.

Cutler, I. (1998) *A Flat Man* (reissue). Arc Publications.

Cutler, I. (1999) *South American Bookworms*. Arc Publications.

Cutler, I. (2001) *Under the Spigot*. Arc Publications.

Cutler, I. (2003) *Scots Wa' Straw*. Arc Publications.

Cutler, I. and Barton, J. (illus.) (1991) *Grape Zoo*. Walker Books.

Cutler, I. and Benge, A. (illus.) (1984) *Herbert the Chicken*. Walker Books.

Cutler, I. and Benge, A. (illus.) (1984) *Herbert the Elephant*. Walker Books.

Cutler, I. and Benson, P. (illus.) (1988) *Herbert: Five Stories*. Walker Books.

Cutler, I. and Honeysett, M. (illus.) (1984) *Life in a Scotch Sitting Room Vol. 2*. Methuen.

Cutler, I. and Honeysett, M. (illus.) (1986) *Gruts*. Methuen.

Cutler, I. and Honeysett, M. (illus.) (1987) *One and a Quarter*. Andre Deutsch.

Cutler, I. and Honeysett, M. (illus.) (1987) *Fremsley*. Methuen.

Cutler, I. and Honeysett, M. (illus.) (1991) *Fly Sandwich and Other Menu*. Methuen.

Cutler, I. and Honeysett, M. (illus.) (1992) *Befriend a Bacterium: Stickies by Ivor Cutler*. Pickpocket Books.

Cutler I. and Honeysett, M. (illus.) (1998) *Glasgow Dreamer*. Methuen. First published 1990.

Cutler I. and Lithgow, K. (photog.) (1994) *A Stuggy Pren*. Arc Publications.

Cutler, I. and Muñoz, C. (illus.) (1992) *Doris*. Heinemann.

Cutler, I. and Muñoz, C. (illus.) (1995) *The New Dress*. The Bodley Head.

Cutler, I. and Oxenbury, H. (illus.) (1971) *Meal One*. Heinemann.

Cutler, I. and Oxenbury, H. (illus.) (1975) *Balooky Klujypop*. Heinemann.

Cutler, I. and Oxenbury, H. (illus.) (1976) *The Animal House*. Armada Lions.

Davies, H. (2016) *The Beatles Book*. Ebury Press.

Eiseman, C. S. and Lonsdale, O. (2018) "New State and Host Records for Agromyzidae (Diptera) in the United States, with the Description of Thirty New Species." *Zootaxa* 4479: 1–156.

Farnes, Norma (2004) *Spike: An Intimate Memoir*. Harper Perennial.

Frank, F. (2012) "An Outsider Wherever I Am?: Transmission of Jewish Identity through Five Generations of a Scottish Jewish Family." Unpublished PhD thesis, University of Strathclyde.

Garner, K. (2007) *The Peel Sessions*. BBC Books.

Gayford, M. (2019) *Modernists & Mavericks. Bacon, Freud, Hockney & the London Painters*. Thames & Hudson.

Glasser, R. (1987) *Growing Up in the Gorbals*. Pan Books.

Hayward, K. (2013) *Tin Pan Alley: The Rise of Elton John*. Soundcheck Books.

Hennessy, V. (1989) *A Little Light Friction*. Harrap.

Hoare, N. (ed.) (2018) *Y'Hup: Ivor Cutler*. Goldsmiths Press.

Hussey, M. (2021) *Clive Bell and the Making of Modernism: A Biography*. Bloomsbury Publishing.

Kershaw, A. (2012) *No Off Switch*. Virgin Books.

King, P.A. (1978) *Dust*. Morden Tower Publications.

King, P (1980) *Close Views*. Morden Tower Publications.

Lindsay, B. (2020) *Two Bold Singermen and the English Folk Revival: The Lives, Song Traditions and Legacies of Sam Larner and Harry Cox*. Equinox Publishing.

MacDonald, I. (2005) *Revolution in the Head: The Beatles' Records and the Sixties* (second edition). Pimlico.

MacQueen, A. (2011) *Private Eye: The First 50 Years*. Private Eye Productions.

Miles, B. (1997) *Paul McCartney: Many Years from Now*. Secker & Warburg.

Miller, D. and Price, R. (2006) *British Poetry Magazines 1914–2000: A History and Bibliography of "Little Magazines"*. British Library/Oak Knoll Press.

Milligan, S. (1973) *More Goon Show Scripts*. Woburn Press.

Mitchell, A. (2004) *The Shadow Knows*. Bloodaxe Books.

Pattinson, J. (2016) "'Shirkers', 'Scrimjacks' and 'Scrimshanks'?: British Civilian Masculinity and Reserved Occupations, 1914–1945." *Gender & History* 28(3): 709–727.

Peel, J. and Ravenscroft, S. (2005) *Margrave of the Marshes*. Bantam Press.

Randall, L. and Welch, C. (2001) *Ginger Geezer: The Life of Vivian Stanshall*. Fourth Estate.

Saxon, P. (1997) "The Second World War." In *A History of Navigation in the Royal Air Force: RAF Historical Seminar*, 52–62. Royal Air Force Historical Society.

Sherrin, N. (2005) *Ned Sherrin: The Autobiography*. Little Brown.

Sugarman, M. (2002) "More than Just a Few: Jewish Pilots and Aircrew in the Battle of Britain." *Jewish Historical Studies* 38: 183–204.

Taylor, A. (2014) "'Are You a Billy, or a Dan, or an Old Tin Can?': Street Violence and Relations between Catholics, Jews and Protestants in the Gorbals during the Inter-war Years." *Urban History* 41(1): 124–140.

Vowles, C.J. (2006) "The Little Become Big? *Ambit* and London's Little Magazines, 1959–1999." Unpublished PhD thesis, Goldsmiths College, University of London.

Willetts, P. (2013) *The Look of Love: The Life and Times of Paul Raymond, Soho's King of Clubs*. Serpent's Tail.

Wyatt, R. and Benge, A. (2020) *Side by Side: Selected Lyrics*. Faber & Faber.

Index

www.ingramcontent.com/pod-product-compliance
Lightning Source LLC
Chambersburg PA
CBHW040419110426
42813CB00013B/2702